Brief Contents

P9-DNA-689

Contents

Successful Business Communication

Bridging the Gap

Deborah Luchuk

OXFORD
UNIVERSITY PRESS

OXFORD

UNIVERSITY PRESS

Oxford University Press is a department of the University of Oxford.
It furthers the University's objective of excellence in research, scholarship,
and education by publishing worldwide. Oxford is a registered trade mark of
Oxford University Press in the UK and in certain other countries.

Published in Canada by
Oxford University Press
8 Sampson Mews, Suite 204,
Don Mills, Ontario M3C 0H5 Canada

www.oupcanada.com

Library and Archives Canada Cataloguing in Publication
Luchuk, Deborah
Successful business communication : bridging the
gap / Deborah Luchuk.
Includes bibliographical references and index.
ISBN 978-0-19-544655-5
1. Business communication—Canada—Textbooks. I. Title.

HF5718.2.C3L82 2013   651.7   C2012-906232-4

Cover image: Maarten Wouters/Stone/Getty Images

This book is printed on permanent (acid-free) paper ⊖ which
contains a minimum of 10% post-consumer waste.

Printed and bound in the United States of America

2 3 4 — 16 15 14

CHAPTER 2   Memos, Email Messages, and Social Media   28

CHAPTER 3   Business Letters   60

CHAPTER 7 Team Communications Projects 156

CHAPTER 8 Informal Reports 170

CHAPTER 9 Formal Reports 202

CHAPTER 10 Informal Proposals 228

CHAPTER 11 Formal Proposals 258

CHAPTER 14 Job and Informational Interviews 346

APPENDIX A Grammar Handbook 371

APPENDIX B Guidelines for Documenting Sources 405

From the Publisher

In today's fast-paced world of business, where reports are constantly coming due, meetings happen every few hours, and emails flow in a steady stream, having effective communication skills is critical to success. Focusing on real-world application, *Successful Business Communication: Bridging the Gap* provides all the essentials of business communication that students will need to hit the ground running in the workplace.

Using a hands-on approach, this text engages readers with lively, classroom-tested instruction, as well as ample opportunities to practise the industry-relevant concepts they have learned. Bridging the gap between the classroom and the business world, *Successful Business Communication* helps students develop the practical skills employers need them to have today and a foundation for effective workplace communication they can depend on in future.

Key Features

⇨ **"Learning Objectives"** and **"Essential Employability Skills" sections** help students set study goals and highlight key competencies they will develop based on The Conference Board of Canada's "Employability Skills 2000+" benchmarks for workplace success.

LEARNING OBJECTIVES

In this chapter, you will learn:

- What business letters are and when it is appropriate to use letters to communicate
- How to write short, concise, informative letters to internal and external readers based on their information needs and the information you want to convey
- Appropriate protocol for business letters
- How to organize and write business letters for good or bad news
- How to organize and write business letters as short, informal reports

ESSENTIAL EMPLOYABILITY SKILLS

2000+ Employability Skills — The Conference Board of Canada has identified certain essential employability skills (EES) as benchmarks for performance in the workplace. You will learn the following EES skills in this chapter:

THINK AND SOLVE PROBLEMS

- Can assess situations and identify problems
- Can seek different points of view and evaluate them based on facts
- Can recognize the human, interpersonal, technical, scientific, and mathematical dimensions of a problem
- Can identify the root cause of a problem
- Can be creative and innovative in exploring possible solutions
- Can evaluate solutions to make recommendations or decisions

COMMUNICATE

- Can read and understand information presented in a variety of forms (e.g., words, graphs, charts, diagrams)
- Can write and speak so others pay attention and understand
- Can listen and ask questions to understand and appreciate the points of view of others

⇨ **Chapter-opening case studies** detail realistic situations based on chapter themes and are accompanied by questions that encourage applied, critical thinking.

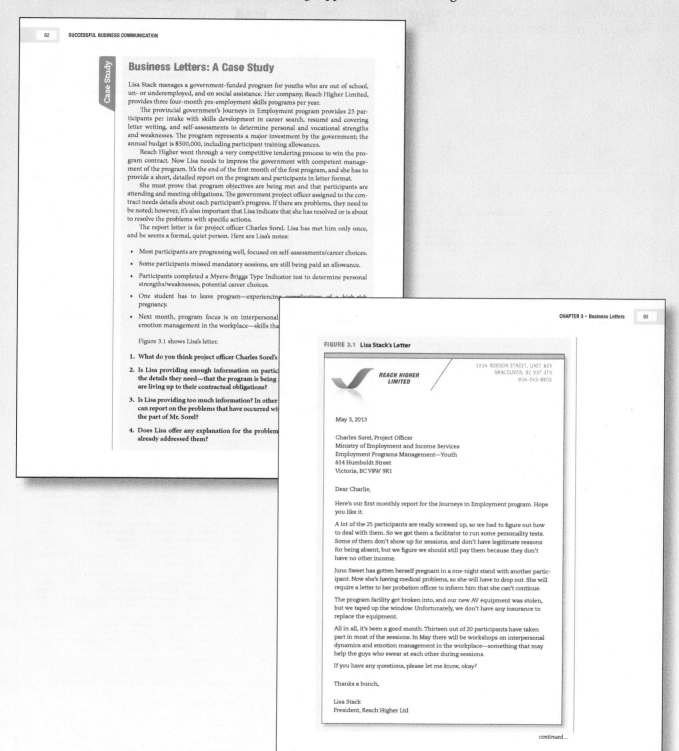

62   SUCCESSFUL BUSINESS COMMUNICATION

Case Study

Business Letters: A Case Study

Lisa Stack manages a government-funded program for youths who are out of school, un- or underemployed, and on social assistance. Her company, Reach Higher Limited, provides three four-month pre-employment skills programs per year.

The provincial government's Journeys in Employment program provides 25 participants per intake with skills development in career search, resumé and covering letter writing, and self-assessments to determine personal and vocational strengths and weaknesses. The program represents a major investment by the government; the annual budget is $500,000, including participant training allowances.

Reach Higher went through a very competitive tendering process to win the program contract. Now Lisa needs to impress the government with competent management of the program. It's the end of the first month of the first program, and she has to provide a short, detailed report on the program and participants in letter format.

She must prove that program objectives are being met and that participants are attending and meeting obligations. The government project officer assigned to the contract needs details about each participant's progress. If there are problems, they need to be noted; however, it's also important that Lisa indicate that she has resolved or is about to resolve the problems with specific actions.

The report letter is for project officer Charles Sorel. Lisa has met him only once, and he seems a formal, quiet person. Here are Lisa's notes:

- Most participants are progressing well, focused on self-assessments/career choices.
- Some participants missed mandatory sessions, are still being paid an allowance.
- Participants completed a Myers-Briggs Type Indicator test to determine personal strengths/weaknesses, potential career choices.
- One student has to leave program—experiencing complications of a high-risk pregnancy.
- Next month, program focus is on interpersonal emotion management in the workplace—skills tha

Figure 3.1 shows Lisa's letter.

1. What do you think project officer Charles Sorel's

2. Is Lisa providing enough information on partic the details they need—that the program is being are living up to their contractual obligations?

3. Is Lisa providing too much information? In other can report on the problems that have occurred wit the part of Mr. Sorel?

4. Does Lisa offer any explanation for the problem already addressed them?

CHAPTER 3 ▪ Business Letters   63

FIGURE 3.1   Lisa Stack's Letter

REACH HIGHER LIMITED

1234 ROBSON STREET, UNIT #25
VANCOUVER, BC V3T 3T5
604-743-8903

May 3, 2013

Charles Sorel, Project Officer
Ministry of Employment and Income Services
Employment Programs Management—Youth
614 Humboldt Street
Victoria, BC V8W 9R1

Dear Charlie,

Here's our first monthly report for the Journeys in Employment program. Hope you like it.

A lot of the 25 participants are really screwed up, so we had to figure out how to deal with them. So we got them a facilitator to run some personality tests. Some of them don't show up for sessions, and don't have legitimate reasons for being absent, but we figure we should still pay them because they don't have no other income.

Juno Sweet has gotten herself pregnant in a one-night stand with another participant. Now she's having medical problems, so she will have to drop out. She will require a letter to her probation officer to inform him that she can't continue.

The program facility got broken into, and our new AV equipment was stolen, but we taped up the window. Unfortunately, we don't have any insurance to replace the equipment.

All in all, it's been a good month. Thirteen out of 20 participants have taken part in most of the sessions. In May there will be workshops on interpersonal dynamics and emotion management in the workplace—something that may help the guys who swear at each other during sessions.

If you have any questions, please let me know, okay?

Thanks a bunch,

Lisa Stack
President, Reach Higher Ltd

continued...

⇒ **"Idiom Alert" boxes** help ESL and native-English speakers alike understand the meaning of figures of speech and other commonly used vocabulary in the workplace and beyond.

Idiom Alert

short and sweet – Completed quickly and easily.

checking your ego/agenda at the door – Not imposing your views or needs on others but putting them aside in favour of working as a group.

fuzzy sandwich head – The sleepy feeling you get after eating a large lunch.

ditto – The same.

stickhandling – What hockey players do in a fast-paced game, adeptly moving their sticks around to make a play or a score a goal. In the business sense, when someone is stickhandling, he or she is completing a complex set of tasks or responsibilities with deft decisions and actions.

TGIF – Stands for "Thank goodness it's Friday" (and the weekend is almost here).

comfy – Comfortable.

doze off – Fall asleep.

off-track (discussion) – Not following what the group or individuals intended to discuss; that is, the discussion has moved to subjects or topics other than what was planned.

parking lot – Put off to a later time. When a discussion of certain matters is put into a parking lot, the discussion is deferred—to later in the meeting, to the next meeting, or to a more appropriate time.

visioning – Brainstorming about what could be, how to best solve a problem, future possibilities, and so on.

⇒ **Annotated sample documents** drawn from real business practice reinforce concepts and provide students with models to guide their own writing.

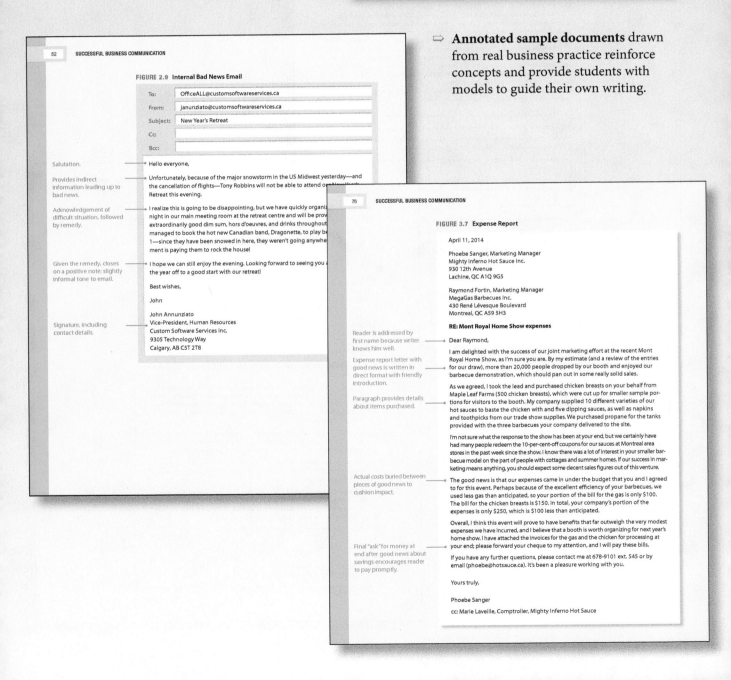

52   SUCCESSFUL BUSINESS COMMUNICATION

FIGURE 2.9 Internal Bad News Email

To:	OfficeALL@customsoftwareservices.ca
From:	janunziato@customsoftwareservices.ca
Subject:	New Year's Retreat
Cc:	
Bcc:	

Salutation. → Hello everyone,

Provides indirect information leading up to bad news. → Unfortunately, because of the major snowstorm in the US Midwest yesterday—and the cancellation of flights—Tony Robbins will not be able to attend our New Year's Retreat this evening.

Acknowledgement of difficult situation, followed by remedy. → I realize this is going to be disappointing, but we have quickly organiz[ed] night in our main meeting room at the retreat centre and will be prov[ided] extraordinarily good dim sum, hors d'oeuvres, and drinks throughout [the] managed to book the hot new Canadian band, Dragonette, to play be[tween] 1—since they have been snowed in here, they weren't going anywhe[re] ment is paying them to rock the house!

Given the remedy, closes on a positive note; slightly informal tone to email. → I hope we can still enjoy the evening. Looking forward to seeing you a[nd] the year off to a good start with our retreat!

Best wishes,

John

Signature, including contact details. → John Annunziato
Vice-President, Human Resources
Custom Software Services Inc.
9305 Technology Way
Calgary, AB C5T 2T8

76   SUCCESSFUL BUSINESS COMMUNICATION

FIGURE 3.7 Expense Report

April 11, 2014

Phoebe Sanger, Marketing Manager
Mighty Inferno Hot Sauce Inc.
930 12th Avenue
Lachine, QC A1Q 9G5

Raymond Fortin, Marketing Manager
MegaGas Barbecues Inc.
430 René Lévesque Boulevard
Montreal, QC A59 5H3

RE: Mont Royal Home Show expenses

Reader is addressed by first name because writer knows him well. → Dear Raymond,

Expense report letter with good news is written in direct format with friendly introduction. → I am delighted with the success of our joint marketing effort at the recent Mont Royal Home Show, as I'm sure you are. By my estimate (and a review of the entries for our draw), more than 20,000 people dropped by our booth and enjoyed our barbecue demonstration, which should pan out in some really solid sales.

Paragraph provides details about items purchased. → As we agreed, I took the lead and purchased chicken breasts on your behalf from Maple Leaf Farms (500 chicken breasts), which were cut up for smaller sample portions for visitors to the booth. My company supplied 10 different varieties of our hot sauces to baste the chicken with and five dipping sauces, as well as napkins and toothpicks from our trade show supplies. We purchased propane for the tanks provided with the three barbecues your company delivered to the site.

I'm not sure what the response to the show has been at your end, but we certainly have had many people redeem the 10-per-cent-off coupons for our sauces at Montreal area stores in the past week since the show. I know there was a lot of interest in your smaller barbecue model on the part of people with cottages and summer homes. If our success in marketing means anything, you should expect some decent sales figures out of this venture.

Actual costs buried between pieces of good news to cushion impact. → The good news is that our expenses came in under the budget that you and I agreed to for this event. Perhaps because of the excellent efficiency of your barbecues, we used less gas than anticipated, so your portion of the bill for the gas is only $100. The bill for the chicken breasts is $150. In total, your company's portion of the expenses is only $250, which is $100 less than anticipated.

Overall, I think this event will prove to have benefits that far outweigh the very modest expenses we have incurred, and I believe that a booth is worth organizing for next year's home show. I have attached the invoices for the gas and the chicken for processing at your end; please forward your cheque to my attention, and I will pay these bills.

Final "ask" for money at end after good news about savings encourages reader to pay promptly. → If you have any further questions, please contact me at 678-9101 ext. 545 or by email (phoebe@hotsauce.ca). It's been a pleasure working with you.

Yours truly,

Phoebe Sanger

cc: Marie Laveille, Comptroller, Mighty Inferno Hot Sauce

⇨ **Coverage of current trends in business**, including instruction on social media and intercultural communication, helps students succeed in an increasingly digital, networked, and global workplace.

---

6. When in doubt about posting a link to an image or article, email the author or photographer, and ask whether you can feature them in a blog post. Chances are they will be happy to have the free publicity. *Always* ask the originator of any full article, written piece, or image/photo if you plan to post the article or image in your blog (to do otherwise is to steal their work).

Caution! road hazards ahead: Avoiding social media mistakes

The main challenge with any social media initiative is the transparency it involves, but transparency can provide the best rewards. Customers are always impressed when you are clear about your business and don't try to hide anything. It shows that you not only have nothing to hide but are comfortable enough with your business to be open on a social media level. That being said, it is important to be careful when it comes to social media communication and what you choose to say online. Here are a few tips to keep in mind:

1. Remember that it is a two-way interaction. Don't just spit out information, but rather try to create a conversation with your followers and those you follow. Posting information or news about your business is one way to use these tools, but they are most valuable when you use them as discussion tools for exchanging information and opinion with your customers.

2. Not every message will be positive. Once you open yourself up to feedback in online social networking applications, you are just as likely to receive negative comment from a dissatisfied customer. It is how you deal with these situations that will set you apart from your competitors. Do not try to hide the problem or pretend it does not exist. Deal with it head-on, and your customers will respect you for it. Conveying a positive image *does not* mean that you can "delete" customer complaints while leaving positive reviews in the public eye, since the point of using

these social media applications is to make your business as transparent as possible to your customers.

How you handle both the positive and negative feedback is, therefore, on display in a public venue, whereas it would have been a little more private in the past. You may find this a bit scary at first, but if you are able to deal with such situations well, the outcome will be extremely positive, and you will earn the respect of other customers.

3. You should deal with negative feedback in a timely way, first acknowledging any fault or mistakes and then outlining the solution to the problem so that other readers can see that your company is conscientious about following through. However, this approach may not resolve the problem, so it's important to monitor each situation to see whether it needs to be taken "offline" to a private conversation, depending on the severity and content of the matter.

4. Time management is very important. It is very easy to get buried in u[...] itiatives and not r[...] As with all aspects [...] schedule time for [...] keting. There are v[...] ment of social me[...] you can work with [...] necting different a[...] together automat[...]

The culture of time

Linear (monochromic) time cultures focus on time as moving forward in a step-by-step process from point A to B to C and so on. Planned timelines for a project are often projected from start to finish, with all the details in between plotted according to dates/times as interim steps. There is no going "backward." The theory is that by following steps in chronological, logical order, you will complete a project successfully—as long as you allow extra time for inevitable problems or challenges that might arise. Deadlines are extremely important in this culture, mostly found in North America, northern Europe, Australia, and New Zealand. Don't change the schedule unless a major catastrophe forces you to do so!

In a flexible (polychromic) time culture, as in southern Europe, and Central and South America, projects are managed through multi-tasking, valuing "people time" (which is often indeterminate) over non-human work. Schedules are observed more or less, but if an opportunity to meet and discuss with others comes up, the schedule is modified. Relationships and emotions are more important than sticking to an "artificial" deadline, and if it takes longer to work out details of a contract or business decision through discussion, so be it. Those who view time flexibly also tend to live in the moment and are comparatively less concerned about the future. Enjoying the people you are with and going with the flow of what might come up are key to getting the most out of life and work. Deadlines are flexible and can be altered for more important priorities such as the needs of the people involved.

A cyclical time culture can be found in First Nations, African, and Asian cultures. As the name suggests, time is viewed as a circle or even a spiral; events move matters forward but circle around while doing so. In each season, we expect a certain kind of weather, but it may differ in intensity from the weather during the same season the year before (winter, for example, can have more or less snow). Influenced by such natural cycles of life, those in a cyclical time culture are comparatively less anxious about the future and not much concerned about the past. With less concern about past, present, or future, they make decisions after giving more time to reflection—consideration of what was done before and the consequences; the current situation, resources, and facts available; and potential future outcomes. Such decision-making does not occur in a step-by-step fashion; sometimes, what in a linear culture might be seen as "going backward" is in fact a means of ensuring the best possible outcome. In a cyclical time culture, a schedule is not a fixed, forward-moving scheme that must be followed precisely (linear), nor is it forward-moving but fluid to allow more time for people (flexible). Rather, there is an end result to be achieved, but even this end result may be altered as work and efforts evolve and new factors emerge, requiring those involved to move "backward," "sideways," or "forward" to achieve a desired outcome.

The bottom line of culturally sensitive communication

The most important point to keep in mind about culturally sensitive communication is to *never assume*

Globalization makes the world seem smaller, and this is particularly true for business. When communicating with international colleagues or clients, be proactive—consider cultural contexts, and be prepared to adapt to local communication conventions.

⇨ **Helpful tips and "insider information"** drawn from actual industry experience show students the etiquette and professional touches they can use to make the right impression in the workplace.

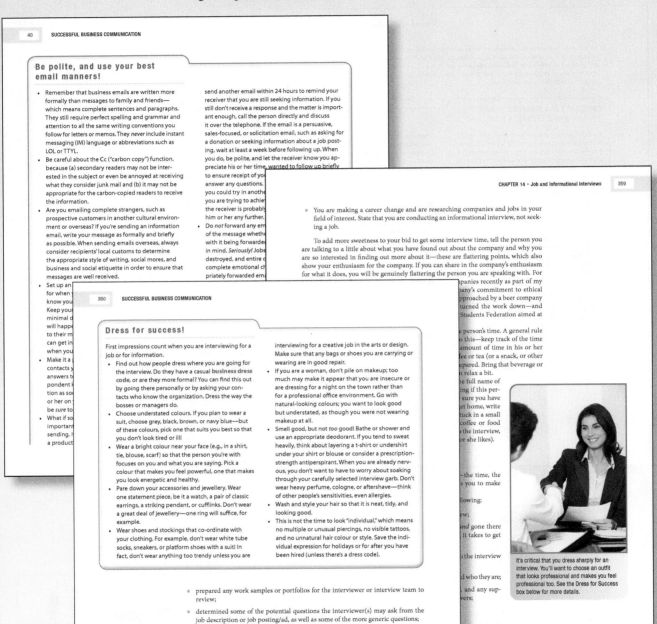

40   SUCCESSFUL BUSINESS COMMUNICATION

Be polite, and use your best email manners!

- Remember that business emails are written more formally than messages to family and friends—which means complete sentences and paragraphs. They still require perfect spelling and grammar and attention to all the same writing conventions you follow for letters or memos. They *never* include instant messaging (IM) language or abbreviations such as LOL or TTYL.
- Be careful about the Cc ("carbon copy") function, because (a) secondary readers may not be interested in the subject or even be annoyed at receiving what they consider junk mail and (b) it may not be appropriate for the carbon-copied readers to receive the information.
- Are you emailing complete strangers, such as prospective customers in another cultural environment or overseas? If you're sending an information email, write your message as formally and briefly as possible. When sending emails overseas, always consider recipients' local customs to determine the appropriate style of writing, social mores, and business and social etiquette in order to ensure that messages will be well received.
- Set up an [...] for when [...] know you [...] Keep your [...] minimal [...] will happe[...] to their m[...] can get in[...] when you[...]
- Make it a [...] contacts y[...] answers t[...] pondent [...] tion as so[...] or her on [...] be *sure* to [...]
- What if so[...] important[...] sending. I[...] a product[...]

send another email within 24 hours to remind your receiver that you are still seeking information. If you still don't receive a response and the matter is important enough, call the person directly and discuss it over the telephone. If the email is a persuasive, sales-focused, or solicitation email, such as asking for a donation or seeking information about a job posting, wait at least a week before following up. When you do, be polite, and let the receiver know you appreciate his or her time, wanted to follow up briefly to ensure receipt of yo[...] answer any questions. [...] you could try in anothe[...] you are trying to achie[...] the receiver is probably [...] him or her any further. [...]
- Do *not* forward any em[...] of the message whethe[...] with it being forwarded[...] in mind. *Seriously!* Jobs [...] destroyed, and entire c[...] complete emotional ch[...] priately forwarded em[...]

CHAPTER 14 • Job and Informational Interviews   359

- You are making a career change and are researching companies and jobs in your field of interest. State that you are conducting an informational interview, not seeking a job.

To add more sweetness to your bid to get some interview time, tell the person you are talking to a little about what you have found out about the company and why you are so interested in finding out more about it—these are flattering points, which also show your enthusiasm for the company. If you can share in the company's enthusiasm for what it does, you will be genuinely flattering the person you are speaking with. For [...]panies recently as part of my [...]pany's commitment to ethical [...]pproached by a beer company [...]turned the work down—and [...]Students Federation aimed at [...]

[...]e person's time. A general rule [...] to this—keep track of the time [...] amount of time in his or her [...]ee or tea (or a snack, or other [...]epared. Bring that beverage or [...]n relax a bit. [...]he full name of [...]ing if this per- [...] sure you have [...]get home, write [...]tuck in a small [...]coffee or food [...]e the interview, [...]r she likes).

[...]—the time, the [...]s you to make

[...]iew;

[...] *and* gone there [...] it takes to get

[...]o the interview

[...]d who they are; [...], and any sup- [...]vers;

---

360   SUCCESSFUL BUSINESS COMMUNICATION

Dress for success!

First impressions count when you are interviewing for a job or for information.

- Find out how people dress where you are going for the interview. Do they have a casual **business dress code**, or are they more formal? You can find this out by going there personally or by asking your contacts who know the organization. Dress the way the bosses or managers do.
- Choose understated colours. If you plan to wear a suit, choose grey, black, brown, or navy blue—but of these colours, pick one that suits you best so that you don't look tired or ill!
- Wear a bright colour near your face (e.g., in a shirt, tie, blouse, scarf) so that the person you're with focuses on you and what you are saying. Pick a colour that makes you feel powerful, one that makes you look energetic and healthy.
- Pare down your accessories and jewellery. Wear one statement piece, be it a watch, a pair of classic earrings, a striking pendant, or cufflinks. Don't wear a great deal of jewellery—one ring will suffice, for example.
- Wear shoes and stockings that co-ordinate with your clothing. For example, don't wear white tube socks, sneakers, or platform shoes with a suit! In fact, don't wear anything too trendy unless you are

interviewing for a creative job in the arts or design. Make sure that any bags or shoes you are carrying or wearing are in good repair.

- If you are a woman, don't pile on makeup; too much may make it appear that you are insecure or are dressing for a night on the town rather than for a professional office environment. Go with natural-looking colours; you want to look good but understated, as though you were not wearing makeup at all.
- Smell good, but not *too* good! Bathe or shower and use an appropriate deodorant. If you tend to sweat heavily, think about layering a t-shirt or undershirt under your shirt or blouse or consider a prescription-strength antiperspirant. When you are already nervous, you don't want to have to worry about soaking through your carefully selected interview garb. Don't wear heavy perfume, cologne, or aftershave—think of other people's sensitivities, even allergies.
- Wash and style your hair so that it is neat, tidy, and looking good.
- This is not the time to look "individual," which means no multiple or unusual piercings, no visible tattoos, and no unnatural hair colour or style. Save the individual expression for holidays or for after you have been hired (unless there's a dress code).

⦿ prepared any work samples or portfolios for the interviewer or interview team to review;

⦿ determined some of the potential questions the interviewer(s) may ask from the job description or job posting/ad, as well as some of the more generic questions;

⦿ practised answering these questions with family and friends;

⦿ planned—and prepared—your interview outfit and accessories the night before (see the Dress for Success box for tips and tricks on what to wear for interview success).

POTENTIAL QUESTIONS: INFORMATIONAL INTERVIEW

In the informational interview, *you* will be asking the questions of a potential employer, a decision-maker in the company you want to work for. At the end of the interview, or even during, the person you are interviewing may ask you some questions about yourself and why you are there.

It's critical that you dress sharply for an interview. You'll want to choose an outfit that looks professional and makes you feel professional too. See the Dress for Success box below for more details.

⇨ **A contemporary, full-colour design** makes chapter content approachable and visually appealing.

⇨ **Effective end-of-chapter pedagogy**—including chapter summaries, practical checklists, debate and discussion starters, suggestions for further reading, and exercises—supports student learning.

CHECKLIST FOR team communications

☐ Has your team reviewed the demands and purpose of the project?

☐ Has your team reviewed the needs of the audience (using Starting Point questions in Chapter 1)? Has your team considered whether the audience is culturally diverse and thus requires a different approach?

☐ Have you prepared a team contract to improve the functioning of your writing team?

☐ Have you decided on a team writing model—collaboration, consensus, or delegation?

☐ Have you decided who will do which parts of the research?

☐ Has everyone recorded source information for citations?

☐ Have you conducted a final meeting to bring all research together and address information gaps before you start writing?

☐ If you are each writing specific parts of the final document, have you agreed on such details as length (or word count), tone, style, and the details needed for each section?

☐ Have you met as a group to review your draft document once all sections are in place?

☐ Have you conducted a group edit of the document?

☐ Have you decided on one final editor to go through the entire document after the team editing process? Has the editor followed all of the steps for editing noted in this chapter?

☐ Has the team reviewed the edited document for: format; content; documentation; unified voice, tone, and style; and grammar and spelling errors?

☐ Once it has been printed, have you double-checked the document for any possible errors?

☐ Has the document been produced according to the format, number of copies, an required by the readers/receivers?

☐ Have you delivered the final product to the appropriate people?

☐ Have you determined whether there is to be an oral presentation? If there is, hav support your document as appropriate in the presentation?

Chapter Summary

In this chapter, you have learned that there are several writing a report as a team—consensus, delegation, ar own strengths and weaknesses and each appropriate for You discovered that each of these three methods invo ing to which you will have to adapt. Collaborative rep ers in addition to the primary ones. You found that w regularly, meet frequently, and review the research tog writing of the first draft. You learned step by step how into a cohesive and professional whole through editing cycling and a review chain can help to improve your pr troubleshooting strategies to overcome challenges comm

---

SUGGESTIONS for Further Reading

Alred, G.J., Brusaw, C.T., and Oliu, W.E. (2010). *Writing that works: Communicating effectively on the job [with team writing]*. (10th ed.). New York, NY: Bedford/St. Martin's Press.
——— (2011). *The business writer's handbook*. (10th ed.). New York, NY: Bedford/St. Martin's Press.
Harris, T.E., and Sherblom, J.C. (2010). *Small group and team communication*. (5th ed.). Toronto, ON: Allyn & Bacon/Pearson Higher Education.
Kolin, P. C. (2011). *Successful writing at work: Concise edition*. Independence, KY: Cengage/ Wadsworth.
Lumsden, G., Lumsden, D., and Wiethoff, C. (2009). *Communicating in groups and teams: Sharing leadership*. (9th ed.). Independence, KY: Cengage/Wadsworth.
Wolfe, J. (2010). *Team writing: A guide to writing in groups*. New York, NY: St. Martin's Press.

DEBATE and Discussion Starters

1. What would be the benefits of each model of team writing if you were working on a student team to produce a report and/or oral presentation as part of a course?

2. Which model do you think would have worked best in a past team effort that perhaps didn't go so well? Which model might you try in a team project you have coming up in a course you are currently taking? Why?

3. In the industry or sector you anticipate working in after graduation, which model do you think would work best? Why? Which would be least useful or helpful? Why? (Perhaps you should research the field you have in mind.)

4. Which team model would you prefer to work with? Which one would be the least appealing? Why?

PRACTISING What You Have Learned

1. a. For your next *team writing project*, create a team contract for your group as described in this chapter and in Chapter 6. (Your instructor may have a specific project in mind to which you should apply the principles of this chapter.)

   b. Conduct the research and writing, using the steps outlined in this chapter, and apply the style appropriate for the particular written product (e.g., informal or formal report, informal or formal proposal, business plan, marketing plan). Refer to the chapters in this textbook covering each type of written product for guidance in determining research, writing, format, and editing requirements.

   c. At the end of the project, conduct an evaluation process with your team to assess how well you did and what you would do differently next time (in this team or another).

2. a. For your next *team oral presentation*, create a team contract for your group as described in this chapter and in Chapter 6. (Your instructor may have a specific project in mind to which you should apply the principles of this chapter.)

   b. Conduct the research and writing, using the steps outlined in this chapter and those necessary for the particular written product (e.g., informal or formal report, informal or formal proposal). Refer to the chapters in this textbook covering each type of written product for guidance in determining research, writing, format, and editing requirements.

   c. At the end of the project, conduct an evaluation process with your team to assess how well you did and what you would do differently next time (in this team or another).

⇨ **"Grammar Handbook"** and **"Guidelines for Documenting Sources"** appendices offer guidance on grammar and reference styles, as well as abundant exercises to help students polish their writing.

APPENDIX **A**

Grammar Handbook

Parts of Speech 101

For the purposes of your writing in business, here are the basic parts of speech you need to be most concerned with when writing sentences.

Noun: a person, place, or thing; can be a subject of the sentence—doing the ma[...] action of the sentence—or can be an object of the sentence—having something [...] done to it, receiving the action.

Verb: asserts or asks something about the subject; can be a verb that represents [...] the main action of the sentence done by the subject.

Pronoun: a word that stands in for a proper or defined noun. For example, the [...] pronoun "he" can stand in for the noun "John," and the pronoun "it" can stand [...] for the noun "cat."

Preposition: a word that indicates a relationship between a noun/pronoun and [...] other words in a sentence (such as "by," "like," "as," "to," "toward," "of," "for," "out o[...]

Interjection: an emotional or emphatic exclamation "injected" into a sentence [...] and followed by an exclamation point, such as "Ouch!" and "Good!"

Article: a word that defines a subject or object, such as "a" or "an" (an indefinite, no[...] specific, noun, such as "*a* cat") or "the" (definite, very specific noun, such as "*the* cat[...]

Adjective: a word that describes and gives more detail about a noun (e.g., the [...]

1. Jorge's car died on the side of the busy highway last night.
2. The car was jammed with too many passengers—students who [...] from the pub.
3. So overloaded was the car's rear end, it was scraping the asph[...] flying from the exhaust pipe.
4. The billowing smoke coming from under the hood was a sig[...] should vacate the car immediately.
5. They all leapt out of the car and dove into the snowy ditch; th[...] the car burst into flames.
6. All Jorge could think about was his parents' reaction when th[...] was totaled and he hadn't been maintaining it properly.
7. Someone had called 911, but the fire trucks arrived about 20 [...] find a smouldering hulk of twisted metal.
8. The police arrived around the same time and recorded the de[...] then arranged for a van to transport the students back to their [...]
9. It was difficult to determine the cause of the blaze, but the fac[...] changed the oil in a year probably had something to do with it; [...] ed to take the car to a mechanic when he was seeing puddles [...] the residence parking lot.
10. Needless to say, Jorge's parents were not pleased, but he an[...] instead to buy shares in AutoShare for future transportation so t[...] to worry about maintenance again.

Pronoun-Antecedent Agreement

Another sticky situation for writers is ensuring that a pronoun agrees with its antecedent. The antecedent is the word (a noun, pronoun, or other substantive) to which a pronoun refers in a sentence. Here is a sentence in which the writer got horribly muddled in connecting the pronoun with the antecedent:

After the long, hot convocation event, when they had finally gotten rid of their steamy robes and donned cooler clothing, cars of students and families headed to the town's many restaurants.

Read this long sentence carefully. Because the pronoun *they* is used in the second clause we aren't sure who *they* are. It appears that the *cars* were attending the convocation and were wearing steamy robes. Chances are the writer intended to say that the *students* had disrobed and changed into cooler duds.

Now the sentence makes sense, though it's still a bit longer than you'd want to use in a business communication:

After the long, hot convocation event, when STUDENTS had finally gotten rid of their steamy robes and donned cooler clothing, cars of students and families headed to the town's many restaurants.

The subject is the noun (person, place, or thing) that is doing the action (the verb). To write a complete sentence, you can't have one without the other. The subject and the verb are, in a sense, married to each other. They can be separated by other modifying information in a clause, but they still must agree with each other.

For example:

The yellow cat excitedly chased the squeaking mouse across the floor.
      (S)   (V)

For example:

Jane waited three hours for her date to show up, but in the meantime, was entertained by
  (S)   (V)   (V)
three other attractive young men.

For example:

The weary student, exhausted after writing three essays in one week, slept for 24 hours
      (S)   (V)
straight.

Confusing a Subject with an Object

One of the most common errors people make in identifying subjects and verbs is confusing them with objects, or adjectives or adverbs. It's easy to be confused about which word is the subject (the noun doing the action) and which is the object or objects (the noun or nouns having the action done *to* them). Both are nouns!

Consider the following example:

The professor told the class that a pop quiz would be held at the end of the lecture.

"Professor" is the subject. He or she is doing (did) the action "told" to "the class," which is the direct object (or main receiver of the action). The "quiz" is also a noun, as is "lecture," but these are indirect objects involving further details about what is going on.

Remember: the **subject** is the noun (person, place, thing) doing the action (the verb) to the **direct object** (noun: person, place, or thing receiving or being affected by the action of the subject) and the **indirect object** (further nouns that define more of the details of the sentence—the object[s] of the direct object!)

Therefore the previous sentence could be described as below:

The professor told the class that a pop quiz would be held at the end of the lecture.
    (S)   (V)   (DO)   (IO)   (IO)   (IO)

Online Supplements

⇨ **Resources for every instructor.** A rich array of ancillaries makes this text suitable for both seasoned and new instructors teaching students with a wide range of learning needs.

- *An instructor's manual* offers engaging overviews of chapter material alongside suggested classroom activities, discussion questions, annotated further resources, and marking rubrics.
- *Power Point slides* summarize the main points in each chapter in a clear and accessible manner.
- *A test generator* provides a comprehensive set of multiple-choice, true-or-false, and short-answer questions to assess students' skills.
- *Six full-length chapters* offer instruction on promotional communications, marketing plans, advertising communications, public relations, business plans, and writing for the web.

⇨ **Learning tools and examples for every student.** Supplements designed with the diverse needs of students in mind make this textbook appropriate for readers from a range of study streams, levels, and career directions.

- *A student study guide* offers chapter summaries, key concepts, self-testing study questions, and a helpful listing of relevant resources.
- *An example bank* includes model documents from a wide range of workplace settings and contexts.
- *A style appendix* offers instruction and exercises on stylistic conventions as well as strategies to help students improve the tone and clarity of their writing.

COMPANION WEBSITE

Deborah Luchuk

Successful Business Communication
ISBN 13: 9780195446555

Successful Business
Communication

Bridging the Gap

Deborah Luchuk

Inspection copy request

Ordering information

Contact & Comments

About the Book

Successful Business Communication: Bridging the Gap offers a classroom-tested educational framework that takes a career-ready approach to business communication. Using a conversational tone that will be appropriate for students of all levels, Luchuk provides step-by-step instruction on the common forms of business communication that students will encounter in the workplace, as well as a practical examination of how these forms are actually used. Luchuk also underscores the importance of adapting to recent trends in business, offering guidance on cross-cultural communication in a global context and instruction on using social media and other digital technologies as tools for business communication.

Instructor Resources

You need a password to access these resources. Please contact your local Sales and Editorial Representative for more information.

Student Resources

www.oupcanada.com/Luchuk

Preface

Successful Business Communication: Bridging the Gap guides student business communicators as they master the basics while learning "insider" information—tips and tricks of professionals who are currently writing for and presenting to business audiences.

This book is a conversation and a starting point for your adventures in business communication. It was written by a college instructor and entrepreneur who is engaged in business communication for a variety of business and not-for-profit organizations. The book's goal is to focus on the basics that you need to create every kind of important business communication in a wide range of work environments.

Experienced business professionals know that when it comes to business communication, there is *always* something new to learn about how to communicate better, faster, and more effectively. The environment of business and work is constantly changing, so we have to keep up with the latest trends in our field. Take this textbook as a starting point for your journey, and build on what you learn in these pages by doing your own observation, research, and reading.

Learning how to write and prepare communications is much like learning how to cook or bake: you need to learn the basic recipe and why you must follow certain preparation steps in order to master the dish and be able to prepare it in future. Once you have learned how to prepare a dish without looking at the recipe, you can then innovate and add your own style and the suggestions of other cooks or bakers. Learn how to prepare a wide range of business communications, learn from trial and error, and then you can develop your own methods for getting the job done.

Note to Instructors

As an instructor with more than 13 years' experience teaching in both college and university, I know how hard it is to find a textbook that students *might* read and possibly find useful. While you and I generally enjoy reading and learning, we know that many of our students do not want to bury their heads in a book. Increasingly, students are active, kinesthetic, and inter- or intrapersonal learners—which means that wading through a book written more for instructors and intellects in any discipline is not a high priority.

And yet we need to have some tangible resources for our students to work with so that they have access to more information than we can possibly pass on or elaborate on in our brief time with them in the classroom or lecture hall.

I've written this book with students in mind, so you may find this text somewhat unorthodox in its tone, approach, and material. However, it meets the needs of students who are looking for hands-on, experiential learning. They want us to show them what to do and to share with them our rationale for producing a particular communication in a particular way. They want to get in and get out with their learning—show us, then let us work with the concepts, make mistakes, get feedback to improve, and move on.

It's my hope that this book will help you to meet your course or program's learning objectives by providing practical and student-friendly tools for effective communication based on actual business communication practice. The book has been tested with students of widely varying interests, academic achievement levels, and capacity for learning—from mature students and career changers through to students with learning disabilities and ESL challenges. It was tweaked and adjusted as it was being written to accommodate their feedback. Overall, they have said they found the book easy to read because it's written in an informal tone from the perspective of someone who actually "does this stuff" for a living.

The book lends itself to several communication courses, so it can be reused by students and instructors; it has been conceived as a reference resource so that students can keep and use it in their future careers, wherever their path may take them.

Note to Students

As someone who has recently been on both sides of the classroom—as an instructor and as a student—I know that if we can have a laugh or giggle while learning, we will actually retain more of what we are reading. Nothing like having to wade through a lot of dry, boring stuff that doesn't seem to relate to the real world to put you off reading your textbook! Therefore, I've done my best to keep this book lighthearted, integrating some of the more humorous aspects of everyday business life into the basics of business communication.

This textbook is based on real-life experience—I've been a business communicator for more than 24 years while continuing to teach and work with students of all ages. I'm just sharing what I've learned over the years to help you with your own doing and observing.

This is the beginning of your journey as an effective communicator. Not all of you will love, or even like, producing business communications, and some of you will be fortunate enough to have others who can do this work for you in the future. However, good communication is essential to business success. Having the right tools and recipes for effective communication will allow you to make good decisions about what, where, when, why, and how to communicate with whoever you need to communicate with.

It's my hope that you will find this text a breath of fresh air when it comes to the reading you have to do for your studies. It's written in an informal to moderately informal tone, so you can easily learn the basics and then apply them yourself. Once you've learned the basics, you can mess around with the finer points of communication to suit the needs of your readers or receivers, your message, and your own personality.

Let me know what you think about this textbook and the resources you'll find online. I'd like to know if I've helped you to get through, or even enjoy, your communications studies. Email me at deb@luchuk.ca, and I'll do my best to get back to you if you want a response.

Acknowledgements

There are many people to acknowledge and thank for the help, encouragement, and constructive criticism they offered while I was writing this book. A book is truly the result of a collaboration among many people and experiences; it is not just something dreamt up and worked through by one person alone. The saying "It takes a village to raise a child" resonates with me as I wrap up writing this text—it has taken a wide community and collected experience to "raise" this book to the point where it can venture out into the wide world!

At the risk of sounding like a breathy Hollywood starlet accepting an award, there are many people I'd like to thank in particular. I hope I haven't missed anyone; mea culpa if I have.

- Professor Lawrence Gulston, Sir Sandford Fleming College, for mentorship, moral support, and major assistance with copy editing, revisions, and technology meltdowns.

- Caitlin Christoff-Taillon of Take Root Creative, Uxbridge, Ontario, for the professional, technical guidance in social media peppered throughout this book, particularly in Chapter 2.

- Dr. Greg Conchelos, M.A., M.Ed., Ph.D. (Adult Education), for the early, extensive, helpful master review and critique of chapters as they were produced and for his encouragement through the process.

- Fellow professors at Sir Sandford Fleming College in communications, organizational behaviour, and business and in the programs I have taught in, with particular thanks to Professors Melanie Isaac, Tracy Partridge, Dale Northey, Rose Manser, and Roberta Legacy and the fabulous professors in Academic Upgrading.

- My business partner and friend, Nicole Andrews, of Interconnection Research International, Port Perry, Ontario, for her moral support, encouragement, material contributions to several chapters, and advice.

- Ted Dyment, of Altermedia, Millbrook, Ontario, for providing technical support when the computer disagreed with me, professional advice and information to support marketing, promotional, and Web-writing chapters, moral support and encouragement, and the design of sample promotional materials.

- Anthony Gulston for his sage and light-hearted review of materials from the student perspective but particularly for the adept writing of many examples for the online example bank.

- Kathleen Barnett for her enthusiastic support of me and this text, and expertise in providing many testbank questions.

- Dr. Suzanne Bailey, an enthusiastic reader of the manuscript and esteemed Trent University Department of English faculty member, who provided not only a thorough review and suggestions regarding the publishing process but also truly supportive encouragement.

- Joanne Luchuk for consulting on writing and communications in the governmental sector, copy editing, and example writing.

- My students at Sir Sandford Fleming College for providing the inspiration for writing this book, for putting up with my off-the-wall humour, and for keeping me relevant and real in the classroom. You are too many to list, but you know who you are.

- Participants in the Government of Canada's Durham Region Youth Entrepreneurship Program and Youth Employment Readiness Program in Oshawa/Whitby, Ontario. You have been a major source of inspiration and feedback on the book as it progressed.

- My family and friends, who have listened to my ideas, critiqued the writing, provided moral support and a kick in bottom when needed, and tried to keep me balanced throughout.

I also wish to thank the reviewers for initial comments and suggestions:

K. Brillinger, Conestoga College

Daniel Guo, Conestoga College

Melanie Isaac, Sir Sandford Fleming College

Joyce Wade, Sir Sandford Fleming College

Peter Miller, Seneca College

Helen Ziral, Seneca College

C. Legebow, St. Clair College

Neil Randall, University of Waterloo

Marcella LaFever, University of the Fraser Valley

Sonia Bookman, SAIT Polytechnic

Dana Hansen, Humber College

Donna Finkleman, Red River College

Alane Duschene, Algonquin College

Zsolt Szigetvari, Concordia University

Thanks are also extended to the editorial and production team at Oxford University Press.

Finally, this book is dedicated to the memory and living spirit of my sister, Katherine Luchuk, who was an inspiration, a bedrock, and a very effective business communicator in her 30 short years on this Earth.

About the Author

Deborah Luchuk has engaged in business communication and development, marketing, and adult education/training in career development and entrepreneurship for more than 20 years and for the past eight years under the auspices of her own company, Luchuk Communications Incorporated. In recent years, she has developed a highly successful training program in youth entrepreneurship that has mentored over 150 businesses—enterprises that continue to expand, grow, and evolve with young adults at the helm. Deb has a particular passion for helping small to medium-sized businesses achieve success through business diagnostics, strategic planning and marketing, and coaching entrepreneurs to success.

In a past life, Deb also published and edited an acclaimed community newspaper, *The Green Hills Gazette*, in Millbrook, Ontario, engaged in technical writing and editing for a variety of scientific and industrial customers, and wrote a book on Canadian Christian feminism.

As a college professor and university instructor, Deb has taught at Sir Sandford Fleming College and Trent University, Peterborough, Ontario. At the post-secondary level, Deb has also taught more than 30 different courses across disciplines and programs in business and technical communication, organizational behaviour, business management and plan development, marketing, customer service, academic upgrading, creative and travel writing, critical thinking, and Canadian politics. She experiences teaching as a vocation, facilitating "a synergy and exchange of intellectual energy between professor and students" and asserts that she learns far more from her students than she can ever possibly impart. "There are no experts—only people with expertise who (one hopes) continue to grapple with what they don't know for continual evolution. In other words, we are all learners and instructors helping each other to develop and master skills for ongoing growth and learning."

Want Deb to speak to your class or help you develop new programs or courses? Contact Deborah Luchuk at deb@luchuk.ca.

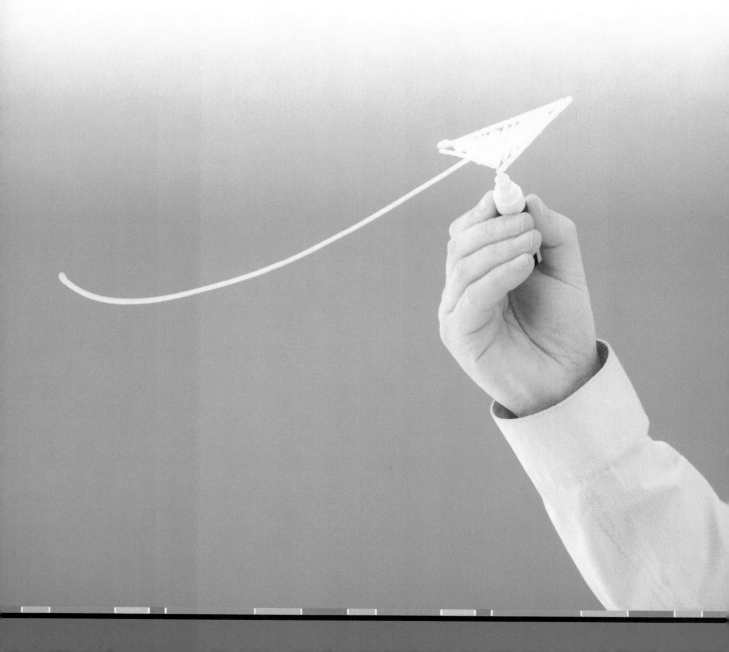

CHAPTER 1

Starting Points for Business Communication

LEARNING OBJECTIVES

In this chapter, you will learn:

- ⊚ How to write effectively to meet the needs, interests, and understanding of readers and receivers

- ⊚ How to conduct needed research using reputable, reliable sources

- ⊚ How to clearly define your message and the information you need to convey

- ⊚ Documentation, research, writing style and tone, formatting, and presentation tips for professional results

- ⊚ How to communicate more effectively in a global cultural context

Before You Begin . . .

As in preparing to cook a dish, you must assemble the tools you will need when you prepare for writing or presenting your **business communication product**. In this chapter, you will find some basic tools that will help you to work with the chapters that follow—and to prepare business communications after your time in college or university.

As a "set-up" or framework for the rest of the book, this chapter will help you to effectively apply what you will learn in the following chapters.

Starting Point Questions

It is crucial that you address certain questions before starting any business communication, whether oral or written. If you don't know who your audience is—or who else *might* see your document or hear your presentation—then it is very likely they will not "get" the message you are trying to communicate. You must present your message in a way that readers understand so that they will appreciate, integrate, and endorse it—and will respond to you in the way you need to fulfill your purpose!

Most important, you need to know *why* you are writing or presenting. What is your purpose? What do you hope to achieve?

These Starting Point questions will trigger other questions (and answers!) specific to your communication project that will help you to further focus and refine your message to readers and receivers for best results and outcomes.

WHO IS THE READER OR LISTENER? WHO ELSE MIGHT READ YOUR WRITING OR HEAR YOUR PRESENTATION *OTHER* THAN THE INTENDED AUDIENCE?

You need to know as much as possible about your reader so that you can write toward what this person is expecting. You need to take into consideration your reader's interests, concerns, understanding of the topic, position in the organization, level of involvement in any planned work, and so on *before* you write. The more information you have about the person you are communicating with, the better. Even seemingly trivial information about the person's hobbies, family life, or preference for tea over coffee could potentially be useful.

For example, if you were writing an unsolicited proposal to the CEO (chief executive officer) of your company to propose a new childcare program at your workplace, it would be good to know if the CEO has children, particularly if they are still preschoolers. It would be good to know how family-friendly the CEO has been in terms of setting policies for employee leave, family time, and so on. It would be good to know if he or she sits on any boards of directors for organizations working with children.

If you found out that the CEO has teenaged children, you could include a subtle message that happy, healthy teens are the result of creative and enriching early childhood education activities. You could also give a subtle reminder of "the old days" when the CEO might have struggled with working and parenting concurrently and had concerns about finding and paying for quality childcare.

If you found out that the CEO has no children and probably little or no experience with having to find childcare, you wouldn't give up. What you would do then is create the message that workers with preschool children are more productive and motivated when they are not worried about who is looking after their children or what their children are doing all day. You could also convey the message that early childhood development activities have been shown to reduce later social, psychological, and emotional issues, leading to a more productive and self-sufficient society and workforce.

In other words, having as much information as possible helps you to pitch or convey your information effectively to the audience and overcome such obstacles as a lack of understanding or even opposition to the topic you are presenting. The old saying "forewarned is forearmed" explains why we need to know as much as possible about our readers—if we know all we can, we will be far more effective in having them understand our message—and having them act on it if we need them to.

When thinking about who your reader is, particularly in the growing world of international trade and transactions, it's essential to consider his or her cultural context so that you communicate not only effectively but respectfully and positively. In general, no matter where your reader is situated, he or she will come from a low- or high-context culture, an individualist or collectivist culture, low- or high-power distance culture, and a linear, flexible, or cyclical time culture.

Low-context vs. high-context cultures

A low-context culture is one in which readers/receivers expect direct communication and don't want to have to "read between the lines" as in a more indirect style to derive meaning: "So, bottom line—what are you talking about? How does it affect me?" Those in low-context cultures don't tend to pay as much attention to non-verbal communication (i.e., eye contact, facial or body gestures) as those in high-context cultures would. Those in a low-context culture would generally expect any hiring or spending decisions to be based on impartial factors—and would be opposed to decisions based on perceived or actual nepotism. Low-context is characteristic of North American, northern European, and UK (British) culture.

In a high-context culture, as found in many Middle Eastern or Asian countries, there tends to be more emphasis on implied meaning in communication—not just the words on the page but the subtle, unsaid message or meaning as well. Therefore, a high-context culture prefers an indirect style of communication and holistic problem solving, which means you must take more time to consider all aspects of a challenge, problem, or project before proceeding: "So what are all the possibilities of this proposal? How does it affect everyone involved/the team?" This is more circular rather than the linear, "point A to point B" method of decision-making favoured by low-context cultures. Business decisions are often made based on relationships, rewarding those who work for the good of the "family" or team.

Individualist vs. collectivist cultures

The definition of individualist versus collectivist cultures runs roughly along the same lines as high-context and low-context cultures.

Individualist cultures (such as in North America, western Europe, Australia, and New Zealand) focus on the needs and aspirations of the individual over those of the community or collective. This culture values individual expression, and people are expected to be independent and self-reliant. Decisions about careers and business transactions are generally based on individual needs, not on the needs of the community, with individual rights taking precedence over those of the community or group. Contracts can be broken if an individual needs to do so on the basis of his or her own needs. Those in an individualist culture don't expect to mix business with pleasure—in other words, there is no expectation of lifelong, meaningful relationships with business contacts and connections. Communication is therefore direct, personal, and explicit; in general, business communication style is straightforward—get to the point quickly and ask for action or response.

Collectivist cultures generally value the group, clan, or business more than the individual. Members of the collective are valued for their loyalty and for consulting the rest of the team before making any decisions. To do otherwise is viewed as selfish and self-centred, and someone acting in this way would soon find him- or herself ostracized. In this culture, "there is no 'I' in 'we.'" Collectivist cultures value harmony, dignity, respect for elders, and an equal distribution of resources and wealth.

High- vs. low-power distance cultures

There are two general cultural expressions of how we view power: high- and low-power distance cultures. When a strict hierarchy (like the command-and-control or autocratic model of management you may have studied in management courses) is generally enforced and communication is only top-down, the culture is described as high-power distance. Not much communication, if any, moves back up the hierarchy from the lowest level of the organization. There is not much that is democratic within such a hierarchical structure.

In a high-power distance culture, such factors as family connections, gender, age, dialect or accent, dress, education and profession, and titles are very important. In some cultures, women do not have the same rights to power as men; in most high-power distance cultures, age is revered as evidence of wisdom.

However, there are important variations between people from different language or dialect groups even in an overall high-power distance culture. An individual with a more "educated"-sounding accent or diction may be given more power than one who has a "less educated, rural" accent or diction. What you wear also affects your power position. Wear the wrong clothing, and you will be disrespected! In a high-power distance culture, you are expected to greet individuals with their title, such as Ms, Mr., Professor, or Doctor. *Only if the individual indicates you can use his or her first name should you ever use it!*

A low-power distance culture can be found in northern Europe, North America, Australia, and New Zealand. Organizations have become "flatter" over the past 25 years, emphasizing teamwork and shallower management hierarchies—at least superficially, businesses have recognized that greater productivity in low-context, individualist business cultures results when individual workers' input and ideas are valued and acted on. Communication—at least in theory—also moves from the grassroots back up to managers at middle and upper levels. The low-power distance culture is considered more democratic, allowing individuals to give their input.

However, variations also exist within low-power distance cultures. For example, the military and police forces have high-power distance structures, with distinctly defined hierarchies and top-down communication.

The culture of time

Linear (monochromic) time cultures focus on time as moving forward in a step-by-step process from point A to B to C and so on. Planned timelines for a project are often projected from start to finish, with all the details in between plotted according to dates/times as interim steps. There is no going "backward." The theory is that by following steps in chronological, logical order, you will complete a project successfully—as long as you allow extra time for inevitable problems or challenges that might arise. Deadlines are extremely important in this culture, mostly found in North America, northern Europe, Australia, and New Zealand. Don't change the schedule unless a major catastrophe forces you to do so!

In a flexible (polychromic) time culture, as in southern Europe, and Central and South America, projects are managed through multi-tasking, valuing "people time" (which is often indeterminate) over non-human work. Schedules are observed more or less, but if an opportunity to meet and discuss with others comes up, the schedule is modified. Relationships and emotions are more important than sticking to an "artificial" deadline, and if it takes longer to work out details of a contract or business decision through discussion, so be it. Those who view time flexibly also tend to live in the moment and are comparatively less concerned about the future. Enjoying the people you are with and going with the flow of what might come up are key to getting the most out of life and work. Deadlines are flexible and can be altered for more important priorities such as the needs of the people involved.

A cyclical time culture can be found in First Nations, African, and Asian cultures. As the name suggests, time is viewed as a circle or even as a spiral; events move matters forward but circle around while doing so. In each season, we expect a certain kind of weather, but it may differ in intensity from the weather during the same season the year before (winter, for example, can have more or less snow). Influenced by such natural cycles of life, those in a cyclical time culture are comparatively less anxious about the future and not much concerned about the past. With less concern about past, present, or future, they make decisions after giving more time to reflection—consideration of what was done before and the consequences; the current situation, resources, and facts available; and potential future outcomes. Such decision-making does not occur in a step-by-step fashion; sometimes, what in a linear culture might be seen as "going backward" is in fact a means of ensuring the best possible outcome. In a cyclical time culture, a schedule is not a fixed, forward-moving scheme that must be followed precisely (linear), nor is it forward-moving but fluid to allow more time for people (flexible). Rather, there is an end result to be achieved, but even this end result may be altered as work and efforts evolve and new factors emerge, requiring those involved to move "backward," "sideways," or "forward" to achieve a desired outcome.

The bottom line of culturally sensitive communication

The most important point to keep in mind about culturally sensitive communication is to *never assume*

Globalization makes the world seem smaller, and this is particularly true for business. When communicating with international colleagues or clients, be proactive—consider cultural contexts, and be prepared to adapt to local communication conventions.

anything about other cultures. Apply the Starting Point questions, then do your research about the country, region, cultural group, and company you are working with to determine whether you are working with a low- or high-context culture, an individualist or collectivist culture, a low- or high-power distance culture, or a linear, flexible, or cyclical time culture. This is the minimum preparation you should do to be culturally aware before communicating.

However, you have to keep in mind that, as noted above, individual and organizational cultures can differ within the overall cultural context that you have identified in your research. There is a real risk of becoming ethnocentric or stereotyping when you rely on generalizations to understand and communicate with those of other cultures, causing offence even in a subtle way. Culture is dynamic—and really, each individual blends cultural influences from his or her environment differently based on such factors as personality, gender, age, education, and sexual orientation—and you won't necessarily be able to determine the precise culture of individuals or even organizations as well as you'd like before communicating. Therefore, keep an open mind, and think before speaking; thoroughly edit your writing to ensure no bias, stereotyping, or ethnocentrism in your communication. Be prepared to adopt the attitude of being ready to learn about the culture of your reader/receiver, and be willing to adjust and adapt your communication style to ensure that your communication messages are respectful and well-received by your reader or receiver.

WHAT DOES THE READER KNOW ABOUT THE TOPIC? ABOUT THE INFORMATION TO BE INCLUDED?

You need to know what the reader knows about the purpose and scope of the communication. What is his or her knowledge of the details, statistics, or research on the topic?

If the reader knows a lot about the topic (as is often the case when information or a proposal has been solicited from you), you can briefly restate what is already known and expand upon the information the reader is not familiar with. In other words, you acknowledge the reader's understanding of the topic and then provide further details in a way that respects his or her position, education, intelligence, and experience with the topic.

If your reader does not know much (or anything) about the topic, you would provide as much detail as possible in terms of the scope of the written or oral communication piece. (Obviously, if you are writing a memo or email, you do not include 20 pages of statistics; you could send a **backgrounder** separately if this information is truly needed.) You may have to explain concepts and ideas in more detail than you are used to, since you may know more about the topic than the reader does.

A word of caution: When you *do* know more about the topic than your reader does, it is easy to mistakenly assume that the specific terminology or jargon you might use will be understood. Always be sure to explain the information in terms the reader will understand completely. If you must use jargon or an industry-specific term, explain it the first time you use it.

Conversely, it's also very important that the reader not feel talked down to. Presumably you are dealing with an intelligent person, so make sure that your style, tone, and word choice pertain to the reader's level of education, experience, and other related knowledge.

HOW WILL THE READER (AND THE COMPANY, DEPARTMENT, AND SO ON) BENEFIT FROM THE INFORMATION OR PROPOSAL YOU ARE PRESENTING?

Knowing the expected or hoped-for benefits of the information you are providing will help you to communicate more effectively with your audience.

If you are conveying straightforward information and not trying to persuade the reader to endorse or buy something, then the benefits of the information may not be apparent. But think about how the information might be used, immediately or in the future. Will this information help your reader to be more productive, make more money, or improve a product or service? Will it help to improve the work of his or her organization or help to prevent a crisis?

If you know how the reader will use or benefit from the information, then you can include messages suggesting how it can be used in or applied to the reader's activities or the company's work. While you don't want to be perceived as telling people what to do, giving subtle suggestions will prompt readers to realize the information they are receiving can be applied in a useful way to one or more areas of activity.

WHAT IS THE READER'S POSITION AND RESPONSIBILITIES?

Knowing the reader's position and responsibilities in the organization will make you more aware of how the communication will be received and what the reader hopes it will provide. You want to give evidence that the information will help the reader in some way with his or her work or position within the organization.

WHAT ARE THE BENEFITS OF THE COMMUNICATION TO THE READERS OR RECEIVERS?

In other words, what is the purpose of your document or presentation? What does the reader or receiver hope to gain from the communication?

If it is unsolicited, you must ask yourself why the audience would be willing to read or listen to your communication—what is the benefit to them? An unsolicited communication must include facts, statistics, and other proof to back up what you are presenting, even if your purpose is just to inform rather than to persuade. Because no one has solicited the information from you, you not only have to present what you want to communicate but must also demonstrate why the recipient should even bother to read what you have written or listen to your presentation.

WHAT INTERESTS OR CONCERNS THE READER?

Knowing what interests or concerns your readers—what gets them excited or what causes them fear and trepidation in the work context and beyond—is helpful as you choose your words, tone, and slant for writing or preparing communication products.

If you know that a reader is very interested in new technology, for example, and you are writing a proposal to investigate a new piece of machinery or technological concept, then you would highlight the innovative features of the technology. If the reader tends to worry about making large purchases, you would highlight specifically and in monetary terms how the new technology would be cost effective.

WHAT IS YOUR EXPERIENCE OR RELATIONSHIP WITH THE READER? HOW DO YOU KNOW EACH OTHER?

If your reader works closely with you and knows you well, you can generally write in a more informal tone than you would for someone you don't know. If this person knows you and trusts you for your knowledge or expertise, you do not have to explain how you acquired the information or why you are the person for the job, for example.

If you and the reader don't know each other, you may have to share (briefly!) more about who you are, why you are qualified to present information or a proposal, and what your interest is in the topic. You may have to build credibility for what you are saying into the communication itself.

WHAT ARE SOME OF THE LARGER ISSUES FACING THE READER AND THE READER'S DEPARTMENT OR SECTOR OF THE ORGANIZATION—THAT IS, WHAT IS THE BIG PICTURE?

Knowing the context of your reader—and of the company or organization in the marketplace and corporate climate—can help you to address concerns, hopes, and needs that are generated by this context. For example, if the company and your supervisor are facing some major budget cutbacks, any expense you are proposing must offer some major benefits for the company.

In order to have your proposal or information adopted or used by the reader, you will have to highlight and detail the benefits of the subject or topic to his or her business or organization.

WHERE WILL THIS COMMUNICATION BE PRESENTED? WHICH DEPARTMENTS OR SECTORS OF THE ORGANIZATION WILL BE AFFECTED BY THIS INFORMATION OR PROPOSAL?

Knowing where the information will be presented—and which departments or sectors will be affected by it—will also help you to write persuasively or effectively, not just to the needs and wants of the intended audience but also to those of the secondary audience (or other people who could be affected).

WHEN IS THE COMMUNICATION DUE?

Knowing when the communication is due allows you to plan for your research, information gathering, and, of course, the writing. Even if your communication is unsolicited and therefore not deadline-specific, you will want to present it at the most appropriate time in order to ensure the best outcome.

WHEN WOULD THE PROJECT OR PROPOSED WORK START?

Knowing when the work would start also helps you to write persuasively. For example, if the company is having a problem with production or workflow—and it's causing major financial losses with every day that goes by—then a project to resolve the issue that starts right away will meet that need.

WHY ARE YOU WRITING OR PRESENTING THIS COMMUNICATION?

This is a most important question—*why* answers not just the purpose of your communication but incorporates all of the information that you have just gathered by asking and answering the previous questions. If the communication was solicited, *why* was it solicited? What are the obvious, stated reasons for the request—and further, what are the less obvious, underlying reasons?

For example, perhaps you have been asked to write a proposal to develop a new product for your company. After further research, you find out that the underlying reason for the development is that your company wants to regain market share from a competitor that has a similar product on the market.

When you write the proposal, you would not only give all the information requested to help the reader plan for and begin manufacturing the new product but also provide some evidence of how the new product will help the company achieve a stronger standing with consumers (and in the marketplace). You would not particularly want to stress that the company would be in trouble if they *don't* introduce the new product; rather, you would emphasize that the company will benefit greatly from improved sales and revenues by developing it. The *implied* message is that the company will be able to overtake its competitor, while at the same time you do not risk upsetting the reader by directly referring to the negative aspects of the situation.

If you know the reader's motivation and concern for the proposed project and the larger context (beyond the expressed reason for writing), you have a much stronger chance of having the proposal accepted and adopted.

Finally, once you have thoroughly addressed these Starting Point questions—and others that you generated yourself—you can create a **purpose statement**, focusing on why you are writing. The purpose statement will keep you on track and help you to refocus if you lose your way in researching, writing, or preparing the communication. To create a purpose statement, answer the following questions:

1. What is the purpose of this proposal?

2. What is the scope of this proposal: What will be addressed? What will not be addressed? What are the limitations of what you will include or address?

Research

WHAT IS PRIMARY AND SECONDARY RESEARCH?

To obtain the data you need to write most business communication products, you need to conduct research. While you may have been asked to write or present information because you are so very talented and good at what you do, readers and receivers are not going to "just take your word for it." If you intend to make any statements or assertions in your writing, particularly if you are trying to write persuasively, you must back up your thoughts with the facts, experience, and research of others in your profession, industry, or sector or noted experts in the field.

Primary research is information you gather firsthand: on-the-street or in-the-mall marketing surveys; data from online surveys through your website; or personal interviews with customers or clients, bank managers, or personnel officers, for example. This is your own gathered information, so it does not need citations; however, you should specify in your writing what you did to gather this primary information (e.g., "A survey with our regular customers was conducted to determine how we could improve our service").

Secondary research is information already published: it can be found in a library, on the Internet, in corporate information centres, or in your own office filing cabinets. Someone else wrote it; you did not conduct the research or do the work that went into it. Because it is not your information, you must cite the source whenever you use it in your business communication and accompanying documents (see the next section, Documentation and Citations, for more information).

ACCEPTABLE, RELIABLE RESEARCH SOURCES

Library resources

Library resources are the most reliable and authoritative, although print resources may not always be as up-to-date as you require if you are looking for the latest statistics or viewpoints in a specific area. Not every library is capable of continually organizing the flood of printed information now available in every field of human knowledge! Look for published books, newspapers, business and popular periodicals, scholarly journals, video presentations, and file boxes containing loose brochures, reports, newsletters, and bulletins.

Most public libraries have extensive business reference materials, such as *Scott's Industrial Index*, and some have specialized reference sources, such as government maps and regulatory guidelines. They also have computerized catalogue systems. Get to know the layout and catalogue in your local library—and its librarians. They are friendly, helpful people who, believe it or not, love to look up information. Many libraries subscribe to online periodical databases containing valuable, otherwise hard-to-find business marketing and statistical information, as well as every journal or newspaper you might want, from the *New York Times* to the *Red Deer Advocate*. For business research, ask the research librarian to direct you to the best sources of information for your needs, which might include a sizeable business section, complete with databases, usually found in major city libraries.

Online/internet resources

Internet resources are quick and easy to search, but beware: most are too shallow to meet the needs of a good business plan or proposal, and some are downright wrong! The most reputable are websites maintained by governments and corporations, such as Industry Canada (http://www.strategis.gc.ca) or Statistics Canada (http://www. statcan.ca). Industry Canada's website provides a wide variety of very relevant and useful business information, statistics, and marketing and demographic data sufficient for most business communication needs. Statistics Canada provides invaluable demographic information, which helps in market research and analysis, and also publishes an important periodical, *The Daily*, in which you'll find an abundance of excellent articles based on government and business statistical research that may be very helpful for your business communication project. Past articles are available through the publication's searchable database.

You can use an Internet search engine to narrow a search by using specific keywords. Many consider Google the best search engine, since it usually returns accurate search results in less than a second. However, note that even Google can't keep up with all the information on the Internet, so don't assume that you've found everything available, and don't be afraid to delve deep into the search results to find what you're looking for.

Directories like the Open Directory Project (http://www.dmoz.org) select websites and list them in subject categories, with descriptions of their content. No two directories use the same set of categories, and they vary widely in quality and amount of commercial sponsorship. However, they are useful for expanding your search into several related subject areas. The quality of the selected websites depends on the quality of the editors reviewing content—some are better than others. About.com is both a directory with sponsored links and an encyclopedia with signed articles on many topics.

Most experienced Web users look for pages of moderated links. These pages are created and maintained by experts in specific fields; the links are more likely to be current (no "Error 404: Not Found"!) and useful (websites with lots of reliable information, organized and cross-linked).

A caution about Wikipedia

Wikipedia, the open-source encyclopedia, is quick and easy to use, and it provides detail on some subjects. However, many articles are underdeveloped or biased, especially if the subject is controversial. Remember that it is just another encyclopedia, although a most interesting and ambitious one. Use it to *begin* your research, to get a handle on your subject, but always *confirm* and *build* on what you find in Wikipedia with other credible, reliable sources.

Never use Wikipedia as one of your sources of information in internal citations or on a works-cited, references, or information sources page. Like using an encyclopedia as a primary source of information, it's just not done.

Business organization resources

Business organizations and associations in your community can also provide useful business information—organizations such as chambers of commerce, business improvement associations, other business networking groups, and business advisory centres sponsored by provincial and federal governments.

Business advisory centres (or similar institutions), often found in larger cities, can not only offer locally relevant research sources for business but also give you access to excellent print libraries and exclusive databases that can help you with your research. Their helpful staff can steer you through the resources and provide guidance if you have a hard time finding information you can use.

Chambers of commerce, business improvement associations, and other business networking groups can be found in most communities and are worth joining if you have your own business. If you are working for someone else and they have a membership, you should have access to a wide variety of information, particularly

Local chambers of commerce offer excellent opportunities for meeting new business contacts. Such contacts can not only be a rich source of primary research for projects but may also open the door to a potential job or informational interview down the road (see Chapter 14 for details).

on local business topics and statistics. Besides serving as secondary sources of information, these organizations give you an opportunity to conduct primary research by interviewing and networking with other members. They can provide especially invaluable help when you are researching local business issues. But keep in mind that federal and provincial chambers of commerce can broaden your search for information even further.

Trade- or sector-specific resources

Trade- and sector-specific organizations may also offer useful information and sources pertaining to your business research: organizations such as the Retail Council of Canada, Imagine Canada (for not-for-profits), the Automotive Parts Manufacturers' Association, and the Canadian Marketing Association. Most of these organizations have websites, and many offer membership to appropriate businesses, organizations, or industries.

HOW TO ORGANIZE YOUR RESEARCH

The more detail you have to write about, the greater will be your need to organize. Give your reader a break from page after page of text. Organize your information under plenty of descriptive headings arranged in a logical order. It is easier for your reader to find specifics in an orderly, categorized text than in an endless sea of words.

How do you do that? *Create an outline!* Here are four easy steps:

1. Read over your research notes to get a good idea of their extent.

2. Using keywords from your notes (words and phrases repeated in several places), identify three or four main ideas, and write a descriptive heading for each of them (this is the trickiest part of the process—you may need two or three attempts to get it right).

3. Break each main subject area into more specific segments. Give each segment a descriptive heading. Continue until you have about three or four paragraphs of ideas under each heading. Then stop!

4. Check your outline for the logical order of your headings and for completeness. Have you included all the important information from your notes?

The outline can help you plan for writing. Take your research notes, and insert them into the outline of your communication product.

Organizing your research in this way will help you stay focused as you apply the information to the appropriate sections in your outline. Whether or not you put the outline headings into your document depends on your audience, your purpose, and the length of the document (longer pieces generally have many headings).

Documentation and Citations

WHY DOCUMENT SOURCES?

While you are conducting your research, it is a good idea to write down all the source information (such as author, title, date accessed, issue number, publisher, and so on) in a notebook or in your notes so that you don't have to try to remember later—or look it all up again.

Yes, you do need to give credit where credit is due—in other words, you need to let the reader know what the source is and who created it and provide complete details at the end of your written piece or presentation.

But why would you need to cite sources in the text or at the end of a written piece or presentation in the business context? Isn't that just for academic papers?

First of all, the business reader, while not (usually) an academic, is someone who has an interest in what you are communicating and could want more information about your subject than your communication contains. By supplying information about sources of information, you are providing a summary of where to find additional information that may help your reader make a decision, do further research, or plan a project or business activity. With this information, you are providing **added value** to your already well-written document or presentation—and the reader will see you as a valuable resource person.

Second, when you indicate to the reader that you have conducted extensive research into the subject, you are providing evidence that you are a professional dedicated to obtaining as much information as you can so that you can present the best, most comprehensive oral or written communication product possible. This increases your credibility as a professional, someone who is not afraid of the hard work involved in generating quality communications.

Third, providing citations for the information you use when writing persuasively (as in a proposal or even advertising copy) generates confidence in the reader, who may be a potential customer or client. If you provide many sources of information to support your assertions and claims for a product or service, the potential client or customer is more likely to feel confident they are not being sold something that will not do or offer what it claims. For example, if you were considering the purchase of a diet supplement, would you trust the cited testimony of the Canadian Medical Association or the manufacturer's insistence (with no cited outside professionals' endorsement) that it is guaranteed to help you lose weight?

Finally, you provide source information to your reader or receiver because taking credit for someone else's research or work is unethical. It also exposes you and your organization to a possible lawsuit from the originator of the information you misrepresented as your own. You may get away with representing others' efforts as your own in the short term, but eventually you will be caught. Whatever benefit you might hope for, it is not worth the damage it could cause you, your career, your employer, or the credibility of your industry or sector.

SO WHAT DOCUMENTATION SYSTEM DO I USE?

Informal vs. formal documentation systems

Many business communicators do not follow a formal documentation system such as the American Psychological Association (APA) or Modern Languages Association (MLA) systems. In practice, many communicators merely state the source of the information

The information funnel

Business communications typically start with more information than is actually needed and end as refined into clear, concise, and to-the-point prose that meets the reader's needs.

It's helpful to envision the research and writing process as a funnel.

First, you start with the idea, concept, or message that is to be communicated. You refine it by applying the Starting Point questions to determine the needs, concerns, and understanding of the audience and by asking questions to narrow the purpose of the document or presentation.

Second, you often have to conduct research, which means gathering as much information as you can on the topic or purpose of the communication, then winnowing it down to the points that will be most relevant to the purpose, the audience's needs, and the type of communication.

Finally, you revise and refine the communication so that it is laser-focused on the purpose, the audience's needs, and the type of communication. The final product is the point at which the document or presentation connects with the audience in the best possible way.

FIGURE 1.1 Information Funnel

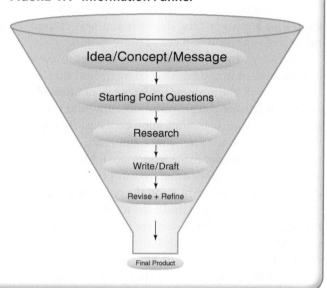

in brackets after the information or quote is used (e.g., "Saving our children," *Globe and Mail* 25 April 2013). In other instances, the writer incorporates information about the source in a sentence (e.g., "According to the *Globe and Mail* article 'Saving our children,' 25 April 2013, researchers have found . . ."). In subsequent mentions of the source, the writer often abbreviates the whole citation into a shorter form ("Saving our children").

Few business writers include a works-cited, bibliography, or sources section at the end of the document, since they have provided the source information within the document itself. However, when writing more formal proposals or reports, an end-of-work list of sources may be required or at least very useful for meeting the information needs or interests of readers.

However, there's a caveat to the informal citation method. While in practice many business communicators do not use a formal documentation system, your college or university may require that you formally document your sources. And while you may groan about this extra work, learning a documentation system will give you yet another important item in your toolbox as a business communicator. Essential while you are in school, this skill may also prove to be a helpful asset in the future.

APA or MLA?

When business writers do choose a formal documentation system for their writing, the APA documentation style is generally preferred, because it is simpler and easier to use in the business context than MLA. MLA is more appropriate for research papers in the arts and humanities.

The APA system uses a simple, uncluttered author–date style of internal documentation, with just two or three brief pieces of information in brackets following the use of the source, like this: (James, 2013: 38–9). This keeps distractions to a minimum for the business reader, who just wants the facts, quickly and efficiently.

The references or works-cited section lists sources in a basic alphabetical format and is relatively easy to use to document all of the potential types of research sources a business communicator might use.

No matter how you decide to document your source information, you must be consistent in the format you choose so that your reader can absorb your message without being distracted by a variety of citation methods. The content, not the format, is the primary concern of the reader, of course, but the format of your writing, and how you document sources, should provide a helpful framework, allowing you to get your message across so that it will be understood.

For more information about documentation, see Appendix B, Guidelines for Documenting Sources.

Writing

RESOURCES

The grammar appendix—in this book!

Do you have problems with grammar? Are you afraid of punctuation? Do you frequently confuse words like *their*, *they're*, and *there*? Not sure how to connect a pronoun or antecedent—or wonder what the heck such things are?

Flip to the back of this book to the handy Appendix A for some helpful, humorous guidance and practice so that you can finally slay your grammar dragons!

The thesaurus

Your choice of words for expressing yourself in any business communication is critical to the professional quality of your work.

If you, like many writers, find yourself using the same words over and over, you need to find others to substitute for the overworked ones. Sometimes you can stare at one word on your computer screen for a long time, your eyes watering, smoke coming out of your ears, trying to find a better word than *nice*, *pretty*, *stuff*, *thing*, *good*, *bad*, and so on. And by the way, using the word *stuff* is a definite mistake in any business communication—unless you are writing about stuffing pillows, down garments, or turkeys or any other situation in which stuffing happens. *Stuff*, and other nondescript words such as *nice* or *good*, are "empty calorie" words: they may fatten up your writing or presentation, but they leave the reader feeling empty. When you haven't "fed" your readers detailed, descriptive information, they may question your reputation as a professional or authority on the topic—or your work ethic, concluding that you are too lazy to find a more appropriate word.

If you want your readers to be well fed with the very important information or proposal you are writing or presenting, give them plenty to ponder by using a variety of words. However, avoid anything too exotic—they may really want just a hamburger, not an ostrich steak. Choose your words carefully to match what you learned about your reader in the Starting Point questions. Don't use obscure or academic terminology if your reader doesn't have the education or expertise to understand these words— you will come across as an arrogant know-it-all. Conversely, simple words might bore a more literate reader. When it comes to choosing the best words from your thesaurus, it's a case of knowing your reader. You must tailor your writing to your audience.

A thesaurus offers another benefit: it not only gives you similar words to replace the overused ones but may also inspire you to think of a completely different way of expressing your thoughts or ideas—just as the Starting Point questions may prompt you to come up with more questions.

The standard Canadian dictionary

Very few business communicators are human dictionaries or lexicographers (writers of dictionaries), so most of us can be flummoxed by certain words. Perhaps you found a word in your thesaurus that you think might be the right one, but you want to be certain that the word will work in the context in which you want to use it.

That is why a standard Canadian dictionary is a must, and there are many to choose between, such as the *Canadian Oxford Dictionary* and the *Gage Canadian Dictionary*. They not only give you the meaning of a word but provide the correct Canadian spelling and sometimes the common Canadian usage of the word as well. Ask your professor or instructor which dictionary he or she would recommend.

One of the biggest challenges in writing or communicating in Canada is the pervasive influence of American spelling, grammar rules, and style conventions (e.g., many Americans use an apostrophe when spelling a plural acronym—*ATV's*—while many Canadians do not—*ATVs*). In fact, the spell- and grammar-check features of many North American word-processing programs come with "American" as the default setting; the Canadian writer has to override this choice with a Canadian setting, if available. Unfortunately, if the only choice is between an "American" and a "British" setting, neither is a completely satisfactory solution.

Whether you are writing for an American or a British audience, you should conform to American or British writing, spelling, and word usage style. In each case, be sure to obtain the relevant dictionaries and other helpful writing guides.

When you are unsure of a word's meaning, always consult a dictionary. Using a word incorrectly might make you look not only inept but very foolish if the word is completely inappropriate for the context.

However, sometimes communicators are afraid of words they do not know. That's why your elementary schoolteachers were right when they encouraged you to learn a new word on a regular basis (even daily!)—they were trying to get you to love—or at least like—playing with language. Don't be afraid: commit to learning new words and using them correctly for variety.

Industry- or sector-specific dictionaries

Are you new to your job, industry, or sector? Are you nervous about using terminology correctly? Do you want to look competent and professional and impress your new boss? Are you an experienced professional in what you do but working on a project that requires you to stretch your communication skills into areas that are new to you? Have you come across jargon that you don't understand but are expected to know?

An industry- or subject-specific dictionary can help to ease your fears about using the correct terminology for your communication project. Have you ever heard the expression "Fake it till you make it"? While you don't want to misrepresent your skills and abilities, you can successfully write or present something that is just outside of your experience or education by learning how to use certain terms correctly. You may not know *everything* about the topic or subject you are writing about, but if you learn how to use the key words and phrases that the audience assumes you know, you are well on your way to convincing them that you are experienced.

There are many dictionaries that address terminology and word usage in specific subject areas, sectors, or industries, including medicine, law enforcement, history, finance, marketing, and technology. While such specialized dictionaries may not always be found on the shelves of your favourite bookstores, an online search will give you their titles and publication information, and you can then ask your local bookseller to order them or order them online yourself.

Style guides

In business communication, you always want to be in style—the correct business style for your sector or industry, that is!

Style guides provide helpful direction for business communicators to refine the content and style of their writing or presentations. There are many to choose between, but seek out Canadian over American style guides if you are working in Canada.

The *Globe and Mail* and Canadian Press style guides are favourites for general writing, because they are particularly helpful for Canadian usage of words and phrases. They also detail politically correct usage of words and phrases, which will help you to avoid embarrassing mistakes, especially when you are writing about socially or politically controversial topics.

The Canadian Style: A Guide to Writing and Editing is an excellent resource on English language usage in Canada. It will instruct you on the correct way to use abbreviations, italics, bibliographies, and geographical terms, as well as specific Canadian grammar conventions. The book also provides some guidance for creating letters, memos, and reports, with various formats suggested.

Although it's an American resource, Strunk and White's *The Elements of Style* is a no-nonsense style guide that has been used by generations of writers (since 1918!) in a wide variety of contexts. As a general resource, this book can be helpful in your writing and refining process.

USING IN-HOUSE COMMUNICATION STYLE

Remember that expression "Fake it till you make it"? Well, it also applies to the style of written communications and oral presentations that is commonly used in your organization. Imitation is not only the sincerest form of flattery—it can help you to communicate more effectively with your audience. If you can identify a style or mode of writing or speaking that is common to most internal and external communications, you can reasonably assume that this style is considered effective; otherwise, the various communicators in your organization would not use it. Why reinvent what is already working well?

Obtain several samples of the type of communication you are planning to write or prepare before you start so that you can identify any specific protocols and styles for writing or speaking. Create a file of these samples, and consult it frequently, particularly if you are new to the organization or business. While you don't want to create communication that is exactly the same as that of someone else, you want to be sure your communication is not wildly different in style.

EDITING AND REFINING YOUR WRITING

Editing and polishing your work is a vital step in the communication process. Chapter 4 will help you revise and refine your writing or presentation so that it positively shines with your innate intelligence and hard work. The editing and refining step should not be glossed over, rushed, or skipped—it is your final opportunity to prepare your communication so that it will be understood and acted on as you wish.

STYLE AND TONE CONSIDERATIONS

Several writing style and tone considerations should be taken into account when you are preparing business communications.

Formality in style and tone

First, be sure to consider the reader's needs regarding formality in style and tone. If the reader is well known to you, in the same organization, and on the same level in the organizational hierarchy, then you should be able to use a moderately informal tone, language, and style—while remaining professional, of course. However, write more formally if this person tends to be more formal.

If your reader is higher in the organizational hierarchy than you are (for example, your boss) or is outside your organization, assume a more formal style than you would use with colleagues.

You should definitely avoid idiom unless you are absolutely sure that your readers, internal or external, understand these terms—and even if you are fairly sure they do, it is wise to avoid using idiom in business communications. If you must use industry-specific jargon or abbreviations, be sure to explain these terms when you first use them in your communication project.

Avoiding idiom

As mentioned above, idiom—clichés, colloquial expressions, or jargon—should be avoided, particularly when you are dealing with an external audience, people you don't know well, or those in authority over you.

Idiom assumes a level of familiarity that is appropriate for close friends or colleagues, but in the workplace, using idiomatic words or phrases can be considered poor business etiquette.

You will notice that this book does contain some idiomatic phrases and words. This is intended to make the writing more interesting and fun for you, the reader, than it might otherwise be. But it is also meant to present you with idiom that you might encounter informally in the Canadian workplace. Like it or not, idiom is a fact, and it does add welcome colour and texture when you want to use an informal style of communication.

If you do choose to include idiom, be absolutely sure that your audience will understand it. If they differ from you in culture, language, gender, age, or experience, they might have difficulty understanding what you are trying to communicate. In fact, you run the risk of causing offence if they misunderstand an expression. Remember, your audience will interpret what you are writing or saying through their own cultural experience.

Culturally sensitive communications

We've already discussed how important it is to avoid using any kind of language that expresses a bias and would result in offensive ethnocentricity or stereotypical communication. Whether you are writing for the culturally diverse audience in Canada or an international audience, using neutral language to represent race, ethnicity, gender, ability, and other cultural identities and factors will go a long way toward ensuring that your communication is respectful and well received.

Beyond writing in a neutral tone, when you are writing in an international context, be sure to find out about local communication conventions and context so that you avoid any major embarrassing faux-pas or miscommunication. (Tip: you can find out a great deal about how people communicate in writing by looking at any available literature, such as promotional material or reports, from the company or individuals you will be working with. Study this material to see how technical terms, jargon, acronyms, and level of formality are used.)

Direct versus indirect writing style, tone, and organization

As suggested earlier, North American business culture (low-context) values direct messages: using active voice, who-did-what-to-whom-or-to-what sentences. It puts individuals at the centre of the action and tends to value *doing* over *being*. However, even if they are communicating in English, writers in high-context cultures (such as southern European or Central American) prefer indirect messages. Because relationships are considered the foundation on which business transactions are conducted, they may find a written communication not as valuable as in-person communication, and they may take the use of a direct voice in writing as outright rude and cold, indicating that the writer doesn't want or value the relationship.

Writing indirectly means first expressing pleasantries (greetings to the reader, reference to a recent meeting you had with them, and so on) and/or explaining the reason that you are writing (events or actions leading to the point of this communication). Only after you have communicated this information do you get into writing about what you really need a response to, such as information you are reporting, a persuasive message, or a bad-news message. Typically, in our low-context culture, business people expect to receive information "upfront" and immediately and would only use the indirect format of writing when delivering bad news. (For more guidance on indirect writing style, see how to deliver bad news in a letter in Chapter 3.)

In cultures prioritizing relationships over time and action, business writing may be more descriptive, "flowery," and verbose. For example, in Mediterranean cultures where relationships must be developed before a transaction, the writing style is vague and sometimes ambiguous, the object being to praise or show esteem for the reader or to avoid offending or disturbing him or her with overly blatant facts or concerns. It is particularly evident in communications involving conflict or negative information. This writing style encourages readers to "read between the lines" for the writer's underlying message.

Again, do your research to find out what is most appropriate within the context you will be working in, since there are variations by region and cultural group within countries. Studying the communications you receive to determine their level of directness can also help you to adopt the appropriate style in your own communications.

GREAT! SO HOW DO WE COMMUNICATE EFFECTIVELY?

You may throw your hands up in the air in resignation and sarcastically say, "Gee— *thanks* for the information. So how do I make sense of it all and use it to communicate effectively, especially with all the cultural groups I may come across?"

First, apply the Starting Point questions found in this chapter. Regardless of a person's culture, these questions will help you to uncover important information about your reader's identity, culture, understanding of information to be communicated, and their social and business context in relation to the information.

Once you have found out as much as possible about your reader from the Starting Point questions process, then you should consider the following:

Does the receiver come from a high- or low-context culture?

North American writers come from a low-context culture, which encourages direct and succinct writing, while those from high-context cultures expect you to be more emotional and personal in your writing style while moderately formal in tone (befitting the business environment and respect for the reader), the idea being to build the relationship. Consider writing in an indirect voice to build a friendly rapport.

What is the convention for organizing information in communication within his or her cultural context?

Many European cultures emphasize writing with rhetorical style, meaning that they acknowledge all sides of a problem or concern equally while emphasizing what they feel is the best solution or idea. Some writers from high-context cultures may restate the history of your relationship or transactions—rather like a "Background" section in a report—before getting into the specifics of the current communication with you. Even cultural groups within low-context cultures may organize information differently from the way we do.

In some cultures, it is appropriate to organize information in order of priority or importance, numerically or by theme, while other cultures place a higher value on written information presented in chronological order, from the time that your relationship with the other party began through to the present.

Which would be better received by your reader—an email, a letter, or neither?

Some readers would prefer receiving a letter, because they consider it more respectful and official in business, while others would be fine with an email, because they prefer a more informal means of communication. You will have to research to determine the best approach. For a start, ask other people in your organization what their best practices have been.

Ensure that your written documents can be read easily.
This means double-spacing, clear paragraph indentation or spacing, and wide margins for notes or translation services (if needed by your readers). Headings and subheadings will help your international readers—as well as those at the desk next to you—read and grasp the information contained in your text.

Always double-check the spelling of your correspondents' names, and ensure that you have their correct position or title.
Making a mistake in spelling a name or title can be considered doubly offensive in a culture where there is emphasis on hierarchy (as in high-power distance cultures).

Be sure to use the same local technical conventions that your readers do.
What are technical conventions anyway, you ask? They are the symbols, abbreviations, and numbers used to express concepts like time, date, measurements, temperature, monetary amounts, or quantities. For example, you would not include metric quantities or measurements in communications with an American businessperson. The US uses the imperial system of measurement for quantities, distance, and temperature; you would convert metric measurements to imperial. While Americans express dates in month/day/year order, Europeans use day/month/year (and you will probably see dates expressed either way across Canada—and even across town, from one retailer's receipt to another's). Some countries use a 24-hour clock to describe time, such as 18:00 instead of 6 p.m.

Avoid slang and colloquialism.
Be aware of the idiomatic, colloquial language you may use every day in your workplace—and don't use it when writing to those of other cultures or language backgrounds. Idiom is one of the hardest aspects of any language to learn, and it is often the last aspect learned when studying English as a second language. Besides, it can be easily misconstrued. Use your best writing manners in such situations, and write more formally than you would for colleagues in your own business context.

Document Organization and Presentation

COVER PAGE

A cover page is required for formal reports and proposals, business plans, and marketing plans. Depending on the needs of your readers, you may also include a cover page at the front of an informal report or proposal, but it's not expected.

In the formal report, proposal, marketing plan, or business plan, the cover page is the first page of your document. It is stapled or bound to the rest of the document. The transmittal memo or letter (if required) and then the executive summary (separate sheets) are attached to the front of the entire document with a paper clip.

Figure 1.2 shows a suggested format for a cover page; you should determine whether your readers require a different format. If you are presenting the document to someone within your organization, you should look for examples in your workplace so that you can create your title page according to that style.

FIGURE 1.2 Cover Page Outline

TITLE OF REPORT
Subtitle (if using)
Date

Your name, position (if required)

Your organization/business name

Street/postal address

City, province, and postal code

TABLE OF CONTENTS

The table of contents is essential to helping your readers progress through any document of more than five pages, particularly formal reports and proposals, marketing plans, and business plans (see Figure 1.3 for an example). It may pain you to know that your audience might not read all that you have written, but providing a table of contents will help your readers to find the sections that are most important to them. (They may read the rest later or not at all.)

FIGURE 1.3 Table of Contents

TABLE OF CONTENTS

1.	Mission Statement	1
2.	Goals and Objectives	1
3.	Business Concept	1
4.	Market Analysis	3
	Customer Analysis	3
	Competitive Analysis	5
	Overall Market Analysis	7
	Competitive Strategy	9
5.	Marketing Plan	12
	Advertising Plan	12
	Promotional Plan	14
	Marketing Plan Budget	16
6.	Personnel	18
7.	Financial Plan Narrative	19
8.	Financial Plan Spreadsheets	20

APPENDICES

A.	Article on Popularity of Barbecued Chicken	24
B.	Statistics Canada Report (July 2014): Outdoor Entertainment Trends	25
C.	Ipsos-Reid Poll (August 2014): Outdoor Entertainment Trends	26

For example, in the case of a business plan presented to a bank in an application for financing, the manager's priority in reading will be the business concept, the financial plan, and then the market analysis and marketing plan. Depending on the manager's thoroughness, the other sections may be read after it has been ascertained that the business is worth considering for financing.

Note that the table of contents in Figure 1.3 lists numbered sections and their subsections. Page numbers start after the front-attached transmittal memo or letter and executive summary and after the first few pages of the document itself—the cover page and the table of contents.

SECTION AND SUBSECTION NUMBERING

An effective way to organize information—and help your reader to process it—is to organize sections and subsections with a numbering system.

Main sections can be numbered with whole numbers—1, 2, 3, 4, and so on. Subsections, which are subdivisions of information covered in the main sections, can then be numbered according to their order under the main section number. For example, subsections of section 1 would be numbered 1.1, 1.2, 1.3, 1.4, and so on.

While you may use different fonts in a variety of sizes and emphasis styles (such as bold, italics, underlined) to demarcate main and subsections, numbering provides a further assist to readers working their way through a lot of complicated text.

This means of organization is strictly followed in technical writing, so if your readers have a technical background (e.g., engineering, science, skilled trades), a numbering system would likely be appreciated.

PROFESSIONAL DOCUMENT PRESENTATION

After you have done all the hard work of researching, writing, revising, editing, page setup, numbering, and so on, it would be a shame to waste this effort by presenting a sloppy-looking document. First impressions count—not just when meeting people but also in written communications. You may have created the most thoroughly researched and brilliantly written report ever, but if it's packaged badly, it won't be taken seriously.

Shorter documents (letters, memos, informal reports, informal proposals) may not be as long as formal pieces, but you will still want to pay attention to small details that impress your reader.

- Choose good quality paper.

- Staple pages (unless otherwise directed) if there is more than one page.

- Present or mail any hard-copy document in a clean envelope, even if it's an internal communication.

- Match the envelope to the paper for a classy touch when sending out an external document.

- Consider choosing a neutral-coloured paper other than white: off-white, pale grey, pale blue (particularly important when preparing covering letters and resumés for work applications so that yours stands out from the rest).

- Use textured paper—such as "resumé" weight—to impress an external reader, particularly someone to whom you are applying for a job or submitting a proposal.

- Don't print on an inkjet printer if you can avoid it, because if the document gets wet, it will smudge.

Longer documents with multiple pages should be presented as noted above, but there are a few other considerations:

- Stapling is not going to work for a very long, multiple-page document. Consider some form of neat binding, such as Cerlox (plastic ring) binding. Visit an office supply or printing store to investigate options; they usually have samples you can look at.

- Covers of proposals, plans, and reports should be created using card stock, a heavier-weight paper than the stock used for the pages of your document.

- The colour of the cover can either match or differ from that of the document's pages. Consider, for example, a subtle, businesslike navy, dark green, burgundy, dark brown, or black.

- Very large documents should be professionally printed (remember, avoid inkjet printing).

- You may want to hire a graphic designer to improve the appearance of your report with better-quality fonts and improved graphic elements such as textboxes, charts, and graphs. While you can put your own reports together using your own word-processing software, if you really want to impress your reader a more professional presentation may be best.

- If the document is very thick in its final form and you have to mail it, post it in a sturdy, bubble-wrap-lined envelope or even a box.

- If you do not trust the mail to get the document to your reader by a deadline (or to get it there in one piece!), use a courier service.

ELECTRONIC TRANSMISSION OR SUBMISSION OF DOCUMENTS

It frequently happens that a report, proposal, or similar document must reach someone more quickly than regular mail or even an overnight courier can manage. Tight time-lines are often the norm for many business writers.

To get your document to the recipient(s) in good order, consider these suggestions. If your document is an internal memo or an informal, short report or proposal, you can relatively safely send it electronically in MS Word to the intended receivers. However, if there is any chance that someone may alter the contents of your document—as is possible with a Word document—then you may want to save the document as a PDF (portable document format). While those who know how to use Adobe Acrobat can alter a PDF, it is not as easy to do as with a document in Word. You can also digitally sign or password-protect a PDF file to further reduce the risk of tampering.

You may be confident enough about your work environment that you feel comfortable sending your internal document in Word, and if it is of a neutral or positive nature, you should be able to do so without worrying. But if it contains something that may be construed as negative by any reader or something that may cause consternation to anyone who might even inadvertently intercept the communication, put it into PDF, and consider password protection.

Sending important documents outside of your organization would warrant saving the report, proposal, or similar document in PDF, simply because details might be garbled in transmission. (There's nothing quite like the embarrassment of a missing chart, illustration, or graph in an important document, particularly when one is trying to persuade someone else to endorse or buy into a proposal.) Blaming your technology, or the recipient(s), for the omission of important information or illustrations is not professional—even if the technology *is* at fault.

After you email a document either internally or externally, be sure to follow up with a phone call to the recipient(s) right away if delivery was urgent to ensure that the document arrived in their inbox. If delivery was not particularly urgent, you could email the recipient(s) later in the day to confirm receipt. If your recipient(s) are internal and/or expecting your report, then phone if you do not receive email confirmation within 24 hours.

If you sent a document externally and it was solicited communication, then do follow up with a phone call if an email confirmation doesn't come through. Give your email at least a few hours to get through to the recipient(s), because sometimes emails take time to arrive at the destination. If no email confirmation is forthcoming within a reasonable amount of time, phone. However, if the document was not solicited by the external recipient(s), a follow-up email on the day of transmission and then another within a week is acceptable. However, badgering the recipient(s) for a response by phone is *not* a good idea. If you don't receive any kind of response to your message and document within a week, you could make a friendly inquiry by telephone. If there is still no response, give it two weeks before calling again. After that, you can probably assume that the recipient(s) are not interested in what you sent.

Chapter Summary

In this chapter, you were introduced to the principles of writing effectively to meet the needs, interests, and understanding of readers and receivers of business communications. You discovered how important it is to clearly define your message and the information you need to convey and how to do that effectively. For you to achieve positive and professional results, you will have to attend to the details of research and documentation of sources, writing style and tone, and the formatting of your presentation. You were also given tips for making your presentations stand out from the crowd. Finally, you learned some important aspects of cross-cultural communication and how to communicate more effectively in a global context.

■■ SUGGESTIONS *for Further Reading*

Cambie, S., and Ooi, Y.M. (2009). *International communications strategy: Developments in cross-cultural communications, PR and social media*. London, UK: Kogan Page.

Dignan, B. (2012). *Collins effective business communication*. New York, NY: Collins.

Reid, M. (2012). *Report writing*. Basingstoke, UK: Palgrave Macmillan.

Warren, T.L. (2005). *Cross-cultural communication: Perspectives in theory and practice*. Amityville, NY: Baywood.

CHAPTER 2

Memos, Email Messages, and Social Media

LEARNING OBJECTIVES

In this chapter, you will learn:

- What memoranda (memos) and emails are
- When it is appropriate to use memos or emails to communicate information
- How to write short, concise, and informative memos and emails to internal and external readers based on their information needs and the information you want to convey

- Appropriate protocol for business emails
- Appropriate protocols and considerations for business communications via social media platforms
- How to write appealing text for Facebook or blog posts or brief messages for Twitter

ESSENTIAL EMPLOYABILITY SKILLS

2000+ Employability Skills The Conference Board of Canada has identified certain essential employability skills (EES) as benchmarks for performance in the workplace. You will learn the following EES skills in this chapter:

THINK AND SOLVE PROBLEMS
- Can assess situations and identify problems
- Can seek different points of view and evaluate them based on facts

- Can recognize human, interpersonal, technical, scientific, and mathematical dimensions of a problem
- Can identify the root cause of a problem
- Can be creative and innovative in exploring possible solutions
- Can evaluate solutions to make recommendations or decisions

Memos, Email, and Social Media Messages: A Case Study

Case Study

Nicole Parks, the CEO of Interprovincial Youth Works Ltd., manages program administration and facilitation at 20 youth recreational centres across Ontario and Manitoba.

Nicole tries to stay out of locally arising issues and concerns, deferring instead to centre managers she supervises. However, recent complaints from parents and other community members have been sent directly to Nicole; apparently, evening programs at several centres have been left unsupervised.

Nicole decides to send out a memorandum by mail to all managers, regardless of whether there have been any negative reports about their centres (see Figure 2.1).

FIGURE 2.1 Nicole's Memo

INTERPROVINCIAL
YOUR WORKS LIMITED

121 ONTARIO STREET
LONDON, ONTARIO
L4H 141
555-983-4567
800-983-4566
WWW.INTERPROVYOUTH.CA

MEMORANDUM

DATE: March 23, 2014
TO: All youth centre managers
FROM: Nicole Park, CEO
SUBJECT: Supervisory issues—evening programs

Congratulations on a job well done in developing evening program attendance to full capacity!

While most centres have been doing an excellent job of managing evening programs, some have not been providing adequate supervision. This office has received letters of complaint or phone calls from parents/guardians, as well as unhappy neighbours concerned about noise or teenagers on their property.

As you know, our insurance dictates one adult supervisor per eight teens on the premises or grounds. No one is to enter the facility without supervisors present.

Effective immediately, any centre that does not comply with these rules will have its evening programs suspended until further notice.

If you have any questions, please contact me by telephone on our toll-free line between 9 and 5, Monday to Friday, or by email at nicpark@interprovyouth.ca.

She feels it's better to address evening supervision now to avoid further complaints in future.

A week passes, and in a subsequent video conference, 19 managers confirm improved supervision. Many are planning unannounced evening visits to ensure that regulations are being followed.

However, the manager of the Kinmount Youth Centre, April Brock, does not take part in the meeting. Kinmount Youth Centre has been the focus of several complaints. Nicole leaves three telephone messages for April, asking her to get in touch, but receives no reply. As they are "friends" on Facebook, Nicole logs into her Facebook account and sends April a private message, requesting that she contact her immediately by phone.

A week later, Nicole still has not heard from April. A registered letter from a neighbour of the Kinmount Youth Centre arrives, complaining of vandalism to her garage and garden. Bertha McGuinty says the police were called but that charges were not laid because the youths involved could not be identified. She says teens have been at the centre for the past week without supervision; she found a group smoking on her property next to the garage the night before the vandalism happened. She asked them to leave, and they swore at her and threatened to harm her cat.

The envelope also contains a letter from McGuinty's lawyer, indicating that if supervision at Kinmount Youth Centre is not improved, Interprovincial will be taken to court for damages.

Nicole tries again to contact April, but there is still no reply. She decides to send an email, marked *urgent* and with a mail receipt, to April and to the assistant manager of the centre in case April does not get the email (see Figure 2.2). To further ensure a response from April, Nicole posts a message on the "wall" of April's personal Facebook account: "Please get in touch ASAP about the Kinmount Youth Centre issue before we get sued."

1. **Is a memo an appropriate form of communication for Nicole to convey to her managers what she wants to happen regarding evening supervision? Should this communication be conveyed in a more formal letter?**

2. **Would an email be a better way of reaching the managers of the youth centres? Would it be guaranteed to reach them all? Why or why not?**

3. **Given the situation (the letters from Mrs. McGuinty and her lawyer) and the lack of contact with April Brock, should Nicole have emailed April the message she did? Should it have been sent as a letter and couriered?**

4. **Do you think it was appropriate to send a copy of the email to the assistant manager of the Kinmount Youth Centre? Why or why not?**

5. **Having exhausted all other forms of communication with April with no result, what should Nicole's next step be: a registered letter? a personal visit?**

6. **Was it appropriate for Nicole to send a private message to April via Facebook? Was it appropriate for her to post a (public) message on April's Facebook page "wall"?**

(continued)

FIGURE 2.2 Nicole's Email

To:	abrock@kinmountyouthcentre.org
From:	nicpark@interprovyouth.ca
Subject:	Vandalism and evening supervision
Cc:	asstmanger@kinmountyouthcentre.org
Bcc:	

Dear April,

I have tried several times over the past couple of weeks to connect with you by telephone about program supervision.

I received a letter today from Mrs. Bertha McGuinty, one of your centre's neighbours, who has experienced vandalism and harassment from allegedly unsupervised youths. Her lawyer, John Talbot, has also sent us a letter stating that if supervision is not improved, his client will proceed with legal action for damages.

We will not tolerate this behaviour on the part of any participants, nor the lack of supervision. If this situation is not addressed, the centre will be closed until further notice, and you will be dismissed.

Please contact me by telephone by this Friday, 9 March, to discuss the matter. You may call me during regular office hours at the toll-free number, 1-800-983-4566, or at home at 555-123-4567 after hours.

Yours truly,

Nicole Park
Interprovincial Youth Works
121 Ontario Street
London, ON
L4H 141
555-983-4567
800-983-4566
nicpark@interprovyouth.ca

Before You Begin . . .

Got a question you need someone in your organization to answer? Need to let people know when a meeting will be held? How about notifying staff about a change in parking outside your building?

One of the fastest and most effective ways of conveying information within an organization is the memorandum, or memo. It's fast—similar to an email—but because it is produced in hard copy (print) and circulated through an internal mail system and/or by postering on bulletin boards or in other places people gather, it is less likely to be lost. (And it helps you to bypass people's excuses that they didn't get the email!)

An email is an even faster way to send out information quickly. For business purposes, it can follow the same format as a memo if the content is like a short report, but most often an email is a quick note to another person with as little content as possible. An email should be short, succinct, and to the point; problems arise when people put in too much content, which can lead to misunderstandings and possibly even conflict. Err on the side of putting only the bare facts into an email, and never, ever convey major bad news, such as firing someone, in an email. Business etiquette requires that you save such bad news for an in-person meeting.

Finally, another quick method used for communication, particularly in marketing, is messaging via Facebook, Twitter, or other social media. Many companies have their own Facebook page and use it to communicate quickly with "fans" about time-sensitive promotions, important developments, or even pop-up (one-time/one day only) stores, restaurants, or venues. These messages have to be very short, because (a) people may be reading them on a mobile device with a small screen and (b) the program may limit the number of characters or words you can use ("tweets" are typically very brief). You wouldn't use social media to communicate internally with staff or colleagues, but you might do so in the public sphere. And that brings up another important point: anything you put on a social media site *is* public, so you must be very careful to post only information that you want the public to know.

A memo is not a letter. They differ in length (letters are usually longer), readership (memos are strictly internal; they are *never* sent to people outside your organization), and formality.

An email can be sent inside or outside your organization. **Internal emails** are usually less formal in tone and content but still must adhere to business etiquette. **External emails** can be more formal in tone and content, and they usually are used to merely introduce an attachment or to confirm something like a meeting time or contact information. Anything more involved in terms of information should be conveyed in a letter (which could be attached to an email) or in person.

Business emails never, *ever* include the instant messaging (IM) language or abbreviations that you and your friends may use when online together. Whether internal or external, an email must be written in a moderately informal or formal tone, and it must contain complete sentences and paragraphs. Spelling and grammar rules still apply. The goal is to provide clear, easy-to-understand information in a quick format, regardless of whether the reader is within or outside your organization.

Memos containing good news and neutral information may be sent to individuals or groups of people in your organization. Because memos are generally more informal than letters, any human resources issues pertaining to specific individuals (unless the matter is very routine) should not be included in a memo. In fact, no difficult or potentially conflict-causing information should go into a memo (or an email). Rather, these matters belong in a letter delivered confidentially, in a sealed envelope, to the person(s) in question. Bad news memos or emails are usually directed at groups of people and would only be directed to an individual if the information wasn't terribly serious or the news wouldn't really upset anyone.

The memo or email should be written in a brief, factual style. It is a brief *who, what, where, when, and why*, written carefully, clearly, and concisely to get the message across with a minimum potential for misunderstanding.

The order of the text of a memo varies depending on the nature of the news you need to convey to your reader(s). You would use a *direct* format for good news or routine content and an *indirect* format for bad news. Because emails deal primarily with good or neutral news, you would use a direct format; you can use an indirect format if you are delivering bad news that has a minimal impact on people. (It bears repeating: never convey seriously bad news to anyone via email, whether the recipient is an internal or an external reader.)

As with emails and memos, text for a social media site or message (such as Twitter or Facebook) is also written in a brief, factual style. The who, what, where, when, and why must be included, but typically you have even less space in which to convey essential information. Emails and memos are not technically limited in the number of words you can use (although if you are writing more than a few pages, you should put the information in a letter). However, because the physical space for your text can be limited on social media, particularly on Twitter, you need to identify the most important points of your communication before writing and uploading.

Depending on the goal of your communication, you would use a direct or indirect format, as you would in an email, memo, or letter. Direct format is very important when you are writing a promotional or persuasive message you want readers to act on—usually because you are letting them know about something that is time-limited (such as a one-day sale or pop-up store). It is also the expected format for routine good or neutral news.

Idiom Alert

breaking the news – Letting someone know what has happened, is happening, or will happen. The expression often refers to delivering bad news to someone, but it can also be used in a happy situation, such as breaking the news that you've just been hired for a wonderful new job.

postering – Affixing posters to surfaces such as bulletin boards, walls, store windows, or telephone poles (as seen in many cities). Many entertainment organizations pay people to do the postering work—putting posters up on almost any available surface!

report back – Provide a report after you have been asked to investigate a matter further or gather more information about something. When you report back, you give an update on the information people had before, perhaps at a previous meeting.

Your Starting Point

To begin, you should apply the Starting Point questions in Chapter 1 to primary and secondary readers of your memo or email.

Once you are clear on who your readers are and what they need from you, consider what you want the outcome of this communication to be. What response do you need? Write a purpose statement defining why you are writing the memo or email and answering the *who, what, where, when,* and *why* questions.

You may say, "If it's just an email, do I really have to go through all of this stuff to write a few lines?" Well, if it's a quick *internal* email, you might simply give some thought to the person to whom you are sending it. You probably know the person, at least a little, so you know how well he or she is likely to understand the information you are about to convey. For external emails to people you don't know well, though, it's wise to consider the Starting Point questions carefully until you get to know them better.

Creating the Written Product: How to Do It

MEMO FORMAT

Memo format is quite different from letter format. For example, a memo doesn't have an opening salutation or a complimentary close, and a memo's text tends to be brief enough to fit on one page. Memos use **block format**, meaning that the first line of each paragraph is not indented and there is a line space between paragraphs. Letters can also use block format.

If you are making several important points in one memo, you can add subheadings within the text to separate the various points and help the reader to absorb information about each one. The main sections of a memo are introduction, body/discussion, and conclusion, but these terms should not be used as actual headings in the memo.

Some organizations have stationery specifically designed for memos, while others simply use their standard letterhead. Figure 2.3 shows a standard memo format; the letterhead information and/or logo would go at the top of the page.

FIGURE 2.3 Memo Format

DATE:
TO:
FROM:
SUBJECT:
_____
Text of the memo goes here.
There is no complimentary close (e.g., *Yours truly*) after the text of a memo.

Introduction

The introduction section of your memo covers all that the reader needs to know about what he or she is about to read. It's brief and to the point, covering the following aspects. (Keep in mind, however, that just as "introduction" should not be used as a heading in your memos, neither would you use "purpose," "scope," "background," or "timelines.")

Purpose: Why you are writing; a brief statement about the information that is to follow. If this is a bad news memo, you will probably try to play down the purpose until you get further into the report, where you will expand on it.

Scope: What you will and will not report or include; the limitations of the information you are about to share or ask for a response on.

Background: The background or context of why you are writing; the event or action that led you to write this memo (e.g., a meeting after which you were to report back on something or a memo that asked you to look into the costs of certain supplies). Background information is not always available, but if you have it, include it in the introduction.

Timelines: Any scheduling information that is relevant to your reader so that he or she can better understand your memo's contents (e.g., a memo about progress so far in planning the company picnic).

You don't need to be tied to presenting information in this order, although the purpose and scope should appear early in the introduction section so that the reader knows exactly what he or she is about to read.

Discussion

The discussion section of your report is where you will provide information about your topic.

To communicate effectively, you need to know who your readers are and, most importantly, what they know about the information or request you are about to convey. If your readers are already quite familiar with your subject matter, then you do not need to be particularly explicit or detailed. However, if you are writing to readers who have less experience with or understanding of your topic, you need to be more explicit, and you probably need to write at greater length so that they will understand. It is very important not to use jargon (specific technical terms only you and others with your training or experience understand), particularly if your readers are not familiar with these terms. It's also important to spell out any acronyms or initialisms (short forms) so that readers understand what they represent. You may have to give readers a bit of an education or an explanation about specific terms or concepts before you launch into your discussion.

Paragraphs should be brief—often only one long (compound) sentence or a couple of shorter sentences. This enables the reader to scan the memo quickly and understand the information or questions it contains at little more than a glance.

In a good news or routine memo, you would use **direct format** for delivering the information. This means that you present the information or query at the beginning of the discussion section. You don't have to worry about a negative reaction from your readers, because the information or questions you are going to convey are either routine (eliciting a neutral emotional response) or good news (in which case, you would convey the information quickly to elicit a positive emotional response).

In a bad news memo, you would use an **indirect format**. Because you are "breaking the news" to someone who will be upset, you first try to convey something positive or at least neutral, then deliver the bad news. Acknowledge what the impact of the bad news will be on the reader. By doing so, you gain the attention of the reader and at least partially cushion the blow of the bad news so that he or she can deal with it more positively. ("I've got good news, and I've got bad news. First, the good news . . .")

If there is any way you can make the situation better, such as offering an alternative, then include the details shortly after you deliver the bad news. If there's nothing at all you can do to make things better, then it's a good idea to express your regret gracefully and sensitively, without resorting to overly emotional language. Let's face it: delivering bad news is no fun at all, and it requires careful thought and consideration of the significance of the bad news, the reader's potential reaction, your own situation and the organization's, and what you can or cannot do about it. This requires practice, unfortunately. But remember: *never* use a memo to deliver any bad news that will generate strong emotions or responses or that is of a confidential nature. Save such messages for formal letters or in-person meetings.

When delivering bad news, it is a very good idea to use non-emotional language. Keep your words emotionally neutral. Avoid laying blame or personalizing problems—identify the problem, not specific people.

Until you get quite familiar with writing memos, it's a good idea to organize your discussion information into points in a template, as in the accompanying box.

Good news/Routine news

1. News to be delivered or question(s) for the reader to respond to

   Paragraph

   Paragraph

   Paragraph

2. More details about the news or questions that the reader needs to know so that he or she fully understands (remember what the reader knows or does not know)

   Paragraph

   Paragraph

   Paragraph

Bad news

1. Good news or neutral news—anything you can report on that isn't the bad news

   Paragraph

   Paragraph

   Paragraph

2. The bad news, delivered in as unemotional a way as possible, using emotion-neutral words and avoiding blame or the first- or second-person case (such as I, me, you, your). You do, however, try to show empathy and express your regrets for the situation where appropriate.

   Paragraph

   Paragraph

   Paragraph

3. Offer an alternative, if possible or relevant.

FIGURE 2.4 Memo Header Format

SUBJECT LINE: *briefly written*

DATE:

PAGE NUMBER:

_____

or

SUBJECT LINE: *briefly written*

DATE:

PAGE NUMBER:

_____

Conclusion

The conclusion of the memo restates your purpose and scope and provides a satisfying ending to the memo. It neatly ties up the details by briefly restating the main points you covered in the discussion section. It may ask the reader for a response or answers to questions, if applicable. Lastly, the conclusion offers a contact name and information in case the reader has any more questions or needs to respond to something in the memo.

A complimentary close, such as "Yours truly," is *never* included in a memo. Sometimes the author of the memo will sign or initial the bottom, but this is not generally the practice in business communications.

If your memo runs to more than one page, insert a header at the top of each subsequent page (see Figure 2.4 for examples).

EMAIL FORMAT

As mentioned earlier in this chapter, emails are brief, to-the-point messages conveying good news, neutral information, or minimally bad news. They can go to an internal or external audience. They are written in full sentences and paragraphs and with correct spelling and grammar rules applied. They can follow the same format as a memo if presented in a brief report style (as noted in the previous section), but usually a memo is created as a separate file and attached to an email serving as a "covering letter."

In terms of the order of the information, you should use the same direct and indirect information delivery patterns that apply to memos. Most of the time, since emails don't deliver seriously bad news, information will be presented in a direct order.

Unlike memos, emails, whether internal or external, usually start with a **salutation** and should always end with a **complimentary close** and contact information "signature" (including your full name and title) so that the receiver can contact you with any questions or concerns. (You can create a signature in your email program that will be automatically applied in your emails.)

However, external emails are more formally worded and usually start with the kind of salutation you would use in a letter ("Dear Mr. Jones" or "Dear Robert"). The format is very similar to that of a business letter, but the text is very brief, direct, and to the point. Use the same direct or indirect format as for an internal email, but make sure you have used a more formal tone and language.

Good news email

Emails to an internal reader are generally less formal in tone and language than those going to an external reader, but both follow a specific pattern:

> Salutation
>
> Introduction—direct information—message
>
> Details on initial information
>
> Closing sentence/conclusion
>
> Signature/contact information

Bad news email

As mentioned, the only bad news you should communicate by email is news that is relatively harmless—it may generate mild annoyance but will not have any major emotional impact. Use the indirect format:

> Salutation
>
> Introduction—indirect information leading up to bad news
>
> Bad news information, presented neutrally
>
> Acknowledgement of difficult situation, disappointment
>
> Remedy, if any
>
> Conclusion—closing with regrets (if appropriate)
>
> Signature/contact information

Be polite, and use your best email manners!

- Remember that business emails are written more formally than messages to family and friends—which means complete sentences and paragraphs. They still require perfect spelling and grammar and attention to all the same writing conventions you follow for letters or memos. They *never* include instant messaging (IM) language or abbreviations such as LOL or TTYL.

- Be careful about the Cc ("carbon copy") function, because (a) secondary readers may not be interested in the subject or even be annoyed at receiving what they consider junk mail and (b) it may not be appropriate for the carbon-copied readers to receive the information.

- Are you emailing complete strangers, such as prospective customers in another cultural environment or overseas? If you're sending an information email, write your message as formally and briefly as possible. When sending emails overseas, always consider recipients' local customs to determine the appropriate style of writing, social mores, and business and social etiquette in order to ensure that messages are well received.

- Set up an automatic out-of-office email response for when you're away so that colleagues and clients know you are not simply ignoring their emails. Keep your out-of-office response very simple, with minimal details. Let people know you are away, what will happen with their email, when you will respond to their message, whether there is anyone else they can get in touch with for help in the meantime, and when you will return.

- Make it a policy to get back to someone who contacts you within 24 hours even if you don't have answers to his or her questions yet. Let your correspondent know that you will send needed information as soon as possible and that you will update him or her on your progress within a certain time—and be *sure* to follow up!

- What if some rogue has not responded to the important email you sent? It depends what you are sending. If the email requests information, such as a product price or the status of an account, then send another email within 24 hours to remind your receiver that you are still seeking information. If you still don't receive a response and the matter is important enough, call the person directly and discuss it over the telephone. If the email is a persuasive, sales-focused, or solicitation email, such as asking for a donation or seeking information about a job posting, wait at least a week before following up. When you do, be polite, and let the receiver know you appreciate his or her time, wanted to follow up briefly to ensure receipt of your previous message, and will answer any questions. If there is still no response, you could try in another week—depending on what you are trying to achieve. If there is still no response, the receiver is probably not interested. Don't harass him or her any further.

- Do *not* forward any email without asking the sender of the message whether he or she is comfortable with it being forwarded it to whomever you have in mind. *Seriously!* Jobs have been lost, friendships destroyed, and entire departments stricken with complete emotional chaos because of one inappropriately forwarded email. An exception might be a *clean*, workplace-appropriate joke that a colleague might enjoy—but do keep in mind that many workplaces frown on use of the business email or Intranet for such frivolity, so get to know your company's policy on such messages.

- What should you do if you send an email to the entire listserve when you meant it to go to just your office mate in the next cubicle? First of all, avoid doing this altogether by double-checking the "To" line of your email, as well as the Cc and Bcc lines. *Never* hit "reply all" to a message that was sent to an entire listserve or distribution list! If you inadvertently sent an email to a list, you're in luck if the information wasn't controversial or damning of anyone else in your organization. Just be prepared to blush when someone else brings it up, admit the dumb mistake, and then move on or change the subject. If you *did* send something that could be perceived as negative, sensitive, or confidential, speak immediately to all concerned, and apologize—profusely. Be prepared for any feedback from your boss or business leadership if they are, unfortunately, involved. The best way to do damage control is to admit your mistake and try to make amends sincerely as soon as you realize what happened.

- Subject lines of emails should be short and to the point but clearly indicate what the email is about. "Requesting a day off to have warts removed from my left foot" is not only probably too long but definitely too much information! Instead, your brief email asking for time off for a medical appointment (please leave out your warts!) should have a subject line like this: "Request to leave early—Tuesday." Keep your subject line to about five words or less, and save the details for the text of the message. In fact, writing the message first might help you to write a more succinct subject line to sum up what you just wrote.

- Use the "urgent/important" flag sparingly—only identify an email as important if it is *truly* urgent (and you can't phone). If you mark all of your emails with an urgent flag, then eventually no one will take your messages seriously anymore, because chances are your messages are not *all* urgent.

- Got a lot of information to send? Be polite, and don't clog up or stop your receiver's email box with a long message or cause eye strain or frustration by making the font smaller to fit. (Reading tiny text in an email may even infuriate some readers who might like to keep their vision for another day.)

- Unless what you are copying into your email is a brief quote or a small image, attach it as a Word, PDF, or JPEG file. Send multiple documents in multiple emails, but identify each email in the subject line so that the receiver knows each subsequent email is a continuation of previous messages.

- If you have a smart phone, people may feel entitled to a response from you 24/7. You are not required, however, to sleep with your devices and respond to every message, even if you have customers overseas! Make clear to correspondents the hours during which you will respond. If email from work is forwarded to you through your smart phone, consider putting a message about when you will respond to your messages in your signature at the bottom of each email. This should minimize frustration on the part of colleagues, customers, or clients and allow you to actually have some downtime—and sleep time!

SOCIAL MEDIA

Beyond email and memos, businesses can connect with potential and current customers and the general public almost immediately using social media with Internet applications such as Facebook, Twitter, and LinkedIn. With most people carrying at least one mobile device at all times, important information can be almost immediately picked up by the people you most want to see it.

Typically, social media are used in marketing and promotion:

- as a way of quickly announcing a new product or service launch (before it is advertised in print, online, or on TV or radio);

- to generate feedback on products or services;

- to build a "fan" base to help in determining what consumers want from your company (market research) or to develop a database of contacts for future promotions;

- to offer tempting and time-limited promotions and sales to build customer loyalty or attract new customers;

- to invite customers and the public to events designed to build customer interest or challenge the competition.

Another important function of social media in business communication is to communicate your company's message quickly, particularly when there is a problem or issue

Social media conversations can move at a lightning-fast pace. If you're handling social media content for your organization, remember to keep Twitter, blogs, and Facebook pages up to date and to provide new content on a regular basis so that readers will stay engaged.

with products and/or services or customer service. A public or media relations person, or a decision-maker at your company, can react more quickly to any negative news about your company by posting to Facebook or Twitter. If company spokespersons have to wait until the next newspaper comes out or until television or radio news programs report on the matter to get their message across, your company might lose the opportunity to do damage control.

Every type of business communication you embark on requires a tailored message, and marketing through social media is no different. The rules of traditional marketing still apply, but there are a few other points to keep in mind:

1. Our attention span online is much shorter than it is for print or in person. Applications such as Twitter and Facebook require your message to be fairly brief, but you should aim to keep it even shorter than the maximum characters allowed. The content should be carefully edited so that it is entirely to the point. Even though you may have many different things to say, you should cover just one message/theme/idea per post.

2. Keep it relevant to the reader. So much content is available on the Internet that you must give the reader good reason to linger over your message rather than going on to something else. Think about what he or she can get out of your post. Whether it is a direct benefit, such as a coupon code for discount, or an indirect benefit, such as a helpful or practical fact or idea, make sure that it will interest the reader.

3. Spelling and grammar rules still apply. Even if it's appropriate to use short forms (only you can decide this, based on what you know about your clientele—your readership), bad spelling and poor grammar are *never* acceptable. Carefully edit any content you are preparing to place online before you hit "enter."

4. Give credit where credit is due. If you find something interesting in a blog or on a website and use it in your post, be sure to reference the website or author in your tweet or post, and include the link to the full article.

5. Remember the difference between private and public and formal and informal when writing for social media. Public posts (as on a Facebook page or in a Twitter feed) are generally reserved for informal, positive, or neutral comments or questions, such as thanking a customer who posts a positive comment about your product or service on his or her public Facebook or Twitter account. Although many social media platforms offer options for sending a private message to an individual or business, these types of messages are still considered informal when compared to an email. As a rule of thumb, use an email when confidentiality or professionalism is required in your communication with someone else.

6. Remember that everything you post online is *forever*—even if you delete it afterwards. There have been many precedent-setting cases before the courts in which people have

been sued for defamation because of something they posted online, even though it may have been "deleted." Keep any negative comments offline. It is *never* a good idea to post a negative image of or information about anyone online, because it almost always backfires—people will rally to the defence of the person you are attacking, to your detriment. (In other words, if you don't have anything good to say, don't say anything!)

Social networking can also be used among employees as a way to break down communication barriers, encourage networking, and help to "humanize" managers with whom employees may have little interaction. LinkedIn offers options for the creation of employee groups under company profiles, and Facebook has the option of private groups as a forum for employees to have discussions, share thoughts and ideas, and post internal news about events such as barbeques and fundraising initiatives.

You would write content for employees on Facebook in much the same way that you would write content for customers—you would include articles on topics that interest them. To do this, you should apply the Starting Point questions to employees (if many people are involved, consider them as a group) to learn more about them. If you can, obtain non-confidential psychographic data about employees from your boss or human resources staff to learn what interests, concerns, hopes, and fears the employees might have not only at work but in their non-working lives as well. (Try applying customer research strategies to discover employees' psychographic and demographic qualities.) Even better, form a committee of interested employees who can provide guidance on content, and query employees about what they want to read through a print or online survey. (A program like Survey Monkey, which your company or department can subscribe to or use occasionally, can help you to set up an easy-to-complete online survey.) Ask for ongoing feedback or article ideas from employees.

Facebook

Facebook is a social networking platform that allows users to set up their own page on which they can interact with friends, businesses, organizations, and brands of their choice. Businesses often set up a Facebook page, which they can use to offer coupons or discounts, handle product or service feedback, and, most important, create a personal connection between the business and the customer. Users who "like" a particular business page receive updates from that business in their newsfeed, which is a constantly updated homepage of information based on the users' friends and "likes." The text included on the Facebook page can be advertising-focused—as in letting followers or fans know about a sale—or it can feature a posting that has nothing to do with selling and everything to do with providing useful information to potential or current customers. As with other social media, Facebook readers expect short and succinct text and pictures or images that can also be uploaded.

Most businesses, when they begin using any social marketing or communication platform, tend to discuss themselves. This information is important, but it should definitely not constitute the bulk of the postings. Posts should be informative, but they also should be fun for the reader. As when writing for an employee Facebook page, you need to know who your customers or potential customers are. Apply the Starting Point questions to your primary customers at the outset to learn how old they are, what they do for a living, and so on. Consult your company's marketing department or specialists to determine the psychographics of your customers—what makes them tick, their hopes, fears, and dreams, and most of all their interests. Write posts and updates that will appeal to parts of the customer's life other than the area your company serves.

Here are some examples regarding a local bakery:

1. **Write a post with a link to a great recipe someone could try at home.**
   The first thing you might ask is "Why would I post a recipe—when I want people to buy food at my bakery instead of cooking?" Well, of course you wouldn't post a recipe for something you sell in the bakery but rather for something else that is easy to make. Your reason is that a potential customer who tries this recipe and enjoys the results will remember your bakery when he or she is short of time and needs to pick up a dessert or rolls for a dinner party.

2. **If you watch one of the many reality shows focused on baking and catering, post a comment about a recent episode.**
   Chances are that if you enjoyed the show, your Facebook page followers would have as well, because it is related to your business and the products or services you provide. You could also refer to something on the show that is similar to a product you offer, such as a unique cake design. By connecting in a friendly way with potential customers, offering something of value, you should receive comments on your post and build rapport.

3. **Trying a new recipe? Let your followers know how it is working out.**
   Even if the recipe is a flop, keep your followers up-to-date. They know that to err is human, and your honesty shows that you are trying new things and not afraid of a challenge. If it's a success, take a photo and show it off.

4. **Offer a Facebook-followers-only coupon.**
   Post a message in the morning to say that a coupon for $5 off a purchase will be available at, say, 1:00 p.m. that day for two hours only. At 1:00 p.m., post the image of a coupon for your followers to print and bring to your store. Once the two hours are up, delete the post and create a new one to tell other followers about the deal they missed and to stay tuned for another one soon. If you have an online store, this technique is perfect for time-sensitive offerings, since people are already sitting at their computer when they receive news of the coupon or sale.

Twitter

Twitter, originally invented for social networking with mobile devices, is another form of communication involving short messages (140 characters or less). This very brief messaging is what distinguishes Twitter from Facebook or blogs. Users create an account, which other Twitter users follow. They post brief messages, called *tweets*, that are viewed by their followers.

Twitter, often considered the most up-to-date form of receiving news, can be used by businesses to convey messages on such topics as new product or service launches and sales events as well as to interact with customers—or to manage any negative events by getting the company's position on the situation out to the public before the media weigh in.

Tweets should be a phrase or sentence that focuses on something that interests the reader enough to follow up on it. A marketing example would be *Free lunches to 1st 100 customers today 1–2 p.m.* To promote your business by building a relationship with your customers, or to promote a better relationship with employees, you might tweet about something of interest to your followers that has nothing to do with your company (as was noted for Facebook, above). For example, a health food store with customers concerned about the health of their feet might like this tweet: *50% off on Birkenstocks at ABC Footwear today only.*

Some of the things you can do with Twitter include:

- Re-tweeting something interesting from someone you follow to your own followers. For example, if you are a florist and one of your customers tweeted about another local business (say, a gift shop) that carries beautiful vases, you could re-tweet this to your followers. Even if you carry some vases in your shop, the benefit here is that you are sharing relevant, useful information to your followers while showing support for another local business at the same time.

- Mention someone in a tweet by typing the @ symbol, and then start typing their username and choose from the drop-down menu. This is a way to connect with other businesses as well as non-business customers. For example, if you were a photographer and one of your followers recommended a great printing house, you could thank them with a tweet such as "Thanks to @photoguy for recommending @theprintinghouse."

- Contribute to existing topics, or start your own. Twitter works on something called **hashtags**, which are # followed by the topic such as #herbaltea or #summervacation. You can post a tweet and use a trending hashtag (as seen on the right of your Twitter homepage) or start your own topic.

- Read what followers are posting for future posting ideas based on their interests and concerns. This is an easy kind of market research that will further enhance sales strategy and service for your company's customer base.

- To save time, you can link your Facebook business page with your Twitter account so that when one updates, the other one does as well.

LinkedIn

LinkedIn is a communication platform geared toward professionals who want to network in a controlled environment online. It is similar to Facebook in that users create a profile and then add friends and colleagues to their network. You can add your resumé, skills, and achievements to your profile. LinkedIn can help you find professional services or help others to find you. Recently, LinkedIn added a feature for businesses to create their own page separate from personal profiles (something like a Facebook page, following similar content and text posting protocols). As with Facebook, users can follow these business pages to receive updates.

One way you can stay connected with colleagues, potential customers, and those in your field is through the Status Update (or Network Update) feature of LinkedIn, found in Your Profile. You can revise the status update at any time and as often as you like. When you update your status, everyone in your network is "pinged" or notified of your update through their home page. (A caution: If you update too often, those in your network may become annoyed by the frequent contact, so consider who is in your network and whether they would really be interested in such changes in your status.)

Your update is limited to 140 characters (like Twitter), so your message must be very concise and to the point. Keep that in mind, particularly when cutting and pasting information into your status update "window." Don't make the mistake of using the update to continually brag about your achievements. (Something like "Just added 40 new clients!" might be okay to post now and then, but be sure to vary your posts with useful or relevant information or links.) Rather, use the update as a tool to build confidence or interest in what you or your company have to say by—you guessed it!—offering added-value information useful to those in the network to help you to build a great relationship. (If your network thinks you are working *with* and *for* them by helping them with their personal or work lives, they are more likely to pass on your information to someone who might hire you or your company.)

Some content ideas include a link to a website or article helpful to those in your network; a pithy, relevant quote; brief advice your network can really use; and a link to news, an article, or website that mentions you or your company. For ideas, look at the LinkedIn profiles of your competitors or others in your network to see what they are posting in their Status Updates.

Blogs

A blog is a regularly updated journal of posts (messages), usually the work of one person who might share their daily or weekly diary of activities with the public. It is also a good way for a company to promote its products or services. A blog can be situated on its own webpage and URL, or it can be connected to a company's existing website. A company can use a blog themed on a specific subject to post helpful or entertaining information for potential or current customers. Popular blogs are interactive (allowing people to leave comments); they combine text, images, and links to other sites, blogs, or media (such as YouTube). A blog should *never* be an advertorial, because that turns readers off, making it unlikely that they will return and read anything else on the site. In fact, a blog's primary purpose is to build a relationship with readers and thus create a loyal following, which will indirectly lead to better sales.

Here are some questions to ask when drafting a blog post:

1. Who is your target market? Who are the regular readers of your blog, and what makes them come back to read each post you write?

2. What message are you trying to convey? Are you informing the reader about an aspect of your business, offering a promotion, or featuring someone else in your industry or related to the products or services you offer?

3. What action do you want the reader to take? Will they be better informed about an aspect of your business? Decide whether there should be a direct action as a result. For example, would the person see your post and want to purchase a product discussed? On the other hand, are you looking for an indirect response, such as potential customers learning why your product is important in a specific scenario and remembering that in the future?

4. Keep the text brief and to the point. Even a blog post (which is usually significantly longer than a tweet or Facebook update) should always be carefully edited into a concise message. Large blocks of text are intimidating and will often be glanced over but not entirely absorbed.

5. Make your blog visually appealing. Images are always more appealing than text alone, but not all successful blogs feature photos in every post. If your blog is not conducive to visual posts, be sure to format the text in a way that is appealing. Short paragraphs make text-only blog posts easier to read; consider formatting options such as bullet points to keep text brief.

6. When in doubt about posting a link to an image or article, email the author or photographer, and ask whether you can feature them in a blog post. Chances are they will be happy to have the free publicity. *Always* ask the originator of any full article, written piece, or image/photo if you plan to post the article or image in your blog (to do otherwise is to steal their work).

Caution! Road hazards ahead: Avoiding social media mistakes

The main challenge with any social media initiative is the transparency it involves, but transparency can provide the best rewards. Customers are always impressed when you are clear about your business and don't try to hide anything. It shows that you not only have nothing to hide but are comfortable enough with your business to be open on a social media level. That being said, it is important to be careful when it comes to social media communication and what you choose to say online. Here are a few tips to keep in mind:

1. Remember that it is a two-way interaction. Don't just spit out information, but rather try to create a conversation with your followers and those you follow. Posting information or news about your business is one way to use these tools, but they are most valuable when you use them as discussion tools for exchanging information and opinion with your customers.

2. Not every message will be positive. Once you open yourself up to feedback in online social networking applications, you are just as likely to receive negative comment from a dissatisfied customer. It is how you deal with these situations that will set you apart from your competitors. Do not try to hide the problem or pretend it does not exist. Deal with it head-on, and your customers will respect you for it. Conveying a positive image *does not* mean that you "delete" customer complaints while leaving positive reviews in the public eye, since the point of using these social media applications is to make your business as transparent as possible to your customers.

    How you handle both the positive and negative feedback is, therefore, on display in a public venue, whereas it would have been a little more private in the past. You may find this a bit scary at first, but if you are able to deal with such situations well, the outcome will be extremely positive, and you will earn the respect of other customers.

3. You should deal with negative feedback in a timely way, first acknowledging any fault or mistakes and then outlining the solution to the problem so that other readers can see that your company is conscientious about following through. However, this approach may not resolve the problem, so it's important to monitor each situation to see whether it needs to be taken "offline" to a private conversation, depending on the severity and content of the matter.

4. Time management is very important. It is very easy to get buried in updating your social marketing initiatives and not realize how much time has passed. As with all aspects of your business, it is important to schedule time for handling this aspect of your marketing. There are various ways of making management of social media easier, such as mobile versions you can work with on the go and techniques for connecting different applications so that they update together automatically.

Sample Documents

FIGURE 2.5 Good News Memo, No Letterhead

MEMORANDUM

Date, to, from, subject may be in different order depending on workplace conventions.

DATE: November 1, 2013

TO: All employees

FROM: Operations Management

SUBJECT: Seasonal holiday closure

Introduction provides purpose of memo.

Many of you are planning for your holidays, so the executive has met, discussed, and decided on the dates for the annual holiday closure at the Peterborough office.

Background to the information is ordered in the second paragraph.

In the past, we have planned our closure to include Christmas Eve (or the Friday before) through to January 2. This has allowed everyone to spend a holiday of about 10 days with their family and friends.

Good news is conveyed here to provide happy surprise for readers (morale building).

This year, we will be closing on December 20 (to coincide with children starting their school holiday) and reopening on January 6. You will receive full holiday pay, as per previous years. This two-week time frame for shutdown is necessary for our IT service company to come in and install new computers and an Internet network before we return to work in January.

Last paragraph always provides contact information for further questions/ information.

Should you have any questions about our holiday closure period, or about the planned IT work, please contact Alison Jones at ext. 202 or ajones@ourcompany.ca.

FIGURE 2.6 Neutral News Memo, with Letterhead

THE FEEL-GOOD AGENCY
2123 14TH AVENUE SW
CALGARY, AB T2T 0A7

Letterhead can be included in a memo.

MEMORANDUM

DATE: September 12, 2014

TO: José Cuerpo

FROM: Jane Greenstein, Facilities Management

SUBJECT: Fall parking permit

Thank you for your recent payment for a Fall 2014 parking permit in Lot A. You can pick up your parking permit, as well as users' rules and regulations, from our office in Room 202.

Direct delivery of information in an informational memo; starts with pleasant thank you.

Please hang your parking permit on your rear-view mirror so it is clearly visible at all times to parking security staff. If you require any assistance at any time, or have an emergency in Lot A, a phone booth is available at the northwest corner of the lot, near the walkway.

Informational memo provides further instructions (neutral news) in subsequent paragraphs.

Drop by the office at any time during regular working hours if you have a question or concern, or contact me at ext. 123 or jgreen@feelgoodagency.ca. I hope you enjoy the convenience of our new lot!

A pleasant close leaves the reader feeling positive about information.

FIGURE 2.7 Bad News Memo, No Letterhead

MEMORANDUM

DATE: November 3, 2014

TO: John Li-Han

FROM: Elizabeth Smart, Software Services

SUBJECT: Adobe Illustrator

Thank you for your recent inquiry about purchasing Adobe Illustrator software for your desktop computer.

As you may know, with our sales down in 2014, we have to reduce spending in all departments. Unfortunately, we will not be able to purchase this software for you at this time, although I can appreciate that Illustrator would be very helpful to your work here.

While this isn't a perfect solution, if you are able to cover the cost of the software upfront, we may be able to reimburse you at the end of 2014 once all expense accounts and savings have been reviewed and finalized by the comptroller. I can't guarantee a full or even partial reimbursement, but if you are willing to take the risk, I'd be happy to make a note to review the situation at the end of the year.

I understand that the software is currently on sale at Sal's Computers downtown, if that helps.

Thank you for your understanding and patience.

Margin annotations:

Good idea to open bad news memo with first paragraph as pleasantry (indirect format).

Bad news delivered here, but acknowledges impact of bad news (empathy).

A possible solution suggested here cushions the bad news.

Always close a bad news memo with a thank you.

FIGURE 2.8 Internal Good News Email

To:	jmorrow@abccorp.ca
From:	lurquhar@abccorp.ca
Subject:	2013–14 Sales Report
Cc:	
Bcc:	

Hi Jane, — Salutation.

I've finally completed last year's sales statistics, and they look great! — Direct format; provides good news in introduction.

I've attached the 2013–14 Sales Report to this email for you to look over. Please let me know if you can't open the attachment, or email/phone me, or drop by my office with any questions. — Provides further details on initial information.

Here's to a fantastic 2014–15 sales year! — Collegial closing sentence.

Cheers, — Overall tone to email and closing is slightly informal.

Lawrie

Lawrie Urquhart
Senior Sales Manager
ABC Corporation — Includes contact details in email signature.
158 Bay Street
Toronto, ON L5N 2B8

FIGURE 2.9 Internal Bad News Email

To:	OfficeALL@customsoftwareservices.ca
From:	janunziato@customsoftwareservices.ca
Subject:	New Year's Retreat
Cc:	
Bcc:	

Salutation.

Provides indirect information leading up to bad news.

Acknowledgement of difficult situation, followed by remedy.

Given the remedy, closes on a positive note; slightly informal tone to email.

Signature, including contact details.

Hello everyone,

Unfortunately, because of the major snowstorm in the US Midwest yesterday—and the cancellation of flights—Tony Robbins will not be able to attend our New Year's Retreat this evening.

I realize this is going to be disappointing, but we have quickly organized a social night in our main meeting room at the retreat centre and will be providing extraordinarily good dim sum, hors d'oeuvres, and drinks throughout. We have also managed to book the hot new Canadian band, Dragonette, to play between 9 and 1—since they have been snowed in here, they weren't going anywhere, so management is paying them to rock the house!

I hope we can still enjoy the evening. Looking forward to seeing you all, and getting the year off to a good start with our retreat!

Best wishes,

John

John Annunziato
Vice-President, Human Resources
Custom Software Services Inc.
9305 Technology Way
Calgary, AB C5T 2T8

FIGURE 2.10 External Neutral News Email

To:	janeway@ottawafamilymed.ca
From:	caravelli@naturalpharmaceuticals.ca
Subject:	Peppy Zippy medication query
Cc:	
Bcc:	

Dear Dr. Janeway, •————— Formal salutation.

Thank you for your recent inquiry regarding Peppy Zippy medication for elderly patients experiencing seasonal affective disorder (SAD).

•————— Begins with a pleasant 'thank you'; direct delivery format.

As a medication that is a blend of traditional herbal remedies, Peppy Zippy pills should be well tolerated by older patients who also take drugs for a variety of chronic health conditions and diseases. In our research, drug interactions are minimal. However, we invite you to read the clinical monograph and information for doctors attached in PDF format files to determine whether this medication would be suitable for your specific patient profile.

•————— Provides details in a neutral voice; formal tone throughout email.

Once you have reviewed this information, we would be more than happy to send our regional sales representative, Ziggy Blair, to meet with you and provide some free samples for suitable individuals to try.

Again, thank you for your interest in Peppy Zippy and in Natural Pharmaceuticals. Should you have any questions, or to book a meeting with Mr. Blair, please email or phone me at the contact information noted below.

•————— Pleasant closing.

Yours truly, •————— Formal complimentary close; much like a business letter.

Dr. Robert Caravelli
Manager, Physician Relations
Natural Pharmaceuticals Inc.
8200 Industrial Way
Whitehorse, YT Y0T 8M7

1-800-555-9862 (toll-free)
caravelli@naturalpharmaceuticals.ca

•————— Signature contains contact details.

FIGURE 2.11 Blog Post

Blog is brief, just over 400 words, to keep reader attention.

The topic is relevant to entrepreneurs but also to anyone at the beginning of a new year.

The writer uses first person to engage readers in a friendly way so they can relate.

Each point is brief, with main idea highlighted and then elaborated upon in just a few words.

Writer gives credit where credit is due, by referring to her sources of information.

Writer continues to engage readers with use of first person, as if she were conversing with them.

Tone throughout is friendly, upbeat; text does not contain anything inappropriate for a wide audience.

NEW YEAR RESOLUTIONS

There is something very refreshing about starting a new year when you own a small business. It's the anticipation of what the year will bring and the opportunity to set new goals. It can also be overwhelming because of the pressure to use this fresh start to your advantage. Here at Take Root Creative, I tried to create some goals that are easily achievable, while others will take a little work. I believe that all of these things will have a positive impact on the business and myself, so here's to 2012!

1. **Read one article a week about an inspiring entrepreneur**
    When I do take the time to read about other entrepreneurs (usually in the *National Post*, *Globe and Mail*, or *Mashable*), it always gives me new energy and drive, so why not have that every week?

2. **Create one new offering a month for my clients**
    This is easier when you have a retail operation. As a service-based business, it takes some brainstorming, but the end result is worth it!

3. **Engage more with other professionals in my industry on Twitter**
    I currently use Twitter for research, posting my own thoughts and responding to other people, but there is a lot more engaging on important topics that could be happening.

4. **Attend at least one design conference**
    Living within about an hour of Toronto, I have no excuse to not do this!

5. **Take lots of photos and become more observant of the world around me**
    I have heard more than one person say that when they stop their daily rush to take a photo, you not only get inspired by the little things in your everyday life, but you appreciate them more too.

6. **Learn how to make cinemagraphs (Not sure what these are? Click here and here to see the work of a master in the field. PS: it is not a video)**
    This is a big challenge, since I would want to do it effectively.

7. **Visit other local designers/artists in their studios**
    There are a lot of blogs that showcase creative people in their studios, and I find it incredibly inspiring. Why not do that locally—instead of in front of my computer, where I already spend a lot of time?

Do you have your own business resolutions? Personal ones? Print them off or write them down, and stick them in a place where you'll see them everyday. It will take you one step closer to making it happen.

Source: Caitlin Christoff-Taillon, Take Root Creative, www.takerootcreative.blogspot.ca.

Want to see more examples?

For more examples of memos, emails, and social media posts, see this text's website at **www.oupcanada.com/Luchuk**.

Checking Your Work

Ensure that you have written a complete, concise memo or email or social media text for your purposes. Why did you write the memo, email, or social media text? What was the outcome you were hoping to achieve? Did you write your post or tweet to address the interests and concerns of your fans, followers, and readers?

To be sure that your message meets the needs and understanding or knowledge level of your reader(s), review what you have written with the Starting Point questions in mind. Yes, do a quick read of even a short email considering the Starting Point questions as they apply to your reader. This will not take long if you are emailing an internal person you know well but may take longer if you are writing to an internal or external person you don't know well. Once you have addressed any missing information or format issues, do a careful copy edit for spelling, grammar, and mechanical errors as well as writing style issues. Writing errors will lower your credibility and possibly give the impression that you were just too lazy to present your very best, professional writing. (Did we mention that you must eliminate any slang or instant messaging abbreviations?!)

Before you hit the "send" button on an email, make sure that your message observes the appropriate "net-iquette." See the "Be polite and use your best email manners!" and "Beware the *send* button" boxes for further details.

Beware the *send* button!

Emails are meant to be quick forms of sharing information or messages with others. However, in the business context it pays to be careful about what you send. Sending emails on the fly can end in embarrassment, hurt feelings, anger, and possibly even the loss of your job! Before you send your message, follow these steps:

1. Draft your email message.

2. Do not send it! Put it in a Drafts folder.

3. Return to the email message when you need to send it (with luck, a reasonable amount of time will have passed).

4. Reread your message. Does it make sense to you? Will it make sense to the receiver?

5. Reread it again. Is there anything in it that might be misunderstood negatively?

6. Reread it *again*. Is it too long? If it's too long, it might be confusing, or the meaning might be misunderstood.

7. Make any necessary revisions. Do not send it yet!

8. If you are responding to an email, check the To address: will it go to just the person you want—or to a list (that is, other people who shouldn't get the email)?

9. Think again—do you want to send this message to this person or these people?

10. If the answer is yes, *then* hit the send button!

CHECKLIST FOR memos

- ☐ Have you applied the Starting Point questions so that you to know your reader(s) better?
- ☐ Are you clear about the message or information you need to communicate? The purpose and the desired outcome? (See Chapter 1 for help with this.)
- ☐ If you're communicating good or neutral news, have you followed direct format?
- ☐ If you're communicating bad news, have you followed indirect format to deliver information as politely and carefully as possible? Have you used a calm tone and unemotional language?
- ☐ Does your memo have a clear introduction, discussion, and conclusion?
- ☐ Have you included all the information you need to communicate?
- ☐ Is there anything that might confuse your reader(s)? Put yourself in their shoes, and consider what you know about them—and what they know about your message or information.
- ☐ Are you quite sure that your memo does not contain any grammar or spelling errors, including the recipient's name and other names within the text?
- ☐ Is the memo in the correct format as described in this chapter?

CHECKLIST FOR emails

- ☐ Have you applied the Starting Point questions so that you know your reader(s) better?
- ☐ Are you clear on the message or information you need to communicate? The purpose and the desired outcome? (See Chapter 1 for help with this.)
- ☐ Is the email to be sent internally (within your organization) or externally (e.g., to a customer)? Have you chosen the correct tone and style for an internal or external readership?
- ☐ If you are sending a good news or neutral email, have you followed direct format?
- ☐ If you are sending a bad news email, have you followed indirect format to deliver negative news as politely and carefully as possible? Have you used a calm tone and unemotional language?
- ☐ If it's bad news, should you communicate it via email? Should it be conveyed in a letter or in person instead?
- ☐ Does the message have a clear introduction, discussion, and conclusion?
- ☐ Have you included all the information you need to communicate?
- ☐ Is there anything that might confuse your reader(s)? Put yourself in their shoes, and consider what you know about them—and what they know about your message or information.
- ☐ Are you quite sure that the email does not contain any grammar or spelling errors, including the recipient's name and other names within the text?
- ☐ Are you sure that you have not used any instant messaging jargon or abbreviations in your email? Have you used complete words and sentences?

CHECKLIST FOR social media

- ☐ Have you applied the Starting Point questions so that you know your readers better?
- ☐ Have you reviewed any available marketing or psychographic research into primary and secondary customers to determine key interests and concerns you could write about in posts?
- ☐ Are you clear on the message or information you need to communicate? The purpose and the desired outcome? (See Chapter 1 for help with this.)
- ☐ Is the message short, meeting the specifications of the form of social media?
- ☐ If you are posting good or neutral news or information, have you followed direct format?
- ☐ If you are posting a response to bad news, such as an incident or accident at your company, have you followed indirect format to deliver negative news as politely and carefully as possible? Have you used a calm tone and unemotional language?
- ☐ Have you covered the basic who, what, where, when, why, and how in your posting or tweet so that customers know what to do with the information?
- ☐ Have you included all the information you need to communicate?
- ☐ Is there anything that might confuse your readers? Put yourself in their shoes, and consider what you know about them—and what they know about your message or information.
- ☐ Are you quite sure that the post or tweet does not contain any grammar or spelling errors?

Chapter Summary

In this chapter, you have learned suitable forms and business functions for memos, emails, and social media. You have also learned when in a business context it is appropriate to choose an email or a memo to communicate information and how to apply appropriate protocols for business emails. You have become skilled at writing short, concise, informative memos and emails to readers inside and outside your organization, based on your readers' need for information and on your own need to convey information. Finally, you have learned more about how and when to use social media in business communication and marketing and how to craft messages in post or tweet form.

▮▮ SUGGESTIONS *for Further Reading*

Baer, J., and Naslund, A. (2011). *The NOW revolution: 7 shifts to make your business faster, smarter and more social.* New York, NY: Wiley Publishing.

Gillin, P., and Schwartzman, E. (2011). *Social marketing to the business customer: Listen to your B2B market, generate major account leads, and build client relationships.* New York, NY: Wiley Publishing.

Macy, B., and Thompson, T. (2010). *The power of real-time social media marketing: How to attract and retain customers and grow the bottom line in the globally connected world.* New York, NY: McGraw-Hill.

Metz, A. (2011). *The social customer: How brands can use social CRM to acquire, monetize, and retain fans, friends, and followers.* New York, NY: McGraw-Hill.

Zarella, D. (2009). *The social media marketing book.* Sebastopol, CA: O'Reilly Publishing.

◼◼◼ DEBATE *and Discussion Starters*

1. Is it ever appropriate to send bad news by email or memo? In what situations would it be appropriate? Inappropriate? Discuss.

2. How would you handle the situation if you accidentally sent an email intended for one colleague to the entire distribution list—including your boss—and in the email you complained about a decision the boss had made?

3. What kind of information is appropriate for your personal Facebook page—particularly when you will be looking for work in your field following graduation or are trying to find work while in school? What kind of information would be inappropriate for a business Facebook page?

4. Do you agree that "once it's out there, it's permanent" when it comes to information posted on social media? Why or why not?

◼◼◼ PRACTISING *What You Have Learned*

1. You are in charge of your organization's annual barbecue. Write a routine memo (using direct format) to your fellow employees and management about what they need to bring to the barbecue, directions to the locale, and the activities planned. (Hint: This would be a good time to think about using subheadings to break up the information in the discussion portion of the memo.)

    Use your imagination to dream up a location, directions, and activities.

2. Because of a major increase in sales—and revenues—over the past year, your company's CEO has decided to award everyone in the company (from the janitorial staff to senior managers) a bonus of $1,000. The bonus will be included in the last paycheques of the year, just before the break for the holidays.

    As the CEO's executive assistant, it is your job to write a memo sharing the good news with all employees. Use your imagination to come up with the details as to why the company was successful in the past year, what the employees contributed to this success, and so on.

3. The company Intranet system will be out of service for the entire day on Thursday, which means that no one will be able to use email or the Internet between 8:00 a.m. and 6:00 p.m.

    This will particularly affect the sales department, since they are currently engaged in an email marketing campaign. Write a bad news memo advising the sales department of the shutdown, and let them know there will be a group visioning meeting in the corporate boardroom instead, complete with snacks and beverages (they will need to bring a lunch).

4. Write an email to employees to let them know that the company will be receiving new computers and peripherals for each workstation next month (February). Tell them as well that installation day is February 14, and because this means that no one will be able to work on a computer at the office, employees can have the day off (perfect for Valentine's Day celebrations with someone special, family, or friends).

5. Write an email responding to a potential client or customer (an external reader) who has inquired about a specific product or service your company sells. Give the customer information about the product or service, keeping in mind what the customer would consider important and what would encourage this person to buy the product or service. Use your imagination to come up with the name of the company, what it sells or provides, and the details you will provide to the customer.

6. Write an email letting your colleague on the social committee know that the restaurant you have been trying to book for the company Christmas party is already booked. Give information about two other options, and suggest that the two of you go to these restaurants so that you can determine which would be best for the company's needs. Ask your colleague to choose a specific time when you can do this together.

7. Write a memo to all employees advising them of the discount parking permits that are available for parking in the municipal lot adjacent to the office. Since there are only four spaces in the company parking area and they are taken by salespeople who need to be in and out of the office frequently, everyone else has been parking wherever they can (and getting a lot of parking tickets). The permits will cost $20 a month (a saving of $10 per month over the full rate); payment can be debited automatically from the employee's bank account (they should contact the Parking Department at city hall) or can be made at city hall by the last day of each month for the following month.

8. Write a blog or Facebook post about good and bad customer service and what businesses can do about poor customer service when they have a negative reputation.

CHAPTER 3

Business Letters

LEARNING OBJECTIVES

In this chapter, you will learn:

- What business letters are and when it is appropriate to use letters to communicate

- How to write short, concise, informative letters to internal and external readers based on their information needs and the information you want to convey

- Appropriate protocol for business letters

- How to organize and write business letters for good or bad news

- How to organize and write business letters as short, informal reports

ESSENTIAL EMPLOYABILITY SKILLS

2000+ Employability Skills The Conference Board of Canada has identified certain essential employability skills (EES) as benchmarks for performance in the workplace. You will learn the following EES skills in this chapter:

THINK AND SOLVE PROBLEMS

- Can assess situations and identify problems
- Can seek different points of view and evaluate them based on facts
- Can recognize the human, interpersonal, technical, scientific, and mathematical dimensions of a problem
- Can identify the root cause of a problem

- Can be creative and innovative in exploring possible solutions
- Can evaluate solutions to make recommendations or decisions

COMMUNICATE

- Can read and understand information presented in a variety of forms (e.g., words, graphs, charts, diagrams)
- Can write and speak so others pay attention and understand
- Can listen and ask questions to understand and appreciate the points of view of others

Case Study

Business Letters: A Case Study

Lisa Stack manages a government-funded program for youths who are out of school, un- or underemployed, and on social assistance. Her company, Reach Higher Limited, provides three four-month pre-employment skills programs per year.

The provincial government's Journeys in Employment program provides 25 participants per intake with skills development in career search, resumé and covering letter writing, and self-assessments to determine personal and vocational strengths and weaknesses. The program represents a major investment by the government; the annual budget is $500,000, including participant training allowances.

Reach Higher went through a very competitive tendering process to win the program contract. Now Lisa needs to impress the government with competent management of the program. It's the end of the first month of the first program, and she has to provide a short, detailed report on the program and participants in letter format.

She must prove that program objectives are being met and that participants are attending and meeting obligations. The government project officer assigned to the contract needs details about each participant's progress. If there are problems, they need to be noted; however, it's also important that Lisa indicate that she has resolved or is about to resolve the problems with specific actions.

The report letter is for project officer Charles Sorel. Lisa has met him only once, and he seems a formal, quiet person. Here are Lisa's notes:

- Most participants are progressing well, focused on self-assessments/career choices.

- Some participants missed mandatory sessions, are still being paid an allowance.

- Participants completed a Myers-Briggs Type Indicator test to determine personal strengths/weaknesses, potential career choices.

- One student has to leave program—experiencing complications of a high-risk pregnancy.

- Next month, program focus is on interpersonal dynamics, conflict resolution, emotion management in the workplace—skills that many are lacking.

Figure 3.1 shows Lisa's letter.

1. What do you think project officer Charles Sorel's reaction will be to this letter?

2. Is Lisa providing enough information on participants to give the government the details they need—that the program is being managed well and participants are living up to their contractual obligations?

3. Is Lisa providing too much information? In other words, is there a better way she can report on the problems that have occurred without raising major concern on the part of Mr. Sorel?

4. Does Lisa offer any explanation for the problems and how she plans to or has already addressed them?

FIGURE 3.1 Lisa Stack's Letter

REACH HIGHER LIMITED

1234 ROBSON STREET, UNIT #25
VANCOUVER, BC V3T 3T5
604-743-8903

May 3, 2013

Charles Sorel, Project Officer
Ministry of Employment and Income Services
Employment Programs Management—Youth
614 Humboldt Street
Victoria, BC V8W 9R1

Dear Charlie,

Here's our first monthly report for the Journeys in Employment program. Hope you like it.

A lot of the 25 participants are really screwed up, so we had to figure out how to deal with them. So we got them a facilitator to run some personality tests. Some of them don't show up for sessions, and don't have legitimate reasons for being absent, but we figure we should still pay them because they don't have no other income.

Juno Sweet has gotten herself pregnant in a one-night stand with another participant. Now she's having medical problems, so she will have to drop out. She will require a letter to her probation officer to inform him that she can't continue.

The program facility got broken into, and our new AV equipment was stolen, but we taped up the window. Unfortunately, we don't have any insurance to replace the equipment.

All in all, it's been a good month. Thirteen out of 20 participants have taken part in most of the sessions. In May there will be workshops on interpersonal dynamics and emotion management in the workplace—something that may help the guys who swear at each other during sessions.

If you have any questions, please let me know, okay?

Thanks a bunch,

Lisa Stack
President, Reach Higher Ltd

(continued)

5. Is the tone and style of this letter appropriate for a government official, especially one who has a formal personality?

6. Rewrite the letter so that it is appropriate for the information needs and concerns of the reader, Charles Sorel, and possible secondary readers (others in the Ministry of Employment and Income Services). Revisit the Starting Point questions in Chapter 1, and apply them to this case to determine how to write the letter so that it conveys the necessary information and meets the needs of Mr. Sorel.

Before You Begin . . .

Want to communicate with an organization or individual outside your own business, organization, or workplace? A business letter communicates or solicits information; persuades the reader to endorse, buy, or support something; or delivers less-than-good news.

Letters written to deliver what can be classified as good or neutral news convey brief information to an outside reader, much as you would use a memo for the same purpose for readers within your organization. Therefore, business letters can be used for communications on progress, evaluation, information, incidents, or expenses, for example.

You can also use a letter for a persuasive or promotional purpose. If you are trying to get another organization or individual to support a new initiative, a program, or the work of your organization, to buy from you, or to join you in a project or plan (an alliance or business relationship), you would write a letter using a persuasive tone and language. In this regard, persuasive letters are written much like proposals, business plans, and marketing plans—they are aimed at winning a "buy-in" from the reader and the reader's organization or business.

Finally, a business letter is also used to deliver bad news to potential and current clients or customers, as well as others outside your organization. An example of a bad news letter would be one that denies a customer a refund on a product because the product had been used improperly, making the warranty invalid. Bad news letters are extremely important in customer service situations where one has to deliver bad news but still maintain a positive customer relationship. Therefore, these letters have to be written with great care and attention to tone, word choice, and level of formality. Unfortunately, bad news travels faster than good news in the realm of customer service.

A letter is also used *within* an organization when the subject involves a serious internal matter. For example, a letter is more appropriate than a memo for communicating with an employee about **disciplinary action**. A confidential letter is sent to the employee, is often copied to a supervisor, and is kept for the record in the employee's **human resources file**. Letters rather than memos are also used when there is a matter of legal concern. Check with your supervisor or someone else in your organization to find out the protocol on using letters for formal communications within your organization.

Remember—memos are for internal audiences only. Letters are for external readers or for very serious internal matters.

Your Starting Point

When writing a letter, you need to know all about your reader—and why you are writing. Go back to the Starting Point questions in Chapter 1 to clearly establish who the reader or readers are and why you are writing the letter. With this information, you will be able to clearly plan what information to include (and exclude) in the letter and how to position it.

For example, you find out that the reader is expecting a letter outlining progress to date on a project. There have been several delays in completing the work, so you will want to put the more positive information about progress earlier in the letter, with the less-than-happy information later on. (This is the basic format of a bad news letter, which we will cover later in this chapter.)

As another example, you have been asked to send your bosses an evaluation of three different options for a new computer system for the office. Your bosses are not very computer- or techno-savvy, so you will have to avoid using jargon and put all the information in simple yet intelligent terms that they will be able to understand.

Think about this process as similar to preparing for a special meal or a do-it-yourself project. You would find out what the project or meal is, determine what ingredients are needed to make it a success, and then organize these elements so that everything turns out well.

Creating the Written Product: How to Do It

PREPARING TO WRITE

Research

As one of the brief forms of business communication, letters usually do not require a lot of research to produce, much like internal memos. Routine letters (for good or neutral news) include only brief, targeted information, which doesn't require much research.

Idiom Alert

you know the drill – In the armed forces, personnel perform what are known as drills (such as marching) every day. If you do a drill often enough, you can remember almost automatically what to do without really thinking about it. If you know the drill when it comes to a task or activity, it means that you've done it so many times that you can do it automatically.

in-house – Specific to your workplace.

buy-in – When someone "buys in" to your idea or proposal, they are not just endorsing it but have had an emotional response to it, which makes them support it enthusiastically.

super-duper – Excellent.

putting yourself in someone else's shoes – Being empathetic; trying to appreciate and understand a situation from the other person's perspective.

softening the blow – Delivering the news in such a way as to minimize the negative emotional impact.

savvy – Knowledgeable about a subject (e.g., computer-savvy, techno-savvy).

de-icer – A substance that is placed on icy surfaces to melt it. Salt is a traditional de-icer used to make roadways and walkways safer for drivers and pedestrians.

However, the quantity of information needed depends on the purpose of the letter and on the reader(s). You may start with a lot more information than you need or than the reader can understand, so you must winnow down the information until you have the best, clearest message.

Bad news letters, such as those refusing to give a refund, require that you stick to the facts about the situation; often, you must also offer a solid rationale for the bad news. While the final letter will be brief, succinctly stating the bad news and the reason for it, you need to gather whatever information is necessary to meet the needs of the reader (and your company).

If the reader has requested a letter outlining some information about a new product the company can retail to consumers, then you will want to gather as much information as you can about the product before you begin writing. Be sure to keep detailed notes on your information sources so that you can tell the reader where you got the information (see the section on citations in Chapter 1). However, you will need to review all of the researched material carefully to determine what information is really relevant to the reader's needs and level of understanding, since you want to keep the letter brief and to the point and ensure that the reader understands everything that is included. In an **information report** letter (one that states only the facts you want to communicate and doesn't try to persuade), use only the information that gives the reader the most complete picture in the fewest words possible.

If you are writing a **progress report** letter (in which you detail your or your team's progress to date in completing a project), you would obtain as much information as the reader can digest and tailor it to fit the reader's needs. You also need to know how the information will affect him or her. For example, if the project is behind schedule and you know the reader may be negatively affected by the delay, you would want to be sure to highlight the positive information and minimize the negative. The trick is in making sure the reader understands that there is a delay without causing undue alarm or upset. You also need to let the reader know how you are dealing with the causes of the delay. Again, obtain more information than you need, and sift out what you feel is most relevant to the needs of your readers and their concerns.

An **evaluation report** letter (in which you give the reader your opinion on the pros and cons of something and possibly make a suggestion for action, based on your research), as in an informal memo-format report (see Chapter 8), must provide detailed, balanced information on each choice or product being considered so that all are given equal consideration, letting the reader make the choice. If you are asked to decide which option is best for your organization, you will need to prove *why* your choice is best with appropriate information and documentation. Since you may have a lot of ground to cover in terms of evaluating various options, you must ensure that you take all of your information and deliberately narrow it down to suit the needs of the reader—and the length of the letter.

An **incident report** letter (in which you give the details and facts concerning an incident or event) should provide all the details of the incident and nothing more. Be sure to meet all of the reader's information needs—you can learn what these needs are by finding out why he or she has requested the report—and be sure to use several good sources if possible so that your reader knows that you were very thorough and considered as many facts as possible in your investigation. If you are asked to make recommendations or assign fault for the incident, be sure to back up your opinions with facts from credible information sources.

In an **expense report** letter (in which you give details about money spent and benefits to the company), as in an informal memo-format report (see Chapter 8), you provide as much information as the reader needs to know about what you spent, why, and what the benefit is. Keep it short and to the point, but include documentation to show what you spent the money on.

Research sources (depending on the purpose of your letter) can include:

- interviews with individuals involved (bad news letters; progress, incident, and possibly evaluation report letters);

- company policy documents (bad news letters; progress, incident, and information report letters);

- libraries (particularly for report letters);

- online business and information resources such as databases, websites, blogs (good and bad news letters; report letters);

- a helpful reference librarian (all!);

- print or online information about the external company or organization you are preparing the letter for (all!);

- your own observations (bad news letters; progress, incident, evaluation, information, and expense reports).

PREPARING FOR CITATIONS

To prevent aggravation later on—and to avoid spending far too much time on a brief letter—make sure that you keep all information about your sources in one place. Yes, it's a letter, and you may be wondering why you have to cite your sources. However, as with any other form of business communication, it's important to give credit where credit is due—and to prove your brilliance and competence by providing the best information possible to your reader from appropriate sources.

By now, you probably know the drill. If *all* the information about your sources is in one place—in a file folder, for instance—you can readily put your hands on it when the time comes to write the letter.

ORGANIZING INFORMATION AND WRITING: FORMAT

Figure 3.2 shows a **full-block format** for a business letter. All letters must be left-justified; most start about eight line spaces down from the top of the page. (There are several other formats for business letters, including **semi-block form** and simplified formats, and your instructor may have others for you to work with. Once you get into a workplace, find out what format is used there for a letter. Many workplaces have their own in-house format and style that you should follow.)

If you are using a letterhead, leave at least five line spaces after the letterhead information before you type the date. The letterhead includes your company's basic contact information.

Good news letters

Letters conveying good (or neutral) news use a simple, direct format, because there is no reason to cushion the reader from what is being delivered, as is necessary in bad news letters.

In accordance with the basic format for letters, the introductory paragraph outlines the purpose (why you are writing), scope (what you will or will not cover in the letter), timelines (if applicable), and background (if applicable to the purpose of the letter).

FIGURE 3.2 Business Letter Format

Letterhead here, if using. ———

LETTERHEAD

Leave five to eight line spaces here.

Date is left-justified; some workplaces right-justify date.

Date:

Leave five line spaces here.———

If not using letterhead, insert your contact information here.

Your name (and position)
Your company/organization
Company address
City, province, postal code

Leave three line spaces here.

Name of person you are writing to (and position)
Their company/organization
Company address
City, province, postal code

Leave three line spaces here.

Bold and/or underline RE: line to stand out as subject of letter.

RE: Reason for letter

Leave two line spaces here.

Dear (name of reader—Mr./Ms/Dr. last name),

Leave two line spaces here.———

Do not indent paragraphs; use left-justified format, double-space between paragraphs.

Introductory brief paragraph 1: purpose, scope, timelines, and background if applicable

Leave one line between paragraphs.

Brief paragraph 2

Brief paragraph 3

Closing, brief paragraph: restates purpose, scope, and main points of letter; gives contact information

Leave three line spaces before complimentary close.

Yours truly,

This is the complimentary close (best choice: *Yours truly*).

Leave three line spaces here; your signature goes here.

Name is *typed* here. ———

Your name

Leave two line spaces here.———

Your initials in CAPS; initials of anyone preparing for you follow in lower case.

Encl: note anything enclosed with/attached to letter.

DL/kl

Encl: Article ABC

Cc: "*carbon copy*" was given to another reader.

Cc: Name of person or people being copied on the letter

The next paragraph or section tells the reader the good or neutral news, briefly and in such a way that he or she will quickly grasp the important details (e.g., "We are pleased to inform you that you have won the Super-Duper Gas Barbecue in the draw at the Home Show held on August 4").

Subsequent paragraphs continue with additional details needed by the reader (e.g., where and how to collect a prize).

The closing paragraph restates the purpose and scope of the letter (but in different words), the main points of the letter, and then ends with the offer of more information and contact information (e.g., "For more information, please contact me at 111-2222 ext. 123 or by email at name@company.com").

As in the basic format, you then sign off the letter with a complimentary close (e.g., "Yours truly,") and your signature, name, and title.

One of your goals as a business communicator is to ensure that readers respond well to messages you write. Organizing your business letters to fit a direct or indirect format depending on content and context will help you achieve this goal.

Bad news letters

Because they deliver news that the reader is not going to be happy about, bad news letters need to be written in an *indirect* format. This cushions the blow of the bad news in that it allows for as much positive or neutral information as possible at the beginning of the letter before the less-than-happy news, thereby minimizing the reader's negative reaction.

Think what a friend might say when delivering bad news to you: "I've got good news and bad news. First, the good news . . ." Your friend will try to soften the blow of the bad news by telling you something positive first. Try to put yourself in the shoes of the reader—and empathize—before you begin to write a bad news letter, even if the person you are writing to has not been an easy person to deal with. How would you like to be treated in a similar situation?

The opening paragraph usually starts with some good or neutral news or a statement such as "At Skippy's Used Furniture Emporium, we value your continued business as a loyal customer over the past decade." This is to build a positive connection with your reader.

The next paragraph states the purpose, the scope, and the background for the letter: "I am writing to you to follow up on your request for a refund on the recliner chair you purchased last month at our Zephyr store. It is our understanding that the recliner mechanism malfunctioned and the occupant of the chair fell backwards."

The following paragraph will then begin to deliver the bad news in as neutral a tone as possible. You need to be very careful not to assign blame or to use negative or emotionally inflaming statements, such as "If the occupant had not weighed 700 pounds, the mechanism would not have malfunctioned."

Instead, if the person who had occupied the chair was large, you would say, "In our investigation of the incident and review of the owner's manual provided with the sale of the chair, it came to our attention that the occupant's weight exceeded the manufacturer's guidelines for safe use of the chair."

Then you would follow the stated facts with the refusal for the refund: "Unfortunately, because of the manufacturer's warranty specifications, we are unable to offer a refund for the chair. The warranty does not cover malfunctions related to excessive weight applied to the chair."

The reader is going to be unhappy, even if you delivered the news as carefully as possible. If you can, now is the time to offer something to cheer the person up—and possibly recover their future business. "While we cannot offer you a refund at this time, we do value your business. Consequently, we would be pleased to provide you with one of our new, weight-tested recliner chairs at a discount of 25 per cent. These chairs come with a five-year manufacturer's warranty covering all failures."

While this offer may not resolve the problem exactly the way the customer wants, you have at least made an effort at customer service that may pay off later. When you close your letter, express empathy with the reader, and apologize for inconvenience, where appropriate.

Report letters

Brief reports to outside readers are not as common as those that are requested by someone within your organization. However, if you or your organization is working with another individual or organization on a project of some kind, you may be asked to provide a brief progress, information, evaluation, or budget report in a letter. You may also need to produce a letter for a brief incident report, particularly if reporting to the authorities is required.

For details on information to include in the report letter, review the formats and notes on how to compose these letters in Chapter 8, Informal Reports. The key difference is, of course, that any short report going to an outside reader is written in the letter format previously described—not *ever* in a memo format, which is reserved for internal readers only.

While subheadings were not included in the sample outline for a letter presented earlier in this chapter (Figure 3.2), you may want to use subheadings to organize information in the same way that you do for an informal, memo-format report. However, as you can see from the sample letters that follow (Figures 3.3 to 3.8), the headings are not used in the letters themselves; rather, they are tools you would use to organize the information before you begin to write.

Table 3.1 shows the formats for short reports; for greater detail and more in-depth how-tos, see the formats and notes in Chapter 8.

TABLE 3.1	**Formats for Short Reports**		
PROGRESS REPORT	**INCIDENT REPORT**	**EXPENSE REPORT**	**INFORMATION/ EVALUATION REPORT**
Summary	Introduction	Introduction	Introduction
Background	Investigation	Activities (or items purchased)	Overview (or background)
Progress	Assessment		Methodology
• Planned work	Conclusion	Benefits	Findings
• Work completed	Recommendations (if required)	Cost(s)	• Option A
• Challenges		Conclusion	• Option B
• Schedule		Recommendations	• Option C (and so on)
Future plans		Attachments (if required)	Assessment/recommendations
Conclusion			Conclusion
Evidence (if required)			

Sample Documents

FIGURE 3.3 Good News Letter

August 4, 2014 ●─────────────────────────────── Date is left-justified here.

Ron Gosbee, Owner
College Street Computers Inc.
123 College Street
Toronto, ON M2X 1Q1

Jane Doer
85 Bridge Street
Mississauga, ON L1E 2X0

RE: Macintosh computer draw ●──────── RE: line **bolded** so that
                                          reason for letter stands out.

Dear Ms Doer:

It is our great pleasure to inform you that you are the winner of the draw we held at ● Opens with good news;
the Technology Expo at the Toronto Trade Centre on July 15.   information is in direct for-
                                                                 mat and provides purpose
                                                                 and scope.

Your prize includes a complete iMac system with the OS-X (10.4) operating system,
as well as Office for Mac (Word, PowerPoint, and Excel) and a one-year subscription
to the iTunes online service. We are happy to provide setup services at your home or
office so that you may be "up and running" as quickly and painlessly as possible.

So that you may enjoy all that iTunes has to offer, we are also adding some excellent ● Second and third para-
Harman Kardon speakers to the package.   graphs provide more infor-
                                                                mation about good news.

In order to claim your prize, simply contact us by telephone before the end of
September 2014 to arrange for setup at the location of your choice. ● This paragraph tells the
                                                                     reader how to claim the prize
                                                                     (what to do, where, when).

Once again, congratulations on winning the prize, and we look forward to providing
you with other quality technology products in the future. Should you have any
questions or require further information, please contact me at 555-1234 ext. 444 or ● Restates purpose and
by email at ron@collegecomputers.com.   scope of letter and closes
                                                                   with contact details.

Yours truly,

Ron Gosbee

FIGURE 3.4 Bad News Letter

May 26, 2014

Kaitlin Vennini-Patrick, Spa Manager
Lotus Day Spa
123 Stone Creek Drive
Oshawa, ON L1G 3M1

Butterfly Brown
33 Beatrice Street
Oshawa, ON L1H 7M8

RE: Spa treatments

Dear Ms Brown,

Thank you for your recent booking of spa services for your wedding party. We appreciate your ongoing patronage of our spa for the past five years.

Unfortunately, on May 15 we experienced a major fire at the spa facility, which has left two of our treatment rooms completely out of service. The repair and renovation work will not be complete until September.

Since your wedding party's spa treatments were booked for Friday, August 17, we will not be able to accommodate you in our spa facility. We can fully appreciate how upsetting this would be for you on the day before your wedding.

We do, however, have an alternative we would like you to consider that might help you and your wedding party relax and unwind before the big day. We would like to send three of our top estheticians to your home or another suitable location of your choice. We do have a completely equipped mobile service with all the equipment and tools you have come to expect at Lotus Day Spa, which we would make available for the day.

If this arrangement would be satisfactory for you, please contact me at 123-4567 as soon as possible. I will personally visit your chosen location for the spa treatments and decide the best way to set it up so that you and your party get the treatment you would have received if you were at our spa facility.

Once again, we are deeply sorry for any inconvenience or concern this may cause you and hope we can work with you to give you the same quality services in the scenario I have described. Please contact me at your earliest convenience so that we can make your time with your wedding party as relaxing and fun as possible.

Yours truly,

Kaitlin Vennini-Patrick

Ms is always the best address for an adult female.

Thank you in first paragraph cushions impact of coming bad news, builds positive connection.

Second paragraph suggests purpose, scope, and background of letter.

Here's the bad news, particularly for a nervous bride-to-be! Tone is neutral.

Immediately following bad news, writer suggests alternative solution.

Provides further assurance to reader about the solution.

Always apologize for inconvenience or upset; restate any resolution or alternative (if available).

FIGURE 3.5 Progress Report

July 15, 2014

Kristen Paynter, Chair
Cavan Family Centre
25 Hwy #7
Cavan, ON L0A 1C0

Dale Elliott-Hijikoop
Ontario Trillium Foundation
123 Charles Street, Unit 4
Toronto, ON L59 2W6

RE: Cavan Toy Lending Library project—progress report

Dear Ms Elliott-Hijikoop,

As requested, this letter is to inform you of the progress made thus far in developing the Cavan Toy Lending Library's resources and related programming that is being funded by the Trillium Foundation. We are currently at the six-month point of the one-year initiative.

As you know, the lending library project was initiated by several rural families in the Cavan area who feel there is a need for toys, learning resources, and activities for children to enjoy while in their homes in isolated parts of the township. These families approached the Cavan Family Centre for their assistance in developing the library and in obtaining appropriate seed funding and corporate sponsorship. Trillium has graciously provided the seed capital needed to hire a fundraising consultant who will help us obtain sustainable funding from corporate and government sources and to help purchase the toys and materials to create an initial lending offering of 25 themed learning kits.

The work planned for the first six months of the lending library project was to hire a fundraising consultant, identify appropriate sources of sustainable corporate and government funding, and write at least two major proposals for funding for submission to these funders.

As soon as we received funding from Trillium, we hired Jemi Echevarria, a fundraising consultant and proposal writer with more than 20 years' experience.

To date, Ms Echevarria and the family centre board have identified 10 sources of funding for the lending library. Of these, three have deadlines for application by the end of July. We expect to submit the proposals a few days before this deadline.

The only challenge encountered thus far has been the timing of proposals to suit funding agencies' submission dates and deadlines. We have addressed this challenge by applying to the agencies with the earliest application deadlines first.

The appropriate address for an adult female is *Ms*, unless otherwise directed.

Instead of summary, letter opens with background for progress report to follow.

Further background on how funding will be used.

Planned work is outlined; paragraph restates expected timelines and objectives to be achieved.

Succinctly outlines work completed.

Challenge is outlined, immediately followed by resolution, reassuring reader.

(continued)

Seven of the funding agencies we identified as suitable for this project have deadlines for application on September 1. We have narrowed down these options to the two most likely to offer substantial funding to the lending library. The consultant will focus on the writing of these proposals in August, incorporating research and data obtained in the work leading up to the submission of the earlier proposals.

Schedule and plans; more details of work completed, providing reassurance to reader.

We also anticipate submitting applications to agencies with floating application deadlines while the consultant completes her contract in December 2014. These agencies would provide funding for very specific applications, such as the purchase of books for the resource boxes. Our board will also apply to a number of toy, educational resource, and children's music production companies to obtain donated materials for the resource boxes.

Good news in conclusion here provides satisfying close of information.

We are pleased that the project has progressed smoothly to date and that our consultant has actually completed more applications for funding than originally anticipated in our contract with Trillium. We anticipate submission of a total of at least five major funding proposals by September 1, with the remaining time in our contract with Trillium being focused on obtaining specific funding for certain aspects of the lending library project and obtaining donated toys and educational and music resources.

No promise of completion but reasonable assurance work should be completed on time.

Should you have any questions about progress to date, or any other aspect of the operation of our contract with Trillium, please contact me at my home at 705-111-2222, on my cell at 705-222-3333, or by email (kpaynter@hotmail.com).

Yours truly,

Kristen Paynter

FIGURE 3.6 Incident Report Letter

January 15, 2014

George Luchuk, Manager
Get Outdoors Inc.
111 King Street,
Woodstock, ON
L2G 4T7

Michael Persichetti, President
Get Outdoors Inc.
1001 Bloor Street West, Suite 200
Toronto, ON
M3T 5X8

RE: Greenberg customer service incident and follow-up

Dear Mr. Persichetti,

In response to your request, the following details results of my fact-finding into the customer service complaint of December 21, 2013.

At around 1 pm on December 21, Ms. Janet Greenberg was in our store shopping for equipment for an upcoming adventure trip to Mongolia. She asked Jim Williams, one of our senior customer service reps, for help in selecting an ergonomically adjustable backpack.

It was a busy day in the store, so several customer service representatives were working with other customers to address their needs. I was off that day, so did not witness the incident. However, I have interviewed several witnesses who verified that Jim did, indeed, touch Ms. Greenberg inappropriately whilst adjusting one of the harnesses on a travel pack. One customer clearly heard Jim whisper to Ms. Greenberg, "I'd love to take *you* on an adventure."

According to one of our customer service representatives, Ms. Greenberg said in a low voice, "Get your hands off me, you creep!" and as soon as she could get out of the pack harness, she marched up to the counter and demanded to speak with me. Unfortunately, I was not there so the assistant manager, Tonia Colombo, said she would report the incident to me.

When I arrived the next day, December 22, Jim was not working, but as previously mentioned, I did interview witnesses for details.

From my research, it is clear Jim was, indeed, acting inappropriately and in a sexually harassing manner. I interviewed Jim by telephone on December 23; he said he was just adjusting the travel pack harness – nothing else.

Until you decide what is to be done about Jim Williams, his employment status is on hold (no more shifts). I have contacted Ms. Greenberg to assure her steps are being taken. In the meantime, I will provide any further information or research you need to make decisions about Mr. Williams' future with the company. I am available at (514) 555-7777 during business hours or on my cell at (514) 333-4444 after hours.

Yours truly,

George Luchuk

RE line precisely refers to incident and what the letter is about.

First line clearly states what letter is about, and nature/date of incident (**introduction**).

Paragraph starts the **investigation** section of the report.

Combines **conclusion** (what the manager is/will be doing) and **recommendation** (what he needs the president to do).

FIGURE 3.7 Expense Report

April 11, 2014

Phoebe Sanger, Marketing Manager
Mighty Inferno Hot Sauce Inc.
930 12th Avenue
Lachine, QC A1Q 9G5

Raymond Fortin, Marketing Manager
MegaGas Barbecues Inc.
430 René Lévesque Boulevard
Montreal, QC A59 5H3

RE: Mont Royal Home Show expenses

Dear Raymond,

I am delighted with the success of our joint marketing effort at the recent Mont Royal Home Show, as I'm sure you are. By my estimate (and a review of the entries for our draw), more than 20,000 people dropped by our booth and enjoyed our barbecue demonstration, which should pan out in some really solid sales.

As we agreed, I took the lead and purchased chicken breasts on your behalf from Maple Leaf Farms (500 chicken breasts), which were cut up for smaller sample portions for visitors to the booth. My company supplied 10 different varieties of our hot sauces to baste the chicken with and five dipping sauces, as well as napkins and toothpicks from our trade show supplies. We purchased propane for the tanks provided with the three barbecues your company delivered to the site.

I'm not sure what the response to the show has been at your end, but we certainly have had many people redeem the 10-per-cent-off coupons for our sauces at Montreal area stores in the past week since the show. I know there was a lot of interest in your smaller barbecue model on the part of people with cottages and summer homes. If our success in marketing means anything, you should expect some decent sales figures out of this venture.

The good news is that our expenses came in under the budget that you and I agreed to for this event. Perhaps because of the excellent efficiency of your barbecues, we used less gas than anticipated, so your portion of the bill for the gas is only $100. The bill for the chicken breasts is $150. In total, your company's portion of the expenses is only $250, which is $100 less than anticipated.

Overall, I think this event will prove to have benefits that far outweigh the very modest expenses we have incurred, and I believe that a booth is worth organizing for next year's home show. I have attached the invoices for the gas and the chicken for processing at your end; please forward your cheque to my attention, and I will pay these bills.

If you have any further questions, please contact me at 678-9101 ext. 545 or by email (phoebe@hotsauce.ca). It's been a pleasure working with you.

Yours truly,

Phoebe Sanger

cc: Marie Laveille, Comptroller, Mighty Inferno Hot Sauce

Reader is addressed by first name because writer knows him well.

Expense report letter with good news is written in direct format with friendly introduction.

Paragraph provides details about items purchased.

Actual costs buried between pieces of good news to cushion impact.

Final "ask" for money at end after good news about savings encourages reader to pay promptly.

FIGURE 3.8 Informational Report

October 24, 2014

Michelle Cook, Consultant
Cook's Professional Training Services
78 Queen Street
Fredericton, NB T5G 9T9

James Leblanc, Vice-President, Human Resources
Taste of the East Restaurants
360 Water Street
Saint John, NB T9Y 4P7

RE: Customer service training packages

Dear Mr. Leblanc,

Thank you for considering Cook's for your company's customer service training needs. I am pleased to provide you with two choices for the training of your restaurant staff, and trust that one of them will meet your criteria.

In terms of the criteria you and I discussed last month, the following training packages are offered to 30 people over three days mid-week (to avoid taking staff out of restaurants during busy weekends) and are situated at a retreat-style venue (Camp Getaway) so that social activities can be incorporated into your time together. • ——— *Opening provides background information and scope (direct format). Methodology is implied.*

With any of the choices noted below, there is significant time built in for your group to take part in any activities you choose to develop or plan beyond the training. Camp Getaway has a good variety of outdoor activities, walking trails, and quiet spaces for reading or relaxation.

Package A • ——— *Findings section outlines options, described neutrally to avoid leading reader into a conclusion.*

Training package A takes three full days and is suitable for staff who are new to your organization and each other. The first half-day is focused on icebreakers and individual activities to help your staff appreciate their personal strengths and weaknesses (personality assessment). The second half of that day is focused on how staff can make their differences and similarities work together for optimum productivity and individual/group fulfillment on the job.

The subsequent two days are focused on teamwork, conflict resolution, and the development of a customer service "code" that all participants take part in developing so that everyone can fully support customer service activities while on the job.

Package A costs $5,500 plus HST.

(continued)

Package B

Package B takes two and a half days and is suitable for staff who have worked together for some time and are fairly cohesive in their work together but need improvement in the area of conflict resolution. The first day (an afternoon) is focused on individual personality assessment (Myers-Briggs), followed by group work introducing each person's strengths and weaknesses. These qualities are mapped out in terms of the Myers-Briggs types, and then workshop participants are guided through an exploration of the ways these types will work best together.

The following two days focus on how the Myers-Briggs types apply to customers. Topics cover how staff can identify the types of their customers to better serve them (and enjoy doing so); conflict resolution with customers and fellow staff based on types; and finally, the development of a code of customer service that all participants will create together and endorse.

Package B costs $5,525, including the licensed Myers-Briggs tests and materials; HST is extra.

Please let me know which package would best suit the customer service training needs of your staff group and at least three dates that would work, and we will handle all of the booking arrangements at Camp Getaway. Once we have made the arrangements, I will be in touch with you again for more specific information about particular customer service training needs so that we can further customize whichever package you choose.

Yours truly,

Michelle Cook

Provides costing for each option so reader can fairly assess benefits before costs.

Informational (not evaluation) report gives no assessment. Conclusion ties up report neatly.

Want to see more examples?

For more examples of good news, bad news, and report letters see this text's website at **www.oupcanada.com/Luchuk**.

Checking Your Work

CONTENT EDITING, COPY EDITING, AND FORMATTING REVIEW

As you would with an informal, memo-format report for an **internal readership**, make sure that you have included all the information needed by your reader (review your answers to the Starting Point questions), have met the information demands for the purpose of the letter, and have formatted the letter as described in this chapter.

Letters sent to an **external readership** will not be taken seriously if there are spelling, grammar, or mechanical mistakes. Be extra careful when copy editing your work—and don't just rely on your computer's spell checker and grammar checker. (If you know you have issues when it comes to your grammar, why not check out the grammar appendix in this text to finally slay your writing dragons? We promise: the description of what points of grammar are and how to use them is simple and quick—and there's ample opportunity to practise what you've just learned.) It's a good idea to give the letter to someone else in your organization so that a second set of eyes will review it before you send it to the designated external reader or readers. Your reputation—and that of your organization or company—will be at stake in the quality of your writing.

Oral Presentation of the Business Letter

An oral presentation of a generic good or bad news letter is highly unlikely, but there is a chance that you might be asked to make a presentation to an individual or small group based on a report letter you have sent to an external reader.

This presentation would not be as in-depth or formal as it would be for a formal report to an external audience, but you will need to review all of the research you did for the report letter so that you are very familiar with the background of the topic when you make your presentation. Even if it's just an informal meeting over coffee, make sure that you have all of the information in your head—and possibly in packages for those meeting with you—so that you can make a professional presentation.

A review of the oral presentation guidelines in Chapter 12 would also be a good idea if you were asked to meet with the readers of your letter.

Electronic Submission of Business Letters

Sometimes regular "snail mail" or even a courier will not get a business letter to an external or internal reader in time for a desired response or to meet a deadline. (Because so many people have to multitask in today's business environment, you might have had too much to do and too little time to do it in—and got the letter done later than you would have liked.)

If you are emailing your letter, it's a good idea to at least put it into a PDF format and perhaps into a password-protected, "locked" PDF format for further security.

CHECKLIST FOR letters

☐ Have you applied the Starting Point questions to know your reader(s) better?

☐ Are you clear about the message/information you need to communicate? The purpose and the desired outcome? (See Chapter 1 for help with this.)

☐ If you're communicating good or neutral news, have you followed direct format?

☐ If you're communicating bad news, have you followed indirect format to deliver information as politely and carefully as possible? Have you used a calm tone and unemotional language?

☐ If bad news, is it appropriate to communicate it in a letter? Should it be conveyed in person instead?)

☐ Does your letter have a clear introduction, discussion, and conclusion?

☐ Have you included all the information you need to communicate?

☐ Is there anything that might confuse your readers? Put yourself in their shoes, and consider what you know about them—and what they know about your message or information.

☐ If this is a progress report letter, have you organized the information into summary, background, progress, future plans, conclusion, and evidence (if required) sections?

☐ If this is an incident report letter, have you organized the information into introduction, investigation, assessment, conclusion, and recommendations (if required) sections?

☐ If this is an expense report letter, have you organized the information into introduction, activities (or items purchased), benefits, cost(s), conclusion, and recommendations sections?

☐ If this is an information/evaluation report letter, have you organized the information into introduction, overview (or background), methodology, findings, assessment, and conclusion sections?

☐ Are you quite sure that your letter does not contain any grammar or spelling errors, including the recipient's name and other names within the text?

☐ Is the letter in the correct format as described in this chapter?

Chapter Summary

In this chapter, you have learned that you can use business letters to communicate with, solicit, or persuade readers outside your organization. They can report on progress, evaluation, information, incidents, or expenses. You have found that letters can also be used for special purposes inside your organization. You have learned the importance of doing your research to ensure that the content of your letter is accurate and complete and then the importance of revising and editing to make your letter concise and to the point. This chapter also provided examples of common letter protocols. You've found that the type of information and its sequencing for letters that express good news are different from those for letters that express bad news. Finally, you learned how to organize an informal report in letter form.

▪▪▪ SUGGESTIONS *for Further Reading*

Bond, A., and Schuman, N. (2010). *300+ successful business letters for all occasions.* (3rd ed.). Hauppauge, NY: Barron's Educational Series.

Geffner, A.B. (2007). *How to write better business letters.* (4th ed.). Hauppauge, NY: Barron's Educational Series.

Lindsell-Roberts, S. (2004). *Strategic business letters and e-mail: Hundreds of model letters.* Boston, MA: Houghton-Mifflin.

Minden, C., and Roth, K. (2012). *How to write a business letter.* North Mankato, MN: Cherry Lake Publishing.

Seglin, J.L., and Coleman, E. (2012). *AMA handbook of business letters.* (4th ed.). New York, NY: AMACOM Press.

Taylor, S. (2012). *Model business letters, emails and other business documents.* Upper Saddle River, NJ: FT Press.

▪▪▪ PRACTISING *What You Have Learned*

1. Karl Schmidt, a long-time loyal customer of your company, has recently been promoted to vice-president of his company. Karl was the person who vouched for your company when it was new and untested, encouraging his company to buy exclusively from yours. The relationship has been extremely beneficial to your own work and to the company's fortunes. On a personal level, you have gotten to know him quite well, and during the winter months you play in a darts league together. Write a letter of congratulations to Karl on his promotion.

2. Jennifer Guyan has applied to your company for a position in the sales department. However, you have decided to award the position to another candidate who has more experience in selling your company's products. Jennifer is the marketing manager's niece, so it is very important that you give Jennifer some feedback about why she was not chosen (she needs more experience with selling your particular products and services and would also benefit from a training course offered by your head office). While you want to give her constructive feedback in the letter, it is also a good idea to invite her to speak with you if she wants further advice to help her apply for future openings with your company. Write the letter to Jennifer, remembering to use the indirect format indicated for bad news communications.

3. Your company has been working on developing a new service with the specific needs of another company in mind. Your company and the other have been working together in a supplier–customer relationship for several years, so the other company knows you have a solid reputation for quality work and effort. However, they are anxious to have the new service, and they would like a progress report detailing where you are in the development process and when they might receive what they have ordered. Write a progress report letter to the company, and specify when the project will be completed.

4. Alpha Corporation and Beta Limited were hosting a fundraising barbecue for the United Way in their community. Alpha's staff looked after cooking the meat, while Beta's staff co-ordinated the event and served desserts and drinks to the public. A female member

of the Alpha staff, dressed in minimal clothing because of the extreme heat that day, approached the barbecue area for a hamburger, and a male Beta employee commented on her dress being "like the ladies who work the street across from the office." Several employees of both companies overheard the comment, but according to the woman involved, he also made other derogatory comments of a harassing nature.

You are the manager of Alpha Corporation, and the woman has reported the incident to you, hoping that she can get a written apology from the man who insulted her. Write a letter describing the incident from this employee's perspective to your counterpart at Beta Limited, and indicate what your employee would like as compensation (the letter of apology).

5. With the financial assistance of your professional association, you have recently completed a training course to improve your work skills in your management position. (The association covered the cost of your books and half the course fee.) Write an expense report letter to this organization, explaining specifically how the course has benefited or will benefit you in your work and detailing how much was spent on the course and books.

6. You have been asked by your manager to review three different choices for uniforms that are to be worn by your sales team when they are in the office. The uniform needs to be business casual (e.g., plain pants and a top with a logo), since customers would be put off by anything too formal. The company does not want to spend more than $100 per complete uniform per person (but individuals can purchase additional tops or pants on their own, so a discount for these purchases would be a good idea). Because your 20-person sales staff comes in all shapes and sizes, the uniforms have to be suitable and flattering to all, and obviously they need to come in a variety of sizes.

Write a letter to your manager evaluating the three uniform choices, and using the criteria mentioned above, decide which uniform choice would be most appropriate. Back up your recommendation with concrete reasons, referring to the company's criteria for the uniforms and any added-value features you have uncovered.

7. Your town's minor hockey association has asked your company for a donation of $1,000 to help the association acquire equipment and pay team fees for children who cannot afford to play hockey.

In January of each year, your company decides on a focus for its charitable giving, and this year the decision was to support children's activities and programs in the community. However, it's now August, and the company has already donated $7,000 of the total $10,000 available for charitable giving. You also know that an annual request for $1,250 from the community early learning centre (a cause the CEO is passionate about) is coming up in September. On top of that commitment, you really do need some money in the bank in case something else arises toward the end of the year (for example, before Christmas there are often appeals for food bank donations).

You have decided to give the minor hockey association $750 rather than $1,000 so that you can meet the other charitable obligation and keep some money in the bank. As manager of public relations, respond to Kristina LeMay, chair of the hockey association, with your decision. It's not entirely bad news, but at the same time it is less money than the association asked for. Use a direct approach, but after you state the good news, explain that the smaller donation is necessary because of other charitable commitments to child-focused groups at this time of the year.

8. Recently, your nationwide cleaning supply company has been in the news, and the media coverage has, in your opinion, not been fair. Your company has been accused of contributing to pollution of waterways and the environment in general by providing what are perceived to be non-biodegradable cleaning products to businesses and industries.

   The truth of the matter is that six months ago, your company quietly reformulated all of its cleaning products. All products are now biodegradable and are composed of plant-based surfactants and cleaning agents. However, this good news has not yet been promoted to the media, because the public relations department has had to handle a variety of other issues and crises.

   While your public relations department has been mobilized to send out media packages and to conduct a television advertising campaign highlighting your company's new products and commitment to the environment, as CEO you have decided to write a letter to the editor of a national newspaper to provide the public with the facts. Your letter is directed to the editor of the newspaper.

CHAPTER 4

Writing Clearly: Editing for Effective Writing

In this chapter, you will learn:

- ⊙ Why editing business writing is essential for professional communications and impact

- ⊙ How to edit written products for content, organization, documentation, style, grammar, and mechanics

- ⊙ A three-step editing process for reviewing, revising, and refining your writing

- ⊙ Considerations for editing documents for an international readership

- ⊙ Tips to help you edit more thoroughly and correctly

ESSENTIAL EMPLOYABILITY SKILLS

2ooo+ Employability Skills The Conference Board of Canada has identified certain essential employability skills (EES) as benchmarks for performance in the workplace. You will learn the following EES skills in this chapter:

COMMUNICATE

- ⊙ Can write and speak so others pay attention and understand
- ⊙ Can listen and ask questions to understand and appreciate the points of view of others
- ⊙ Can read and understand information presented in a variety of forms (e.g., words, graphs, charts, diagrams)

MANAGE INFORMATION

- ⊙ Can access, analyze, and apply knowledge and skills from various disciplines (e.g., the arts, languages, science, technology, mathematics, social sciences, and the humanities)

THINK AND SOLVE PROBLEMS

- ⊙ Can assess situations and identify problems
- ⊙ Can seek different points of view and evaluate them based on facts
- ⊙ Can recognize the human, interpersonal, technical, scientific, and mathematical dimensions of a problem
- ⊙ Can identify the root cause of a problem
- ⊙ Can be creative and innovative in exploring possible solutions
- ⊙ Can evaluate solutions to make recommendations or decisions

Writing Clearly: A Case Study

As customer service manager for his employer, Morton's Munchies, Matt White is responsible for all correspondence with customers. He does not have an administrative assistant, so not only does he write letters, he is also required to edit them before he mails them. Sometimes he has a colleague, Michelle Adams, review letters before he sends them out, because Matt is not a great writer and Michelle has an English degree.

However, Matt has to respond quickly to a recent customer complaint before it ends up in court. Elsie LeBlanc recently bought a box of Morton's premium chocolate truffles and found a desiccated bumblebee in the rum and raisin variety—but not before she bit into the dead bug. She says she has been afraid to eat any chocolate since the incident, and she wants to know how the bee "raisin" ended up in her candy.

Matt has thoroughly investigated the incident and has determined how the bee got into the truffle. Apparently, the bee was dried along with the grapes at the raisin supplier, and because it looked like a raisin, it was missed in the quality-control process.

FIGURE 4.1   Matt's Letter

June 17, 2014

Matthew White, Customer Service Manager
Morton's Munchies
4546 Ocean St.
Moncton, NB B1H 2V0

Ms Elsie LeBlanc
7890 Acadia Ave.
Moncton, NB B4G 2L6

RE: Bee in chocolate incident

Dear Ms Leblanc,

Unfortunately, we can't do much for you pain and sufferin from eating a bee in a rum and raisin trufle. I've investigated the matter and the bee came from the raisins we use.We hope you will find the attached coupon helpful for you to eat more chocolates in future.

Your's truly,

Matthew White

Matt's supervisor has said that he does not want to have to pay the customer compensation and that Matt should thoroughly explain the problem and reassure the customer that the problem has been resolved (a new raisin supplier has been engaged).

Matt quickly writes a letter and mails it minutes after he has written it (see Figure 4.1).

1. **Do you think this letter is acceptable as it is? Why or why not?**

2. **If anything is missing, what information needs to be included? What information needs to be conveyed to the customer?**

3. **While Matt can't give out a huge monetary settlement for Elsie's upset, what do you think he should do—and include—in this letter?**

4. **Is the order and tone of this letter appropriate for the delivery of bad news? Why or why not? (Hint: Check out the guidelines for writing bad news letters in Chapter 3.)**

5. **Are there spelling and grammar errors in this letter? Identify them.**

6. **Help Matt out! Rewrite this letter so that it reflects the information he has to share with Ms Maille and satisfies her need for an explanation.**

Before You Begin . . .

Once upon a time, managers—and sometimes their underlings—had what were called secretaries to take dictation of their letters, reports, and memos. These stalwart and literate people (often women) then took their notes (written in shorthand, a cryptic-looking code) and translated their boss's musings (or rants) into polished, professional copy that made him (usually a "him") and the company look good.

That was when the Earth was still cooling. Today, with the dinosaurs long gone—along with personal secretaries, dictation, manual typewriters, and shorthand—you are in charge of your own letters, memos, and often reports or proposals. You are both writer and editor, so you don't have someone with a brilliant turn of phrase who will take your humble words and turn them into gold or check to ensure that the writing is perfect before sending it out into the world.

So what, exactly, is editing? Editing is not just putting your copy through a spell checker and calling it a day. It's a "re-seeing," not a "re-copying" of exactly the same thing you started with. You read and reread the copy in various ways to review the following:

- Content—determining whether you included all information necessary for the purpose of the document and the reader's needs

- Organization—determining whether you have organized your document according to the correct format and have used paragraphs appropriately

- Documentation—determining whether you have correctly and thoroughly documented any information or quotes from others

- Style—determining whether you have used appropriate tone, word choices, and writing style for the purpose of the document and the reader

- Mechanics—ensuring that spelling, punctuation, word choice, and sentence structure is flawless

The goal of editing is to refine your writing until it says what you want it to say—and says it in such a way that your readers can understand your message. If you are to communicate effectively, you need to revise from your readers' perspective. A first draft is often what is in *your* mind, but the final copy should state what you want your readers to have in *their* mind. For in-depth instructions on polishing the mechanics and style of your writing, please see the user-friendly Grammar Handbook at the end of this textbook.

Idiom Alert

underling – A subordinate, someone who is at the bottom of a hierarchy

rant – When someone speaks (or writes) excessively about a topic that excites or upset him or her. A rant is different from an argument in that the rant is only from the perspective of the person ranting; it does not take into consideration the other side's point of

view or position. A rant is considered self-focused and self-serving, while an argument is two or more people engaging in a conflict dialogue.

have in mind – Think about or consider a certain action or activity

typo – Short for typographical error

Your Starting Point

In order to begin the editing process, you need to review who is reading your written piece and what the document's purpose is.

If you have planned your writing well, you will have applied the Starting Point questions in Chapter 1—what you learned about your reader—to what you have written so that he or she will thoroughly understand and be able to apply your communication appropriately. Pull out your answers to these questions about your reader, and refer to them while reviewing your document to check whether you have met his or her information needs.

Editing works so much better when you take the time to create an outline for your document—*before* you write it. Retrieve your outline, and print a hard copy so that you can refer to it to see whether you followed the plan as you originally intended. Checking against the plan is a good way to spot whether you have forgotten something important or have gotten way off track on some tangent or another.

Along with your Starting Point answers and the outline for the document, be sure to have a thesaurus and dictionary at hand. If you find that you have used boring, nondescript words or have repeated the same words many times, you should use a thesaurus to help you find more appropriate words for what you are trying to express. For example, there are apparently more than 200 words that you can use instead of the word "said." (Check out http://writingfix.com/PDFs/Writing_Tools/said_synonyms.pdf.)

Follow the example of countless editors—have coloured pens at the ready to mark up your hard copy of the document with any changes you need to make. Red is one of the most visible colours, and especially when you are tired, you will be glad you used a bright colour so that you can clearly see what changes need to be made.

If you have quoted from or used anyone else's material or information, make sure you have your notes about the sources and materials you used close at hand. This way you can quickly find the information you need to create a citation if one is missing.

Finally, do print a hard copy of your document to edit. Yes, you can edit on your computer, but staring at a screen for any length of time can lead to your eyes crossing and a splitting headache. For the first round of editing at least, use a hard copy, and edit with your trusty red pen.

With your red pen in hand, you'll be ready to edit your written work. Remember to first look at the *overall picture* (content, organization, documentation) of your document before moving on to the finer *details* (mechanics).

Editing the Written Product: How to Do It

There are three basic steps to the editing process: reviewing, revising, and refining. Depending on the importance of the document and its size, you may go through these three steps three times (or more!) to ensure that the result is as flawless and professional as possible.

REVIEW

The first step in editing is reviewing the document—reading it for content, organization, documentation, style, and mechanics.

Try reading it forward first—you'll catch the most obvious errors or omissions—and mark up your hard copy as you go. Then try reading it backwards to catch, in particular, grammar and mechanical errors.

Reading the document out loud to yourself, slowly and deliberately, making the appropriate pauses where punctuation has been used, helps you to catch such errors as sentence fragments, run-on sentences (you will soon find yourself out of breath when you read these sentences!), and punctuation errors (pausing where you used a comma inappropriately will be a clue that it doesn't belong).

Reading the piece out loud to someone else, someone who hasn't been privy to your writing and is quite unconnected to what you are doing, can help you to catch still more errors ("Read that again," the person will say. "Something doesn't sound quite right . . ."). Giving your written piece to someone else to read, someone who hasn't spent hours on it—and, better still, isn't really familiar with the topic or purpose of the document—can uncover more errors. Having another reviewer helps to ensure that the information can be easily understood by a reader who does not have your background or information on the subject you are writing about.

Content

Refer to the outline for your document, the notes on materials you planned to include, and the Starting Point answers about your reader(s) to ensure that you have met **content** demands for the document.

- Did you include all of the information you intended to?
- Is there material included that shouldn't be included or that isn't necessary?
- Has the content met the purpose of the written piece?
- Has the content met the demands and needs of the reader(s)?

Organization

In terms of **organization** of headings, subheadings, and paragraphs, review the outline for the document, and consult generic outlines for the type of document you are producing (letter, memo, report, proposal, and so on).

- Have you organized your entire piece and sections, if applicable, according to the appropriate format?
- Have you used headings and subheadings, if appropriate, in such a way that the reader can easily follow the information through to the conclusion? Does the information flow so that the reader can clearly understand it?
- Have you used short, concise paragraphs so that the reader is not bogged down in wordy density?

Documentation

Have your list of information about your sources available (title, author, publisher, website information, and so on) so that you can quickly insert the correct citation information if you find a spot where you have not documented the use of someone else's information or words.

- If you are using someone else's ideas or direct quotes, have you documented this information thoroughly and properly in the body of the text and in the works-cited section (if applicable)?

For more information about **documentation**, please see Appendix B: Guidelines for Documenting Sources at the end of this textbook, or ask your instructor for further direction.

Style

The question of appropriate **style** in your document very much depends on who your reader is and the purpose of your document. For example, if your reader requires or prefers a more formal style of writing (with more formal word choices, for example), does your document reflect this preference? Is the style and tone in keeping with the purpose of the document? You would not want to use an **informal tone** or style, for instance, in a written piece that could become a legal document. Conversely, you wouldn't want to use a very **formal tone** in a memo about the company golf tournament if you work in a relaxed, informal environment.

Longer paragraphs mean more words, and verbiage is often considered "more formal." Unfortunately, when trying to explain or express something that the reader may not understand, many writers tend to use too many words. Keep your writing tight and concise, *especially* if your reader does not know much about the subject matter.

- Is your style and tone appropriate for the purpose of the document, the organization, and the reader?
- Have you ensured that you are not using **jargon** or technical terms that the reader will not understand?
- If you have used **acronyms** or initialisms, have you included the long form at the first use (e.g., all-terrain vehicle [ATV]; United Nations Children's Fund [UNICEF])?
- Have you used a variety of words? Have you chosen words that will be understood by the reader and that are professional, intelligent, and meaningful?
- Did you use a thesaurus to avoid such "garbage words" as *nice*, *stuff*, or *things*?
- Have you used certain words repeatedly? (If so, use a thesaurus to find other suitable words.)

Editing for international communications

Good-quality, close editing of documents is essential no matter where you and your readership are in the world. That's a given! However, editing should be even more stringent and take into consideration the English used by your readers if they live in another country or belong to a different culture. It's a worthwhile investment of time to look up conventions for the use of English in the countries or cultures where your readers are situated. There may be important variations in how certain concepts or ideas should be expressed to avoid cultural or social miscommunication.

In many countries around the globe, the English used or adopted as a second language is British. British English has a generally more formal tone, particularly in business communication, and avoids use of acronyms, first- or second-person pronouns, and jargon (unless the reader clearly understands the jargon). The international business culture is, overall, more formal than the North American. While American English and a more informal communication style are being adopted by some internationally (because of the globalization of business and commerce), it's safer to assume you are communicating with an audience that has adopted a more formal, British English with all of the associated conventions and considerations (Algeo, 2006).

British spelling is similar to Canadian, although Canadian spelling is now heavily influenced by American English because of the use of American spell-check programs and the influx of information, media, and advertising from the US. Canadian English can be considered a hybrid of British and US spelling and style, with our own variations included. Err on the side of British spelling when editing. If your word-processing program includes it, select British English as the language of editing when using spell and grammar check. In most cases, this should help you to revise according to what the international reader is expecting.

Because British English and the international business culture are generally formal, you must be doubly sure that what you are sending or mailing has *no* spelling, grammar, or mechanical errors. The international business community does not appreciate such errors, and sloppy or disrespectful writing will reflect badly on you and your organization.

Editing on your computer is similar to editing "by hand." Review content, organization, and documentation first, then mechanics and grammar. Be sure to use "track changes" if your editing will be reviewed by other team members.

Mechanics

Nothing will sink the credibility of your writing faster than misspelled words, incorrect word choices, punctuation errors, or run-on or incomplete sentences. You could write a singularly brilliant missive to an outside reader—in terms of content—and have it completely discredited because you made spelling errors. Readers get annoyed when they see such errors, because it makes them feel that you are too lazy to provide them with the very best writing and information.

Do not *ever* count on spelling and grammar checkers to catch all of your errors. At this point, the editing process has only just begun! A spell checker cannot tell whether you used a word incorrectly, nor will it always catch improper use of commonly confused words (e.g., *there, they're, their*). A grammar checker, unless optimized (see the sidebar in this chapter for help in Word), will miss many errors—and even when optimized, it should not be relied upon as an absolute editor because its database of information does not include all possible errors.

This is one of those times when having someone else read your document—particularly someone who is a good writer and editor—is worth the extra time. Another pair of eyes can catch **mechanics** errors you have overlooked in several rounds of editing.

- Has everything been spelled and punctuated correctly? If you are unsure, consult a dictionary (either printed or online) or a punctuation manual.

- Have you used complete sentences? (Look for any that lack a subject, a verb, or both.)

- Do your sentences go on forever, leaving your reader breathless (run-on sentences)?

- Did you choose the right word for the context? Watch out for commonly confused words.

- Are there any typos in your document?

Optimizing spelling and grammar check in Microsoft Word

To make the most of the spelling and grammar check available in Microsoft Word, it's important to set it up so that it can identify the widest possible range of grammar, punctuation, and spelling errors. (The following are instructions for Word 2010 for PC; if you have a Macintosh computer, the instructions are similar.)

First, set the language the checker will use to evaluate your writing. To set language:

1. Choose the "Review" tab on the Word ribbon.

2. Click "Language," then click "Set Proofing Language."

3. Choose "English (Canada)" from the list.

Second, to check for almost anything that might be an error, you must optimize language settings (and if you have challenges with your writing, you will *want* to do this):

1. Choose the "File" tab on the Word ribbon.

2. Click "Options," then "Proofing."

3. In the "Proofing" box, select "Settings" under the heading "When correcting spelling and grammar in Word." The "Grammar Settings" box will appear. We suggest that you check all of the options, but if there are some things you don't want flagged, simply don't check those boxes. (For example, if you are writing in the first person for an assignment, having grammar check flag all instances of first-person use will make you crazy!)

Once you have set up spelling and grammar check to look for the errors you want to avoid, you should only have to reset certain parameters—such as formality (see above)—when you are writing for a specific audience. But in general, once you have set up the parameters, you will be able to improve your editing process.

However—and this is a *big* however—you cannot rely on spell checkers and grammar checkers to perfect your writing. These tools will only suggest possible errors that need fixing. You still need to know correct spelling and grammar in order to make the best choices from the options the programs suggest. Sometimes they suggest something nonsensical or, more commonly, an American spelling to replace a Canadian spelling (unless you are using a Canadian dictionary in your Word program).

Always subject your writing to an old-fashioned, hard-copy review with red pen in hand after you use spelling and grammar checkers. Read the copy backwards and forward. Read it out loud. Get a friend to read it, preferably someone who hasn't seen the writing before or someone who does not know what you are writing about. You want to find *every* error before you print and send your final copy!

REVISE

Once you have noted errors in a colour (preferably red—yellow is just too hard to see!) on your hard copy, you can begin revising.

It's also a good idea to write corrections in red so that you can easily see what to do to fix problems. This can get a bit messy if you have single-spaced your draft; if this is the case, write changes in the margins, and use arrows to point to where the correction should go.

If you want to keep the original file of the document and edit a copy of the original, save yourself major aggravation and *rename* the new file (e.g., Report1.doc, Report2.doc). If you are in a rush to print your document, you might accidentally print the earlier, unedited version if you are not clear on which one is which!

With a hard copy of your revised version at hand, make the necessary changes to your word-processed document. Don't forget to save it!

REFINE

The final stage—at least in your first round of editing—is refining the written document. Refining requires that you read the entire document again to ensure that content, organization, style, grammar, mechanics, and relevant documentation have been addressed and corrected.

When you inputted changes into your document at the revision stage, it's entirely possible that you also incorporated some new errors, so run a spelling and grammar check to catch anything obvious. Once you have completed this process, save changes and then print.

Then—yes, I can hear you groaning now—you will read the document through *again*. By this point, you may be heartily sick of the piece, but this process is what separates the polished from the mediocre. Reading it backwards can be especially helpful at this point, since you may now find it more difficult to spot errors after working on the writing for what seems like an eternity. Having someone else read it silently or aloud, noting any questions or corrections, can also help immeasurably.

If any changes need to be made, incorporate them, run another spelling and grammar check, and then review the text again.

Depending on how important this document is to your career, your work, your boss, or your company, you will go through the reviewing, revising, and refining stages a number of times before the writing can be released to the reader(s).

Figure 4.2 shows an incident report letter, complete with errors; the revised and corrected version appears in Figure 4.3. This figure shows a letter that was quickly edited for mechanics (spelling and basic grammar) but not particularly for style.

The letter could be further refined and edited, but the writer decided that a quick run-through of all of the editing stages was appropriate because he needed to get his observations of the incident to the reader immediately. This could be the case when you have to dash off a letter quickly, with no time to spare. If time is of the essence, be sure to at least run a spelling and grammar check, print the letter, and read through it carefully to find any errors, then incorporate corrections, run yet another spelling and grammar check, and read through your final copy. Perfection is seldom possible, but you should always strive for competency in your writing.

When writing a document such as an incident letter, which has to be written immediately after the episode and could become a legal document, it's important that grammar, spelling, mechanics, format, tone, and style be as appropriate and correct as possible. Unfortunately, editors sometimes have to decide not to do any further editing, even if they are *sure* it would make the writing better, because a deadline looms.

That being said, further refining your writing is important if you have more time—tightening and brightening sentence structure, word choices, and so on. You should certainly take the time to refine your writing if the document is a report or proposal of major importance—or if you need to appear especially professional or literate.

Sample Documents

FIGURE 4.2 Incident Report Letter (with errors noted in red)

February 18, 2014

Jim Doherty, Manager
S&G Music Store
39 Kings St ●————————————————— Spelling error.
Prince George, BC T1Z 2A8

Marley Cho, Manager
City of Prince Gorge Roads Dept. ●————————— Spelling error.
85 Maintenance St
Prince George, BC T2U 5Q9

RE: An old man's fall on the sidewalk ●——————— Needs to be shorter.

Dear Marley: ●—————————————————————— Using the reader's first
name is too informal in a
business letter.

Per your request, this letter will detail the facts as I know them regarding Mr. Tiller's fall
when he cracked open his head and bled a lot and then moaned on the sidewalk in front
of my store on January 25, 2014. ●———————————— Excessively wordy; provides unnecessary details.

At approximately 11:00 a.m. that day, Mr. Tiller, an elderly man, was walking along the
sidewalk. apparently on his way to Sullivan's Drug Store which is located next door to my ●——— Sentence fragment; needs
business to pick up his medication.   a subject (*Mr. Tiller* or *He*).

There were 2 patrons in the store at the time, as well as I, who saw Mr. Tiller lose his ●——— Numbers under 10 should
footing and fall to the pavement. It appeared he slipped on a patch of ice that had not   be spelled out.
been de-iced yet that day the two patrons, I immediately rushed to his aid and called 911
for assistance. ●——————————————————————————— Run-on sentence.

I arrived at my shop at 9:00 a.m. that day to do some bookkeeping before opening ●——— Unnecessary details.
the store at 10:00 a.m., and from that time to the time of the incident I did not see any
municipal employees putting de-icer on the sidewalk. There had been quite a bit of
freezing rain the night before, so I were surprised that this had not been done before ●——— Subject-verb error.
people came out to shop on King Street.

In my opinion, from my observation of the incident and the lack of de-icing material on
the pavement that morning, I would have to say that the municipality is at fault in this
accident. Had the sidewalk ice been melted, I doubt Mr. Tiller would have fallen. As a
merchant on King Street, I suggest that the municipality direct its roads staff to spread
de-icer on the sidewalks here as soon as freezing rain ends, as this is a very busy
shopping district.

I trust that this information has been helpful to you in your investigation of this unfortunate
accident. Should you require any further information, please contact me in person at my
shop, or call me at 555-7777 between 9:00 a.m. and 5:00 p.m., Monday to Friday.

Thanks a bunch, ●————————————————————————— Too informal.

Jim ●————————————————————————————— Too informal; should
include last name.

FIGURE 4.3 Incident Report Letter (revised)

See how much more professional this letter is? What makes it more professional?

February 18, 2014

Jim Doherty, Manager
S&G Music Store
39 King St
Prince George, BC T1Z 2A8

Marley Cho, Manager
City of Prince George Roads Dept.
85 Maintenance St.
Prince George, BC T2U 5Q9

RE: Sidewalk incident

Dear Mr. Cho:

Per your request, this letter will detail the facts as I know them regarding Mr. Tiller's fall on the sidewalk in front of my store on January 25, 2014.

At approximately 11:00 a.m. that day, Mr. Tiller, an elderly man, was walking along the sidewalk, apparently on his way to Sullivan's Drug Store, which is located next door to my business, to pick up his medication.

There were two patrons in the store at the time, as well as I, who saw Mr. Tiller lose his footing and fall to the pavement. It appeared he slipped on a patch of ice that had not been de-iced yet that day. The two patrons and I immediately rushed to his aid and called 911 for assistance.

I had arrived at my shop at 9:00 a.m. that day, and from that time to the time of the incident I did not see any municipal employees putting de-icer on the sidewalk. There had been quite a bit of freezing rain the night before, so I was surprised that this had not been done before people came out to shop on King Street.

In my opinion, from my observation of the incident and the lack of de-icing material on the pavement that morning, I would have to say that the municipality is at fault in this accident. Had the sidewalk ice been melted, I doubt that Mr. Tiller would have fallen.

As a merchant on King Street, I suggest that the municipality direct its roads staff to spread de-icer on the sidewalks here as soon as freezing rain ends, since this is a very busy shopping district.

I trust that this information has been helpful to you in your investigation of this unfortunate accident. Should you require any further information, please contact me in person at my shop, or call me at 555-7777 between 9:00 a.m. and 5:00 p.m., Monday to Friday.

Yours truly,

Jim Doherty

CHECKLIST FOR editing

Review

- ☐ Did you include all of the information you intended to?
- ☐ Is there material included that shouldn't be included or that isn't necessary?
- ☐ Has the content met the purpose of the written piece?
- ☐ Has the content met the demands and needs of the reader(s)?
- ☐ Have you organized your entire piece and sections, if applicable, according to the appropriate format for a letter, memo, report, or proposal?
- ☐ Have you used headings and subheadings, if appropriate, in such a way that the reader can easily follow the information through to the conclusion? Does the information flow so that the reader can clearly understand the information?
- ☐ Have you used short, concise paragraphs so that the reader is not bogged down in wordy density?
- ☐ If you are using someone else's ideas or direct quotes, have you documented this information thoroughly and properly in the body of the text and in the works-cited section (if applicable)?
- ☐ Is your style and tone appropriate for the purpose of the document, the organization, and the reader?
- ☐ Have you ensured that you are not using jargon or technical terms that the reader will not understand?
- ☐ If you have used acronyms or initialisms, have you included the long form at the first use (e.g., all-terrain vehicle [ATV], United Nations Children's Fund [UNICEF])?
- ☐ Have you used a variety of words? Have you chosen words that will be understood by the reader and that are professional, intelligent, and meaningful?
- ☐ Did you use a thesaurus to avoid such "garbage words" as *nice, stuff,* or *things*?
- ☐ Have you used certain words repeatedly? (If so, use a thesaurus to find a different suitable word.)
- ☐ Has everything been spelled and punctuated correctly?
- ☐ Have you used complete sentences? (Look for any that lack a subject, a verb, or both.)
- ☐ Do your sentences go on forever, leaving your reader breathless (run-on sentences)?
- ☐ Did you choose the right word for the context? Watch out for commonly confused words.
- ☐ Are there any typos in your document?

Revise

- ☐ Have you noted errors in a colour on hard copy?
- ☐ Have you noted more extensive changes in the margins?
- ☐ If you are keeping your original file, have you renamed the edited version to avoid confusion later?

Refine

☐ Have you read the entire document again, ensuring content, organization, style, grammar, mechanics, and relevant documentation are addressed and corrected as necessary?

☐ After you made changes, did you put the document through another spelling and grammar check?

☐ Did you read through the document again to spot any errors that you might have missed during the entire process?

Chapter Summary

In this chapter, you have learned how important editing really is: essential in making your written product connect with its audience. You learned that editing is something you have to do *yourself* and that editing is a complex process. You have to look repeatedly at a written draft, reviewing all aspects of the written product: completeness and accuracy of content, logical sequence of its organization, careful documenting of its information sources, writing style that's appropriate for your reader, and all the issues of the mechanics of the language, including spelling, punctuation, and sentence syntax. As Donald Murray says in his landmark essay, "The maker's eye," "The maker's eye is never satisfied, for each word has the potential to ignite new meaning." Get comfortable diving back into your drafts to pursue excellence in the written product. After all, it has your name on it.

◼◼◼ SUGGESTIONS *for Further Reading*

Barber, K. (2004). *Canadian Oxford dictionary*. (2nd ed.). Toronto, ON: Oxford University Press.

Dundurn Press and Public Works and Government Services Canada Translation Bureau. (1997). *The Canadian style: A guide to writing and editing*. Toronto, ON: Dundurn Press.

Editors' Association of Canada. (2000). *Editing Canadian English*. (2nd rev. ed.). Toronto, ON: Macfarlane Walter & Ross Publishers.

◼◼◼ DEBATE *and Discussion Starters*

1. You are sending an incident report to your boss about an accident that occurred in your department. What would this person require in terms of information? What is required of an incident report? What tone should you use? Based on this tone choice, what should you look for when conducting content, mechanics, organization, and style reviews and edits?

2. Your employer's legal department has sent you an internal memo with their judgment about what to offer an angry client. It's your job to communicate with the client in a manner that he will understand. The client bought an item from your company, it was defective, and he has threatened your company with legal action if he does not receive a full refund and damages. The legal department determined that the product failure was due

to customer error in use and has indicated that the company will not pay for damages or provide a refund. What do you need to consider in terms of tone, style, organization, and mechanics when delivering this information to the client? (Remember that this is also a bad news letter. Refer to information about bad news communication in this textbook.)

3. You are sending a report to all staff members about venue choices for the company's annual awards banquet. This is an information report and is to outline what each venue offers in terms of food, entertainment, physical space, and cost per person. What level of formality should be used in writing this report, and why? Given that you are sending it to many different people with differing levels of interest, knowledge, and experience, what are some of the other editing considerations to keep in mind?

4. You are writing a letter to a long-time colleague who is also your friend. This person has just been transferred to a branch office in London, England. You are filling him or her in on what's been happening at your facility and checking in to see how he or she is doing. What are your considerations for editing before sending?

▮▮ PRACTISING *What You Have Learned*

1. Apply the three-step review, revise, and refine process to the following documents that you have written for any course in the past or that you are about to submit. Remember to consider your readers when reviewing content, style, tone, and word choice.

   a. memo/email message
   b. letter
   c. informal report
   d. formal report
   e. informal proposal
   f. formal proposal
   g. research essay for another course

2. Once you have edited your written work, swap it for someone else's. Can the two of you find content, organization, documentation, or style errors in each other's work? Conduct the three-step process on the documents, and give them back with errors clearly marked in a coloured pen so that you can both learn what your most common content, formatting, grammar, and spelling errors are.

3. Apply the three-step review, revise, and refine process to an unedited document written by a fellow student (choose from the list below). Note any needed changes with a coloured pen before you hand it back. Remember to consider the intended reader(s) when reviewing content, style, tone, and word choice.

   a. memo/email message
   b. letter
   c. informal report
   d. formal report
   e. informal proposal
   f. formal proposal
   g. research essay for another course

CHAPTER 5

Everyday Oral Communications

In this chapter, you will learn:

- ◉ How to plan, organize, and prepare for a meeting
- ◉ How to create an effective meeting agenda
- ◉ How to facilitate a meeting (and deal with challenges)

- ◉ How to effectively use teleconferencing, videoconferencing, and instant messaging technologies for meetings
- ◉ How to record and circulate minutes of a meeting

ESSENTIAL EMPLOYABILITY SKILLS

2ooo+ Employability Skills

The Conference Board of Canada has identified certain essential employability skills (EES) as benchmarks for performance in the workplace. You will learn the following EES skills in this chapter:

COMMUNICATE

- ◉ Can read and understand information presented in a variety of forms (e.g., words, graphs, charts, diagrams)
- ◉ Can listen and ask questions to understand and appreciate the points of view of others.

THINK AND SOLVE PROBLEMS

- ◉ Can assess situations and identify problems
- ◉ Can identify the root cause of a problem

MANAGE INFORMATION

- ◉ Can locate, gather, and organize information using appropriate technology and information systems
- ◉ Can access, analyze, and apply knowledge and skills from various disciplines (e.g., the arts, languages, science, technology, mathematics, social sciences, and the humanities)

WORK WITH OTHERS

- ◉ Can recognize and respect people's diversity, individual differences, and perspectives
- ◉ Can understand and work within the dynamics of a group

BE RESPONSIBLE

- ◉ Can plan and manage time, money, and other resources to achieve goals

Meetings and Minute-Taking: A Case Study

In April, out of concern about the rising rates of childhood diabetes, the City of Saskatoon Council directed the Greater Saskatoon Regional Health Unit to conduct a survey on the incidence of childhood obesity in the community. The health unit expects to receive funding for the survey by June, so a meeting with all stakeholders has to be held in May to discuss the organization, conduct, and processing of the survey and a final report. The survey is to be completed by December, with a report of findings and recommendations to be presented to the council next February.

As the manager of the unit's Child Health Department, Jennifer Willis has the responsibility for organizing and facilitating the meeting. Her agenda for the meeting is shown in Figure 5.1.

Jennifer sends this agenda by email at 4 p.m. the day before the meeting to the stakeholders, some of whom have never been to the Greater Saskatoon Health Unit before. Most of these people are health professionals, school board representatives, and child/youth organization representatives; most work 9 to 5. No directions to the facility are included in the email.

At the meeting, Jennifer is asked whether there is any coffee or tea. She has not provided any, which prompts a few people to leave and run next door to Tim Hortons, not returning for 15 minutes. She has not printed copies of the agenda, so those who neglected to print it and bring it along are forced to share with the few attendees who did. The room chosen is quite large for the group that is attending—only five of an expected 20—so people are spread apart around a large table. The room is too cold. The chairs are rigid and uncomfortable.

Jennifer starts the meeting without the three people who left for Tim Hortons—leaving only two participants besides herself. Jennifer begins by saying that she really doesn't know what council is looking for, other than a survey to document how many fat children there are in the community. The two other people in the room shift about

FIGURE 5.1 Jennifer's Meeting Agenda

Childhood Obesity Survey
22 May 2014
GSHU
3:00 p.m.

Agenda

1. Introductions
2. Mandate of survey
3. What we need to find out about fat children
4. Who will do what
5. When the survey is due
6. The final report
7. Adjournment and next meeting

uncomfortably at the use of the word "fat," and there is a long pause. When the other three return, Jennifer repeats herself, and one plus-sized attendee angrily challenges Jennifer on her use of the word "fat" as insulting.

A heated discussion ensues about how the survey should be conducted so that people are not offended in the process and about how the information should be used. The plus-sized woman dominates the discussion, and Jennifer has lost control of the meeting entirely as the group goes off on a tangent, questioning why the survey should be done and whether the results could be used by the local government to single out and victimize overweight people in general.

At 5:00 p.m., nothing on the agenda has been achieved. Two people declare that their organizations will have nothing to do with such an ill-conceived project and walk out. The other three quietly tell Jennifer that they need more information about the parameters of the project and how their organizations should contribute to the study.

Because she did not arrange for a recorder, no minutes were taken, so Jennifer summarizes the meeting in an email a week later, saying that a discussion was held and that three organization representatives agreed to work on the project. One of these people responds that she did not agree to take part but rather merely indicated that she wanted more information about the project and her organization's expected role.

1. Overall, what went wrong with the planning, organization, communication, and facilitation of this meeting?

2. How could Jennifer have ensured that the agenda, meeting, and follow-up were successful in moving the project to the next step? What would you do differently?

3. How could Jennifer have improved attendance? How could she have better engaged the participants and built their enthusiasm for the project?

4. Looking into the future, what do you think will happen with this project if the first meeting is any indicator of future success?

Before You Begin . . .

Few things in business are more disliked than meetings. They can feel like a waste of time; it seems as though nothing gets done and that everyone is bored beyond description. Meetings, meetings, meetings—sometimes we feel as though we meet just to meet!

However, in any organization made up of more than one person, visioning, planning, problem-solving, and decision-making are generally done by a group. The meeting (while not always appreciated by those who must attend!) is necessary for getting work done and increasing productivity and profits.

When properly planned and facilitated, meetings can be short, sweet, productive, dynamic, energetic, and—dare we say it—fun.

This chapter will help you to plan and facilitate meetings that you and your co-workers will appreciate, if not like, and it will guide you through recording and writing clear and informative minutes of those meeting.

Idiom Alert

short and sweet – Completed quickly and easily.

checking your ego/agenda at the door – Not imposing your views or needs on others but putting them aside in favour of working as a group.

fuzzy sandwich head – The sleepy feeling you get after eating a large lunch.

ditto – The same.

stickhandling – What hockey players do in a fast-paced game, adeptly moving their sticks around to make a play or a score a goal. In the business sense, when someone is stickhandling, he or she is completing a complex set of tasks or responsibilities with deft decisions and actions.

TGIF – Stands for "Thank goodness it's Friday" (and the weekend is almost here).

comfy – Comfortable.

doze off – Fall asleep.

off-track (discussion) – Not following what the group or individuals intended to discuss; that is, the discussion has moved to subjects or topics other than what was planned.

parking lot – Put off to a later time. When a discussion of certain matters is put into a parking lot, the discussion is deferred—to later in the meeting, to the next meeting, or to a more appropriate time.

visioning – Brainstorming about what could be, how to best solve a problem, future possibilities, and so on.

Your Starting Point

When it comes to writing agendas for meetings, facilitating meetings, and writing minutes of meetings, you need to know who is attending and what their interest is in the topics or issues being discussed. This will help you to plan the meeting effectively, facilitate for best results, and finally, produce minutes that highlight the main points of the meeting and meet the needs and preferences of those receiving the minutes.

Of special note: you need to know who will read the minutes. Often, it's not just those who attended the meeting. Be sure to find out who will receive the minutes.

For agenda-writing, facilitation, and minute-writing tasks, review the Starting Point questions in Chapter 1 to clearly establish who the attendees are and who will receive the minutes so that you can plan for, manage, and record the details of the meeting appropriately according to the needs of the meeting group and readers of the minutes.

Creating the Oral/Written Product: How to Do It

PREPARING TO WRITE

Research

As usual, a bit of research is not going to hurt when planning a meeting. Look into your company's history on the project or issue you are meeting about, as well as any individuals' involvement in the issue or concern. Get as much information as you can before you set an agenda and conduct the meeting so that you are well versed in the background to the meeting and have a handle on the varying perspectives and viewpoints that may be discussed. Make copies of relevant reports, memos, letters, and studies that may be of use in the meeting. You can refer to these documents as needed when discussion is taking place and people need clarification.

Depending on the purpose of the meeting, research sources can include:

- interviews with individuals who will participate in the meeting;

- interviews with individuals who will not participate but who have relevant information or background;

- company policy documents and historical documents;

- internal or outside reports, analyses, studies, and such;

- libraries (particularly helpful with business databases and periodicals);

- online information resources such as databases, websites, and blogs;

- reports or information (print and online) on competitors or other companies dealing with similar issues and considerations.

PREPARING FOR CITATIONS

If you intend to introduce information from other sources, be sure to let people know where the information comes from by mentioning the source, even if it is an internal document. Yes, it's a good idea to have the information about these sources close to hand, as it is when you are writing a report, proposal, letter, or memo.

ORGANIZING INFORMATION AND WRITING: FORMAT

Planning the meeting

Meetings are often considered a boring waste of time, when people don't get anything done, and a waste of money.

So why meet? No one wants to meet just to meet—think of the comic strips, such as Dilbert, that suggest organizations hold meetings simply for the sake of meeting.

Have a clear purpose and scope

No meeting should be held without a clear purpose, a rationale that those attending can agree on and work with. The purpose is a theme, a project, or tasks that the gathered group will discuss and work through. Having a purpose usually implies specific work that can be completed. The purpose needs to be something that is achievable—if not right away, at least at some foreseeable point in the future.

Meetings should not be held, however, if individuals can get the work done on their own, perhaps connecting with each other by email or in a very brief conference call to agree on who is doing what for a project or task. A meeting in this situation would be a waste of time that everyone could otherwise use to work on his or her assigned tasks or responsibilities. A meeting might be appropriate after the tasks are completed so that people can come together to share their completed work and bring a project to completion.

Choose the right participants

Participants in the meeting should be people who can actually do the work that relates to the purpose of the meeting. The people involved also have to be willing to work

Hands across the gap? Non-verbal communication across cultures

Has someone ever become annoyed with you because that person thinks you looked at them "funny"? Did you ever wonder whether a friend was about to deliver bad news when he or she paused in conversation a bit too long?

In these situations, you have been an unwitting victim of non-verbal *mis*-communication! It can be difficult even for people of the same culture to accurately translate someone else's non-verbal or "body" language; there are many forms of emotional, social, and physical interference that can lead to misunderstanding.

In a cross-cultural context, what you say may be completely misconstrued if your non-verbal language is interpreted through the receiver's cultural perspective differently from what you intended.

Eye contact helps us to convey and receive messages. As children, we learn appropriate eye contact from observing and mimicking adults. However, even in North America we manage to misunderstand eye contact. Generally, we don't maintain eye contact while talking to someone; we look at the listener intermittently to ensure that he or she is listening. When listening, you learn to maintain eye contact to demonstrate your interest.

However, the reverse is often true in communication with or between North Americans of African descent; in general, one maintains eye contact during speaking and looks away when listening. Some cultures value constant eye contact, as in Arab cultures. In First Nations culture, as a sign of respect, children learn to lower their eyes when addressed by an elder or other adult.

In cultures with a well-established power hierarchy, making direct eye contact with a perceived "superior" is inappropriate. Looking away or breaking eye contact is expected when one addresses a boss or authority figure in many cultures.

Ever notice how babies' facial expressions give away exactly what they are thinking and feeling? Sadly, as we grow up we learn from our culture which expressions are appropriate. In some cultures, smiling is a sign of fear or insecurity, while in others a smile is a way of making the other person feel comfortable and safe.

Hand gestures or gesticulations can also cause problems if inappropriate for the context. Even in North American society, we can't agree on appropriate physical touching, particularly in a business setting. Because of concerns about appropriate behaviour between genders, men and women may avoid hugging, even if they know each other well. Even a pat on the back or a touch on the arm can be construed as inappropriate or harassing.

Those of Anglo-Saxon background use hand gestures infrequently compared to people in more demonstrative cultures such as Latin American or Mediterranean. In many cultures, people readily hold hands, including with people of the same gender; however, in some (for example, Arab culture), touching between non-family members of the opposite gender is strictly forbidden.

Pointing at someone is considered rude in most cultures. Gesturing anything with the left hand can be considered unclean in Muslim and Hindu cultures. You might think things are okay and make the "okay" sign with your thumb and first finger, but in some cultures, such as Russian, this gesture can represent something vulgar—not *okay* at all!

As a child, were you ever told by your grandmother to "sit up straight!"? In grandma's generation, straight posture indicated confidence and respect. While a casual slump may be interpreted as being relaxed, in most cultures a resigned-looking posture expresses defeat. So maybe grandma was right!

Have you ever found yourself backing away when someone approached you to converse? While the other person's halitosis may have made you recoil, more likely you backed away because you felt vaguely uncomfortable. This vague discomfort occurs when our personal space feels "invaded." In cross-cultural contexts, use research and observation to determine the appropriate conversational distance. In some cultures, people need to stand several feet apart—far enough for personal space but close enough to hear each other. In other cultures, if you are not standing close together, you are perceived as standoffish.

Is a handshake always a great way to greet someone? In many regions of the world where North American business culture has been adopted, a handshake may be just fine, but never assume. A firm handshake shows sincerity and confidence here, but in Asia a lighter handshake is often more appropriate. In Japan, bowing is a more customary greeting, and bowing deeper than someone perceived to be a superior is essential to demonstrate respect.

Business attire is another form of communication. Generally, stick to conservative business attire, but again, observe and research the context in which you are doing business. For example, in conservative Muslim countries, women are expected to cover their hair with a scarf or hat and ensure that cleavage, arms, and legs are covered.

collaboratively—to check their egos (as well as their positions and the hierarchical structure) at the door. This will allow everyone to work toward action or solutions with others who may have different opinions or a different reason for taking part in the meeting.

The number of participants in a meeting should be carefully considered. For a small meeting, having any more than five people means that the meeting can be dominated by just a few, with some of the others really just warming seats. Two to five people is an optimum size, unless you are holding a larger meeting or conference-style gathering and plan to break out into smaller work groups (two to five people per group) to focus on specific issues or tasks.

Choose the best time of day for meeting

The choice of meeting time is also very important. You do not want to schedule a meeting at the beginning of the workday without allowing at least half an hour for coffee and a transition to the tasks of the meeting. (This also gives the inevitable late-comers time to arrive and get settled.)

Meeting after lunch (when people have "fuzzy sandwich head") or right before the end of the day should also be avoided. At the end of the day, when people want to get out of the meeting as soon as possible, they are not as likely to focus on the tasks at hand, because their minds are on what they'll be doing after work. The best times for meeting are from 9:30 to 11:00 a.m. and from 2:00 to 3:30 p.m. If you have no choice about the time of your meeting, keep in mind the distractions mentioned above, and plan strategies to keep people's attention.

Another consideration is energy level. If you are going to meet first thing in the morning, provide coffee and a snack (in case people didn't have breakfast) so that participants will feel more alert. Ditto any time after 3:00 p.m.: typically, people's blood sugar levels crash in mid-afternoon, which is why many workplaces have coffee breaks at this time. Late-afternoon meetings should be kept very focused and brief so that you get the best out of the many people who are distracted at that time of day.

Mondays are generally tough days for people to meet, because they are often busy dealing with "after the weekend" problems that have piled up or stickhandling through such tasks as orders and shipments. As for Fridays—well, "TGIF" should tell you something: it's downhill to the weekend, baby! If you must meet on a Friday, be sure to do so in the morning.

Keep meetings short and on time

The length of a meeting is also important. Meetings longer than two hours are problematic, particularly if there is no hourly break. If you plan to meet for longer than two hours, schedule a sizable break after the first two hours (such as an hour to an hour and a half for lunch or dinner). Alternatively, schedule something completely different for participants; this is particularly important when meeting over a weekend. Break up meeting times with fun activities or free time so that participants will come back refreshed and ready to work again.

Hold meetings in comfortable and appropriate locations

Location, location, location: where you hold a meeting is critical to its success. If people feel *too* comfortable, they may fall asleep. On the other hand, if participants have to sit on stiff, hard chairs that have absolutely nothing ergonomic about them (think wooden or metal stacking chairs), they will be shifting around in discomfort, if not pain, and be unable to focus.

Choose a smaller room if your meeting is small. A room too large for a group has a cold and impersonal environment that does not foster collegiality. Conversely, too many people jammed into a small room will feel suffocating.

Meeting around a table on reasonably comfy chairs is great if your group is small—as long as the table isn't so large that you must shout to be heard by people at the other end. Round or oval tables are best, because you can make eye contact and note body language. At the very least, you want to position people around whatever table you have in such a way that everyone can more or less see one another.

Larger meetings, such as those taking place at a convention, conference, or retreat, need a large space for full-group meetings and breakout spaces for smaller groups to meet and discuss agenda items.

The temperature of the space is also a factor in keeping people's attention. Cranked-up air conditioning may make people shiver and eventually ache with the cold, while hot rooms may make people doze off.

Agendas

Agendas give attendees a clear and brief explanation of what is to be discussed at a meeting. This information allows attendees to think about their roles and positions on various issues ahead of time so that they can better prepare to be productive.

Once the purpose of a meeting has been agreed to and established, an agenda can and must be created. Based on that purpose, the agenda will lay out what the meeting will (and, by omission, what it will not) cover. Agenda-less meetings often cause worry ahead of time as attendees wonder what is going to come up. Further, agenda-less meetings are hard to facilitate, because there is no roadmap for the group to agree on and work through and no clear way to get out at a reasonable hour. People tend to bring their pet issues or concerns to meetings, while some may feel that they have been ambushed by information they are not ready to address. Indeed, a meeting without an agreed-to purpose can and often does cause more problems than it solves, because participants do not have a clear expectation of what is to be achieved and what their roles are. (You *could* set the agenda when you all get together, but it is better to have at least a partial agenda ahead of time to frame the work of the meeting.)

So that participants can prepare for the meeting, the agenda should be emailed or otherwise circulated to everyone involved, along with a memo or email notice of the meeting (time, date, and place). Include meeting **ground rules** if you feel they are necessary. Additional pieces of information (such as studies or past reports) that participants would find helpful to read before the meeting can be emailed or circulated in hard copy ahead of the meeting date.

A well-articulated agenda may specify the amount of time that will be spent on discussion of each item. This is helpful if you have several equally important items to discuss that must be addressed in a timely way. New issues, items, or topics brought to the meeting itself can be introduced under the "new business" section of the agenda; these matters are usually considered *after* all of the planned items have been discussed. The group must agree to add these items to the agenda at the beginning of the meeting, and it's often a good idea to designate the amount of time available to discuss them so that your meeting does not run overtime.

Often, certain agenda items will require more time than even the most seasoned meeting planner or **facilitator** could have anticipated, particularly items that the participants are passionate or enthusiastic about. You should check with the group members to find out how they want to continue the discussion (e.g., defer some other items to the next meeting). If the group agrees, the meeting's agenda can be modified yet still fit the timeline for the gathering, allowing people to leave when they expect to. The group may agree to extend the meeting until all items are dealt with; in that case, the timeline for the meeting will expand. (You will need to keep checking with participants to see whether they are still willing to continue discussion and get through all the agenda items.)

If you adhere too strictly to the agenda, participants may miss out on some fruitful discussion that appears to take the group off-track but could be helpful in finding creative solutions or ideas. As facilitator, you will have to use your discretion and consult everyone involved in the meeting to determine if the off-track discussion is going in a direction they wish.

Finally, the agenda will help you (or a recording secretary) to organize the information under discussion as the meeting evolves when it comes to writing the minutes later on. In your notes, apply the same headings used for the various agenda items. Your notes, written beneath the headings, will easily form the basis of the minutes. This is particularly important if you assign the writing of the minutes to someone else.

Agenda format

Agenda formats vary from business to business and organization to organization. If you are planning the agenda for a meeting, consult agendas created for past, similar meetings and meeting topics at your place of business to get a feel for how time and discussion items are organized.

Ask some questions: How long are meetings, typically? How many items are included on most agendas? What do your co-workers think makes a productive and satisfying meeting? What drives them crazy?

As you become more familiar with your organization's culture and experience of meetings, you will find it easier to set an agenda that everyone can work with. See Figure 5.2 for a basic agenda format that you may want to use as a general template when you are getting started. Note, however, that organization of headings and topics will very much depend on how your company conducts meetings, the level of formality, and the information to be covered in the meeting. Just remember to be uniform and organized in whatever format you choose.

FIGURE 5.2 Agenda Format

The title of the agenda describes what the meeting is about.

Date, location, and time noted at top so that attendees know when/where to go.

TITLE OF MEETING
Date
Location
Time

AGENDA

1. Review of agenda
2. Additions to agenda
3. Approval of agenda
4. Approval of (previous) minutes (if applicable)

Information reports discussed first, since late-comers still arriving.

INFORMATION ONLY

5. Report #1
6. Report #2
7. Report #3 (and so on)

Action items discussed next after everyone is present and before anyone leaves.

ACTION ITEMS

8. Action item #1
9. Action item #2 (and so on)

New business discussed last, since not everyone has to be present; can be deferred.

NEW BUSINESS

10. New business items (list, if applicable)
11. Next meeting (if applicable)

ADJOURNMENT

12. Adjournment (note time of adjournment in the minutes)

Figure 5.5 shows a sample agenda for a meeting of a for-profit organization, while Figure 5.3 shows a sample agenda for a meeting of a not-for-profit organization (in which headings are ordered slightly differently from those in the general format to suit the needs of the organization). Because the not-for-profit meeting agenda was for an organization comprised entirely of volunteers, the agenda was kept deliberately simple so that discussion would not be constrained by more specific topics. This is quite common in such organizations. Agendas for not-for-profit organizations are often, though not always, written in a somewhat less formal tone than agendas for businesses, because volunteers with little or no experience in a business setting are involved.

Facilitating the meeting

The leader of the meeting needs to be a facilitator—which means checking his or her own agenda and ego at the door. That way, the facilitator will be better able to ensure that the group thoroughly discusses and considers all aspects of an issue, project, or task. The facilitator is there to bring out the best ideas, thoughts, and impressions of the entire group for maximum productivity.

This doesn't mean you will not have a chance to speak. You can offer your own opinion or thoughts, but it's best to do so after others have had a chance.

Manage people to manage the meeting

Facilitators need to be skilled at drawing out quiet (or new to the company) individuals so that their views and ideas are heard. At the same time, a facilitator acts as a referee, managing those who tend to dominate the meeting, either through their positive enthusiasm or in their attempts to run roughshod over others. In other words, a good facilitator makes sure that everyone has a fair chance to speak and be heard.

If you are the facilitator, you will want to make sure that time is managed. Place a watch where you can see it to manage discussion and time appropriately. Keep the agenda next to the watch for reference, and make a mental note as you go along about how much time has passed, moving people along to a new topic or item as needed.

Defer items when necessary

Some issues or items may require more discussion or consideration time than was planned for. This will affect the amount of time for discussion of other items. Check with participants to see whether they want to continue discussing the item and put the other items into a "parking lot," to be considered if there's time at the end of the meeting, or whether they want to resume the discussion at another meeting.

As a meeting facilitator, you can make or break the success of a meeting. The key is to be attentive—be sure to create an environment in which people feel comfortable and that helps you to stay on track with the planned agenda.

Start promptly

It is important to start on time—don't wait for late-comers, because it is disrespect-ful to those who arrive on time (or early). If people don't know each other, use some icebreakers to help people introduce themselves to each other. Icebreakers are com-monly used in longer meetings, seminars, or retreats when many people do not know each other well, if at all. In a smaller group, simply going around the table and having participants introduce themselves (and possibly identifying their department or orga-nization) is sufficient.

Turn cellphones off

Make sure that everyone's cellphone is off or set to etiquette (vibrate) mode. A ringing cellphone is a distraction and an inconsiderate interruption of the meeting. Participants who absolutely must take a call should be seated where they can easily leave the room and should have their phone set to vibrate mode to minimize interruption.

Keep track of time and task

Explain any time considerations for the meeting so that participants will not be offended if you ask them to move on with comments or ask some to hold their com-ments until another time. Ground rules (such as a "no interrupting" rule) are a good idea regardless of how well you know all the participants. These rules allow you to manage the meeting effectively if behaviour is not appropriate; everyone knows what is expected of them.

As you get to know your company's culture and the personalities of people you will be working with in meetings, you will develop a good sense of how to manage individu-als as a facilitator. If you find that a few strong individuals often dominate meetings, you might want to consider using the talking-stick method. This method, which has its origins in Aboriginal culture, is a way of allowing each person in a gathering to speak without interruption. Whoever is holding the talking stick has the floor, and no one else may interrupt.

In a business meeting, you may choose to use an object (e.g., a "talking-stick sta-pler") as a visual reminder to others not to interrupt the speaker, but generally, you can establish the "no interrupting" rule at the beginning of the meeting without designating an object. However, as facilitator you will also have to manage time, so you may have to interrupt politely and ask the speaker to wrap up his or her remarks to allow time for others to speak.

Once everyone who wants to speak has spoken, time can be allocated for people to address what has been said by others (rebuttal) and to add new ideas or thoughts that arose out of what they heard during the meeting. Again, the facilitator may have to set a rule that until everyone has had a chance to speak a second time, no one has a third opportunity, and so on. This may seem a bit stilted and formal, but if you have a num-ber of very passionate, extroverted people in the meeting, it may be the only way to get through your agenda on time and not offend anyone.

Save the handouts for later

Distribute handouts only if they are brief notes to help people follow along (such as during a multimedia or slide presentation). Otherwise, participants might read rather than listen to each other or work on the issues at hand. However, if there is a report to consider or some information to evaluate, get this documentation to all participants ahead of time, and assign it as "homework." It is sometimes helpful to ask everyone to put reports and papers aside for the duration of the meeting. If certain information is under consideration, the facilitator can keep a copy for reference.

If there is a speaker, hand out only the notes for the speaker's slides or overheads. Anything lengthier, such as a report, should be handed out afterwards so that participants are not reading during the presentation.

Check for body language clues

Monitor participants' body language: are they starting to fidget or look at the clock? If people are looking bored, chances are they are! Suggest a short break if time permits, or divert attention to a new discussion.

Make "popcorn" to generate ideas

If your group is in problem-solving or visioning mode, you may want to employ the popcorn approach to generate as many ideas as possible in a short period. Starting with one person and working around the group (much like the talking-stick method), ask each person to briefly offer a new idea or thought. Keep working around the circle or group for a specified time, and have a recorder write down all the ideas without censoring any. Some people will have many ideas, others fewer, and some may take a pass when it's their turn on each round, but the point is to come up with many ideas in a short time in order to prompt some good discussion.

Once you have all of the ideas recorded, go over each one, and discuss them as a group in reference to the issue or problem you are dealing with. Respectfully eliminate items that really will not work, create a list of ideas to consider if all else fails (contingency plan), and make a shortlist of ideas and thoughts worth exploring further. Depending on the time available in the meeting and the willingness of participants, you may continue discussion or hold another meeting to refine the shortlist's application.

Finish when you said you would

Always finish on time, unless you have the group's agreement to stay longer. People appreciate getting in and out of meetings on time. If you decide to stay longer, keep checking with participants at intervals (perhaps every 15 minutes or so). If something appears to require more discussion, you can agree to "parking lot" the information, with recorded notes on discussion that can be brought to another meeting that everyone agrees to.

Recording minutes

As you (or a recording secretary) write notes on the meeting, be sure to use the agenda's topic titles as headers for your notes. This will ensure that the information is well organized, which will save you a major headache if you write the **minutes** a few days later when your memory is not as fresh.

When you can't get together . . .

Often it's impossible to get everyone together in one room. Many companies have offices around the country or the world, and transporting people to one location can be prohibitively expensive. You still have to have everyone's input and contributions, but how do you bring people together?

TELECONFERENCING

One of the easiest, least technologically challenging ways to meet is by **teleconferencing**—that is, holding a conference call. Often, a physical meeting is held (at head office, for example) with people who can attend, while those who cannot be there in person can communicate with other participants by means of a speaker phone on the meeting table.

Once everyone is connected to the meeting, it is important for the participants in the room to introduce themselves. That way, the people on the line are not left wondering whom they are talking to. The people on the phone, in turn, should introduce themselves so that people in the physical meeting and on other phone lines know who is involved in the conversation.

Whenever anyone speaks, that person should state his or her name and then begin (at least until participants begin to recognize each other's voices). This may feel a bit strange at first, but if you are the person on the other end of a telephone line, you may have trouble distinguishing one person's voice from another's, which is quite tiring mentally.

Allowing a pause after each person speaks gives others the opportunity to respond. There may also be a slight delay in transmission for people speaking from the other side of the world.

Interrupting is never polite, but it's even more of a problem in this kind of meeting. Because of the challenges of phone lines, transmission delays, and the feeling of disconnect when you can't see everyone, interruptions make it difficult for everyone to communicate effectively. Interrupting this kind of meeting will interrupt the entire communication flow.

As in a regular meeting where everyone is in the same room, a **moderator** can keep things flowing so that everyone has a chance to speak and can maintain the pauses between speakers so that people whose responses are delayed can still fully participate.

VIDEOCONFERENCING

Videoconferencing is used when people in various locations can connect with each other in real time via their computers' video cameras. In order for this to work, everyone needs access to a reliable computer with a video camera and current videoconferencing software, as well as a reliable high-speed Internet connection.

You (or your company) would use a software application such as AIM or iChat. When you are about to hold a meeting, you log in, and if you have sufficient processor speed, bandwidth, and system software, you can have several individuals or groups (people clustered around the video camera) participating.

As in teleconferencing, pausing after people speak, avoiding interruption, and allowing for delays in transmission will help in making the meeting run smoothly.

Videoconferences (also called group video chats or webinars—web seminars) are particularly suitable for meetings involving numerous individuals who work for large, multi-location companies or government agencies, because more people can interact in more ways than in an audio conference, allowing for rapid exchange of questions and ideas (brainstorming). Seeing people and reading their body language leads to better communication than just hearing them. Participants can also use the technology to share photos, documents, PowerPoint presentations, and video clips. Videoconferences save the considerable costs of airline travel, hotel rooms, and conference venues for seminars and training sessions, and they save the valuable time of busy employees.

INSTANT MESSAGING

A meeting using **instant messaging (IM)** is not the best way to get people together to discuss issues in a formal sense, but the method can be useful in getting a quick decision on an urgent matter when several people have to be involved. Usually, IM is used not for a full meeting but for discussing a few key issues that need input and/or a decision as soon as possible.

Knowing who will read the minutes is your best guide in deciding what to record as notes. What are the information needs of the readers? What are their interests or concerns vis-à-vis the meeting's purpose or agenda items?

Writing good minutes takes practice. Focus on writing brief, to-the-point notes so that you can keep up with the meeting and what is being discussed at the same time. If you take notes frequently, you may find using your own shorthand or abbreviations helpful in recording essential information quickly.

If a participant talks for a long time on one topic, note the main points, and keep any repetition or irrelevant information out of the notes.

There's no such thing as a stupid question when you are recording information. Be sure to ask individuals to repeat important points or pause to confirm who voted on what point, for example. As a backup, many people rely on a tape recorder; the recording will capture the precise wording of an important statement and the flavour of discussion you may find essential to meeting the information needs of those who will read the minutes. (Journalists often use tape recorders so that they get *exact* quotes in an interview; anything less can lead to a lot of problems.)

An important note on recording minutes: the facilitator should never act as recorder, because the facilitator needs to give his or her full attention to the dynamics and flow of the meeting, while the recorder needs to focus on recording all the important details as they unfold.

Telephone communication is an everyday fact of life in business communication. Whether you're speaking one-on-one with a client or participating in a teleconference, you'll want to keep your phone conversations flowing professionally and productively, just as you would if facilitating an in-person meeting. See the box below for specific tips.

Writing and circulating minutes

When you are writing minutes from notes, be sure to use short, concise sentences and paragraphs. Make sure that you have spelled individuals' and organizations' names correctly—and yes, do a thorough edit for other spelling, grammar, and mechanical errors.

Attach a cover page if the minutes are longer than two pages. Otherwise, a title and other details of the meeting typed on the front page is appropriate (see Figure 5.4).

If possible, attach any handouts or materials that were circulated at the meeting; this information can further clarify what was discussed.

Minutes should be circulated in hard copy or by email as soon as possible to those participating (generally within a week after the meeting).

Help others get the message by telephone

One of the ways you will connect with others about an upcoming meeting, or follow up on tasks flowing from the meeting, will be by telephone. As we are such busy people, you may have to leave a message. It may be the bane of your existence, being caught in an endless loop of recorded messages or instructions about how to leave a message for someone. However, a telephone call may be the only or best way to reach someone at that moment.

Generally speaking, it is appropriate to leave telephone messages when the information is neutral or positive or just mildly negative (for example, if you have to turn down an employee's request for the night off).

Do not leave any detailed message if the information is seriously negative or could be construed as such. For example, you would not fire someone over the phone or tell them they are being demoted. You would simply leave a message asking the person to call you back, giving the best time and your phone number or asking him or her whether he or she can meet with you at a specific time and location. Why would you just give the basic information? Simply put, a lot can be read into your tone of voice and whatever message you leave by telephone, because the receiver cannot see your face or body language. What you say can be misinterpreted, much as email messages can be misunderstood. Finally, it's just plain ill-mannered to deliver bad news by an indirect means of communication. You have to summon the courage to say what needs to be said, as neutrally as possible, face-to-face.

Never, ever hide behind a telephone (or email) because you don't want to deal with the emotional fall-out of delivering bad news.

Once you've gotten through to the receiver's voice mailbox, you'll have to let go of your frustration and adopt a clear, upbeat tone of voice. Enunciate your words clearly, and don't speak too quickly. You *must not* express your frustration or negative mood in your tone when you leave a message, because the receiver will react negatively to what you are hoping to communicate.

Don't ramble. If you tend to do so, write out a list of what you need to say, and practise saying it briefly before you call and leave a message. (You might want to avoid reading these notes out loud if you share an office space—your officemates might think you are losing it!) Then focus on the notes when you call.

Always state your name and telephone number and the time of your call when you start the message. This is the most important part of the message. State your purpose in calling—the next most important part of the call. Finally, provide the most important details he or she needs to know, then repeat your name and telephone number for a return call.

It's important to remember that a message does not replace a full conversation by telephone, face-to-face, or by email, since you will not be able to provide all the details you need to communicate. You will need to follow up on your message, usually when the receiver calls you (or otherwise responds) about your communication.

If what you have to say is too much for the messaging time available, simply leave a message for the person to call you back (or email or respond in another way, like dropping by your office) about the topic you wish to discuss, and give a best time to call and the number at which you can be reached.

Sample Documents

FIGURE 5.3 Agenda: Not-for-Profit Organization Example

AGENDA

Brown School Family Centre
Board of Directors' Meeting

November 29, 2013
7:00 p.m.
Brown School, Brownville, ON

1. **Additions to agenda**

2. **Approval of agenda**

3. **Approval of minutes**

4. **Lia Southam, United Way** •———————— Schedule guest speakers early when most people are present, attentive, and energetic.

5. **Chairperson's report** •———————— Items 5–16 are reports from subcommittees or staff with information and/or action required.

6. **Brownville Stay and Play report**

7. **Treasurer's report**

8. **Fundraising Committee**

9. **Program Development Committee**

10. **Early Years Board**

11. **Community funding**

12. **January event**

13. **Strategic plan**

14. **Newsletter**

15. **Trillium Open House**

16. **Internet**

17. **New business items** •———————— New business last (less important); people may be tired or leave early.

18. **Next meeting**

19. **Adjournment**

Minutes created by: (signature, Secretary)
Minutes approved by: (signature, Chairperson)

FIGURE 5.4 Minutes: Not-for-Profit Organization Example

THE BROWN SCHOOL FAMILY CENTRE
BOARD MEETING
November 29, 2013
7:00 p.m.
Brown School, Brownville, ON

Who, what, where, and when details are at top as context for minutes.

ATTENDANCE

List includes those present or arriving late.

Present

Donna Lukinuk
Mary-Jane McRonald
Robert Reach
Jamie Smith
Jacinta Chester
Shanice Bradley
Christine Court
Zahra Abdul
Cristin Armstrong
Melody Winch
David Cuttle

Additions to the agenda are noted briefly and clearly.

1. **Additions to Agenda**
   a) Strategic planning for the United Way
   b) Newsletter
   c) Trillium application

Minute-taker's notes are brief, to the point, to keep reader's attention.

2. **Approval of Agenda**
   A suggestion was made to combine items #7 and #8. A motion was made to adopt the agenda with #7 and #8 combined.
   1st – Melody
   2nd – Mary-Jane
   All in favour

3. **Approval of Minutes**
   1st – Melody
   2nd – Mary-Jane
   All in favour

INFORMATION, ACTION define type of item, useful for readers not attending.

4. **Lia Southam, United Way (INFORMATION)**
   Lia handed out the strategic plan. We are all to read it over, make a list of questions, and then email her. We will contact her for continued training.

5. **Chairperson's Report (INFORMATION)**
   Donna thanked everyone for coming out to United Way training. Jamie will write a thank-you card.

6. **Brownville Stay and Play Report (INFORMATION)**

   It has been very busy. Christmas party will be on Thurs. Dec. 19. Closed on Dec. 26, 27, Jan. 2. Closing at noon on Dec. 6.

   RAPP is being enjoyed, but attendance is sporadic. Funding is for two more full sessions: Thursday mornings and an evening session. Money needs to be used up by June, so evening session will be after March break.

   On Jan. 3, Tim Holland will make a juggler presentation to the Stay and Play group.

7. **Treasurer's Report (INFORMATION/ACTION)** •

   We may have to reduce Jacinta's office hours because of gaps in funds between now and January. **Board members may have to sign up to do tasks.** Mary-Jane will email updates.

   > INFORMATION, ACTION combined in some items because no need for not-for-profit organization minutes to be organized into sections.

8. **Fundraising Committee (INFORMATION/ACTION)**

   Old Time Christmas

   Free hot chocolate with donation. Tickets for cookie baskets—350 to 500. We will do reindeer antlers again. Volunteers are needed. Draw is at 3:00 p.m. after the parade.

   Men's Night

   This is on Dec. 14. Lisa is doing up a flyer to advertise. One or two people are needed.

   Spaghetti Dinner

   Set for Sat. Feb. 8. Looking for a place to hold it. Silent auction with dinner and local talent. Held from 4:30 to 8:30; no sittings, just come and eat. Ask high school, Explorers, and Guides for volunteers. Melodie Beal has done this type of dinner; she will sit down with fundraising committee for ideas. Donna will ask Men's Skating Group to volunteer. Jacinta will make a flyer to give to her husband to pass out at skating. Suggestion to do a raffle rather than a silent auction.

   > Tone ("just come and eat") more informal than in minutes in a business setting.

   Fundraising document

   In theory, it looked good, but this group can only commit to a few. Discussion about lack of volunteers followed. Homework: Think of volunteer strategies. Donna will do a short speech. Sign-up sheets will be posted.

9. **Program Development Committee (INFORMATION/ACTION)**

   Jacinta wants direction on when to go to people for funding for programs. Mary-Jane will email document to Jacinta.

10. **Early Years Board (INFORMATION/ACTION)**

    Jacinta will approach a user about attending their board. We will invite the user to our next meeting.

11. **Community Funding (INFORMATION/ACTION)**

    Due on Friday. Jacinta has it almost done. We will ask parents in Jan. or Feb. to phone council members.

(continued)

12. **January Event (INFORMATION/ACTION)**
Potluck at Donna's on Sun. Jan. 12 at 2:30 p.m.; bring your significant other. Melodie Beal offered to hold it next year. Emails will go out for reminders, and someone will call David.

13. **Strategic Plan (ACTION)**
Read, write up questions, and discuss in January. Allocate an hour every month for planning. Agenda will be put on email so that we can spend more time on planning.

14. **Newsletter (INFORMATION)**
Will be sent out in *Brownville This Week*. Ready to be sent out.

15. **Trillium Open House (INFORMATION/ACTION)**
Talk to Trillium first. We need to call Larissa Scottdale and council members to attend. Jacinta and Mary-Jane will figure out who to call.

16. **Internet**
Called Bell Sympatico because no response to August letter. Elizabeth Stein from Bell said we could partner up with the library but should approach the library to confirm. Waiting to hear from Elizabeth from Bell Sympatico. Trillium money for computer can go toward the router and equipment.

17. **New Business Items**
No new business.

18. **Next meeting (INFORMATION/ACTION)**
Wednesday, January 29, 2014.

19. **Adjournment (ACTION)**
1st – Mel
2nd – Mary-Jane
All in favour. Meeting adjourned at 9:05 p.m.

Tells people whom to contact for more information.

Minutes created by: (signature, Secretary)
Minutes approved by: (signature, Chairperson)

FIGURE 5.5 Agenda: Business Example

AGENDA

Shining Smiles Dental Office Staff Meeting
December 5, 2013
6:00 p.m.
Rock Lobster Seafood Emporium, Antigonish, NS

1. **Attendance**

2. **Approval of agenda**

3. **Adoption of minutes**

4. **Dentists' report**

5. **Financial report**

6. **Correspondence for action**

7. **Correspondence for information**

8. **Community activities**

9. **Nova Scotia Dental Assistants' Convention**

10. **Exchange of Secret Santa gifts** ————————————— Minor issues scheduled last because they are less important than reports and action items.

11. **Next meeting**

12. **Adjournment**

FIGURE 5.6 Minutes: Business Example

Shining Smiles Dental Office
Minutes of the December 5, 2013 Staff Meeting
6:00 p.m. Supper Meeting
Rock Lobster Seafood Emporium, Antigonish, NS

1. **Attendance:** Present were Dr. Jane Nielsen, Dr. Ralph Jeffrey, Valerie Lindt, Krista Kirby, John Cassidy, Hakkim Ahmad, Megan Mallory. Regrets/absent: Lawrie Urquhart, Alice Smyth.

2. **Approval of agenda:** All in favour; no changes or new business added.

3. **Adoption of minutes of November 7, 2013 meeting:** All in favour, no changes needed.

4. **Dentists' report:** Dr. Nielsen reported that the clinic's recent teeth-brushing campaign in local schools was a great hit with children and teachers alike, particularly the very silly songs and antics of Murphy the Molar, who paid several visits to demonstrate the proper way to brush. Because the materials for the campaign (child-friendly toothbrushes, floss, disclosing tablets, toothpaste) were donated by the Canadian Dental Association, and because Dr. Jeffrey had the starring role as Murphy, there were no expenses incurred other than a $50 rental of the costume. There were no other items to report.

5. **Financial report:** Everyone reviewed the November financial operating statements; there were no questions for clarification. While there is not yet a year-end financial statement, it appears we will have to raise our treatment fees by June 2014. This move is particularly essential because we had an unforeseen expense in replacing an x-ray machine that failed safety inspections in October. Dr. Nielsen and Valerie Lindt will investigate recent fee increases at nearby dental offices to assess what a reasonable fee increase will be. They will report at the January meeting. Dr. Jeffrey noted that we have not increased fees since 2006 and that this has probably led to our troubling financial situation, particularly since costs of supplies and required computer systems have increased annual operating expenses.

6. **Correspondence for action:** The Canadian Dental Association requires us to administer a survey with all of our patients as to their leading dental health concerns. This survey will help the association lobby provincial and federal governments for increased funding to subsidize dental care for individuals and families on social assistance.

    Megan Mallory has agreed to take charge of the survey project and to make multiple copies of the survey to give to all patients starting in January. Krista

Many sections like this are wordy, representative of office culture.

Kirby will ensure that each patient completes the survey before or after his or her appointment. The survey should be conducted in January and February; it is to be submitted to the association by March 5, 2014.

7. **Correspondence for information:** A thank-you note was received from the Antigonish Ratepayers' Association for attending a roundtable discussion on community health issues on November 30, 2013. We are quite happy to have been invited and have let the association know we are interested if they hold a similar event in 2014.

8. **Community activities:** Hakkim Ahmad reported that we have collected two refrigerator-sized boxes of food from our month-long food drive for the Antigonish Food Bank, thanks to our generous patients. He will contact the food bank to pick up the food and will suggest they bring several smaller boxes to collect it all. Dr. Nielsen indicated that we still have a number of Murphy the Molar tooth-brushing kits from the recent schools campaign and suggested we donate them to the food bank.

9. **Nova Scotia Dental Assistants' Convention:** The Nova Scotia Dental Assistants' Convention is to be held April 3–5 in Halifax. Discussion about the event took place, and it was decided that Krista Kirby, John Cassidy, and Megan Mallory will attend, since they have never attended before. The office will cover the cost of the conference for all three people, but travel expenses will be the responsibility of those attending.

10. **Exchange of Secret Santa gifts:** Very funny gifts were exchanged between everyone present. Dr. Jeffrey volunteered to deliver the gifts for those who were away on the weekend.

Not much detail in reporting on Santa gifts—not essential to the business.

11. **Next meeting:** Our next meeting is January 14, 2014, noon, at the dental office. (Lunch will be catered by Sandy's Sandwiches and Treats.)

12. **Adjournment:** The meeting was adjourned at 8:30 p.m.

Want to see more examples?

For more examples of agendas and minutes see, this text's website at **www.oupcanada.com/Luchuk.**

Checking Your Work

CONTENT EDITING, COPY EDITING, AND FORMATTING REVIEW

Agenda

When writing the agenda of the meeting, it is still important—as with any other written product—to ensure that you have checked both content and form for errors in information, omissions, or grammar/spelling/mechanical errors.

Check the agenda first to ensure that you have included all of the information that needs to be covered in the meeting. You could also ask someone else who is involved in planning the meeting or who will be attending (and who knows the issues or items to be discussed) to review it. Sometimes another person will find an omission quicker than you will as the writer or organizer.

Once you are sure that you have included all that is needed (and left out what is not necessary to discuss or work on at the meeting), then review your agenda to ensure that correct spelling and grammar is in place. An agenda with misspellings or grammar errors will be taken less seriously—and so will its author—because it will give the impression that it was not important enough to warrant careful editing. It's particularly important to correctly spell the names of anyone presenting or speaking to the group, as well as the names of any outside organizations that might be taking part in your meeting. Misspelling company or individual names is a major faux pas in **business etiquette**.

The format should be an appropriate variation of the agenda outline presented earlier in this chapter (Figure 5.2). It should reflect expectations at your company or organization—check out formats that were used for similar meetings. Aim for simplicity and ease of reading, and don't add notes about any item—save any comment for the meeting itself.

Minutes of meeting

When writing the minutes of the meeting, it's even more important to get spelling, grammar, and content right. The format will follow that of the agenda you have used, but be sure to also include in your minutes any additional items your group agreed to discuss in the meeting (e.g., new business items).

Spelling names correctly reflects your professional attitude to the management of information and polite business etiquette. Not only is misspelling names sloppy, inconsiderate, and unprofessional, but people hate having their names misspelled, so do take the time to double-check. This is especially important when it comes to the names of people "of note," senior executives of your company, or representatives from another organization who may be in attendance.

Be sure to record both first and last names, at least at first mention. If your organization has a more informal culture, it may be acceptable to use first names after the first mention. In a more formal organization, or for a meeting attended by people from outside the company, you would use the formal address of *Mr.* or *Ms* (*Ms* is generally the safest choice for women, since you may not know their marital status or their preference among *Mrs.*, *Miss*, or *Ms*). In industrial, technical, or legal settings, simply using the person's last name after the first mention is often appropriate. Study minutes of other meetings to get an idea of which forms of names and address are appropriate. Or ask someone!

People from outside your organization—or people with a specific position in your own company—should have their position noted at the first mention of them in the minutes (e.g., *Eudora Zolf, Comptroller, Green Thicket Limited*, or merely the position if it's someone from your own company—*Vice-President, Human Resources*).

The content of the meeting minutes is very important, and if you have done your research into who is attending and who will be reading the minutes, you will have a good idea of the information that will be most important to these readers. Obviously, you will want to provide the most important points of what was covered in the meeting, but your decision on whether to include other details will depend on whether you think the readers and attendees who will receive the minutes would find this information helpful or essential.

Again, if the minutes are for a critical meeting within your organization, you might want to double-check that you have covered everything necessary by giving a draft of the minutes to someone who attended the meeting and also has a great memory for detail. This person may be able to fill you in on what you might have missed.

Circulating the Minutes

Once you have edited and proofread your minutes, you should send them out as soon as possible, whether in hard copy or by email. You should also, at the very least, print a few copies of the minutes in case you lose the electronic file or emails are garbled in transmission. Keeping a hard copy of any official documentation, such as minutes, in well-organized and labelled files is a very good backup in case disaster strikes. It can also be helpful if, sometime in the future, another meeting group wants to consider what was done before and the electronic files don't exist anymore.

Oral Presentation of the Minutes

Following the meeting for which minutes are written—for example, at the next sched-uled meeting to discuss progress on a project—you may be asked to orally present the minutes. Hand out copies of the minutes so that people can follow along as you read them.

Often, what happens is that you bring the minutes to the next meeting for peo-ple to review and approve before they move on to the new meeting's work; you may not need to read them aloud unless asked to do so. A quick review by those present will suffice; they can suggest changes if necessary and approve the minutes thereaf-ter. (Because you will have already mailed or emailed the minutes to everyone who attended the meeting, you might hope that they will have read them, but often they will not have done so.)

CHECKLIST FOR meetings

- ☐ Have you applied the Starting Point questions so that you know the participants better?
- ☐ Are you clear about the information you need to communicate and/or discuss in the meeting? The purpose and the desired outcome? (See Chapter 1 for help with this.)
- ☐ Have you planned an agenda that is short and to-the-point to keep the meeting moving along?
- ☐ Does your agenda include all of the most important points that you need to discuss, decide on, and communicate?
- ☐ Have you made a plan to circulate the agenda a week in advance and to email or phone everyone involved the day before?
- ☐ Have you booked an appropriate venue (considering space, comfort, and type of use) for the meeting?
- ☐ Have you made copies of all necessary documents for everyone?
- ☐ Have you planned the meeting for a time of day when people will be most attentive?
- ☐ If you can't avoid meeting at a less than optimum time, have you planned for refreshments to keep people's energy up and attention focused?
- ☐ Have you appointed a facilitator for the meeting (separate from the note-taker)?
- ☐ Have you appointed a note- or minute-taker for the meeting (separate from the facilitator)?
- ☐ Have you considered in advance who will be attending? If you are the facilitator, how you will handle the various personalities and communication styles?

CHECKLIST FOR minutes

- ☐ Have you double-checked and verified the information in the minutes you have recorded?
- ☐ Have you organized the information according to the headings used in the agenda?
- ☐ Have you formatted the minutes with headings bolded and items numbered so that readers can relate the minutes back to the agenda they followed in the meeting?
- ☐ Have you checked the spelling of names and the correct titles of those participating in the meeting?
- ☐ Have you conducted a thorough content and grammar check?
- ☐ Have you checked as to how people want to receive the minutes (i.e., by email or in hard copy), and do you have their contact information?
- ☐ Have you printed and placed copies of the minutes into appropriate files for future reference?

Chapter Summary

In this chapter, you have found out why we have meetings: to vision our work, plan it, solve problems, and make decisions. Meetings get work done and, if properly planned and facilitated, increase productivity and profits. You have learned the principles and the nuts and bolts of how to plan, organize, and prepare for a meeting. You've seen that meetings come in a variety of formats, and as a business leader, you need to know how to facilitate a meeting and deal with its challenges, everything from creating the agenda and checking the minutes to keeping the set timeline and managing the responses of participants. You've learned the key elements of getting to know the participants, recording and circulating the minutes of a meeting, and practising good business etiquette. In the end, good planning and facilitation lead to better meetings: short, energetic, and productive.

■■■ SUGGESTIONS *for Further Reading*

Diamond, L., and Roberts, S. (1996). *Effective videoconferencing: Techniques for better business meetings*. Fredericton, NB: Crisp Publications.

Handford, M. (2010). *The language of business meetings*. Cambridge, UK: Cambridge University Press.

Harvard Business School Press. (2006). *Running meetings: Expert solutions to everyday challenges*. Cambridge, MA: Harvard University Press.

Henkel, S. (2007). *Successful meetings: How to plan, prepare, and execute top-notch business meetings*. Ocala, FL: Atlantic Publishing.

Levasseur, R. (2000). *Breakthrough business meetings*. Bloomington, IN: iUniverse Inc.

Poncini, G. (2007). *Discourse strategies in multicultural business meetings*. New York, NY: Peter Lang Publications.

■■■ PRACTISING *What You Have Learned*

1. If you have a group project, write an agenda for and minutes of each group meeting you have, and submit them weekly (or as often as requested) to your course instructor. You can use the template from this chapter to record all information, using headings.

2. Hold a group meeting to plan a fictitious or real event you could reasonably organize. The information included can be as humorous as you like, but you still have to follow the template. The scenario should include information that would be put under different headings in the template. Here's an example:

   Your student group is planning an end-of-semester pub crawl for all students at your campus. You need to plan this event considering:

   - date and time
   - cost to participate
   - rules for participating in the event
   - places you will visit

- "designated" (non-drinking) transportation
- special contests
- potential crisis management/planning for possible emergencies

You need to know who will do what and specifically what is involved before you proceed. These main points are your agenda for the meeting.

Under new business, include anything else your committee comes up with while you are meeting that they think needs to be addressed in addition to the action items.

Write the minutes for your meeting, and then send them to everyone involved, highlighting what each person agreed to do.

3. You share a house with four other students this year, and your name is on the lease. To ensure that everyone gets along and that all the household tasks are done on a weekly basis, you need to hold a meeting of all roommates to go over the house rules, the cleaning schedule (including how you will divide the tasks fairly), and the consequences for those who don't do their share.

Make a list of all issues and information that need to be covered in the meeting, and write an agenda. Give everyone a copy of the agenda, and then hold the meeting. Give another person the responsibility for recording the minutes, or, if none of your roommates is comfortable doing that, you may have to do it as well. (In this case, it's not a bad idea to tape record your proceedings so that you don't miss anything important—it's difficult to facilitate and write at the same time.)

4. Your sports team needs to do some fundraising to rent facilities, buy uniforms, and pay tournament fees and other expenses. No one really likes fundraising, but it must be done, so you decide that the best way to get everyone on board is to hear what team members are most interested in doing to raise money.

Make a list of the important issues to be covered: how much money needs to be raised (and for what), the deadline for raising the money, and some fundraising suggestions to get the conversation started. It's also not a bad idea to work out what tasks are involved in each suggested fundraising activity so that people can decide whether they can commit to working on one event or another.

Be sure to keep the agenda simple, but set ground rules at the beginning that specify that everyone is to be given a chance to speak on any topic before a second comment or input can be made—otherwise, you might not hear ideas or feedback from everyone.

Stick to a firm timeline, and keep a watch nearby so that you can be sure that all of the agenda items are discussed. Make it clear that by the end of the meeting the group needs to decide specifically what it plans to do to raise the necessary funds (otherwise, this type of meeting tends to drift off, and nothing gets done). Set a date for the next meeting before people leave.

Write the minutes, and send them to everyone who was involved.

5. You and your friends are planning to go away for a week's vacation. Because six of you plan to go on the trip, you need to get organized in terms of your costs, mode of travel, accommodation, schedule of activities, desired activities, and other details.

List all of the information and concerns your group needs to consider, and then create an agenda for a meeting at your house, the pub, or a restaurant.

Facilitate the meeting, but try to get someone else to write the minutes so that you are free to keep everyone on track and discussing all the important issues. It's easy to get off-topic when people are eagerly looking forward to an exciting event.

6. You and some friends from your graduating class have a brilliant idea for a business you would like to start together. You all need to work out the steps involved in investigating whether the business would actually be a viable enterprise—something that would make money. Market research is a lot of work, so you will want to divide the tasks: library visits, research on the Internet, and networking with leaders in the industry. (To get an idea of what is involved in market research for a business, see the supplementary chapters on marketing plans and business plans available on this textbook's companion website: **www.oupcanada.com/Luchuk**.)

   List all the information your group needs to determine whether you have a customer base that will buy from you, who the competition is (and their strengths, weaknesses, opportunities, and threats), and what the overall market is for your products or services. Create an agenda for your first meeting that outlines what types of research need to be done, and where, so that you can discuss assignment of tasks and how to best tackle the work involved. You might also want to include in your agenda discussion of a deadline that everyone can work with—a time by which everyone has their research done and can bring it all together.

   Get someone else in the group to record the minutes. If you have to, write them yourself, making sure that you cover the entire meeting's discussion. Send the minutes to everyone involved.

7. Your grandparents are celebrating a major anniversary, and you and your family and friends want to throw a surprise party for them. Because they have many friends in the community and at work, the potential guest list is huge. There is a lot to organize: an appropriate venue, food, entertainment, gifts, donations, parking, flowers—the list is endless!

   Write down all the items that need to be discussed by the small group of family members and close friends who have agreed to help with the party. (If you are stuck and can't think of what would be needed to plan a party, check the library or Internet for party planning guidelines.)

   Create an agenda incorporating everything that needs to be discussed and an action list so that each person can sign up for planning tasks. (This way, you will know that nothing critical will be missed—like the food or your grandfather's favourite beer!) Have someone else take the minutes, and type them yourself later if you have to. Make sure that everyone gets a copy of the minutes, and highlight in each set of minutes what each person has agreed to do so that he or she will not forget.

8. You and your roommates are moving out of your current home, and you need to organize the move. It is a big house, and a lot of furniture, personal belongings, and appliances have to be moved. Some of you are moving into new, separate apartments. You need to organize the logistics of the move as well as decide who will be responsible for which tasks (such as packing boxes, moving furniture, taking items no longer wanted to Goodwill, and so on).

   Make a list of all of the tasks involved and the timeline for task completion, working backward from the date of the big move. Create an agenda including all of these list items. Ask someone else to be the minute-taker, if possible, while you facilitate the meeting. Write the minutes, and highlight for the individual participants the tasks they agreed to perform before you send them out.

CHAPTER 6

Communicating in Teams and Small Groups

In this chapter you will learn:

- How to create a positive, working team

- The role of a team contract in keeping everyone working together to meet team goals and objectives

- How to manage conflict and challenges as these arise

- How to create a contingency plan (in case you have to change team direction)

- How to manage a team and manage yourself as part of a team

ESSENTIAL EMPLOYABILITY SKILLS

2000+ Employability Skills — The Conference Board of Canada has identified certain essential employability skills (EES) as benchmarks for performance in the workplace. You will learn the following EES skills in this chapter:

THINK AND SOLVE PROBLEMS

- Can assess situations and identify problems
- Can seek different points of view and evaluate them based on facts
- Can recognize the human, interpersonal, technical, scientific, and mathematical dimensions of a problem
- Can identify the root cause of a problem
- Can be creative and innovative in exploring possible solutions
- Can evaluate solutions to make recommendations or decisions

WORK WITH OTHERS

- Can understand and work within the dynamics of a group
- Can ensure that a team's purpose and objectives are clear
- Can be flexible: respect and be open to and supportive of the thoughts, opinions, and contributions of others in a group
- Can recognize and respect people's diversity, individual differences, and perspectives
- Can contribute to a team by sharing information and expertise
- Can lead or support when appropriate, motivating a group for high performance
- Can manage and resolve conflict when appropriate

Communicating in Teams: A Case Study

Jim Jackson and three friends (Marcy LeBoeuf, George Kim, and Shelley Sarasvati) have been interested in the well-being of the elderly ever since they volunteered in high school to take part in a friendly visiting program with Charlottetown seniors.

Motivated by this experience, Jim completed an honours degree in gerontology, focusing his thesis on services to help the elderly stay in their own homes. Knowing his grandmother felt overwhelmed when she had to find a plumber, a reliable contractor for home improvements, or competent homecare for herself, he took on the role of home and personal care manager to save her the worry.

Through this experience, Jim discovered the need for an agency that would help elderly homeowners or renters obtain high-quality, reliable, and safe home maintenance and personal care services. While there were many businesses providing nursing or personal support worker services, there were none combining personal care and home maintenance services for "one-stop shopping."

However, he knew he couldn't start this new business alone. This is where his friends came in; because they all got along so well, Jim was certain that they would work well together. They were all extroverts and very sociable—the life of the party. Having been personal support workers for several agencies over the years, Marcy and George knew the needs of Charlottetown's seniors. Shelley had a diploma in business administration, so she could manage the new agency.

Jim met with his friends over a beer at their favourite pub and laid out his idea. Everyone talked excitedly about next steps. Shelley suggested starting with market analysis to prove the business would work and to identify the target and secondary customers and the competition (which would be mostly indirect). A strengths-weaknesses-opportunities-threats (SWOT) analysis for each competitor would help in determining a competitive strategy.

Using a napkin from the bar, Shelley made a list of who would do what and promised to email everyone their tasks. However, she forgot to do so, and everyone did what they *thought* they should do—which meant that most of their work overlapped and a lot of research was left undone. At their next meeting, the group discussed the situation briefly, and Shelley emailed the task list to everyone the next day. They agreed to get the work done within four weeks.

In the meantime, Marcy met an attractive younger man and all but disappeared from the scene in a love fog. George and Shelley decided they liked each other a lot more than "just friends" and began going out every night. Needless to say, the three did not get much work done, and Jim became increasingly upset and anxious.

Finally, he called his friends and asked to meet them at a local Mexican restaurant. All three apologized for not doing any research. Jim swallowed his anger—because they were his friends, after all.

In the meantime, Marcy's new boyfriend, who also worked in personal support services, talked to a few of his colleagues, and they decided Jim's idea was a good one. This group hired a market research agency for a business feasibility study. They announced their new business in all of the city newspapers, just before the deadline Jim's group was to meet for their market analysis tasks.

Furious, Jim called Marcy and informed her that they were no longer friends. Marcy called George and Shelley. On hearing the news, George told Shelley that Marcy was a traitor for giving away their business idea and said that Shelley would have to choose between her friendship with Marcy and their romantic relationship. Shelley broke up with George.

1. **What do you think went wrong in this story?**

2. **How could the group have organized itself better to get the market research done thoroughly and on time?**

3. **Should there have been group rules set up so that everyone would get their jobs done? Should there have been a confidentiality or non-disclosure agreement signed by all? Would this have helped? Why or why not?**

4. **Do you think it's a good idea to work with family or friends you really like and who are a lot like you? Do you think you can be productive in a work situation if everyone on your team is similar in personality and work style?**

5. **How can a group make sure that all members can speak their truth and address problems as they arise?**

Before You Begin . . .

Why put a chapter about effective teamwork in a communication textbook? It's simple: during your career you will find yourself working in teams on any number of projects involving communication, and you will work collaboratively in teams to produce reports, proposals, and plans. Understanding how teams work can help you to communicate better, which leads to better work and production, including better written or oral communication products.

But why use teams at all? Teams can be especially beneficial, because by combining the talents and brainpower of the individuals involved, they can achieve more than any of the individuals would on their own. This is called synergy, where two plus two equals five—or more!

Most workplaces use teams to get projects completed. It is recognized that an interdisciplinary group of people can complement each other's skill sets to get a project completed quickly and effectively. Group members "spark ideas off each other"—one person puts an idea out there, then others think of other ideas related to that idea, and so on.

Many people find working as part of a team highly motivating. Being able to consult with others about the work helps them to feel more confident about the direction the work is taking and to complete their assigned tasks more easily.

Employers like teams because they are a cost- and time-efficient way to complete complex projects—and the results are often better than if the work were assigned to one person.

Effective team members complement each other's strengths and compensate for individual weaknesses. In other words, in combination it's possible for individuals to cover all the bases in a team.

Unfortunately, teams often get a bad rep, because a team can be highly dysfunctional if the following factors are not managed well:

- personality of team members
- relationships among team members
- the team's place and identity in the organization
- adequate training, funding, and advocacy
- the organization's support for teams

However, failure is not necessarily a bad thing. If a team can catch itself in its own dysfunctional behaviour, the turmoil can lead to creative thinking and an even better outcome for a project or task. Conflict among team members is not always a bad thing, because it too can lead to creative thinking and problem-solving.

You may find yourself in a self-managed team or in one led by a manager in your organization. In either case, a successful team depends on people taking charge of their individual responsibilities within the team, using self-motivation and discipline to get the job done. A leader will not always be around to make sure that you do what you said you would!

The biggest challenges to working effectively with a team are conflict management, confusion over who is doing what, and keeping motivated. You can handle these challenges better if the following elements are in place:

Optimum number of team members for efficiency and effectiveness: In order to function well, teams work best with four or five people. Fewer than four members can mean less efficiency in getting work done, and optimum synergy can be compromised; more than five people can result in an uneven distribution of responsibility, which may lead to conflict, and some members are likely to merely be warming a seat and not contributing meaningfully.

Clear task and work assignments: Members should be assigned—and agree to—equal tasks and work. Everyone on the team needs to be clear on who is doing what.

Complementary skill sets and experience: Teams work better if the team members have skills that complement each other—for example, one team member may be an excellent researcher, while another is better at recording information and writing. If all of the skills and experience needed are not well represented, there can be misunderstandings about who is doing what, resulting in aspects of the work being poorly or incompletely done.

Empowerment by the organization or company: A team will work better if the organization has empowered it to plan, implement, and control its work or project.

SMART goals: A project or work assignment will be completed more efficiently and with less conflict when the team has goals that are SMART: specific, measurable, achievable, realistic, and time-limited.

Sufficient time and resources for the task or project: If the team has enough time and resources (e.g., financial, human) to complete the project, conflict will be minimized and efficiency will be maximized. Take away any essential element for successful completion, or ease of work, and the possibility of conflict increases.

Rewards and incentives for completion and a job well done: If there are rewards and incentives for completing the work and doing a good job, the team will work harder to resolve conflicts or disagreements as they arise. Wanting to "win the prize" as a group can increase unity among team members.

Team and individual commitment to conflict resolution and team-building skills: If the team is committed—as a group and individually—to improving conflict-resolution and team-building skills, it will have sufficient goodwill and energy to resolve issues and challenges as they arise.

Idiom Alert

getting a bad rep – Developing a bad reputation.

growth area – An aspect of a person's personality or behaviour that is perceived as needing improvement.

R & R – Rest and relaxation.

read between the lines – Perceive an additional or alternative message in someone's spoken or written words.

pick up on – Perceive an unspoken or unwritten message (for example, through body language).

love-in – A type of social action that people engaged in during the 1960s in which a group of peace-minded individuals would get together to protest the war in Vietnam and to promote peace and love in general. In a team context, a love-in would mean everyone getting along well and liking each other.

barking – Issuing demands or being insistent about having one's own way (just as a large barking dog—particularly one that is snarling and baring its teeth—generally gets its way).

give and take – Reciprocity; that is, being flexible or accommodating by giving someone what they need in order to get what you need in return.

pushing someone's buttons – Intentionally aggravating, annoying, or harassing someone by deliberately doing something that you know will upset that person.

going above and beyond – Doing far more than is expected; contributing meaningfully and positively to the work of the group or cause.

Your Starting Point

CREATING A TEAM

When you are creating a work team and have the opportunity to select the members—or at least have meaningful input—there are many factors to consider so that the skills, personality, and abilities of all members work synergistically to produce the best possible result.

Some points to consider:

- What is the job or project to be completed?

- What skills or experience will be required to get it done? What skills or experience should at least some of the team members have, ideally?

- Who is available to work on the team? Do they really have the time to dedicate to the project?

- Of the people available, which ones are most likely to work well together? Which ones are not? ("Best friends forever" may have fun but may not accomplish much; sworn enemies won't have fun but probably won't accomplish much either.)

- Which people have the right skills and experience for the job?

- What is the work ethic of these individuals? Are they self-motivated and disciplined? Do they have a record of accomplishment in getting work done well and on time?

- Does anyone you are considering have strong leadership and coaching skills appropriate for leading the team?

DEVELOPING A TEAM MEMBER PROFILE AND SETTING CRITERIA FOR FORMULATING TEAMS

It is a great idea, if you have time, to have each team member participate in an evaluation of their work style (or "personality test") such as the **Myers-Briggs Type Indicator** (MBTI), DiSC, True Colours, or the Enneagram. When each person has a better idea of his or her strengths, weaknesses, and "growth areas" to work on, team members can better understand where they fit into the group and the particular project at hand. If all team members know each other's "type," it's a good idea to use this information to formulate a team contract, which describes how you will work together for maximum effectiveness and possibly even have fun!

Assembling a team can be like putting together a puzzle. It's essential that potential team members reflect on their abilities so that it's clear what "piece of the puzzle" each person brings to the table and how they fit into the team.

CULTURE AND TEAMS

Working on any team requires all members to foster a bias-free and inclusive environment in which everyone feels their contribution is valued and fairly considered. We've just considered synergy—the power of many people putting their talents together for greater results than individuals can achieve on their own. Imagine the potential of even greater synergy when you add people from diverse cultures with a wider perspective on projects, challenges, and issues!

As Canadians, we pride ourselves on our diversity and the breadth of our cultural experience. However, in order to make our differences and similarities work well for optimum productivity, we need to have consensus on an open environment in which anyone can share ideas or concerns from their own cultural perspective. (It's important to note that culture is not just about ethnicity and race but also about other individual factors and experiences such as regional background, physical, social, and emotional abilities, sexual orientation, gender, and personal experience.) The team leader should check with team members at the outset—and at regular intervals—to determine whether anyone has cultural concerns or issues with any aspect of the project or team operations.

The team leader should merely ask individuals about any restrictions or concerns they may have about their role or work on the team or project, reminding everyone that the team is there to support each member in his or her culture as well as personal strengths and limitations. By focusing on individual rather than cultural concerns, the team is able to acknowledge differences but avoid working with limiting cultural stereotypes. Each person should be encouraged to do some self-examination and identify what he or she brings to the team, his or her limitations, and potential for personal growth through the project.

Individual members of the team need to not only acknowledge difference but decide to view difference as an asset to the team and the project. Members of the team should be vigilant with each other about any bias or stereotypes that might arise in working together; whether we want to admit it or not, each of us has consciously or unconsciously absorbed a number of stereotypes through our upbringing, the media, and even education. As soon as we assume something about someone else, not only do we limit what he or she can do or be, but we also limit ourselves in how we are perceived by others and in how our particular strengths and weaknesses are viewed in the context of the team.

We need to avoid making assumptions about anyone else, particularly in terms of their ethnicity, gender, physical abilities, and other personal factors, and allow each other the space to not only meet but exceed expectations for their role(s) and task(s). Check with the other person before assuming that he or she won't be able to do something—for example, just because a member is hearing-impaired, don't assume that he or she cannot be an effective oral communicator for your team. Give everyone equal opportunity to express their personal strengths and capabilities and the chance to accept or decline work or tasks based on what they feel they can achieve.

In general, the information that follows about optimal team functioning and communication applies regardless of the cultural situation of each member.

TEAM-MEMBER ROLES AND RESPONSIBILITIES

In order for the team to function well and complete assigned tasks or projects, all team members should assume a number of formal and informal roles.

Formal, task-focused roles

Formal roles are task-focused positions on the team for which a job or task description could be created. For example, the team leader's job comes with certain tasks and responsibilities, and a job description could be written defining these. (In fact, this is a good idea, as you will read further on in this chapter.)

If a team is small, you may be asked to take on more than one formal, task-oriented role, such as researcher and minute-taker.

Examples of formal work roles

Here are some formal, task-focused positions typically found in work teams focused on a project that includes a written report or proposal. Your team could include positions that are variations on the following or devise others that are more pertinent to your project or work assignment.

Team leader: This person has the responsibility of oversight for the team project, team members, details of work, and expected outcomes. However, the leader must delegate tasks equally and appropriately, with the agreement of all team members, for optimum functioning. (In other words, the team leader is not a dictator, nor does the leader do all the work!) This job requires diplomacy, tact, and discernment to know what to do in various situations and with issues that may arise. The leader may also function as the team's liaison and point of contact with a project manager or supervisor.

Communications co-ordinator: This person makes sure that everyone is communicating with everyone else on the team, whether by email, telephone, or mail. The co-ordinator may work with the team leader to plan meeting agendas and send these out by email or memo to other team members.

Researcher: This person takes on research tasks required for the project. However, this role is usually shared by most or all of the team members. If one person has to do all of the research work, the team will likely break down in chaos,

leading to failure of the project or assigned work. While the position of researcher is not always the most exciting or fun role, it's essential to the success of many projects.

Writer: This person takes the information gathered by other team members and synthesizes it into a unified, written document as required for a project. In a large team project, there may be several writers. See Chapter 7 for more information on writing in teams.

Editor: Before and after the team reviews its written document supporting or elaborating on a project, an editor performs content and copy edits to ensure that the document is polished, error-free, and written appropriately for expected project outcomes. This role may also be shared by several people, particularly for a major document, because several pairs of eyes can catch more errors or content inaccuracies than one pair.

Minute- or note-taker: This person takes minutes or notes at every meeting or work session (as needed or required for the term of the project) and keeps these notes in a file, a binder, or a similar storage device so that the group can refer to past information or discussions as needed. The minute-taker is usually responsible for sending out the minutes as soon as possible after every meeting to remind individuals about tasks they agreed to perform and the entire team about work completed, tasks remaining, and any new directions or decisions that could affect future work.

Informal, team-support roles

In an **informal, team-support role**, individuals assume responsibility for positive, effective teamwork and individual emotional and psychological support throughout a project or series of tasks. As a team member, you may find yourself in any or all of the "unwritten" roles—for which there are no job descriptions—in the box below, sometimes without even really thinking about it.

TEAM CONTRACTS

The **team contract** is a set of rules and operating guidelines for how your group will function. A contract can be drawn up for a long-term work team or for a short-term project team.

Examples of informal team roles

The following is a sampling of some of the informal, team support roles you may assume during the life of your team's project or assigned work. (You may recognize yourself in several of these descriptions!)

Facilitator: This person helps the team to see how various ideas will work in combination and co-ordinates team members' efforts and activities. (This person is often a team leader.)

Cheerleader: This person keeps everyone on the team feeling positive and motivated to get the job done and to reach the team's highest potential in the process.

Visionary or idea-generator: Visionaries come up with new ideas and strategies. They foresee possible changes that might take place if a challenge to the team's work or functioning arises. A visionary can also help the team to imagine how a potential solution or method might work by thinking through possible outcomes.

Clarifier: This person helps the team to sort out confusion and pick apart problems so that members can see challenges in detail. Once this person helps to define the details or aspects of a challenge, it's easier to resolve issues. A clarifier can also help to keep the group on track with its work by alerting team members when the team is working beyond its mandate or assigned tasks.

Evaluator or process technician: This person helps the team to assess how it is functioning in reference to expected project outcomes and in light of the team contract the group has agreed to for optimum functioning.

Peacekeeper: This person mediates differences, helping members of the team to speak their truth, see others' points of view, and be accountable for their own feelings, responses, and actions.

Temperature-taker: This person "takes the temperature" of the team—in other words, he or she gauges the opinions and feelings of individual members on certain challenges, issues, or ways of working and provides feedback on the team's heat or passion or relatively relaxed, cool state as part of the teamwork process.

Backstage support: This person works in the background of the team, gathering resources and performing routine tasks that, while less exciting or glamorous, are essential to the success of the project and the team.

Team player: This person (someone we all *should* be when working in groups) goes along with others and accepts their ideas, listens as others speak, and observes as others act, all in harmony with the prevailing team direction.

The contract should reflect the team's particular personality and work-style mix. As mentioned earlier, it can be based on what you learn about each other in completing assessments or tests such as Myers-Briggs or True Colours. Ultimately, you want the contract to enhance individuals' strengths and help you collectively to work with, through, or around their weaknesses.

For example, if you know that everyone in your team is a major procrastinator, you might want to set some clear guidelines about deadlines and the penalties that will apply when they are not met. If you know that your members have no problem with speaking their minds in meetings (i.e., you are all extroverts), perhaps it would be wise to include a "no interrupting" rule in the contract.

A good contract deals both with operations—the tasks you need to complete so that work is done to specifications and well—and with problem-solving, should any conflicts arise.

Operations can include:

- times, frequency, dates, and locations of meetings
- project details, broken down
- deadlines for completing certain aspects of the project
- detailed lists of who does what (e.g., note-taker, team leader, liaison with decision-makers), including brief job descriptions

Outline for a team contract

WORK PROJECT AND GOALS

This section includes:
- work or project details: who, what, where, when, why, and how
- a short mission statement outlining what the team's mission is for this project
- team goals for the project, making sure they are SMART goals (specific, measurable, attainable, relevant, and time-limited)

TEAM MEMBER PROFILES

Team profiles should be brief descriptions, like mini-biographies, of each member's strengths, skills, abilities, experience, and education related to the work project.

TEAM ROLES AND JOB DESCRIPTIONS

Identify the roles that each team member will assume, such as team leader or co-ordinator, researcher, writer, or minute-taker. (You might want to consider the task roles presented in this chapter as a guide for determining work roles.)

For everyone to work well together, it's important to outline in a brief job description the specific duties and tasks that each role will involve. Then note the names of the people who are taking on each of these roles.

DEADLINES AND RESPONSIBILITIES

List all the tasks that need to be completed, with dates for completion, noting clearly who is responsible for each task.

TEAM GROUND RULES

In this section, you will establish a harmonious and efficient team process by developing statements about expectations for behaviour and performance during the work project. Here are some examples:

All team members will be on time for all meetings and working sessions.

Each team member will be responsible for bringing all relevant resources and information pertaining to his or her tasks on the project to each meeting.

CONSEQUENCES FOR POOR INDIVIDUAL TEAM MEMBER PERFORMANCE

State agreed-upon consequences of unacceptable individual team member conduct. Team members need to agree on clear and specific definitions of:
- the circumstances in which sanctions or discipline will be enacted
- each of the sanctions and how they will be applied
- intermediate steps, if any, that will be taken to deal with a team member's unacceptable performance or actions

CONTACT INFORMATION AND COMMUNICATIONS

Set out details as to how members will keep in touch with one another regularly, as well as how they will be able to monitor the success and elements of the project. This section should include:
- team members' contact information
- procedures for keeping everyone informed of progress and challenges as they arise (e.g., ensuring everyone receives every email sent between members by using a distribution list)
- meeting times and locations

Adapted from Goetsch, 2003.

Add anything else you feel you need to commit to paper so that everyone has the same understanding of what is needed to get the job done.

In terms of problem-solving, you will want to discuss with your team what they are comfortable with if a problem or conflict arises. Decide who will enforce the rules, and reach agreement on appropriate penalties. Later on, you can use these general guidelines if a conflict arises. The box on the previous page presents an outline of what goes into a team contract; Figure 6.1, further on in the chapter, shows an example of a team contract.

CONTINGENCY PLAN

You will also want to create a **contingency plan** in case something goes slightly or horribly awry in the team's completion of the project. To do this, think about anything that could go wrong with each step or part of the project. Granted, this "catastrophizing" (imagining the worst possible scenario) does not exactly fall in line with what the gurus of success say about affirming the best and visualizing a great outcome. However, in business it's good to take a realistic look at what could go wrong so that you can be proactive in preventing or dealing with negative events or situations.

Consider some of the following questions:

- What if the supplies we need are delayed? What if they cannot be obtained at all?

- What will we do if a member gets sick? Who will do that person's work?

- What will we do if we run out of money in the budget?

- What if the initial findings of our research don't match the expectations for the project?

Getting to Work with Your Team

STAGES OF TEAM DEVELOPMENT

Teams go through several **stages of team development**, and they do not necessarily happen in any linear order. While your team may achieve workplace nirvana at one point—everyone loves each other and everything is going wonderfully well—it may experience a crisis at the next point.

According to social psychologist Bruce Tuckman, the stages of development that teams experience are as follows:[1]

Forming: This is described as a period of test and orientation when you are getting to know each other and the project and figuring out where you all are going.

Storming: As the name implies, this is when members work out the details: taking on specific roles and responsibilities, competing for leadership and other

---

[1] Adapted from Bruce Tuckman's original concept (1965).

positions, possibly experiencing interpersonal conflict, and establishing team norms (rules, guidelines, the team contract).

Norming: This is when the group comes together, joining up the pieces that are worked out in storming. Roles are established, and there is consensus around team objectives.

Performing: At this point, team members are focused on accomplishing objectives.

Adjourning: This is the end of the team, usually occurring when the project has been completed. (In the case of "permanent" work teams, this stage may never occur, unless members leave or change jobs.)

While this may seem like a linear sequence, most teams, although they progress through these steps, experience a crisis or setback and have to revert back to an "earlier" stage a number of times before the project is completed.

MANAGING TEAM MEETINGS

Once the team is formed, the contract and contingency plan are worked out, and roles have been decided upon, it's very important to maintain a high level of communication between team members.

In your contract, set out a schedule of team meetings that everyone agrees to. A protocol of how communication takes place between meetings is also a good idea so that people can solve problems and complete their parts of the project when the group is not together. Usually, the team leader will act as a point person for this kind of information traffic, but everyone should agree to terms regarding communication (using email or phone, when to communicate, and so on).

Remember that email can be "a tool for good or evil"! Keep your emails brief and to the point so that there are fewer chances for misunderstanding. When you write too much, the recipient may tend to "read between the lines" and could pick up what he or she perceives as the "real" message or a tone that you never intended. Keep emails focused on tasks, and include only necessary information. We've all experienced having someone misunderstand us or misread us when we're face to face; add the stress of meeting a team deadline and perhaps a few personal issues, and you can see that the recipient of an email is even more likely to perceive some nonexistent slight or unintended insult.

Generally speaking, for longer-term projects lasting several months, it's a good idea to meet at least every other week during the first month or so and then more frequently when there are a lot of tasks to be completed and deadlines to meet. This way, everyone sees the others at least once a week, challenges can be resolved face-to-face, and each member is accountable to the others. (It's hard to confess that your work isn't done when the people who are relying on you are right there in front of you!)

Decide ahead of time who will facilitate the meeting (the same person every time or a different person), who will record minutes or take notes (and keep them in good order!), and how long the meetings will last, and prepare an agenda for the meeting. (See Chapter 5 for help with setting an agenda, note-taking, and facilitation of meetings.)

Virtual teams

When you work with your team members independent of time, space, and sometimes organizational affiliations, you have a **virtual team** connected by communication technology. Such teams may be temporary and may come together to accomplish specific goals and tasks. They have the advantage of being able to access the best available expertise, but they also require strong leadership and team skills.

A common purpose is essential. It holds a virtual team together in the absence of common organizational or personal links.

The virtual team needs good planning—the same team building processes, clearly defined structure, and shared knowledge bases that make a good team. It also needs acknowledgement and acceptance of cultural differences, technical expertise, and consistent team training.

The first team meetings should be face-to-face if at all possible to build interpersonal relationships. If that is not possible, online social networking can help a strong team leadership to focus initially on building social relationships within the team.

Good communication is essential in a virtual team. Team members must be good communicators and have the project-appropriate technologies available to them. The opportunity for the kind of non-verbal communication that takes place in face-to-face meetings may be limited or nonexistent, and that can be a challenge. Humans do communicate better through body language (Pease and Pease, 2006). Thus, the virtual team must anticipate missed or misinterpreted messages and learn how to use feedback to keep it on track. The quality of team leadership is a key factor in promoting good communication. In addition, the competence and commitment of each team member affects the team's ability to accomplish its purpose; one lazy or incompetent member can create a negative atmosphere that is hard to overcome.

The use of video can improve communication across cultural and linguistic boundaries. Being able to see each other's non-verbal (body) language can help us to understand each other's communication more clearly. Electronic communication works better for structured tasks such as routine analysis, while phone or face-to-face communication works better for tasks like brainstorming or managing conflict.

Virtual teams can achieve better productivity (members are not constrained by daily work schedules), extended market opportunities because of members' geographic dispersal, and superior knowledge transfer because team members can join a complex discussion from any part of the world using remote computer access, wireless technology, and conferencing systems.

Compatibility of software and hardware is essential to initiate and maintain communication among members of a virtual team. Various protocols exist for online communication; team leaders must choose the most appropriate. In addition, the team can develop electronic files in various formats, which also must be compatible with the local computer systems used by team members.

The Microsoft Office Suite is commonly used to document team meetings, develop presentations to supervisors, develop knowledge bases, and work out budgetary and technical formulas. The "track changes" feature in MS Word is a particularly useful tool, allowing team members to contribute and to see the contributions of others to a shared document.

Wikis (websites that allow the creation and browsing of interlinked webpages by multiple users) are also excellent tools for virtual team output, potentially on a corporate intranet. Editing rights and access controls allow a team leader to manage a team's progress and outputs. The use of hyperlinks promotes meaningful topic associations that lead to creative thinking and problem-solving. The use of wikis by governments and corporations has become increasingly common as the number of applications has proliferated, including technology, law, medicine, and international security.

Make sure that everyone gets copies of the minutes or notes of each meeting and that each person knows what he or she has committed to completing or doing before the next meeting or before a specific deadline.

Developing conflict management skills

There is no such thing as the perfect team. Don't expect a big love-in all the time when working with others. Even if you are the best of friends inside and outside of the workplace, you will to get on each other's nerves at least from time to time, just like an old married couple.

When people are under stress—as when, say, an expensive project has been derailed by some circumstance and the boss is barking at you that it should have been done by now—they tend to get "crazy." Even the most serene, balanced individual can snap under the strain. So how do you deal with stress in teams?

It starts with you

Remember those individual personality and work-style assessments and how they are great for team-building? Well, these tests also alert you to your *own* buttons and, in particular, which of them are liable to get pushed when you're in a team situation. It's a good idea to suggest to the others in your team what they should avoid doing when you are under stress. That doesn't mean that because you have warned them, you can go ahead and throw a tantrum, but forewarned is forearmed in terms of your teammates.

If you know that you will react negatively to certain things, try to avoid doing or experiencing these things. Of course, sometimes such situations are unavoidable—for instance, when there is a task that no one on the team wants to do but that nevertheless must be done. In that situation, you can let them know that you don't like it but then simply get on with it. Just like eating your Brussels sprouts or having a root canal, the sooner you get it over with, the better you will feel.

Further, you have to take responsibility for your own reactions when things go wrong or when you think they are going wrong. No one can *make* you feel angry, guilty, or stupid—you *choose* to feel that way! So don't choose these feelings; instead, when negative feelings come up, allow yourself to feel them, take note of them, and then put them aside in favour of positive or just neutral feelings about what is happening to you. "Observing" the feelings, standing back from them, and putting them into perspective can be a helpful way to manage stress. It's important to keep in mind that most stressful situations in the workplace are time-limited. The stressor will cease to exist, you will move on to another project with another team, or the project itself will finally be finished.

Now that you've taken stock of yourself and you know what causes you stress and negative emotions, and now that you've learned how to manage situations when there is no choice and you have delegated as much as you can, it's time to consider the rest of your team.

Learning how to give and take

All the members of your team have their own set of personal stressors and hot buttons they have trouble dealing with or don't want to have pushed. After you've taken stock of yourself, you will be hoping that your colleagues have done the same and are reasonably aware of their limitations and how to manage their own stress.

In case of emergency . . .

As suggested above, the first rule of working in a team is to own your feelings and responses to situations. If a colleague is pressing your hot buttons, then *you* have to make a decision about how you will react.

When you feel pushed to the limit, you need to stand back from the problem or person. If you can, tell the person that you are going away for a while because you are too angry, upset, or hurt to discuss the situation with them now. Give a specific time when you will meet to deal with the situation, a time when you will be calmer or more in control of your emotions.

Sometimes, however, this is not possible: the matter is urgent, requiring action *now*. In this case, you may want to practise observing your feelings and then putting the feelings into the background as you concurrently resolve the problem. Yes, this can be a feat requiring muscular emotional control when you are about to lose it and scream at the top of your lungs.

Address the problem, not the colleague. It might feel good in the moment, but it's not going to help matters if you call the other person a jerk—or a more colourful (highly inappropriate!) version of "jerk."

Labelling only puts that person down, when your goal should be to maintain a working relationship, at the very least. If you do damage now, you'll regret it later when your relationship with this person is strained beyond repair.

Focus on the problem, but at the same time acknowledge your own feelings—and those of the other person: "What you just said was really hurtful, and I'd like to talk to you about this later on. However, if we both get upset, we really aren't solving this problem. So what can we do about it right now?" or "I hear your anger, but let's talk about how we feel about this later. What we need to do right now is deal with this issue, because it's going to seriously jeopardize what we need to get done today. What can we do?"

Perhaps the problem is bigger than the particular issue the two of you are having at the moment. This is the time to ask the team leader to get involved to help resolve the problem or perhaps to have a team meeting to air grievances or issues so that everyone can work collaboratively on a solution that supports all parties— while getting the work of the team done.

You can help by checking with your team members frequently. This means asking not just how the work is progressing but how people feel about the work. It could take place in a no-holds-barred session during which team members can ask for what they need in order to feel comfortable, productive, or supported in the process of completing the project. Sometimes using a "talking stick" (see Chapter 5) works as a way of enabling each person to speak uninterrupted and as unemotionally as possible about what they need. While the person speaking holds the talking stick, no one else is allowed to speak or comment. The facilitator and/or note-taker makes a note of all concerns.

An action plan is then drawn up based on what people identify as their needs within the project. A list of tasks that each team member has agreed to take on is generated— including changing the way individuals interact with others with whom they are in conflict. This then becomes somewhat of a contract that everyone agrees to in order to support each other.

Recognizing and rewarding good work

Recognizing and rewarding good work, or completion of a tough task, is something teams often don't do very well. In the workplace, we tend to focus on solving problems

It's important for teams to celebrate successes—give yourselves a round of applause, pat yourselves on the back, and consider holding a team celebration event.

(or "putting out fires") while not acknowledging the positive developments that are probably taking place most of the time. It's important for a team to recognize jobs well done and even to recognize that it has managed to get something done that was really challenging or complex.

Recognition can be as easy as each person taking the time to thank others for their work as the team proceeds through the project. That is something you can remind yourself to do—and giving a genuine compliment or thank-you actually makes you feel quite good yourself. Recognition is important in that not every task a team member does, or the group completes, is noteworthy, yet the work may have involved a lot of quiet effort and determination. Rewards should not be tied only to extraordinary events; at the same time, they should not be so frequent as to make people feel complacent about making an effort to give their best.

Recognition and rewards can also be more formally implemented into the project by establishing benchmarks for performance and timelines. These benchmarks and timelines could be incorporated into your team contract. For example, if the team project was slated to take six months, the completion of certain tasks within each month could be tied to a recreational group event for some R & R. For example, you could go out for dinner, attend a movie together, go out for drinks at a new martini bar, or even have supper at someone's house. In this way, the team can maintain morale and positive interpersonal dynamics by spending time together outside the workplace.

If individuals go above and beyond the call of duty, there should be some form of recognition. For example, in sales work the "salesperson of the month" often gets a reward, such as tickets to a popular upcoming concert or a gift certificate for dinner at a local restaurant. Sometimes the reward is just having the person's picture posted on a "Salesperson of the Month" plaque that customers see when they come to the sales counter.

These individual rewards can be incorporated into the team contract to ensure that individual effort does not go unnoticed.

Wrapping Up Your Team

EVALUATION

Once the team has completed its assigned project or tasks or has achieved its purpose, it's important to evaluate how it worked.

A comprehensive evaluation gives individuals, the entire team, and the company or organization the opportunity to reward excellence, recognize strengths, and look at ways to improve on weaknesses in future work and projects. It is a good idea to decide how your team will evaluate itself and its work before you start a project and to include the details in the team contract.

Many places of employment conduct what is called **360-degree evaluation**. This means that everyone involved has a role to play in evaluating individual work, teamwork, the process, and the outcomes of the project.

Individual evaluation

The evaluation process can start with giving team members the opportunity to evaluate their own performance on the project. To help individuals think about their role in the project, they can use a **SWOT analysis** (strengths, weaknesses, opportunities, and threats).

- What were your specific strengths in this project? What strengths of yours helped the process? Which strengths would you like to enhance or use more when you are in a similar project or teamwork setting?

- What were your weaknesses in this project? What weren't you able to do particularly well or complete properly, and why? What can you do personally to improve the next time around?

- There may have been some opportunities in this project for you to apply your unique skill set or experience to improve how the team worked or how the project was completed. What opportunities did you identify and act on? What opportunities did you see that you were not able to act on or that you missed? How would you pursue such opportunities to add value to the team's work in future?

- What were the threats to your functioning well in the team and to the completion of your own tasks or work? (Threats could include internal issues such as procrastination or external issues such as not being able to obtain needed supplies.) How did you deal with these? What could you do differently next time, if anything?

The answers to these questions could be incorporated into the group evaluation, if team members are comfortable doing so, or kept confidential in whole or in part if the evaluation is intended to improve individual performance in the future.

Group evaluation

A SWOT analysis is also very helpful for team evaluation, and it can be incorporated into a questionnaire for individuals to complete and then be debriefed. The SWOT questions can also be used more informally for a team debriefing and discussion; one member would take notes and write a final report based on these notes. The report would be sent to all members of the team and possibly to supervisors, managers, or others in the organization. (Again, before you start the project, decide on what will be reported and who it will go to, noting what is required by supervisors and the organization.)

Here are some suggested SWOT questions to get the group evaluation process started:

- What were our strengths in this project? What did we do well—or exceptionally well? How did team members' strengths complement each other, specifically? How could we individually and as a group capitalize on each other's strengths in future if we work together again?

- What were our weaknesses in this project? What do we feel we did not do very well or possibly failed in doing? What could we do differently next time (individually and as a group) for a better outcome?

- What opportunities did we identify that would have taken the project to a higher standard of excellence or benefit? Which ones did we act on? What was the outcome? Which ones did we not act on, and what was the outcome? What can we do in future to identify opportunities more quickly and to incorporate them into a project for improved outcomes?

- What were the threats to our completion of this project or to our ability to work well together? Which ones did we deal with well or proactively? Who was involved? How can we apply this problem-solving experience to future projects? Which threats caused problems for the project or in our work together? Why weren't we able to address these threats to resolve problems? What can we do differently next time?

This is a basic evaluation method to work from and modify as needed. A variety of teamwork resources are available through your college or university (entire courses are devoted to the subject) and in books and journals as well as online. You may be able to find other evaluation methods that would be more appropriate to your work and projects.

ADJOURNING THE TEAM

"Our work here is done. . . ." Once your team's work has been completed and evaluated, it's time to adjourn. You have been through a lot together, so just saying "Next!" does not acknowledge the hard work completed.

When the team adjourns, there should be some form of celebration, reward, or recognition. Again, this can be part of your team contract, and it should include specific details—otherwise this part of the agreement might be forgotten as you all move on to other work. Have a party! Go to the spa for the day! At the very least, go out for drinks and snacks. Take the time to thank each other for a job well done and for all that you have learned about yourselves and others in the process.

Sample Documents

The team contract shown in Figure 6.1 is based on a contract prepared by students in a health information management diploma program for their work on a presentation for fellow students in a business teams course.

FIGURE 6.1 Team Contract

WORK PROJECT AND GOALS •————————————

Our topic is a potential flu pandemic, and we hope to provide our class with an informative and educational oral presentation on the flu pandemic.

In terms of an outline for our presentation we will cover the following topics:

- what is a pandemic?
- the history of pandemics
- how to protect yourself in the event of a pandemic
- how to be prepared for a pandemic
- emergency measures/plans worldwide as well as regionally, provincially, and nationally
- flu pandemic vaccine and the health care system
- health information management staff's role during a pandemic

MISSION STATEMENT •————————————

To deliver an educational and interactive presentation to our peers, while modelling positive teamwork skills.

GOALS •————————————

- to achieve an overall mark of 90 per cent
- to complete and meet all expected deadlines
- to work well as a team

TEAM MEMBER PROFILES •————————————

Julia
Julia has a farming/agriculture background, and she previously attended the University of Guelph. She worked in agriculture for six years.

Julia often finds herself in an informal leadership role during projects and tasks at school. She is concerned with communication and people, is optimistic, and is a "people person." She is energized by working with people and enjoys working in groups. She likes a fast-paced environment and becomes agitated with time-wasting activities. Change is a must. She has a difficult time being around negative people and performing routine, detailed tasks.

The top skills she brings to this project are creativity, time management, and an energetic personality. Enhancing these skills, she is also punctual and dependable, and she often takes the initiative.

Provides outline of main project details.

Mission statement to the point; states how team will work while completing project.

Goals briefly written; clearly identify the outcomes desired by the team.

Profiles describe relevant skills and experience of each team member.

(continued)

Amy

Amy was previously a team leader in another course. She is currently the class and program representative for the HIM program and has been a leader of many committees at church. She graduated from the RN program at Seneca College in 1994.

Amy is conscientious and careful. She is very detail-oriented and likes to include everything pertinent to the topic being addressed. She likes to weigh the pros and cons of actions that she takes. Amy follows procedures as closely as possible and doesn't like to deviate from them. She is a perfectionist and strives to do her best. She does have the ability to take over and be the leader, but her choice is to be assigned tasks with clear guidelines and deadlines.

The top skills she brings to the project are attention to detail, dependability, and an ability to work behind the scenes. She is also punctual to a fault.

Heidi

Heidi has worked well with teams in the past. She has met and surpassed her commitments in order to come up with a product she was satisfied with. Heidi's previous experience as a leader was a good confidence-builder, and she has learned how to delegate tasks effectively for best results.

In terms of the skills she brings to the project, Heidi is conscientious, responsible, and accountable for what she does. She will seek help if required and will reciprocate when others need help. However, if people seem unreliable, she will do the task herself because she doesn't always trust that it will be done. She is detail-oriented and something of a perfectionist. That being said, she can be overwhelmed with details and needs grounding. She likes to work with a clear outline of assigned tasks, and she expects that everyone will do what is assigned to them and ask for help if needed. She works best in an environment where everyone is equally committed to tasks and outcomes.

Kylie

Kylie has successfully completed three semesters of HIM. She was a committee leader of the 10th Milton Beavers when her sons were small. She successfully organized a recent college fundraiser that raised more than $2,000 for the Save the Children Fund in the wake of the Burma disaster.

In terms of the skills she brings to the project, Kylie is an adventuresome, inquisitive, and self-assured risk-taker. She prizes honesty, courteousness, and punctuality.

TEAM ROLES AND JOB DESCRIPTIONS

TEAM LEADER
Julia Van Dam
- establish and maintain a positive work environment
- be a liaison between team and project manager
- facilitate meetings

Explained in point form; helps team members quickly review and remind themselves of responsibilities.

- monitor team performance
- demonstrate recognition of team members' good work

SECRETARY

Amy Chow

- record meeting discussions and decisions in order to produce minutes
- email the minutes within two days of meetings
- send a hard copy of minutes to each team member and the project manager

MEETING PLANNER

Kylie Malik

- review meeting minutes and prepare agenda two days prior to the next meeting
- email agenda to all team members
- book a room for meetings if necessary

RESEARCH CO-ORDINATOR

Heidi Heigl

- find possible reference websites and other sources of information
- divide research activities among team members
- complete the formal reference page

PROJECT/WORK DEADLINES AND RESPONSIBILITIES

Lists all tasks with dates, deadlines, responsibilities organized into brief points to keep track of project.

Finalize team contract: Wednesday, January 30, 2013

Commence project tasks: Wednesday, February 6, 2013

Mid-project meeting and review of completed work: Wednesday, March 6, 2013

Meeting to prepare for presentation: Wednesday, March 20, 2013

Presentation to class: Wednesday, March 27, 2013

Weekly meetings: location, days, and times as agreed

Meeting minutes due dates: weekly, within a couple of days of each meeting

TEAM GROUND RULES

Identifies the non-negotiable rules by which all team members agree to function.

1. Members will be present and on time for all scheduled classes and designated meeting dates; if a member must be absent, she will give proper notification (phone call or email).

2. Members will be accountable and complete assigned/agreed-to tasks on time.

3. Members will ask for and offer help as needed within the team.

4. Members agree to handle conflicts in a constructive manner using the "I feel . . ." method of owning their own feelings and emotions.

5. Members have the right and responsibility to address any actual or perceived expression of stereotypes or bias (i.e., insensitivity to diversity such as sexual orientation, abilities, ethnicity) that arises during work on the project or in team operations.

(continued)

Consequences of poor performance are clearly outlined.

CONSEQUENCES FOR POOR INDIVIDUAL TEAM MEMBER PERFORMANCE

1. Missing three meetings without prior notification and justifiable reasons will result in a 5 per cent reduction of the individual's overall mark for the presentation.

2. Failure to produce assigned work will result in a 5 per cent reduction of the individual's overall mark for the presentation (may be combined with #1 for a 10 per cent reduction, if applicable).

3. Failure to handle conflicts appropriately as stated in team ground rule #4 will result in a meeting with the project manager to discuss possible actions.

Effectively outlines how members will regularly keep in touch.

CONTACT INFORMATION AND COMMUNICATIONS

NAME	Work Tel #	Home Tel #	Email	Fax
Julia Van Dam	111-222-3333 x 1234	111-333-4444	**jvandam@company.ca**	N/A
Amy Chow	111-222-3333 x 5678	111-444-5555	**achow@company.ca**	111-123-4567
Kylie Malik	111-222-3333 x 9101	111- 676-7777	**kmalik@company.ca**	N/A
Heidi Heigl	111-222-4900	111-989-1010	**hheigl@subsidiary.ca**	111-222-4910

- Amy will be responsible for sending out weekly emails with updates to all team members.
- It is the individual's responsibility to inform everyone else on the team if she cannot attend meetings, cannot complete assigned work on time, or needs help with tasks or challenges arising.
- If your challenge arises well before a deadline or meeting, please email everyone and request confirmation of receipt to ensure that everyone knows what is going on.
- If the problem is last-minute (i.e., the night before a meeting and you are quite ill), phone Amy (as secretary), and she will inform the others by telephone, if necessary.

MEETING TIMES AND LOCATIONS

Weekly meetings Mondays 3 p.m., Boardroom 101. Other meetings held on dates specified in Project/Work Deadlines or as agreed.

Additional meetings as required will be decided by all team members through email conversation. Any member of the team can suggest a meeting if she feels one is needed.

CHECKLIST FOR optimal teamwork: criteria

- ☐ Are members able to share responsibilities more or less equally?
- ☐ Do members have complementary skills for the tasks to be completed?
- ☐ Do you have the authority from your organization to plan, implement, and control your work?
- ☐ Are your team's goals clear and specific?
- ☐ Do you have adequate time and resources to complete the tasks and the project?
- ☐ Do you have an incentive to get the job done (rewards)?
- ☐ Do you have problem-solving, decision-making, and conflict-resolution skills within your team?
- ☐ Have you created a team contract that all members endorse and can work with?

CHECKLIST FOR team contract

- ☐ Have you included details of the team project (topic, purpose, areas to be discussed, mission statement, team goals)?
- ☐ Have you included profiles of team members (background, personality test characteristics, team skills, behaviours, developmental areas, personal goals)?
- ☐ Have you included team roles (primary roles, duties and tasks, role assignments, job descriptions)?
- ☐ Have team assignments, schedules, and deadlines (including due dates, timelines for all team assignments or tasks) been included?
- ☐ Have team ground rules been included?
- ☐ Have the consequences of unacceptable behaviour been outlined?
- ☐ Have contact information, communication strategy, and meeting information been provided?
- ☐ Do all team members endorse the contract? Have they signed it?

Chapter Summary

In this chapter, you discovered how to create a positive, working team and how to manage conflict and challenges as these arise. You learned the usefulness of a team contract in keeping everyone working together to meet the team's goals and objectives. You learned about the special challenges of working cross-culturally and in virtual teams and how to use technology to communicate and share information more effectively. You found ways to manage a team and manage yourself as part of the team. You've learned how to give and take and how to reward yourself and the members of your team for a job well done. You also read about the value of creating a contingency plan in case you have to change the team's direction. You have learned how to wrap up the team's efforts and evaluate the group and yourself.

■■▌ SUGGESTIONS *for Further Reading*

Goetsch, D. (2003). *Effective teamwork: Ten steps for technical professions.* Upper Saddle River, NJ: Pearson/Prentice-Hall.

Halverson, C., and Tirmizi, S.A. (2008). *Effective multicultural teams: Theory and practice.* New York, NY: Springer Press.

Krzyzewski, H., and Spatola, J.K. (2010). *The gold standard: Building a world-class team.* New York, NY: Business Plus, 2010.

Maxwell, J.C. (2009). *Teamwork 101: What every leader needs to know.* Toronto, ON: Thomas Nelson.

Rosenhauer, S. (2009). *Teams and teamwork as the basis of effectiveness.* Munich: Grin Verlag.

West, M.A. (2012). *Effective teamwork: Practical lessons from organizational research.* (3rd ed.). Hoboken, NJ: Wiley-Blackwell.

■■▌ DEBATE *and Discussion Starters*

1. Is it ever advisable or desirable to have a team leader take on another formal role on the team? Why or why not? What would be the pros and cons of having the team leader wear more than one hat? Do you think other formal role "holders" could have more than one role without any problem? Why or why not?

2. What might be some of the challenges of working with a multicultural team? Why would it be essential to foster a team environment that is open to sensitive, honest, and open discussions about cultural expectations, business conduct, and communication, for example?

3. Can you see any drawbacks to working in a virtual team? What would work well and not so well, in your opinion? What problems could arise, and what kind of contingency plan could you set up to deal with some of the more common problems that might come up?

4. Think about the last time you worked as part of a student team for a course project. How did that go? What went right, and why do you think these aspects of the project worked well? What went wrong, and why do you think these problems arose? How might student team projects turn out better in future?

■■▌ PRACTISING *What You Have Learned*

Choose one of the following scenarios and apply the steps below to practise what you have learned:

- planning a party or event with a committee
- developing and writing a business plan with partners
- planning and organizing a new team or club with a founding group of people
- fundraising for a certain cause or project with a team
- conducting research and writing for a group project at work or at college/university

1. Before you begin work, create a team contract for your group. Include all sections as described in the team contract section of this chapter.

2. Create a contingency plan based on possible challenges or situations that might arise.

3. Select a facilitator or group leader, preferably someone who has demonstrated leadership ability and can motivate and coach others while getting his or her own work done for the project.

4. Appoint someone as the note-taker for each meeting, and make sure minutes are sent to everyone involved (and others, such as managers or instructors as required) as soon as possible after each meeting. This will be great practice for taking minutes in the real world. (If you are stuck, reread the sections in Chapter 5 on recording minutes and facilitating meetings.)

5. Create progress reports, as appropriate, as your project moves forward (your instructor may require that you do so if you are following these steps as part of a course).

6. Complete the project.

7. Conduct an evaluation. Review your team contract and see whether your group actually followed up on what it said it would do. Do a SWOT (strengths, weaknesses, opportunities, and threats) assessment of how well you completed the project, with the goal of understanding what worked, what didn't, and what to do differently next time. Write an evaluation report.

8. Reward the team for a job well done. Even if it was not well done, take the time to acknowledge the hard work that was contributed by doing some kind of adjournment activity together.

CHAPTER 7

Team Communications Projects

In this chapter, you will learn:

- Consensus, delegation, and collaboration methods for team writing

- How to conduct research in teams and groups

- How to write according to the consensus, delegation, and collaboration methods

- How to bring written work together into a cohesive and professional whole through editing

- Troubleshooting strategies to overcome common team writing challenges

ESSENTIAL EMPLOYABILITY SKILLS

2000+ Employability Skills The Conference Board of Canada has identified certain essential employability skills (EES) as benchmarks for performance in the workplace. You will learn the following EES skills in this chapter:

THINK AND SOLVE PROBLEMS

- Can assess situations and identify problems
- Can seek different points of view and evaluate them based on facts
- Can recognize the human, interpersonal, technical, scientific, and mathematical dimensions of a problem
- Can identify the root cause of a problem
- Can be creative and innovative in exploring possible solutions
- Can evaluate solutions to make recommendations and decisions

WORK WITH OTHERS

- Can understand and work within the dynamics of a group

- Can ensure that a team's purpose and objectives are clear
- Can be flexible: respect and be open to and supportive of the thoughts, opinions, and contributions of others in a group
- Can recognize and respect people's diversity, individual differences, and perspectives
- Can contribute to a team by sharing information and expertise
- Can lead or support when appropriate, motivating a group for high performance
- Can manage and resolve conflict when appropriate

COMMUNICATE

- Can read and understand information presented in a variety of forms (e.g., words, graphs, charts, diagrams)
- Can write and speak so others pay attention and understand
- Can listen and ask questions to understand and appreciate the points of view of others

Team Communications Projects: A Case Study

Jaya, Chantal, Misha, and Tamar were working on a business plan for an esthetics and massage therapy spa for their entrepreneurship course. As esthetics students nearing graduation, they were to research, write, and present a business plan for a spa operation in their community.

They wrote a team contract to help them to define responsibilities, a meeting schedule, and deadlines leading up to the time when they would present the plan to their class, and they handed the contract to their professor. Unfortunately, once it was written, it was promptly forgotten.

Team leader Jaya had difficulty getting everyone together for meetings. There was always something occurring that kept team members from getting together, whether it was Misha's bronchitis (a legitimate reason) or Tamar's making excuses at the last minute (the group suspected that her new boyfriend had something to do with this). Jaya resorted to emailing everyone, reminding them of their individual deadlines for completing plan sections, and she urged them to get together two weeks before the assignment deadline to complete the final business plan.

Two weeks before the assignment due date, Jaya, Chantal, and Misha met and exchanged their assigned plan parts. Tamar didn't show up, nor did she call the rest of the group to explain why. Worse still, Tamar was responsible for the market analysis section of the plan, which was to examine the customer demographic, describe the competition, and put forward a competitive strategy for the business. Without this section, the business plan would not be complete, and their professor was expecting not only all of the parts of the plan but a very thorough job of research and documentation to prove a business case.

Fuming, Jaya began to write the market analysis section of the plan, since Tamar didn't return anyone's phone calls or emails. Without the research sources the group had painstakingly vetted for the market analysis section, Jaya was working with what she could remember of group research sessions to fill in information about customers and competition. Because she didn't have the original sources, she could not include any citations for the statistics and facts.

The night before the presentation, the final edit was left to Jaya. Exhausted by work on other assignments and studying for exams, she merely copied and pasted sections supplied by other team members into the plan. At midnight, slumped over her computer, she decided it was good enough. There was no time to do a copy edit, much less a content or style edit.

On the day of the presentation, Jaya and her team members got into a fight. Adding to this tension, Tamar finally showed up and expected to present the plan along with her team members to earn her portion of the marks. Jaya made the presentation by herself, and other team members got up and left. The business plan was handed in and received a zero: there were no internal citations in the market analysis section (indicating plagiarism), each section did not flow well into the next, and major blocks of information were missing. The professor considered the grammar and spelling in two sections "atrocious"—which he wrote in large red letters.

1. What went wrong in this team project? List the factors that contributed to the breakdown of the group and, consequently, of the written project and presentation.

2. Should members of a group ever write parts of a major plan, proposal, or report on their own instead of as a group? Should there be one writer who will pull everyone's research and information together?

3. Could you suggest a step-by-step approach for this group? How could the group members have gotten their project done properly, even if they had differences?

Before You Begin . . .

WHY WORK IN TEAMS ON WRITING PROJECTS?

Ever heard the expression "two heads are better than one"? In teamwork, two plus two really *can* equal five, because the ideas and energies of individuals can produce more when combined than they ever could alone. That's why many workplaces now use teams to produce written documents—for maximum productivity.

There are several models for teams working together to produce written products such as proposals, progress reports, formal and informal reports, and annual reports. Here are three of the most common examples:

- The team works together throughout the document preparation process, researching and writing each section of the written document together. (This is described below as the **consensus model** of team writing.)

- One individual meets with members of the team throughout the document preparation process to ensure that everyone has input (and that no important idea, information, or documentation is missed). Those involved provide their suggested changes to or other feedback on the document and return it to the writer for revisions. (This is described below as the **delegation model** of team writing.)

- The team defines the tasks, creates the outline, and makes major revisions together, but different team members gather information and evidence for various sections of the document and are responsible for drafting and perfecting these sections with revisions. The sections are then brought together into one document, which is then edited by one person. This method is very common in a workplace where several departments or types of expertise are needed to complete tasks or projects. (This model is described below as the **collaboration model**.)

THE CONSENSUS MODEL OF TEAM WRITING

Each method has its pros and cons. When working with the first method—the consensus model—everyone works together on everything in the project until there is consensus, or agreement, about what should be in each section. While this method is admirable and optimal, it generally takes more time than a team has available to complete a project. There is also the potential for major disagreement within the group as it proceeds with the project, which can lead to an interruption or even breakdown of the work process.

THE DELEGATION MODEL OF TEAM WRITING

The second method works well when the company or organization has someone they can employ or designate to do the research (if the team doesn't have time); this person may also do the writing and editing. This is often what happens in a not-for-profit organization governed by a board of directors. The board may know what it wants to include in a funding proposal, for example, but may lack the expertise to professionally research, write, edit, and produce the final document. While the writer is responsible for the final outcome, it is a collaborative process between the writer and the team—in this case, the board of directors. While this can be an efficient way to get the job done—and done well—there can be major misunderstandings and miscommunications, since the people who want to communicate the message or information are not the ones writing it.

THE COLLABORATION MODEL OF TEAM WRITING

The third method is more likely to be used in a business or not-for-profit organization environment in which there are enough people who can be given time, space, and resources to research, write, edit, and produce a report or proposal. While this method still has the potential to break down in terms of communication or task completion, the chance of this happening can be greatly reduced by adhering to a team contract, or version of a contract, as described in Chapter 6. For this method to work well, team members need to be selected carefully for their work style, skills, and abilities as these qualities pertain to the project, and every aspect of the project needs to be documented at the start so that everyone knows what he or she should be doing.

This chapter will focus primarily on the collaboration model of team writing. It's the most commonly used, because it allows for individual work to completed away from the group once each person's roles and tasks have been established and group members are clear on who is doing what (i.e., there is a team contract). Then members can come together for meetings to review progress or work completed to date, edit each other's work, and so on. It's a flexible model of working that can be adapted to both in-person and virtual teams.

WHO ARE YOUR READERS?

Often, collaborative writing means review by known (primary) and unknown (secondary) readers. The **primary readers** might include your boss or manager, his or her boss or manager, or leaders of other departments. The **secondary readers** might be numerous: still other managers, supervisors, or even outside readers—whomever your primary readers decide to share the final report or proposal with.

As when writing any other reports or proposals—or, for that matter, other business documents—you need to plan on your readers being unfamiliar with the purpose, topic, and terminology of the project. Assume that your readers know very little about your subject.

Idiom Alert

two heads are better than one – The idea that two (or more) people working together can be more productive than one person working alone.

the good, the bad, and the ugly – All the positive and negative aspects of a matter.

the "real world" – Often, a colloquial reference to the working world outside of school.

Your Starting Point

You have probably already worked in teams in your course work as a student—or perhaps in a workplace. If so, you have probably already seen "the good, the bad, and the ugly" of teamwork on projects. Many students dislike working in teams—and for good reason—because teams can break down in many spectacularly nasty ways.

Never fear. The best remedy for team dysfunction is to plan to avoid it in the first place. The best-laid plans include selecting people carefully for the best fit in terms of personality, skills, and experience and then creating a team contract.

You may have no choice about who is included in your team, whether at school or in the work environment. However, it's a good idea to get to know who is on the team by at least having everyone conduct a SWOT analysis of himself or herself (personal strengths, weaknesses, opportunities for growth, and threats—that is, what makes the person feel threatened) and sharing this information. That way, everyone will have a better idea of how each person will function best on the team and what each member needs to be most productive and positive about the work.

The team contract should be drawn up before any work is done. Then if something does go wrong, you have a process you all have agreed to in order to resolve the problem.

People (and teams) often fail because people (and teams) fail to plan. Any project, cause, organization, or work with people involved is prone to failure, because we are imperfect beings—so planning for the worst and hoping for the best will greatly increase your team's chances of success.

Remember that one of your starting points for successful group communications projects is to have team members sign a team contract so that roles and responsibilities are clear. See Chapter 6 for an outline of a team contract.

Creating the Written Product: How to Do It

PREPARING TO WRITE

Research

In your team contract, assign to individual members of the team the research for each section of the project. Knowing who is doing what is important so that efforts are not duplicated and people don't upset each other by doing another person's work. At your regular meetings, you can review the research each person has done to ensure that there is no overlap and that all required research is being addressed.

Team members will be able to decide who is best qualified or suited to conduct the research or work on each section of the project once they have reviewed the outline with notes (as included in the team contract) and related these tasks to the skill and experience sets of each team member.

Communicate regularly

It's quite likely that your team writing experience will take place with each of you at your own desks and computers—and perhaps even time zones apart, never mind a short drive away! Throughout the research process, it's absolutely critical to keep lines of communication open through meetings, emails, and telephone calls so that everyone is in the loop at all times. Set up an email distribution list, and make sure that everyone gets the others' emails. (That way, team members can't say they don't know what's going on!) This between-meetings communication is also vital if someone discovers new information that the group should follow up on or encounters a roadblock to getting work done.

As with any business email, remember that messages should be kept brief and to the point, because unintended meaning can be read into longer emails (and you definitely want to minimize misunderstanding among your team members). Stick to the details of the project, and save discussion of concerns or issues with others on the team for face-to-face meetings.

Meet frequently

Meet at least weekly if your project will last a month or longer. The team may wish to use technologies such as videoconferencing and instant messaging to meet virtually (see Chapters 5 and 6 for further details).

Designate someone to take and keep minutes to ensure that all details are documented. If anyone forgets what he or she agreed to do or misses an important deadline, the recorded details will be very helpful. Weekly meetings can help you all to regroup, and if there is a problem with any aspect of research, others can help the individual with the problem, or responsibility for research tasks can be switched around so that someone else takes over the problem area.

You may find that at some point in the research process, you all hit a dead end. This may mean reconsidering the project and what needs to be done, pursuing a different angle for research, or heading off in another direction altogether. Keeping on top of issues with regular meetings should help you to manage the project in a timely and less stressful way. Having a team contract also helps your group should anyone drop the ball on what he or she is supposed to be doing; since the guidelines have been agreed upon in advance, the consequences can be imposed without undue stress or upset.

Review the research

At the end of the research process, hold a longer meeting to conduct a final, comprehensive review of all the information gathered by the group. The meeting should take place with plenty of time to spare before the writing and editing has to be completed. Each group member should provide a summary of what he or she has gathered and be able to explain what the implications of his or her research are for the project as a whole.

Each member should prepare a summary and distribute copies of it to other members so that everyone can see at a glance what each person has gathered. Collecting research and information is a bit like putting a puzzle together with a variety of pieces. When you lay out the pieces, you can see whether any are missing and address the situation as soon as possible by allocating the additional work to everyone to get the job done.

Fill information gaps

Once you have determined what, if anything, is missing, get going on the research work that still needs to be done. If you have planned your time well initially, you should have incorporated some extra time for this kind of work—*before* you start writing as a group.

PREPARING FOR CITATIONS

How you organize citations will depend on the demands of your readers. In some situations, you will need to use an appropriate documentation system—particularly in an academic setting or one that is oriented toward formal research. However, in most business situations, giving credit where credit is due can be achieved by noting the source of the information in an informal way (see Chapter 1 for guidelines on how to do this).

Regardless of how you choose to let the reader know your sources of information, it's important that group members note information about each source as they conduct their research. They should record the author, title, publisher, date, pages, website address, and so on for each source—as much information as possible—so that it is readily available to be incorporated into the appropriate section of the final written document.

Just one member's failure to cite a source can sink the entire team's credibility, so you will want to stress the importance of "giving credit where credit is due" with each member. It's worth including in your team contract.

ORGANIZING INFORMATION AND WRITING: FORMAT

Once members have completed their assigned research and the team has closed any information gaps through a research review meeting and follow-up, you can begin writing.

Each person must have explicit instruction on what needs to be written, both in terms of the information the particular section is to contain and in terms of the entire report.

Everyone needs to see the overall goal and the specific objectives simultaneously. First, review what the project as a whole is intended to achieve, then review how each section contributes to the whole and relates to other sections within the final written product. Make sure that everyone is clear on his or her part and how it relates to the whole project and the work of others. This will facilitate the work of the final editor, who will have to unify the document in tone, style, and voice (more about this later on).

Agree on a general tone and style for the document. While each person will interpret this in his or her own way, it's good to agree on a set of general guidelines so that the writing is similar in each section before it is edited. For example, if the report or proposal is going to an internal audience, you will be pretty safe to go with a moderately informal tone. If the written document or presentation is meant for an external audience, then make sure that you are all using at least a moderately formal style and tone of writing. (See Chapters 8 to 11 on informal and formal reports and proposals for guidelines on tone and style.)

Remind the team to avoid using jargon and colloquialisms in the document and to explain any acronyms, initialisms, and abbreviations. While you all may understand these forms of language and be focused on using them as you work together, remember that some or all of your readers may not know what they mean.

If possible, obtain a copy of a report or proposal that is comparable to what you need to produce. If you all agree to write in a tone, style, and form similar to that of this sample document, you will reduce the work of your final editor in unifying your document.

As has been suggested in other chapters of this textbook, remember that writing for an international readership means that you must pay special attention to the Starting Point questions—and ask questions of the organization or individual who solicited your project if possible. There's guidance in Chapter 1 on how to write for an international audience.

Finally, the designated editor (choose your best editor or writer in the team for the job, and be prepared to provide a lot of support—perhaps lots of treats!) should be sent all members' sections in electronic format for easier assembly of the document. Each section needs to be clearly marked so that this person can put the information where it needs to go according to the outline.

INITIAL EDITING FOR CONTENT

Before you leave the report or proposal with your brilliant wordsmith editor, you all need to review the document. Made up of pieces submitted by members and slapped into the right places in the outline, the document may look a bit like a Frankenstein monster of parts patched together with headings and subheadings.

Everyone should read the document and refer back to the original outline to see that all the information demands of each part are met. Team members should focus particularly on sections that are not their own. (Reading and rereading your own material may be counterproductive at this point.)

If any section or subsection is found to be missing information, the group can then decide who will be responsible for filling in the gaps. If time is short, it may take the combined effort of several people to get the required information. The author of the section in question could be responsible for rewriting the section incorporating the revised information.

Then the revised section goes back to the person—the editor—who pulled all the sections together into one document. The editor is responsible for unifying the document by carefully copy editing it (see Checking Your Work, below). He or she has the right to call on any team member for clarification or further information as needed to improve the document.

Checking Your Work

CONTENT EDITING, COPY EDITING, AND FORMATTING REVIEW

As mentioned previously, one person should be appointed to edit the entire document for style, tone, and voice, as well as conduct a final review to ensure that all content is in place to meet the demands of the receivers or readers of the document. Whoever you choose to do this important job should look at Chapter 4 on revising and editing to help with the process.

Step 1: Review the content

The first step is to conduct another content review. Do all of the sections contain what is needed in terms of required information? Check each section against the agreed-upon outline with notes to ensure that nothing is missed.

Step 2: Read and reread the document

The second step is to read the entire document a couple of times, looking for any writing that appears disjointed. (It is strongly suggested that you print a copy and use a red pen to note areas of concern, then go back and revise as needed in the electronic document.) When each section has been written by a different person, they may be written in a more or less formal tone, depending on the style of the writer. Make sure that each section flows into the next in terms of formal or informal tone, word choices, and style.

Step 3: Double-check documentation of sources

It is also important at this point to ensure that some form of citation is in place for materials that are not yours. In other words, while a business report or proposal may not use MLA or another documentation format, make sure that ideas and quotes taken from others' work are noted. Be sure that the reader knows where your team obtained information so that no one (meaning your entire team, even if just one person slips up in his or her section) can be accused of plagiarism.

Step 4: Revise as needed for unity of writing

Rewrite or edit sections as needed so that the entire document appears to be written by one writer rather than several. This is *unifying* your team writing. The goal is to produce a report that seamlessly and effectively communicates with your readers.

Step 5: Do a comprehensive copy edit

Next, review the document for grammar, spelling, mechanics, and structural (paragraph and sentence) errors. Start with your word-processing program's grammar and spell checkers, then print the document and give it a thorough copy edit on hard copy. Implement the changes in the electronic document, then run another grammar and spelling check to ensure that you didn't mess up the copy further when making changes.

Step 6: Review the document for appearance and presentation

When you review the document for appearance and presentation—the final step—make sure that headings and subheadings stand out by using different-sized typefaces, bolding, or italics as needed. However, you must also make sure that the use of such visual devices is consistent—for example, that subheadings of sections of the same level of importance are the same size and style of typeface. Believe it or not, careless layout of sections will be noticed by the final reader, who may question the validity or professionalism of the team's report or proposal if it appears you were too lazy to pay attention to this kind of detail.

Step 7: Print—and then double-check everything

After you hit the "Print" command, review the document one last time to make sure that it looks professional and is ready for further copying and/or processing with covers, bindings, and so on.

What Happens to Your Document Next?

Once you have completed the document, give it to whoever commissioned or requested it. After that, whether you know it or not, there may be many other readers, so always assume that others will be reading your final product.

Many people may be called upon to review the document before it is endorsed or accepted by your company or organization. This is commonly known as **document cycling**. The report is put into an interoffice envelope and physically circulated through interoffice mail to those who need to see it and comment on it or suggest revisions. Alternatively, the document may be circulated through email for comment and review.

The people who are formally included in the review of the report or proposal constitute a **review chain**. It includes not only the person or people who gave your team the responsibility for creating the written document but also other people with authority or relevant expertise in the organization, such as a lawyer, financial controller, or technical editor. The chain will review your team's work for balance, objectivity, and tone and, in general, ensure that your document truly represents the organization's culture and interests to the people who will ultimately read it. This is particularly important when the topic or focus of your work is governed by the regulations and rules of your industry or by government.

Be prepared from the outset: when your team is assigned the project, ask whether there will be a review chain, and if so, try to find out as much as you can about the readers. But in any case, assume that there will be many readers. Double-check facts, statistics, and statements of fact; check your writing for jargon, abbreviations, and any assumptions of understanding that you may have made in your writing.

Oral Presentation of the Team Project

Your team may be asked to make a presentation of the report or proposal to just a few or to many people—a frequent expectation, because teams are usually assigned weighty or complex projects that involve not only a written product but also a presentation to accompany or support the document.

Your team contract should address who will take what role in the presentation. Together, you should assess the ability of each team member to speak comfortably and well and determine who would be more suited to a supportive role, perhaps managing PowerPoint slides, overheads, or other visuals or distributing materials such as the printed document to those in attendance.

In a professional setting, most teams choose their best speaker and facilitator to do most of the talking, with others speaking to areas in which they have done work or answering questions about the research they have conducted for the project. This is particularly important when you are presenting a proposal or report that is persuasive in nature, such as a sales pitch to a potential major client or customer.

However, if the project is for a course, *every* member of the team may be required to speak or otherwise be active in the presentation so that the instructor can evaluate oral presentation skills. It is important that you know how to speak and conduct yourself in all of the roles required in a team presentation, even if you never have to handle the speaking portion when you are out working in the "real world." Knowing how it should be done is essential in helping—or managing—any project team in the workplace to create and present an excellent presentation.

You should always rehearse an oral presentation, preferably in the location where you plan to deliver it and employing the tools you will use, such as multimedia software. This is even more important for team presentations, because with several people involved, movements and speaking, along with use of any visual aids, will have to be co-ordinated. Where will people stand when they are speaking? Where will others stand or sit when not speaking or actively involved in the presentation? Who will manage the visuals? Where will this person be situated? How will you position yourselves so that the audience can see you?

Have at least one group rehearsal of your presentation, and have someone observe it so that you can judge what it looks like from the audience's perspective. Have this person tell you what you need to do to improve the presentation. If you have a chance to run through it again, you can incorporate the suggested changes. If you can't rehearse in the location where you will be presenting, at least try to pick a venue that is similar so that you all have a feel for what giving the presentation will be like.

Review the guidelines in Chapter 12 for more help in planning and delivering oral presentations. And remember that when you are making a team presentation to an international audience, be sure that it is suitable for and sensitive to the needs of the people who will be attending.

If your team is asked to present its findings, be sure to have a frank discussion with team members ahead of time to determine how best to organize your presentation so that it will be well received.

CHECKLIST FOR team communications

☑ Has your team reviewed the demands and purpose of the project?

☑ Has your team reviewed the needs of the audience (using Starting Point questions in Chapter 1)? Has your team considered whether the audience is culturally diverse and thus requires a different approach?

☑ Have you prepared a team contract to improve the functioning of your writing team?

☑ Have you decided on a team writing model—collaboration, consensus, or delegation?

☑ Have you decided who will do which parts of the research?

☑ Has everyone recorded source information for citations?

☑ Have you conducted a final meeting to bring all research together and address information gaps before you start writing?

☑ If you are each writing specific parts of the final document, have you agreed on such details as length (or word count), tone, style, and the details needed for each section?

☑ Have you met as a group to review your draft document once all sections are in place?

☑ Have you conducted a group edit of the document?

☑ Have you decided on one final editor to go through the entire document after the team editing process? Has the editor followed all of the steps for editing noted in this chapter?

☑ Has the team reviewed the edited document for: format; content; documentation; unified voice, tone, and style; and grammar and spelling errors?

☑ Once it has been printed, have you double-checked the document for any possible errors?

☑ Has the document been produced according to the format, number of copies, and other specifications required by the readers/receivers?

☑ Have you delivered the final product to the appropriate people?

☑ Have you determined whether there is to be an oral presentation? If there is, have you prepared materials to support your document as appropriate in the presentation?

Chapter Summary

In this chapter, you have learned that there are several ways to divide up the work of writing a report as a team—consensus, delegation, and collaboration—each with its own strengths and weaknesses and each appropriate for specific team writing situations. You discovered that each of these three methods involves a particular mode of writing to which you will have to adapt. Collaborative reports may have secondary readers in addition to the primary ones. You found that writing teams must communicate regularly, meet frequently, and review the research together before the organizing and writing of the first draft. You learned step by step how to bring written work together into a cohesive and professional whole through editing. You discovered how document cycling and a review chain can help to improve your product. Finally, you learned some troubleshooting strategies to overcome challenges common in team writing situations.

▉▉ SUGGESTIONS *for Further Reading*

Alred, G.J., Brusaw, C.T., and Oliu, W.E. (2010). *Writing that works: Communicating effectively on the job [with team writing]*. (10th ed.). New York, NY: Bedford/St. Martin's Press.
———. (2011). *The business writer's handbook*. (10th ed.). New York, NY: Bedford/St. Martin's Press.

Harris, T.E., and Sherblom, J.C. (2010). *Small group and team communication*. (5th ed.). Toronto, ON: Allyn & Bacon/Pearson Higher Education.

Kolin, P. C. (2011). *Successful writing at work: Concise edition*. Independence, KY: Cengage/Wadsworth.

Lumsden, G., Lumsden, D., and Wiethoff, C. (2009). *Communicating in groups and teams: Sharing leadership*. (9th ed.). Independence, KY: Cengage/Wadsworth.

Wolfe, J. (2010). *Team writing: A guide to writing in groups*. New York, NY: St. Martin's Press.

▉▉ DEBATE *and Discussion Starters*

1. What would be the benefits of each model of team writing if you were working on a student team to produce a report and/or oral presentation as part of a course?

2. Which model do you think would have worked best in a past team effort that perhaps didn't go so well? Which model might you try in a team project you have coming up in a course you are currently taking? Why?

3. In the industry or sector you anticipate working in after graduation, which model do you think would work best? Why? Which would be least useful or helpful? Why? (Perhaps you should research the field you have in mind.)

4. Which team model would you prefer to work with? Which one would be the least appealing? Why?

▉▉ PRACTISING *What You Have Learned*

1. a. For your next *team writing project*, create a team contract for your group as described in this chapter and in Chapter 6. (Your instructor may have a specific project in mind to which you should apply the principles of this chapter.)
    b. Conduct the research and writing, using the steps outlined in this chapter, and apply the style appropriate for the particular written product (e.g., informal or formal report, informal or formal proposal, business plan, marketing plan). Refer to the chapters in this textbook covering each type of written product for guidance in determining research, writing, format, and editing requirements.
    c. At the end of the project, conduct an evaluation process with your team to assess how well you did and what you would do differently next time (in this team or another).

2. a. For your next *team oral presentation*, create a team contract for your group as described in this chapter and in Chapter 6. (Your instructor may have a specific project in mind to which you should apply the principles of this chapter.)
    b. Conduct the research and writing, using the steps outlined in this chapter and those necessary for the particular written product (e.g., informal or formal report, informal or formal proposal). Refer to the chapters in this textbook covering each type of written product for guidance in determining research, writing, format, and editing requirements.
    c. At the end of the project, conduct an evaluation process with your team to assess how well you did and what you would do differently next time (in this team or another).

CHAPTER 8

Informal Reports

In this chapter, you will learn:

- ⊚ The common types of informal reports and their purpose

- ⊚ When it is appropriate to use each type of report

- ⊚ How to plan for, organize, and write expense reports, progress reports, evaluation and information reports, and incident reports, in an informal format and style

- ⊚ How to edit and review your informal report to ensure that it meets your readers' needs and your reasons for writing

- ⊚ Professional tips on how to effectively communicate the information in each type of report to a business readership

ESSENTIAL EMPLOYABILITY SKILLS

2ooo+ Employability Skills   The Conference Board of Canada has identified certain essential employability skills (EES) as benchmarks for performance in the workplace. You will learn the following EES skills in this chapter:

COMMUNICATE

- ⊚ Can read and understand information presented in a variety of forms (e.g., words, graphs, charts, diagrams)

- ⊚ Can listen and ask questions to understand and appreciate the points of view of others

THINK AND SOLVE PROBLEMS

- ⊚ Can assess situations and identify problems
- ⊚ Can identify the root cause of a problem

MANAGE INFORMATION

- ⊚ Can locate, gather, and organize information using appropriate technology and information systems

- ⊚ Can access, analyze, and apply knowledge and skills from various disciplines (e.g., the arts, languages, science, technology, mathematics, social sciences, and the humanities)

WORK WITH OTHERS

- ⊚ Can recognize and respect people's diversity, individual differences, and perspectives

- ⊚ Can understand and work within the dynamics of a group

BE RESPONSIBLE

- ⊚ Can plan and manage time, money, and other resources to achieve goals

Informal Reports: A Case Study

Tristan Gottlieb is a district sales manager for a major pharmaceutical company, Heartsafe Inc. Heartsafe manufactures and sells medications to manage various forms of heart disease.

Tristan recently attended a North American pharmaceutical sales conference in Miami, Florida. He was attending to learn better strategies for selling to doctors and clinics, since Heartsafe is in heated competition with another company specializing in such medications, Mediheart Ltd. In turn, he was to take his learning from the conference and pass it on to his sales team. Here are the details:

- The conference took place over a three-day weekend, with a social evening the night before for those arriving early.

- There was one seminar per day (10 a.m. to 2 p.m.) with leading sales specialists from across the continent and daily smaller workshops between 2 and 5 p.m.

- The conference cost $1,000 plus airfare.

- Tristan's boss, Jocelyn Braekvelt, expected Tristan to attend all main seminars and a few of the smaller workshops relevant to his work.

- She expected a comprehensive report on what he learned and how it would help Tristan's team to exceed sales projections.

Tristan arrived the night before the conference began and met a few friends who lived in Miami. He celebrated a bit too much and was an hour late for the first seminar, "Overcoming objections and closing the deal," at 10 a.m. on Friday. This seminar focused on typical objections to purchasing pharmaceutical products and how to address these proactively in order to close a deal, something his team needed to know about because sales of their heart medications were down.

At 1:00 p.m., he figured he had gathered all he could from the seminar and went off to nurse his hangover in his room. He missed two smaller workshops but attended "Learn how to read your customers" between 4 and 5 p.m. This workshop focused on ways to identify common types of consumer personalities and how to work with customers based on a good fit with their psychographic profile.

He intended to make it an early night, but his friends came by again, and they all went to a blues bar. Apparently, he gave his cell number to an attractive server, but his friends intervened and took him back to his room. As his friend Travis said, "What happens on the road, stays on the road."

Despite a nasty headache, Tristan made the 10 a.m. seminar on Saturday ("Customer service: keys to better sales") and attended "Winning strategies with doctors" later in the day. From these seminars, he learned new ideas on improving customer retention and more about what medical professionals are seeking in the pharmaceuticals they recommend to patients.

He then went to the hotel spa for a massage at 3 p.m. and didn't return to the conference, instead heading out for dinner with a former girlfriend.

Tristan missed the Sunday session on financial management for sales professionals. As someone with a finance degree, he felt he didn't really need this seminar anyway. He went to brunch with his gal pal, then attended the closing sessions—one-on-one meetings with keynote speakers—between 3 and 5 p.m. This information helped to reinforce what he needed to take back to his team.

Soon after Tristan arrived back at the office on Tuesday, his boss dropped by to remind him she needed a full report of the trip, including any additional expenses, by Thursday's staff meeting, when the report would be presented to his peers. He gathered his expense receipts and determined that he had spent an additional $250 on meals for himself and $50 on taxis. His receipts did not include others' meals or any other expenses, such as the massage.

Tristan struggled with what to write. He had missed parts of the conference, but he did feel that he had derived as much as he could from the opportunity and had learned about some creative strategies that his team could use.

1. Should Tristan include his "non-professional" activities in his report? How could Tristan have handled his experience at the conference more professionally?

2. Tristan needs to let Jocelyn know which sessions he attended and why the learning is essential to himself and his team. Using your imagination and the information available, make a list of what he could have learned from the conference seminars he did attend, and explain how this learning can be translated into action within his sales team.

3. Write the informal report (an expense report) to Jocelyn Braekvelt, National Sales Manager. (You can make up the details that are not included, such as the company address.)

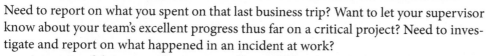

Before You Begin . . .

Need to report on what you spent on that last business trip? Want to let your supervisor know about your team's excellent progress thus far on a critical project? Need to investigate and report on what happened in an incident at work?

Accounts of these everyday events and activities in the workplace are usually given in an informal report. Informal reports are **internal communications**, usually solicited by someone in authority or a peer, that cover routine information for such business functions as operations, planning, or financial management.

The most common types of **informal reports** are incident, progress, expense, or information/evaluation reports.

Incident reports describe something that has happened on a worksite, with a project, or within the work setting—typically an accident but often something less obvious, such as sexual harassment or insubordination, misuse of funds, or even corporate espionage.

Progress reports detail your progress (or your team's progress) on a project or work assignment to date. They are often written when you are taking part in a project that spans at least one month—usually longer. For example, if you were implementing a new one-year marketing plan, you might be asked to report on how well the plan is working and what has been achieved to date at regular intervals set by your boss—monthly, quarterly, or semi-annually.

Expense reports detail what your expenses (or those associated with a project or work assignment) have been. They usually include a written narrative of what was spent on services or items, any cost savings or over-budget expenses, the benefits of the expense to you, the company or organization, or the project, and any recommendations (e.g., where to find a cheaper supplier next time).

Your expense report may need to be somewhat persuasive, particularly if you spent more than was anticipated or planned. If this is the case, you will have to focus in particular on the benefits of the expense(s).

A standard expense report form usually accompanies the report, or the writer generates a spreadsheet (Excel) report detailing expenses and any savings or cost overruns.

Information reports are just that—they provide information on a neutral, relatively routine matter. This type of report does not contain any opinions, nor does it attempt to persuade. The purpose of the information report is to give "just the facts, ma'am" so that the reader can make his or her own judgment.

As an example, if your company was considering buying a new computer system, you might be asked to compile an information report. In it, you would provide the same or similar amounts of information for each brand or supplier being considered—the pros and cons—so that all the choices would get equal consideration and could be compared effectively.

A variation of the information report is the evaluation report. In an evaluation report, you also provide your opinion, but that opinion is backed up by the facts you present about each choice, based on specific criteria.

Brief and to the point, informal reports usually use memo format because these are written for an internal audience and are two pages or fewer in length (see Chapter 2 for memo format.) You would switch to a *formal* report format under the following circumstances:

- The project, work, or tasks are complex, or they involve more than one organization (i.e., there are external readers or stakeholders).

Idiom Alert

cost overrun – An expense that is more than the amount originally budgeted.

dead end – An obstacle or challenge. The expression comes from driving: when you find yourself in a dead end, you cannot proceed further and must turn around or find an alternate route.

"just the facts, ma'am" – Catch phrase indicating a rejection of extraneous or unnecessary details. From "Dragnet," a radio and television show of the 1950s and 1960s, it was the signature line of the main character, a police detective, when questioning a witness to a crime or incident.

stickler (for details) – Focused on the details of a project or product, ensuring a quality outcome and no mistakes.

tight budget – Very limited money allocated for any extra expenses.

downplay – Minimize the importance of something.

spot (v.) – Notice or have brought to one's attention.

- The information included is quite serious and has major implications for the readers, or a significant amount of money is involved.

- You are specifically requested to do so by someone in your organization.

Informal reports are generally organized to include an introduction (purpose, scope), background to the report and its topic, the details of what you have been asked to report on, and a conclusion that restates the purpose, scope, main points, and possibly an evaluation of the information.

Your Starting Point

As with any other form of business writing or oral presentation, you need to know as much as possible about the audience for your communication. And you need to know why you are writing the report.

To get started with an informal report, ask the Starting Point questions found in Chapter 1 about the reader or readers of your report. You need to know as much as possible about your primary and secondary readers if you are to provide the information they need, want, or will be persuaded by.

If you are writing for someone who has solicited the report from you, chances are good that the person knows at least something about the topic you are writing about, but don't assume anything. Unless you are certain that the reader knows your topic very well, write for a moderate level of understanding (assume that the reader knows something about your topic but that you are perhaps more of an expert).

If the report is unsolicited—you are preparing it but have not been asked to do so—it's safer to assume that your readers may not know much about your topic. They may have some idea, but you should write with respect for their position while assuming that they don't know everything about the topic. For example, you might open your report with a line such as "As you know, testing for the XPJ software is almost complete, but we still have a few processes to complete before we can launch it with our business customers." The "as you know" part is politely flattering the reader, indicating you have faith in the person's understanding and intelligence, even if you do proceed to give the kind of detail normally given to someone who knows little or nothing about the topic.

Creating the Written Product: How to Do It

PREPARING TO WRITE

Research

You will need to do some research to obtain all of the information the reader is looking for in your progress, incident, expense, or information report. Whether informal or formal, the quality of your report—and its possible adoption—depends very much on the quality and variety of sources of information you use to provide "just the facts."

As with all written communication products, when preparing an informal report it's critical to ask: Who is the reader and what are the reader's needs? With the answers in mind, you'll be ready to start the process of writing a successful product.

Based on the answers to the Starting Point questions, you will know what kind of information the reader needs in your report. For example:

- Your reader is your supervisor, and you are writing an incident report about an accident that happened to one of your colleagues on the shop floor. Your supervisor has to report, in turn, to her supervisor. Her supervisor is a stickler for details, and because there have been a few such accidents lately, he wants to know what happened, in detail, so that the company's health and safety committee can come up with some means to avoid accidents in the future. Therefore, you know that the reader is quite anxious to have as much information as possible from you—in as much detail as possible—so that she can report to her supervisor as comprehensively as possible. You then know that you are going to have to do some detailed research, including an assessment of the situation and the physical site, and that you will probably need to interview the witnesses or other people involved. You also know that you are expected just to get the facts; the health and safety committee will make the final assessment as to what can be done to improve safety on the shop floor.

- Your reader is budget-conscious, and you recently purchased some new network technology that cost 20 per cent more than the amount originally approved by the purchasing department. Therefore, you know that your budget report will have to make a very solid pitch for the extra expense, outlining the researched benefits of the network system as "value-added" so that your report will be approved and the extra 20 per cent doesn't come out of your pay.

- Your reader is responsible for reporting to a variety of stakeholders about the progress of a project you are working on that is quite complex and involves a team of 20 diverse specialists. He is not very clear on all the details of the project—particularly the scientific data—and was assigned at the last minute to supervise and report back regularly to all stakeholders. He needs you to provide a detailed analysis of the work thus far, including progress, any delays or challenges, and planned work in such a way that he can explain it easily to stakeholders. That means providing as much information as possible but writing in such a way that the reader can fully understand the progress to date and pass on all the important details.

- Your reader needs information about three different catering services for the board of directors' annual meeting. You know that the budget for the event is tight, and you have the details of the activities that will be taking place, as well as the number of people attending, how many are vegetarian, and other logistical details. You know that your information report will focus on comparing the three catering companies using the same criteria so that your reader can make an unbiased decision about which company to choose. Since the reader is quite budget-conscious, you will want to provide the information about the cost of each catering company's services fairly early in the report, since cost is a priority of the reader.

Think about the timelines for your report, and work backward from the deadline to determine how much time you have to write and edit your work—and before that, how much time you will realistically need for research.

Even for a short, informal report, you still need to assume that your research will take longer than you think. While an informal report often deals with routine, mundane information, details are important to the decision-making, implementation of projects, budgets, and operations—and to the health and safety of people in the workplace. If you stint on research and settle for less than accurate, appropriate, and current information, your report may do you more harm than good. Well-researched short reports build your reputation as a conscientious, capable person. Less than stellar fact-finding will sink your reputation.

Yes, research can be as boring as watching paint dry, but it is essential—and, dare we say it, you might even find it interesting once you get into it. Plan for it to take longer than expected, prepare for the inevitable dead-ends, and take a break from time to time and turn your mind to another project or activity.

Research sources include your own observations, telephone or email inquiries, interviews, company records, libraries, and, of course, the Internet. The choice of sources will very much depend on how much detail you need in the information for your report, as well as on the answers to your Starting Point questions about the big picture and your readers.

PREPARING FOR CITATIONS

The professionalism and quality of your report depends on your information sources—even in a short, routine report.

You must be able to tell the reader where you got your information in order to prove that your information is as unbiased as possible and that you have done your job in getting as much information as you can for the purpose of the report.

When you have located information that is useful to the report's purpose, immediately write down everything you can about the source in a place where it can be easily located:

- website address, date accessed, date of the most recent update or launch of the website, the authors (if any) of materials you are using, the name of the organization hosting the website, the titles of articles and information sections, the section or paragraph number on the webpage where the reader can find the information if desired

- title of the print source, chapter name and number (if relevant), names of authors, volume or issue number, series name/number, publisher's name, publication date

- full name and title of the person you spoke with, the organization the person works for or with, the date you spoke with this person, contact information

Keep source information in one location. While for most business audiences you don't need to cite this information as you would in an academic research paper, if your reader asks for more information about your sources, it's best to have it organized and close at hand.

ORGANIZING INFORMATION AND WRITING: FORMAT

How to get started writing any informal report

Write the report first using memo format and the basic template as noted below (in Table 8.1). Once you have organized the information under the appropriate main headings, you then break it up further under subheadings to avoid overwhelming your reader.

The general format of an informal report is simple—introduction, background, the report, and conclusion. If your report will run to three pages or more and cannot be put into a memo format, you need to consider it a formal report in terms of format and length (see Chapter 9 for guidance on how to organize a formal report).

Progress report

Whenever you and/or a team are involved in a project of several weeks, months, or years duration, you may be expected to write **progress reports** at specific intervals to update stakeholders or managers about progress to date. Even if you are not asked to do so, writing a progress report and submitting it unsolicited at appropriate intervals demonstrates to supervisors or stakeholders that you and/or your team are managing the project effectively. (Besides, it's a great way to track what has been done, what needs to be done, any problems, and possible solutions— a document the team can consult in case anyone forgets details or what was done by whom.)

The progress report starts with a very brief summary of the project—what it is and the goals/objectives to be achieved at completion or finish. The background section addresses why the project was initiated and by whom and any other history pertaining to its initiation and start.

The progress section is divided into four subsections. The planned work section outlines the work expected to be completed on the project (from the beginning); work completed explains which tasks and work have been completed to date by you or members of your team. The challenges section outlines any difficulties experienced to date that have affected completion of project tasks but also explains what was done to address the challenges or provides some ideas for solving the problems (to reassure

TABLE 8.1	**Report Formats**		
PROGRESS REPORT	**INCIDENT REPORT**	**EXPENSE REPORT**	**INFORMATION/ EVALUATION REPORT**
Summary	Introduction	Introduction	Introduction
Background	Investigation	Activities (or items purchased)	Overview (or background)
Progress	Assessment	Benefits	Methodology
• Planned work	Conclusion	Cost(s)	Findings
• Work completed	Recommendations (if required)	Conclusion	• Option A
• Challenges		Recommendations	• Option B
• Schedule		Attachments (if required)	• Option C (and so on)
Future plans			Assessment/ recommendations
Conclusion			Conclusion
Evidence (if required)			

readers). Finally, the schedule section outlines the schedule for work going forward, whether altered or not by challenges, and explains any schedule changes.

The future plans section addresses work yet to be completed and may again remind the reader that the schedule has changed and why, if applicable. The conclusion section restates what work was to be completed by the date of the report, work that was

Progress report format

SUMMARY

The summary is what you start with instead of an introduction section. It is a brief synopsis (condensed version) of your entire progress report, which outlines the past, present, and future of your project using the sections noted below. This section should be written last, since it summarizes everything from the background to the evidence section.

BACKGROUND

The background section focuses on the past and describes the situations and events leading up to the report. It briefly states the who, what, where, when, and why of the project.

PROGRESS

This section highlights the work done since the last report or since the project began.

- **Planned work:** This is a description of the work that was planned, whether or not it has been completed yet.
- **Work completed:** This section details the work completed to date, usually tied into your own timelines, schedules, or the client's or boss's expectations.
- **Challenges:** This is where you note anything that has held up the project or created problems. It's especially important not only to tell what the problems are or have been but also to explain how you have resolved the problem or challenge or what you are doing to identify the cause of the problem and find an appropriate resolution. If there have not been any problems, then state that fact (e.g., "To date, we have experienced no difficulties in completing tasks to agreed-upon deadlines.").
- **Schedule:** Here you outline the schedule for the remainder of the project or work. Note any revisions to timelines resulting from such factors as challenges, slowdowns, or changed expectations for the project.

FUTURE PLANS

Focusing on the future, here you note the details of the work that is to be completed in the remaining time allotted and, most important, the expected completion date.

CONCLUSION

The conclusion briefly restates the purpose and scope of the report, touches on the main points of the progress section, and provides a concluding statement to wrap up the report neatly.

EVIDENCE

The evidence section is detailed data, mostly supporting the work completed section. It is not commonly included in a memo-format, informal report, but sometimes the information you used to support your report should be attached. In such cases, because your informal report is to be less than three pages in length, this section can be attached at the end of the memo report as a stand-alone section. If the pieces of evidence are merely copies of other documents, create a separate cover page for the evidence section, and attach the pieces to this cover.

The evidence section should include any relevant materials or information you have gathered thus far to show your boss or client what kinds of materials or findings you have uncovered to date, demonstrating that you are, indeed, working hard on the project.

Consult the directions or agreed-upon parameters for reporting on the project or work to see whether such evidence needs to be supplied with your progress report, or use your best judgment based on the needs of the reader (as identified in your answers to the Starting Point questions) and your reputation.

Depending on the type of report you are writing, you may be required to make assessments and recommendations. Be sure to think critically about the issues at hand, and ensure that the opinions you provide are well supported. Providing a well-reasoned, convincing assessment will build your reputation as a thoughtful communicator.

completed, any problems that arose and how these have or will be resolved, work still to be completed, and the schedule for work yet to be completed.

An evidence section is optional. Like an appendix, this section may provide any statistics or data the reader would appreciate as proof of progress to date; evidence can also document any problems. If you include an evidence section, be sure to mention, in the appropriate earlier section of the report, that additional, relevant information will be provided in that section.

Incident report

Whenever there is a serious issue—such as a malfunction, an accident, a technological issue, or a breach of confidentiality or trade secrets—you may be required to write an **incident report**. First, you investigate the incident, and then you write the report based on your findings.

You may be asked for your opinion based on what you learned about the incident and/or your recommendations, and you would include it in the assessment, conclusion, and recommendations sections of the incident report. However, in some cases, such as in a health-care setting, you are strictly instructed *not* to provide your opinion or recommendations; you are expected merely to present the facts so that others can use the information for further investigation.

It is important to know whether your report requires your opinion, assessment, or recommendations after you have collected the facts, so double-check with the person who asked you to write the report.

Begin your investigation by asking what are known as "journalists' questions" (the basis of your Starting Point questions): *who, what, where, when, why,* and *how*. These are the factual details: who was involved, what happened, where it happened, when it happened, why it happened, and how it happened.

Whether or not you are to provide your opinion in the assessment, conclusion, or recommendations section of the report, at this point you are merely collecting facts and must reserve judgment about the causes of the incident or who is at fault. Think of yourself as a police officer or forensics expert called to a crime scene to collect information and samples before further investigation takes place. You might be involved in assisting the crime investigation team at a later date to determine who or what was at fault, but at first, no blame is laid on anyone or anything until all the facts are known.

If you were asked to do so by the reader who solicited your report, you give your judgment about fault based on the details you have uncovered. This judgment specifies whether any person or process was to blame (thus addressing the *why* question). If you are *not* to give your judgment or assessment, you do *not* include an assessment section. If you *are* to give your judgment or assessment, you provide it in the assessment section— based on and referring to the facts you stated in the investigation section.

In the conclusion section, if you are *not* to give your judgment or assessment, you merely restate the purpose and scope of your report, along with the main points

Incident report format

INTRODUCTION

This section includes the following:

- **Background:** Why the report is required (what happened)
- **Purpose:** The reason for writing the report (e.g., to inform a superior or a department)
- **Scope:** The specific limitations of the report, or what you will and will not address (e.g., an equipment malfunction that took place on a certain date and time)

Do not use *background*, *purpose*, or *scope* as sub-headings; rather, they describe what needs to be included in the introduction section, and you should use them to help you organize information and effectively introduce the reader to what follows.

INVESTIGATION

This section includes answers to these questions:

- **Who** was involved in the incident? Give their names, titles (if any), and position in the workplace or work setting.
- **What** happened? Describe in as much detail as possible the incident itself, without assigning or implying any blame or cause.
- **Where** did the incident occur? (e.g., the physical location, on the telephone, via email, away from the workplace)
- **When** did the incident occur? Give the date, the time of day, or a time span.

It is important that what you write in this section not only is unbiased but also does not imply that anyone or anything is to blame or is the cause of the incident. (That comes later!)

Do not use *who*, *what*, *where*, or *when* as subheadings. These are meant only to help you think about what information to include in this section.

ASSESSMENT

This section answers the *why* question: Why did the incident take place? Who or what is at fault, if anyone or anything? Which people or processes are to blame for the incident or problem?

When you make a judgment about fault, it is important to refer back to the facts you stated in the investigation section. Otherwise, your assessment may not be taken seriously, and your investigation of the situation will appear biased. It would be as though a police officer collected facts for an investigation and then merely relied on a "gut feeling" to assess guilt and make an arrest. Needless to say, such a case would be quickly thrown out of court!

CONCLUSION

The conclusion brings together the purpose and scope of the report (introduction), the facts you have uncovered (investigation), and, if you are to provide one, your judgment about fault or responsibility (assessment). As with any memo or report, it summarizes the entire report and provides the reader with closure.

The final sentence of your conclusion should include an invitation for the reader to contact you for more information and give your contact details.

Unless you have been asked to provide recommendations based on the facts and your assessment, this will be the end of your report.

RECOMMENDATIONS

This section is where you list recommendations for the company, organization, or individual to resolve the issue and to help avoid a similar situation arising in the future. You can do this numerically, in short paragraphs, or use a list, as in the following example:

Problem (Issue): Aging computers not compatible with latest server software.

Recommendation: Purchase new computers in a bulk buy from Skippy's Computer Warehouse to save on this necessary equipment cost.

of information you have uncovered or gathered. If you *are* to give your judgment or assessment, in the conclusion you restate the purpose and scope of the report, the main points of information you have uncovered, and your assessment of fault as described in the assessment section. The conclusion does not introduce any new information but merely brings together the purpose and scope, facts (investigation), and cause of and/ or responsibility for the incident (assessment).

Finally, if you have been asked to do so, based on the facts and your assessment of the situation you make recommendations about what your organization should do now to rectify the situation or impose damage control measures. Your recommendations might also include what the company should do in future to avoid a similar incident.

As noted previously, if the incident is serious or complicated, it should be written in formal report format. A serious incident report would probably include a great deal more information to consider from your investigation, warranting more than the two-page limit of a memo-format report.

Expense report

Whenever you are spending the company's or organization's money or want to claim expenses for reimbursement, someone is going to want to know that the expense was reasonable, documented—and worth it.

Besides the person you are mandated to provide the **expense report** to, there may be several other readers, including your supervisor, the financial controller of the company, or a budget committee.

In writing the expense report, your goal is not only to give the detailed information of exact costs and what was purchased or paid for but, more important, to provide a solid rationale for the expense.

An expense report should do the following:

- tell what was spent—actual dollars and cents of each item or service purchased;

- tell what was accomplished, learned, or purchased to the benefit of yourself, your department or team, and/or the company;

- explain why the expense provided "added value"—in other words, the company got more than it paid for (but don't go too far overboard with this);

- share new information and ideas you learned in spending the money that may benefit the company (e.g., where to go for the best service, the cheapest product);

- provide recommendations, if appropriate (e.g., "It is strongly recommended that the company consider XYZ courier in future, since ABC's timelines don't meet our tight deadlines for delivery").

Some organizations or companies you may work for or with may have their own guidelines for an expense report. However, if they don't, this outline should cover all the bases in terms of the information that decision-makers and managers need to see.

In any case, you should check with the person you are providing the report to about additional information you should attach, such as receipts or a spreadsheet expense report form (which you create or they supply).

As stated previously in this chapter, if your expense report is very detailed (such as one that covers a year's worth of expenses), it may have to be put into a formal report format.

Expense report format

INTRODUCTION

In this section, provide the following:

- **Background:** What led to the writing of this report, such as a planned business trip, a request to purchase items or services, an upcoming conference, or a continuing education event
- **Purpose:** Why you are writing this report and for whom
- **Scope:** What the report covers (dates, projects, types of expenses, and so on)

ACTIVITIES (OR ITEMS PURCHASED)

In this section, describe what you did to incur the expense (e.g., purchased equipment, attended a conference, took a course). Provide as much detail as possible about the items or services purchased.

BENEFITS

In this section, detail the benefits of the expense—to yourself, to the company or organization, to customers or clients. Describe what you learned or the reasons the item you purchased is going to be of benefit to the company.

It is very helpful to answer the Starting Point questions and note the readers' interests or concerns in terms of what they would consider a worthwhile expense, what would satisfy them that the expense was not only warranted but added value. This will help you to figure out what to highlight most prominently as benefits and what to downplay to avoid any negative reaction.

While an expense report is generally considered informational, it does have an element of persuasion. The trick is not to go so far in trying to persuade the reader about the value of the expense that you appear to be "overselling"—this would raise a red flag and concerns about the accuracy of the report.

COST(S)

In this section, tell how much each item or service cost. Use sentence format, not point form. If you attach a company standard expense form or create your own, refer to it in this section.

To further highlight the numbers involved, it's a good idea to attach a spreadsheet; write a title and/or date at the top, and list the type of expense, the cost per unit/service (if applicable), and the total cost. You can attach it to your memo-format expense report. (You can use a software program, such as Excel or Numbers, to easily create your spreadsheet.)

CONCLUSION

In this section, reiterate the purpose and scope of the report, the costs involved, and why the purchase or activity was or will be of benefit to the company. In the last line, provide your contact information, and let the reader know you are available for further information or to answer questions. (The "bean counters" will sometimes need to contact you to verify information about your expense claims.)

RECOMMENDATIONS

If your reader has requested it, or if it's appropriate to the rest of your report, you may make brief recommendations. For example, if you attended an annual programmers' conference at Walt Disney World in Florida and you feel it would be not only educational for people in your department to attend in future but a good morale booster, you may wish to include a statement to that effect. Remember, however, that recommendations in a memo-format report are best kept brief and in point form.

ATTACHMENTS

Attach your expense report and copies or originals of receipts, as required by the person responsible for the expense. Always keep a copy if you are giving away your originals in case they happen to go astray. Unfortunately, even if you hand-deliver an expense report to the appropriate person's desk, paper has a habit of going AWOL—with the result that you may not be reimbursed for what you have spent.

Information and evaluation reports

Information reports include any report on information or research that is not particularly persuasive. You might be asked to gather information comparing three different suppliers of photocopiers, or a couple of different restaurants for the annual company holiday dinner, but not to mention which one you favour. Your supervisor or manager may merely want the information collected so that he or she can make a final decision.

An **evaluation report** goes one step further. Perhaps your supervisor does not have the time or desire to make a final decision on the best photocopier or restaurant, so the task has been delegated to you. Your supervisor wants a report on your findings about each option and then, based on these findings, your recommendation about which option to go with.

To prepare an information report or an evaluation report, you gather information or data within certain categories—the scope of the information collected is limited so that the reader (information report) or you (evaluation report) can quickly make an assessment of the information and decide what to do.

For example, if you were comparing two restaurants for the annual holiday party, you might gather information from each on price per plate, wine service cost, menu options, entertainment, and parking. So that your information or evaluation report is unbiased and complete, you would only consider information on both venues that falls into these categories: you would not collect information about one restaurant's menu options without also collecting information about the other restaurant's menu options as well.

Likewise, you would not include information about either choice that has not been solicited by your reader. For example, you would not comment particularly on the ambience of the restaurants, since it is not one of the factors to consider. Particularly when you are writing a memo-format report, it's important not to add extra details, because your writing needs to be very brief and to the point.

You might consider using a chart or table to set up the information being compared so that the reader can quickly see how each option measures up against the others.

Information and evaluation report format

INTRODUCTION

The introduction to an information or evaluation report tells why you are writing the report, provides the purpose of the report, and describes how you gathered the information for the report (also known as *background*, *objective*, and *methodology*).

OVERVIEW (OR BACKGROUND)

This section describes the situations, products, or services you are investigating (e.g., which three computer systems or which two restaurants) and the factors you are evaluating (e.g., the price and features of the computer systems; the price per plate, wine service, and menu choices of the two restaurants).

This sets the stage for the sections that follow in which you describe how you obtained information and your findings.

METHODOLOGY

This section tells the reader where you got your information, such as printed primary sources (surveys, questionnaires), personal observation, published secondary information sources (newspaper articles), or telephone or email interviews or queries.

Telling the reader how you got the information shows that you gave all the options being assessed equal consideration and that you were thorough in gathering relevant information.

FINDINGS

Here you provide your analysis of each option, comparing them according to the same criteria. To organize this information clearly so that the reader can see at a glance the options under consideration, write the facts about each option in separate paragraphs or subsections, each headed by a subtitle (usually the name of the product or service):

Option A
(Details, according to criteria)

Option B
(Details, according to criteria)

Depending on the type of information, the details might be presented in a table or chart.

ASSESSMENT

This section is only required for evaluation reports, when you have been asked to review all of the data and recommend a choice.

As in an incident report, your opinion must be based on the facts of your research. You must not just state your opinion without referring back to your findings about each option, or it will appear that you didn't do a thorough job of considering all of the options and the criteria involved.

CONCLUSION

The conclusion, as in all other short reports, wraps up the purpose, scope, background, and research into a neat package and invites the reader to contact you for more information. In an evaluation report, the conclusion also includes a reiteration of your recommendations from the assessment section.

Sample Documents

FIGURE 8.1 Progress Report

MEMORANDUM

TO: Wei-Lin Runner, CEO

FROM: Kate Compass, Director of Sales

SUBJECT: Progress report for sales training program

DATE: July 4, 2014

Reason for report, work to date, persuasive start for report.

Summary

The following is the report you requested on the progress of participants in our Sales—Beat the Odds training program.

As you know, the program started May 1 with several weeks of world-renowned motivational speakers, intensive seminars, role-playing, and applied learning to help our sales team achieve their very best. The 20 participants have had a refresher on the entire sales process and have received motivational training to generate further enthusiasm.

Participants have successfully completed this first phase of training and are expected to complete Phase II (mentorship and a final report) by August 30.

Background information provides context for report that follows.

Background

Following what we all agree was not our best first quarter, the executive of Interactive Computing decided our sales team needed some support in the way of a refresher sales course.

This course was to not only review the commonly accepted methods of sales but to apply these tried and true standards to the new demands of sales in the technology industry, as well as to generate new life and enthusiasm in the sales team.

Progress

Planned work describes what was to be done in project.

Planned Work

Following endorsement by the executive management team, it was decided to deliver the sales course as soon as possible, starting May 1 and finishing up by August 29, 2014.

Tasks successfully completed; persuades reader that project has been managed well to date.

Work Completed

To date, participants have had a complete and industry-relevant review of the entire sales process, including market/customer analysis, dealing with objections, closing the sale, and customer retention activities.

It seems that many had lost sight of who our target and secondary customers are and how important it is to understand the motivations and purchasing process of our customers. We are confident this renewed focus on meeting and exceeding customer needs and concerns will result in better sales in the third and final quarters of this year.

Participants have also received motivational training and support from a variety of sales industry and business leaders, including world-renowned Tony Robbins. According to participants, these speakers, as well as a variety of self-reflection and evaluation exercises, have proved invaluable in helping our sales team to overcome their own internal blocks to success.

We are now ready to move on to the mentorship and final reporting phase of the program.

Challenges

To date, we have not experienced any challenges to the presentation or completion of this program within agreed-upon timelines. A minor glitch in scheduling Tony Robbins during Phase I caused some concern, but we merely reorganized the course work with a few extra sessions so that participants could take advantage of this once-in-a-lifetime opportunity to be motivated by Mr. Robbins.

Challenges are described now that reader has been convinced of successful management of project.

Challenge is immediately followed by resolution, to reassure the reader.

Schedule

Because we have not experienced any major challenges to date, the sales course is expected to be completed by August 29.

Schedule is reflected upon here; reader can see project is on track.

Future Plans

Participants will be matched with their sales mentors this coming week to commence their on-the-job training with the mentors' assistance. In this phase, each participant will meet with his or her sales mentor on Friday afternoons to review the week's sales activities and approaches used, which will help us to implement Phase I learning more confidently in future.

Outlines what is yet to be completed but with specific dates to reassure reader.

Participants will each complete a final, cumulative report reflecting on course work and learning by August 15, 2014. A wrap-up wine and cheese celebration will be held on August 29 at my home (directions and details to be supplied at a later date).

Evidence

In the attached Evidence section, you will find a detailed interim sales report for the second quarter that shows a definite increase in sales over the same time period in the first quarter, as well as a couple of rather compelling testimonials written by participants. The investment in this program is definitely paying off!

Evidence supports rest of report (included only if needed for reader comprehension).

Should you require any further information, please contact me at extension 555 or at kcompass@interactivmail.com.

FIGURE 8.2 Incident Report

MEMORANDUM

TO: Marissa Koropatwa, Owner, Genteel Spa

FROM: Lynn Hoogendoorn, Manager

SUBJECT: Incident report: Complaint by Mrs. I. Crab

DATE: May 29, 2014

_____

Introduction covers
background, purpose, and
scope of report.

Introduction

As requested, the following incident report will provide you with the details of
Mrs. I. Crab's recent customer service complaint, my investigation, and suggestions
for the resolution of this situation. Recommendations follow this report to help
our estheticians with any similar situations in future.

Incident described
sparingly to keep reader
focused; covers who, what,
where, when.

Investigation

On May 21, 2014, Mrs. Crab came to our spa for the Rest, Rejuvenation, and
Relaxation half-day treatment package. She was to receive a custom facial, pedicure,
manicure, and complimentary eyebrow waxing.

The estheticians assigned to Mrs. Crab were Gwen Golden, our senior esthetician,
and Patricia Smith, a recent graduate of the ABC Beauty School.

Mrs. Crab arrived at the salon in a disgruntled mood that day, saying that her neighbour's dog had dug up her front flowerbed and that she wished the dog could be
euthanized. Away from the client, I informed the estheticians working with her that
she was clearly upset and advised them to be soothing with her.

The treatments proceeded as planned, and I checked in with the pair to see how
they and Mrs. Crab were doing a couple of times throughout that morning.

However, Mrs. Crab began to scream at around 11:30 that she was being burned,
threatened to sue for permanent scarring that "she was most certainly going to
have," and left the building.

To date, no legal communication has been received.

Succinct details of why
incident took place, rem-
edies undertaken.

Assessment

As soon as Mrs. Crab left the building, I questioned both Gwen and Patricia about
the incident.

Gwen had left the room when Patricia began the waxing. Gwen had personally checked
the wax temperature and consistency and had reviewed the process with Patricia.

Patricia asked Mrs. Crab to close her right eye while she applied the wax and then
quickly pulled off the wax. Mrs. Crab began to scream immediately and smacked
Patricia before running out of the room.

I personally checked that the wax used was appropriate for the eyebrow procedure and had Patricia demonstrate on another esthetician what she did that day. It appears she is quite competent in handling this procedure.

I then consulted Mrs. Crab's health questionnaire completed prior to treatment. The customer did not indicate any allergies, skin, or health conditions that would contraindicate waxing. However, in response to the question, "Have you had these treatments before?" Mrs. Crab indicated that she had not had any waxing previously.

Patricia said she forgot to warn Mrs. Crab about the potential for brief pain during any waxing procedure. The pain experienced by individuals receiving waxing varies widely, so it is our policy to speak candidly about the range of discomfort, particularly with a first-time client so that he or she can assess whether to proceed.

I visited Mrs. Crab at her home two days later, and when she came to the door (to slam it in my face), I did not see any evidence of damage to the eyelid or surrounding skin. The one eyebrow that had been waxed looked quite normal.

While the procedure was correctly delivered, neither esthetician had prepared the client for potential discomfort. We are, therefore, at fault in providing this service without duly warning Mrs. Crab about what she might experience. However, we have not created any physical problems.

Conclusion

Findings restated; call for action on recommendations, probably requested by reader.

In conclusion, it appears that the customer was warranted in being upset about her treatment in that we did not provide adequate warning before the treatment. It appears that we did not physically injure Mrs. Crab, nor were there any allergies or other conditions contraindicating waxing.

We need to respond quickly to manage the situation, thereby providing a positive resolution. If you have any further questions or require more information, please contact me at extension 222 or at 123-4567 at your convenience.

Recommendations

Listing recommendations with bullets helps reader to quickly see/act on them.

I suggest that you, as the owner of the spa, write and send a registered letter to Mrs. Crab acknowledging our fault. To save you time, I have attached a sample letter for your consideration to revise as you see fit.

I strongly suggest that we offer her a full refund, a personal apology from Patricia, and a voucher for another half-day spa package of her choice.

Suggestions for action probably requested by reader; don't include unless requested.

It is strongly recommended that we implement the following as soon as possible:

- a refresher course in waxing and waxing safety for all estheticians
- discussion about procedures, including potential discomfort involved, with all customers who are receiving a procedure for the first time
- a waiver for clients to sign before they receive a potentially uncomfortable procedure, indicating their understanding and acceptance of discomfort

FIGURE 8.3 Expense Report

MEMORANDUM

TO: Jacques Bean, Comptroller

FROM: Roger Cloutier, Manager, Human Resources

SUBJECT: Expense report: Department managers' retreat

DATE: August 1, 2014

States clearly/concisely topics of report, providing context for reader.

Introduction

The following is an expense report detailing the costs, services purchased, and the benefits of the department managers retreat held July 2–7, 2014.

As you know, the retreat was held at Jasper National Park, Alberta, for 20 of our department managers. Because there has been a major reorganization of Imagine Inc.'s departments over the past year, with new people at the helm, it was decided that a retreat would be a good way to build the new management team, create strong relationships, and strengthen commitment to the company's goals.

Provides background details on budget and items covered.

In terms of budget, $35,000 was allocated for participants' lodging, meals, activities, and airfare from Winnipeg.

Writer is persuading reader that expense was justified, with brief yet descriptive passages about activities.

Activities

During the retreat, department managers took part in a variety of workshops, including conflict resolution, customer service excellence, business teams, leadership skills development, and Myers-Briggs typology. A team of four consultants from Proof Positive Inc. facilitated these workshops.

Seminar learning was reinforced by interactive and experiential learning activities such as role-playing, group projects, and one-on-one professional coaching to help participants see their own blocks to success along with ways to overcome challenges in the work setting.

Following workshops, daily hikes to enjoy Jasper's natural beauty were organized as part of the focus on well-being and health in the workplace. Three healthy meals were provided daily, and evening activities were left to participants to organize.

By using persuasive diction, writer is persuading reader of benefits of expense.

Benefits

As you will see in the participant reports recently submitted to you, as well as in this report, the retreat was an overwhelming success for the participants.

Participants felt that the opportunity to spend time with colleagues in a relaxed environment was highly beneficial in resolving conflicts that had arisen and in helping individuals to recognize the talents and strengths of others in the organization.

In the last session of the week, participants quite spontaneously created a new think-tank model in which managers and employees of all departments can be proportionally represented to regularly meet and solve problems, do visioning, and otherwise improve morale and productivity. A description of and flow chart for this new group is attached for your reference.

Given our recent changes in structure, management, and customer base, participants agreed that this new decision-making and visioning model will create more "buy-in" from all employees and managers for the new direction of the company, increasing productivity.

Costs

The approved budget for the retreat was $35,000. We are currently $2,000 over budget for all costs related to the retreat, because we had not anticipated an increase in airport taxes and a small increase in airfares.

However, we are now in the last quarter of the year, and it appears that the budget for continuing education will be $3,000 more than is needed to cover already agreed-to employee courses for fall 2014. I suggest that we transfer $2,000 from the continuing education budget line to cover the extra expenses for the retreat, leaving a cushion of $1,000 for any unexpected costs.

Please see the attached spreadsheet for a detailed breakdown of airfare, transportation, workshop facilitation, accommodations, meals, supplies, and entertainment costs, with GST and applicable RST broken out for your convenience.

Conclusion

To conclude, the department managers' retreat was a great success for all involved, and it is anticipated that the company will benefit greatly from improved morale and commitment to working collaboratively, as well as from the new think-tank model.

Should you require any further information or documentation, please contact me at extension 444 or by email at rcloutier@imaginationincmail.com.

Recommendations

It is strongly recommended that at our next senior managers' meeting we discuss making this retreat an annual event in the lead-up to budget talks. If there is any financial leeway within our HR budget, it would also be beneficial to hold a similar retreat for employees on a rotating, department-by-department basis over the next three years.

Attachments

- Spreadsheet report of expenses

Please also refer to the file of participants' reports I have already submitted for further details on the benefits of this conference, if needed.

Costs listed after persuasive sections so that reader is more disposed to this information.

While budget shortfall is noted, a solution is immediately proposed to keep reader happy.

Conclusion not only restates main points but also mentions benefits to company—final persuasion.

Recommendations probably requested by reader; not always included in expense report.

Budget reports usually have attachments documenting items and expenses.

FIGURE 8.4 Evaluation Report

MEMORANDUM

TO: Richard Lamanna, Vice-President

FROM: Denise Smith, Chair, Social Committee

SUBJECT: Venue choices for holiday event

DATE: October 10, 2014

Introduction

In order to plan this year's company holiday dinner and dance, I have reviewed three suitable venues: the Carlyle Inn, Swingin' Sixties Bar and Grill, and the Palm Bistro.

The three venues have been evaluated on cost (to meet our budgetary restrictions), menu selection, dance facilities, and music options. I have contacted all three restaurants in person, meeting with managers to discuss our criteria for the event.

Background

Last year's seasonal dinner and dance was deemed a great success by all who attended, and many strongly encouraged the social committee to organize a similar event for this year. The beautifully presented, delicious meal options and the elegant ballroom particularly impressed attendees, as well as the big band music provided in house at the Gilded Swan.

Unfortunately, the Gilded Swan closed for renovations in September and is not scheduled to reopen until February. The social committee had to look for another venue that could offer a similarly high level of service and entertainment. After meeting to devise a short list, we decided that the Carlyle Inn, Swingin' Sixties Bar and Grill, and the Palm Bistro would be worth looking into, based on our initial research.

Methodology

As mentioned previously, I met with the managers of all three venues personally to discuss our specific needs and to make as unbiased a decision as possible, based on price (for 75 people), menu options, dance facilities, and music.

I also gathered menus and brochures from each location so that the social committee could see what was on offer.

Findings

The Carlyle Inn

The Carlyle Inn offers a three-course meal, a moderately sized dance floor (accommodates up to 100 people), and an in-house classical string quartet for music during dinner.

Indicates purpose of report and provides overview of background, scope, and methodology.

Reminds reader of previous year's events as background to frame information to be presented.

Briefly outlines steps taken to evaluate choices to reassure reader of appropriate methodology.

Writer lists criteria applied to each option for reader to understand following findings.

Options evaluated with similar number of facts and words to demonstrate lack of bias.

There is no band or musical entertainment to accompany dancing, so we would have to engage a DJ or another band, but the sound equipment is available free of charge for this purpose.

The meal options include a fish- or poultry-focused dinner, with a vegetarian option available upon request.

The cost of the event for 75 people at the Carlyle is $4,000 plus applicable taxes. However, there would be an additional cost for whatever musical accompaniment we engaged for the dance portion of the evening, so the final tally of costs would very much depend on that.

Swingin' Sixties Bar and Grill

Swingin' Sixties Bar and Grill offers a three-course meal and a dance floor that accommodates up to 50 people. They provide a DJ for dances (mostly '50s and '60s rockabilly music, which many in our company appreciate).

The meal options focus on classic diner fare and include a tossed salad, an entrée of choice (e.g., baked macaroni and cheese, Salisbury steak, fish and chips), and a traditional dessert selection (e.g., hot fudge sundae, pie Ã la mode, chocolate cake). Unfortunately, there are few provisions for special diets, and only one option for vegetarians (the macaroni and cheese dinner).

The cost of the event for 75 is a modest $3,500 plus applicable taxes.

The Palm Bistro

The Palm also offers a three-course meal but provides tapas with drinks purchased at the bar before dinner as well. The newly installed dance floor accommodates up to 100 people, and the restaurant has a retainer contract with the Joe Miller Trio, a well-known swing and jazz band quite popular with both younger and older crowds.

For a group our size, there would be a fixed menu, with a choice of chicken or beef, although special arrangements can be made for vegetarians or those on special diets. We would specify by November 1 how many meals of each type are required.

The cost for the event, including the Joe Miller Trio, is $4,000 plus applicable taxes.

Assessment

In terms of menu options, it appears that Swingin' Sixties has the most leeway for individual choices, but there are not many for vegetarians or those on special diets. Because many people who attended last year's event indicated they liked the more formal fare at the Gilded Swan, it is probably safe to assume that the menu at Swingin' Sixties would be too informal for our Christmas event.

Responds to reader's request for writer's evaluation of venues and a recommendation.

This and subsequent paragraphs are brief to highlight pros and cons of each venue.

(continued)

The Carlyle has healthier choices, but it is the opinion of the social committee that many people don't really like fish, so that leaves poultry as the only menu option (turkey or chicken).

The Palm's meal options, while fixed for all except special dietary needs, seem to be not only healthy but innovative in presentation. The free tapas available before dinner is also a classy touch.

Swingin' Sixties has a smaller dance floor, and rockabilly music really does require a lot of room to dance to, particularly in couples. This could pose a hazard.

The Carlyle's dance floor, while ample and beautifully appointed, lacks music for dancing. This additional cost is unknown, and we may have problems booking live or DJ music at this late date.

The Palm's dance floor, newly built (and used for a recent swing dance show), would be ideal for both the quieter and livelier jazz standards played by the Joe Miller Trio. Everyone attending could dance safely and comfortably.

Finally, price is also a consideration. Swingin' Sixties is the cheapest, the Carlyle the most expensive (considering the additional cost of music), and the Palm is middle of the road.

Recommendation made *after* pros/cons to reassure reader of thorough assessment before decision.

Considering its meal choices, music, and dance facilities, as well as cost, it appears that the Palm is the best choice for our dinner/dance.

Neatly restates writer's recommendation; asks for urgent action so reader clearly sees what to do.

Conclusion

In conclusion, the Palm is recommended as the venue for the event. The manager of the facility strongly recommends that we book as soon as possible because of the many events held at this time of year. He has told me he will tentatively reserve Friday, December 5, for us and hold the date until November 1.

Alternate choice recommended to reassure reader if the first venue is not available.

If for any reason we cannot book the Palm, the next choice would be the Carlyle.

Contact information for all three restaurants is attached. Should you require any further information, please contact me at extension 444 or email me at dsmith@finebooksellers.ca.

Want to see more examples?

For more examples of informal reports, see this text's website at www.oupcanada.com/Luchuk.

Checking Your Work

CONTENT EDITING

Once you have written your informal report, the first review you conduct will focus on whether you have answered all of the Starting Point questions in your writing. Did you meet what your reader needs, wants, and understands and the specific instructions for the report (purpose and scope)—or did you get off track?

What was your purpose in writing? Was it to provide information, and did you provide what was needed for your purpose and for the reader's understanding? Was it to give an assessment of a situation or item, and did you provide enough information to assure the reader that your assessment is correct? Was your report intended to persuade the reader of something—and did you achieve that goal?

If you feel that the report meets your reader's needs *and* your purpose for writing, then you can proceed with copy editing.

COPY EDITING

A detailed copy edit is essential once you are satisfied you have met content needs. You may be thinking that because the report is short, a quick editing job (or a run through the spell checker) will be enough.

Wrong! Because your report is so brief, it may be easier for the reader to spot spelling, grammar, or mechanical errors. Any of these errors can bring the authority of your writing into question.

Start with the spelling and grammar checker in your word-processing program. Then put the report aside for a while.

Print a copy, and read it carefully for grammar, spelling, punctuation, and mechanical errors or problems. Get someone else in your organization to review it for copy errors.

FORMATTING REVIEW

Now that you have the copy under control, address format issues:

- Make sure that you have used an easy-to-read font.

- Make sure that the report is in memo format and is less than three pages long.

- Ensure that the report is organized with appropriate headings and subheadings.

- Make sure that you have used different sizes of font and/or bolding or italics to indicate main or subheadings.

- Ensure that your report is left-justified, that paragraphs are flush left (not indented), and that there is a double space between paragraphs.

- Make sure that no headings or subheadings are stranded at the bottom of a page, with the text belonging to these on the next page.

Oral Presentation of the Informal Report

It's rare for the writer of an informal, memo-format report to be asked to make an oral presentation, but it is possible. Follow the rules suggested in Chapter 12. However, unlike a presentation to an external audience, this presentation does not have to be as formal, because your audience probably knows something about you and/or the topic of your report.

Preparing and Sending Your Report

Informal reports do not need to be printed in hard copy unless your supervisor or other reader requests it. Often, there is a sense of urgency in getting the report to someone, such as when you've been asked to write a quick or brief report on your recent business trip or an evaluation of three suppliers in time for a meeting or to meet a deadline. You do need to check which format is most appropriate for your particular business environment and situation, but in general it's usually okay to email the report. It can be sent in the body of the email, using the same headings as in the memo/non-memo format, or as a "stand alone" attachment, formatted in memo or non-memo format. You can keep the original on your computer and print a copy for your files for extra assurance that you won't lose the report (in case technology fails you!). In fact, if you do email your report, always be sure to have a backup or two in case the receiver doesn't get it.

You might also be asked to present your report at a meeting, as noted in the previous section on oral presentation. If so, think about setting it up on PowerPoint slides and handing out hard copies to everyone. They can then look at you and your slides as you talk and review the report itself later on.

Chapter Summary

In this chapter, you learned that there are different kinds of short reports, each intended to meet the needs of a specific business situation: expense reports, progress reports, evaluation reports, information reports, and incident reports. You were shown a detailed schema for each of them. You discovered that research is the key to success: considering the reader when selecting information to include, judging the amount of time available for research and writing, and keeping track of information sources so that they can be documented in the final report. You learned how to format the report, usually as a memo, and how to plan each document, organize its content in standard and logical sequences, and write it in a concise and readable style. You also learned how, if applicable, to transmit it electronically. Finally, you picked up some professional tips on how to effectively communicate the information in each type of report to a business readership.

CHECKLIST FOR informal reports

- ☐ Have you applied the Starting Point questions so that you know your reader(s) better?
- ☐ Are you clear about the message/information you need to communicate? The purpose and the desired outcome? (See Chapter 1 for help with this.)
- ☐ Do you understand the purpose of your report and whether it's an information, evaluation, progress, incident, or expense report?
- ☐ Have you included all the information the reader is looking for?
- ☐ If applicable, is your report persuasive enough to convince the reader of the merits of your information?
- ☐ If it is a budget report, have you included all of the financial information your reader requires? Have you included a spreadsheet budget, or report, if required?
- ☐ If it is a progress report, have you organized the information into summary, background, progress, future plans, conclusion, and evidence (if required) sections?
- ☐ If it is an incident report, have you organized the information into introduction, investigation, assessment, conclusion, and recommendations (if required) sections?
- ☐ If it is an incident report and you are not to evaluate or give your recommendations on the situation, have you been careful to include only the facts and not to give a judgment? Have you avoided laying blame?
- ☐ If it is an expense report, have you organized the information into introduction, activities (or items purchased), benefits, cost(s), conclusion, and recommendations sections?
- ☐ If it is an information or evaluation report, have you organized the information into introduction, overview (or background), methodology, findings, assessment, and conclusion sections?
- ☐ Are you quite sure that your report does not contain any grammar or spelling errors? Including the recipient's name and other names within the text?
- ☐ Is the report in the correct format as described in this chapter?

▬▬ SUGGESTIONS *for Further Reading*

Greenhall, M. (2010). *Report writing skills training course: How to write a report and executive summary, and plan, design and present your report.* Bury, UK: Universe of Learning.

Gulston, L. (2007). *Thomson Nelson guide to report writing.* (2nd ed.). Toronto, ON: Cengage/Nelson College Indigenous Publishing.

Kuiper, S. (2009). *Contemporary business report writing.* (4th ed.). Independence, KY: Cengage/Southwestern College Publishing.

Kupsh, J., and Rhodes, R. (2010). *Report writing.* Bloomington, IN: Xlibris Corporation.

Netzley, M., and Snow, C. (2001). *Guide to report writing.* Upper Saddle River, NJ: Prentice-Hall.

Roy, J.R. (2011). *Sharpen your report writing skills.* Berkeley Heights, NJ: Enslow.

■■ PRACTISING *What You Have Learned*

1. As a workplace health and wellness consultant for Zippy Tool Corporation, you have been asked by your supervisor, Martina Araujo, to research and write a proposal outlining the benefits of an in-house fitness facility for all employees at your London, Ontario, plant. Statistics from Human Resources indicate that many employees have missed work because of injuries on the job attributed to their being overweight or out of shape or to diabetes or heart disease.

    You have three months to complete this project and report your findings in a proposal to the CEO and other executives of the company. It's now one month into the proposal research and writing process, and you have completed the following tasks:

    - One of three planned employee focus groups. The findings from this first group indicate that 70 per cent would use an in-house fitness facility, 67 per cent would like the services of a personal trainer to help with individual fitness goals, and 81 per cent think they would stick to a fitness plan if they didn't have to make a special trip to go to the gym.
    - A plant-wide survey, with similar responses to similar questions.
    - Twenty-five of 135 employee fitness tests with the company nurse and a fitness assessor from the University of Western Ontario's medical school. So far, the results from these tests indicate an employee population in need of weight loss and strength training to help workers stay safe, healthy, and free of injuries.

    You still have to complete a feasibility study for the renovation of a large, seldom-used boardroom for the fitness facility, prepare financial projections for the renovations and cost of operating the program and facility, conduct two more focus groups, and administer the remainder of the employee fitness tests before your proposal is complete. You expect to have the proposal done on time.

    Write a report outlining your progress to date on the proposal.

2. The proposal for the fitness facility has been accepted by upper management, and you have been asked to supervise the renovations and construction work to convert the old boardroom into an in-house fitness facility. The entire project has been scheduled to take place between May and August so that the facility will be ready when employees return after their summer holidays. It is now the beginning of July, and you have been asked for a progress report on the project. Your report needs to tell your supervisor, Martina Araujo, Senior Human Resources Manager, about the progress of the renovations, how much of the $30,000 budget has been used to date, and whether the project will be completed in time for September 1.

    So far, the project is over-budget, and because of a building trades strike in June, construction is two weeks behind. You need to tell Ms Araujo, but remember that you also need to tell her what is being done to resolve the situation. Be sure to address the concerns she will have about the project.

3. You are also to assess three fitness trainers in your community who can provide employees with personalized training plans incorporating use of the new gym facilities as well as other activities such as running, walking, or swimming, along with some fitness classes. You are to compare these three trainers on the following criteria:

    - cost to provide individualized training programs (one per year per employee) for 100 employees;

- how much they will charge to provide 10 hours of group training sessions per week in various fitness activities (over 50 weeks);
- their qualifications and experience.

Write an evaluation report for Ms Araujo, evaluating the three trainers on the criteria noted above. Make a recommendation about which trainer would be most appropriate, and explain why you made that choice.

4. Ms Araujo has to make the final decision on which equipment to buy for the gym, so she has asked you to obtain quotations from three fitness equipment supply companies for 10 complete sets of free weights, 10 weight benches, two universal weight-training machines, 10 inflatable fitness balls, and 10 yoga mats.

Write an information report for Ms Araujo, outlining the quotations from each company and stating whether each of them can provide all of the items (some do not stock all of them). The bottom line is that she is trying to get equipment for as low a cost as possible, but the process also has to be convenient. She doesn't want to have to run around from one distributor to the next to obtain items for the gym, so the company that can provide all or most of these items at a reasonable price is probably the one she will go with.

However, remember that you are merely providing information about each supplier—what they can provide (or not) and the price. You are *not* to give your opinion or a recommendation, because your supervisor will make the final decision herself, based on your information.

5. Unfortunately, there has been an accident at the worksite (where the gym is being built). On July 13, one of the carpenters discharged a nail gun and hit one of the other workers in the forehead. You have been asked by Ms Araujo to investigate the accident, report on what has been done to deal with the situation, determine the cause of or blame for the incident, and, finally, provide recommendations aimed at ensuring that no accidents like this one happen on the project in the future.

6. The four-month (May to August) gym project has been completed, and you now have to file a final budget report. Your original budget (for the renovations only, not the equipment or staff) was set at $30,000. As mentioned previously, the project was over-budget in July. You may have resolved the issue by finding cost savings somewhere or perhaps not. Report to your supervisor on the following:

- labour cost (broken down by hourly rate of pay and number of hours worked);
- any overtime charges;
- cost of materials (e.g., lumber, flooring, paint);
- amount over or under budget.

Of course, if you are over-budget, you will want to persuade your supervisor of the merits of the extra cost so that she is satisfied that you managed the project successfully and well. If you are under-budget, she will no doubt be very pleased (as will the financial controller of the company). Be sure to highlight how the savings were achieved; you might even make a suggestion about using savings for additional equipment you think would be a good choice for the new gym.

7. It's been six months since the fitness centre opened, and Ms Araujo would like a progress report on the use of the facility to date, as well as employee fitness levels.

Since its opening, 83 per cent of the employees have used the facility at least twice a week, 75 per cent of them have met with the fitness trainer for a customized fitness and health plan, and 87 per cent attended a series of nutrition seminars held by the company nurse and the City of London Health Unit to learn more about sensible diet and weight loss strategies. Follow-up fitness tests at three months on the people who were coached weekly by the fitness trainer (75 per cent of employees) indicate a 25 to 40 per cent increase in muscle mass and strength, as well as an average weight loss of seven to 12 pounds.

Overall, the results are encouraging, and Human Resources reports a 32 per cent decrease in accidents attributable to poor fitness and a whopping 35 per cent decrease in missed days due to illness.

8. It's now one year since the fitness centre opened, and the CEO of the company, James Ready, would like a first-year evaluation report of the facility. Combining all of the information in the previous questions and adding any pertinent details you think would make the evaluation report persuasive and positive, write the report for Mr. Ready and his senior executives. They need this report to help them decide whether to increase funding for the centre, thereby allowing new services to be added, or to keep funding at the same level for the second year of operation.

CHAPTER 9

Formal Reports

LEARNING OBJECTIVES

In this chapter, you will learn:

- The differences between formal and informal reports

- When to write a formal report rather than an informal report

- How to prepare for a formal report with research and organization of information

- What content is needed to provide the level of information expected in a formal report

- How to organize information into an appropriate format

- How to edit and review your formal report to ensure that it meets your readers' needs and your reasons for writing

ESSENTIAL EMPLOYABILITY SKILLS

2000+ Employability Skills The Conference Board of Canada has identified certain essential employability skills (EES) as benchmarks for performance in the workplace. You will learn the following EES skills in this chapter:

THINK AND SOLVE PROBLEMS

- Can assess situations and identify problems
- Can seek different points of view and evaluate them based on facts
- Can recognize the human, interpersonal, technical, scientific, and mathematical dimensions of a problem
- Can identify the root cause of a problem

- Can be creative and innovative in exploring possible solutions
- Can evaluate solutions to make recommendations and decisions

COMMUNICATE

- Can read and understand information presented in a variety of forms (e.g., words, graphs, charts, diagrams)
- Can write and speak so others pay attention and understand
- Can listen and ask questions to understand and appreciate the points of view of others

Formal Reports: A Case Study

Greg Chatterton, cytologist and unit manager at MLS Labs Inc., was asked 12 months ago to undertake a pilot project for the company to increase productivity in the cytology labs in the entire Canadian operation (75 in total). MLS is thinking about increasing staffing and shifts in order to meet an increased demand from hospitals and clinics for faster test results. Currently, once a clinic or hospital sends slides, blood, or other cellular samples to the nearest regional lab, results are returned within a week at best—and at worst, up to a month later. The Canadian Medical Association has asked MLS and other testing companies to consider adding more capacity so that tests can be processed faster.

The pilot project included the following:

- in the first two months, creation of a formal information report on operations, staffing, and the finances/budget of each lab to determine current and historical productivity levels;

- implementation of one additional shift per day (a late-afternoon or night shift, depending on each lab's facilities and staffing) over an eight-month period and hiring of additional, contract cytologists as needed in each location;

- concurrent research into best practices of North American and European testing companies and their facilities to provide faster results while maintaining quality assurance.

It is now the end of the pilot project and reporting period, and Greg is required to write a final, formal report to evaluate the entire project and make recommendations. He produced a formal information report on each lab's status at the beginning of the pilot project, has documented changes made at each lab to implement the additional shift (including costs), and has gathered information on best productivity practices of other labs. He has asked each lab for a report that evaluates the success of the additional shift in improving turnaround times for testing and assesses whether the additional expense has improved the lab's profit.

1. Given all of the elements the company wants Greg to report on, how should he organize this final evaluation report with headings and subheadings?

2. What tone should Greg use in his writing? Should it be informal, moderately informal, or formal? Why?

3. What do you think the company is looking for in Greg's report? What do they hope to learn? What is at stake for the company in this project and final report?

Before You Begin . . .

Like their informal cousins, formal reports also encompass progress, incident, expense, information, and evaluation report types. (For a description of these report types, see Chapter 8.)

TABLE 9.1	Differences between Informal and Formal Reports	
	INFORMAL	**FORMAL**
Reader	Internal	External or someone in authority
Table of contents	Not needed	Essential
Report title	In a memo subject line	On a title page
Summary	Depends on report type	Usually an executive summary
Transmittal page	None	Covering letter (external)/memo (internal)
Length	Short, with sections	Long (3 pages +), with sections and subsections

FORMAL REPORTS VS. INFORMAL REPORTS

Informal reports, as you now know, are written for an internal audience—readers within your own organization or business. They are written in a less formal tone because generally the people you are writing for know you and/or know the topic you are writing about. Because informal reports are usually solicited by someone in your organization, less explanation or fewer details are needed; you only include what the reader really needs to know (and you would consult the answers to your Starting Point questions to be sure).

Informal reports are never sent to an external reader and are always written in a memo format (if they are less than three pages long). **Formal reports** are used for an external audience—people outside of your organization—or for an internal audience if the topic is very detailed or serious in nature, covers a long period of time, has some external readers associated with it, or requires a lot of research. Formal reports are written in a more formal tone than informal reports.

ORGANIZING MORE DETAILS IN A FORMAL REPORT

In terms of length, formal reports are at least three pages in length. They are never put into memo format, because this format is too informal for the information contained—and of course, you know by now that you never send a memo to anyone outside of your organization, right?

Formal reports require more parts within their format. Besides the basic informal report template, formal reports need to have a covering letter to introduce the report (attached to the front of your report with a paper clip), a title page, a table of contents, and a summary (or executive summary), which sums up the entire report. (The summary is written last and is attached to the front of the formal report on a separate sheet of paper.)

The **formal report's format** then generally follows the format for progress, incident, expense, information, or evaluation reports. What's different about a formal report is that in the case of longer ones, you need to organize the information under subheadings as well as main headings so that the reader does not become lost in all the additional detail.

Why do you have to include so much information and detail if there is a risk of confusing or overwhelming the reader? Formal reports are more often read not only by the soliciting reader(s) or assumed primary receivers but also by secondary readers. You generally know very little about secondary readers, so you have to assume that they have even less expertise or understanding of the contents of your report. You must write as if you were reporting to someone with very little understanding of your topic(s). On the other hand, because formal reports are most often solicited by specific readers, your first concern is to write for the needs of those primary readers. In order to do so, apply the Starting Point questions to your readers. This will help you to determine what they may or may not know about your topic; however, if the primary readers know the subject better than potential secondary readers, include more background information on the subject matter than you would just for the former.

If the report has to cover a lot of ground or will be particularly detailed, you will need to organize all the details under subheadings to keep the reader moving through the report.

NEVER ASSUME YOUR READER KNOWS ANYTHING!

Since the report is probably going to an external reader, it's hard to know what the reader knows about your report's topic or background information. Applying the Starting Point questions in researching the external reader before you write will help. Once you determine (as best you can) the external reader's knowledge or understanding of the report topic, you will write with more or less detail and explanation as needed to communicate effectively with that reader.

While we are on this topic, it's important to note that a formal report should not be wordy or rambling—or anything like an essay. *Every* business report must be as clear, concise, and brief as possible, even if you have a lot of ground to cover in terms of information and detail. Keep paragraphs short, and make every word you use count.

In the end, writing formal reports requires practice. As you write more of these, your style and formatting skills will improve, as well as your discernment in learning and meeting the needs of the reader and the desired outcome of the report.

Idiom Alert

no-brainer – Something that is obvious.

Reader's Digest condensed version – Information reduced to its most important points (articles in *Reader's Digest* magazine are often condensed versions of longer articles published elsewhere).

Your Starting Point

As with any other form of business writing or oral presentation, you need to know as much as possible about the audience for your communication, and you need to know why you are writing the report.

Begin by reviewing the Starting Point questions in Chapter 1, and answer these questions first before you start to collect information for your formal report. This will save you time, hassle, and certainly misunderstanding on the part of your readers as they read your report.

Creating the Written Product: How to Do It

PREPARING TO WRITE

Research

Doing detailed research is essential when it comes to creating a professional formal report. Your credibility will be on the line as the reader scrutinizes your report for details on the topic or project, so you will need to consult as many sources as possible to show the reader that you have considered the topic or project from all angles.

Preparing the ingredients for a quality report

Consider research for a formal report this way: as though you were preparing a gourmet dinner for a food critic—someone you know by reputation but not personally. The ingredients must be fresh, innovative, and like nothing else the critic has ever tasted. If you use bland, generic, or stale ingredients, the dinner will not make the impression you want. In fact, the food critic may never come back to your restaurant—why eat at your establishment when there are otherwise so many excellent restaurants in the city?

On the other hand, research for an *informal* report is like preparing an informal dinner—while you want the ingredients to be fresh (no mould!) and you want to make sure that everyone has enough to eat, you would not comb farmers' markets and specialty food shops for the ultimate ingredients. An informal report is rather like preparing a casserole for your family—you don't have to wow them every night of the week. They know you well, they're hungry, and they really do like tuna and macaroni with crumbled potato chips on top!

Attention to detail is especially important when you are writing an incident or evaluative report, because the reader will want to know that you have considered all the details and angles before you arrived at your conclusion or recommendation. As for an information report, well, that's a no-brainer: because it's an informational report, you will need to provide as much information as time and research sources allow.

Too many information ingredients can confuse

Being thorough equals being taken seriously. However, you don't want to confuse people! To refer back to the analogy of the food critic, too many ingredients in a special entrée may actually ruin the dish. It's the quality (and, obviously, a certain degree of variety) that really counts when it comes to research sources for your report.

The Internet can be an excellent source of information for formal reports, but don't discount going to the library, where you will be able to consult industry-specific databases as well as trade or business journals that could be relevant to your project.

Just because your sources appear to be literate, credible, or intellectual doesn't mean they are suitable for your report—or your reader. While many sources that seem brilliant may work for a university or higher academic essay or thesis, the reverse is true for a business report. If you use too many sources that your reader will find difficult to understand or appreciate, you could come across as trying to hide something, or, at the very least, you will seem less than credible.

Using the Starting Point questions will help you to determine what kind of information your readers need and will understand and/or appreciate.

Work backward to plan ahead

As when writing an informal report, work backward from the deadline for delivery of the report to the reader, and think realistically about how much time you will need to do the kind of careful research that a formal report requires. When planning an excellent gourmet meal, the chef can go far afield to obtain just the right ingredients and may have to do some research to find out where to buy an elusive element of a recipe. The chef doesn't leave it to the last minute, because the supplier of a certain ingredient might have run out and another source must then be found, or an ingredient that the chef thought would be a good substitute might turn out to be less than wonderful.

Research sources include your own observations, telephone and email inquiries, interviews, company records, libraries, and, of course, the Internet. In some cases, you can find valuable information at the external company or organization that the report is being prepared for.

PREPARING FOR CITATIONS

Here's where we depart from the gourmet dinner analogy. While the chef may keep various ingredients and how they were combined a secret, you will share your information sources with your reader to prove that your formal report's findings, information, or assessment is backed by solid facts and figures the reader can understand and appreciate.

As suggested for other reports and proposals, make sure you write down any and all information about a source as soon as you consult it. Keep this information in a notebook or other secure place so that if you decide to use the source in your writing, you have all the details close at hand for writing simple in-text citations and a bibliography or works-cited page as required. Your readers may also want to do more research on their own using your sources. See Appendix B of this book for more guidance.

ORGANIZING INFORMATION AND WRITING: FORMAT

To get started with writing a formal report, decide first why you are writing the report. This determines which type of report you are writing—progress, expense, incident, information, or evaluation. It may well be that your formal report combines a couple of these types, so you may have to improvise. In this case, you would look at the formats for each type of report and hybridize them, such as the introduction/background when combining aspects of an evaluation and progress report.

No matter what kind of formal report you are preparing, applying a numbering system to your sections is an accepted protocol for organizing information into easily read and followed sections.

If you use subheadings as well as main headings, number them first with the number of the main section they fall under, followed by a period and the number that corresponds to the subheading's placement within the main section (e.g., in the Figure 9.5 example of a progress report, 2.3 identifies subsection 3 in main section 2).

Covering letter

A covering letter is required for formal reports in order to introduce the report and provide some of its most important highlights. The trick is to avoid giving all the details yet give enough information so that the reader will want to read at least the summary, if not the report itself. Follow business letter format as described in Chapter 3. Note that the covering letter is not bound in the report; instead, it should be attached to the front cover of the report with a paper clip.

Title page

The title page comes at the very beginning of your report. It should include the title of your report, centred, bolded, and in a larger font so that it stands out from the rest of the information. Below that, in a much smaller font, centre and type the date (month and year). At the bottom centre, type your name, company name, and full address (see Figure 9.1).

FIGURE 9.1 **Sample Title Page for Formal Report**

SWIFT CURRENT FOOD BANK PILOT PROJECT

Progress Report (January–June 2014)

June 30, 2014

Navid Dhaliwal
Food Insecurity Program Consultant
Swift Current Regional Health Department
Swift Current, SK S1A 2W2
123 Main Street

Summary

Your summary is on a separate page and comes just before your introduction. You shouldn't write it until you have finished the entire report, because it is a summary of all that you have written. When you are writing for a business reader, it's called an executive summary—a brief synopsis of what you are communicating in the report, intended for someone who may not have a lot of time to read the entire report.

To write the summary, go through your entire report, and make some point-form notes for each section. Use these notes to write a very brief statement about the contents of each section, but don't use subheadings, since they will appear in your actual report. The summary is merely a "*Reader's Digest* condensed version" of the entire report.

Table of contents

The table of contents is a professional means of organization that will be welcomed by your readers, because it enables them to go directly to the sections that are of most interest to them (see Figure 9.2).

Introduction

As noted in Chapter 8, the introduction outlines the purpose, scope, any applicable timelines, and more or less background, depending on the purpose of the report.

In progress reports, the background section functions as the introduction but focuses a lot more on background, since it is your starting point for explaining progress on a project to date. The introduction section of an information or evaluation report has three components: the purpose and objective (what you hope to assess and possibly draw a conclusion about); an overview section describing the situation, product, or service you are investigating; and a methodology section describing sources of information and how you used them.

Body of report

The information contained in the body of the report depends on the type of report you are writing. In a progress report, the body includes planned work, work completed, challenges, schedule, and future plans. In an incident report, this section would give details of the investigation, using relevant subheadings to organize the information. The body of an expense report includes details of activities, benefits, and costs. In an information or evaluation report, it details your findings, divided into subsections as necessary. Refer to the outlines for each type of report in Chapter 8 for more details on organizing your headings and subheadings so that you can guide your readers through the information effectively.

Because of their greater length and readers' need for a greater amount of information, formal reports often require more subsections within the main sections than informal reports do. These subheadings need to be relevant to the information you are reporting on or assessing for the reader. Go back to your Starting Point questions: review what the reader really needs from you in this report, and assess how much he or she knows about the topic. This should give you some idea of how to present the information so that he or she can digest it.

If the reader knows little about the topic, you should probably err on the side of more information—but it should be explained as simply as possible so that it can be

FIGURE 9.2 Sample Table of Contents

T of C required on multi-page report to guide reader through text.

Note that Summary page is not numbered.

Table of Contents

Summary

1.0	**Introduction**	1
2.0	**Discussion**	2
	2.1 Subheading 1	3
	2.2 Subheading 2	4
	2.3 Subheading 3	5
	2.4 Subheading 4	6
3.0	**Conclusion**	7
4.0	**Recommendations**	8
Appendix		9

The pages of the appendix section may or may not be numbered.

easily understood. This means dividing it into a number of subsections, using appropriate subheadings to guide the reader through the information.

Especially if the report addresses a very complex project or body of information, it's a good idea to break it down into many subsections so that you avoid large blocks of text that the reader would find hard to wade through.

Conclusion

In the conclusion, you wrap up all of the pieces in a neat package. It incorporates the main points of the introduction and the main points of the report's body (from the point of view of the reader!) and presents a concluding statement to close the report.

Recommendations

A **recommendations** section usually appears only in incident, expense, or evaluation reports. However, if the report was solicited, the person who requested it may ask you to provide recommendations based on your findings, research, or information.

Even if the report was not solicited—for example, you are writing it to show a supervisor that you are being thorough, responsible, and proactive—you may choose to add a recommendations section to further reinforce the purpose of your writing. In other words, a recommendations section may be the added value you give it to impress the reader of an unsolicited report.

Refer to the notes about recommendations sections in Chapter 8 for guidance on how you would structure this section for both a solicited and an unsolicited formal report.

FIGURE 9.3 Sample Annotated Bibliography

ANNOTATED BIBLIOGRAPHY

Osborne, C. (2002). *Dealing with difficult people*. **New York, NY: DK Publishing.**
Dealing with Difficult People offers practical strategies for assessing and analyzing the causes of conflict with difficult people, better communication with these individuals, and methods for resolving issues. I consulted this small book first when I started my research into customer service manuals as a starting point for understanding some of the challenges with customers your company might face. It's a good, quick study of customer service problem resolution that could be inexpensively purchased and put into the hands of all staff who work directly with the public.

Performance Research Associates. (2011). *Delivering knock your socks off service.* **New York, NY: American Management Association (AMACOM).**
This book is an entertaining and highly accessible read that I strongly recommend for all members of your sales and customer service teams. I have used many of the concepts in this book as background for the Customer Service Plan and suggest that your company purchase copies of the book for all of those working with your customers. It covers the background to customer service, the "how-tos" of customer service, problem-solving, and finally, how to bring out the best in oneself and others in the service or sales role.

Thaler, L.K., and Koval, R. 2006. *The power of nice: How to conquer the business world with kindness.* **New York, NY: Doubleday.**
The Power of Nice, another small and easily read book, explains how individuals and businesses can improve their relationships with others by simply being "nice." Of particular interest to the Customer Service Plan project, the book presents a very user-friendly strategy for providing excellent customer service without being a doormat—a win-win situation. I consulted this book for a more philosophical approach to working with clients in a positive way. While this is an excellent book for my purposes, I think it would be considered a bit too "Pollyanna-ish" for general use among your sales staff. However, I strongly suggest that we work some of the key points of this book into the training I will provide to your staff when the Customer Service Plan is ready for implementation.

Annotated bibliography or works-cited page (optional)

Depending on the expressed needs of your reader(s) or your own requirements (e.g., to impress a reader of an unsolicited report), you may include an **annotated bibliography** or works-cited section.

As mentioned elsewhere in this text, you must always let the reader know when you have used information or a direct quotation from another source within the body of the text. That way, you cannot be accused of using someone else's work as your own, and you are citing additional sources of information you used that the reader may wish to consult.

Your instructor or professor should be able to help you with his or her preferred form of works-cited or references page. Figure 9.3 is a model for an annotated bibliography (intended for a progress report on the development of a customer service plan for a medium-sized business).

An annotated bibliography differs from a bibliography or works-cited page in that it not only presents the identifying details (the author, publisher, and so on) for each source but also includes a brief description of what the source is about, information it contains, and how you used the information in your report. The annotations not only indicate to your readers that you did thorough research and consulted a variety of information sources but also will help them in any further research or investigation they may do on their own.

Refer back to your Starting Point questions to see what your readers know about the topic of your report and what they are seeking in terms of information. This will help you to decide what information to include in your annotation for each source.

The annotated bibliography is presented on a separate page, after the conclusion (and recommendations, where applicable). (In some cases, particularly with regard to technical reports, the bibliography comes after the summary.)

Appendix (optional)

The **appendix** section is an add-on section of graphics, maps, charts, and so on, that are too large or wordy to embed in your report. However, every single item in your appendix section needs to *count*—in other words, don't just attach items that you think look good or are remotely interesting. If these items don't highlight what you've written to reinforce your information, points, or evaluation, then don't include them.

You must *always* refer to the items you include in the appendices within the text of your report so that the reader will understand how they are relevant to the report contents. For example, "For further details on the widget machine, please see the Widget Machine Guide brochure in Appendix A." Otherwise, you risk confusing your reader, who may not be able to figure out what the attachments are for—and annoying the reader defeats the purpose of the report, right?

Sample Documents

FIGURE 9.4 **Covering Letter for Progress Report**

July 30, 2014

Frost Professional Consultants
145 Grant Avenue
Calgary, AB A1A 2B2

RE: Progress report, ABC Customer Service Plan and training

Dear Mr. James:

Letter and paragraphs following briefly written to keep the reader moving through text.

We are pleased to present this mid-project report on the progress of ABC's Customer Service Plan and training project.

Provides background on project, to remind/inform reader of context.

As you know, we were contracted to provide research, development, writing, editing, and printing services for your company's new Customer Service Plan manuals and to plan and facilitate customer service training incorporating the new manual by the end of August 2014.

Delays noted after other information to keep reader happy about overall progress.

We are delighted to report that this project is on schedule, despite some small delays in aspects of implementation; further, we are operating well within budget. We are confident that the entire project (with the exception of evaluation) will be completed by the end of August, as agreed. Evaluation will take place in early September.

Providing contact information is essential for any reader follow-up.

Should you require any further information or have any questions about this report or the project itself, please contact me at your convenience at 123-4567.

Yours truly is appropriate closing for business letter.

Yours truly,

Joanne Frost
President, Frost Professional Consultants

FIGURE 9.5 Formal Progress Report

ABC CORPORATION
CUSTOMER SERVICE PLAN

Centre the title of the report at the top of the page.

Frost Professional Consultants
345 King Street
Moncton, NB T4H 5U6
fpc@fpc.ca
www.fpc.ca

Centre the writer/preparing organization's name and address at bottom of page; supplying a URL and/or email optional.

(continued)

Table of Contents

Summary

On June 5, 2014, ABC Corporation (ABC) contracted Frost Professional Consultants (FPC) to provide research, writing, editing, design, and printing services for a customized Customer Service Plan (CSP) for use by ABC's sales and service teams. As part of this project, FPC agreed to provide customer service training to ABC's sales and service staff and managers incorporating the new Customer Service Plan. This training is to take place at the end of August.

To date (July 30), all timelines for completion of research, preparation of an initial draft, and consultation with management on any changes to the content of the plan have been met. These tasks have been fully completed, despite a small delay in obtaining management feedback on the first draft. In order to keep the project on time, we contracted another writer to work with our editor at no additional cost to ABC, thus keeping within the agreed-upon budget for the project.

Still to be completed are the final reviews of text by all designated managers and then final edits and revisions of the text, graphic design, and printing of the Customer Service Plan. The customer service training sessions, based on the new CSP, will be held shortly thereafter with sales and service staff and managers.

While a possible delay is threatened in printing the Customer Service Plan because of a strike, we have set an alternative plan to work with another printer to complete this task on time. With this in mind, and given our work flow to date, we anticipate no further delays or challenges to completing all aspects of the project up to the training by the end of August. Evaluation is scheduled for the week after Labour Day weekend, with a final evaluation report to be completed and distributed to senior management by September 30, 2014.

Summarizes in same order as report so that reader quickly identifies purpose and relevant points.

1

(continued)

Section provides rationale/——•
context for report.

1.0 Background

As requested by the client, ABC Corporation (ABC), the following report represents progress made to date on the development of a Customer Service Plan (CSP) by Frost Professional Consultants (FPC).

FPC was contracted by ABC at the beginning of June 2014 to provide research into and development of a Customer Service Plan appropriate to the needs of ABC and its sales and frontline customer service staff. ABC has never had such a plan, but because of a recent downturn in sales, it was decided by senior management that customer service needed to be improved. Further, some recent serious customer service complaints had been received by the Manager of Customer Service, which took some major effort by senior staff to resolve.

One of the complaints involved a sales representative not providing accurate costing of a service to a valued customer, with the result that the customer refused to pay the extra costs not addressed in the quotation for service. The sales rep argued with the customer about the quotation and insisted that the customer had been informed of the increased cost. However, the customer equally insisted that he was not informed and not only refused to pay the additional cost but advised the president of ABC that he would go out of his way to tell many other key customers to switch to ABC's competition in future.

The company had to take a loss on this contract in order to keep the customer's business and prevent loss of many other key customers. While a couple of staff were fired as a consequence, clearly the increasing frequency of customer complaints across the company's operations indicated a need for further investigation into how service was being delivered to regular and new customers alike.

Senior management contracted a major assessment of customer service using a third-party, "secret customer" service. The "secret customer" uncovered many failings in service standards that could cause further problems with clients or potential clients in future, particularly in reference to problem-solving. Management determined that the entire team (including department managers) should undergo a comprehensive training program to address interpersonal skills and customer service attitudes.

A plan that particularly addressed the interpersonal skills required of all staff in reference to customers and colleagues alike, as well as company-wide customer service standards, was to be the first step of the project. The second, equally important step of customer service training in all departments (but particularly the sales and service teams), integrating the new plan as part of the training process, was to follow shortly after senior management endorsed the plan, The entire project was to be completed and delivered by the last week of August 2014 so that staff would be ready for the peak sales season between September and December.

2.0 Progress

2.1 Planned Work

As noted previously, we were requested to provide a complete, customized Customer Service Plan and deliver training to the appropriate staff at the end of August 2014.

Internally, we decided to research and prepare the plan by July 15, with the remaining month focused on printing and disseminating the plan while planning for and organizing the training for ABC's staff. It was expected that 100 copies of the plan would be printed and Cerlox-bound for each member of the sales and service staff, with an additional 25 to be distributed to managers and some kept in reserve for any new hires.

In consultation with ABC's sales and customer service managers, we decided to have their input on the interim draft before we completed it and sent it to the printers.

The target week for training would be the last week of August, just prior to the Labour Day weekend; in order to make the training as pleasant and motivating as possible, it would be held at the Delta Chelsea hotel and would include spa services, individualized career development planning, and a multicultural pub night.

2.2 Work Completed

Section explains what's been completed to date.

To date (July 30), we have completed research into best practices for customer service, reviewed a wide range of other companies' customer service plans, obtained a copy of ABC's nearest competitor's CSP for reference, and correlated these findings to the specific needs of ABC's sales and service teams—as well as to ABC's 2011–12 business plan.

3

(continued)

Before writing the plan, we reviewed the findings with the managers of the sales and service teams to obtain their thoughts and insights on how they might be applied to ABC's staff and the overall goals of the company. Once we obtained this feedback, we began work on the interim draft (started June 21), completed writing, and then sent the draft back to these managers as well as the CEO for any additional changes, editorial direction, or comment.

There was a delay in receiving the responses to the draft from the CEO, who was away on vacation between June 19 and 27. However, all relevant managers did respond, and we have now incorporated all feedback into the final draft of the CSP. On July 21, it was sent to our copy editor for careful editing.

2.3 Challenges

As mentioned previously, we did experience a delay in receiving feedback from ABC's CEO, John Jones, but we managed to keep the project on agreed-to timelines by subcontracting an additional writer to work with our editor to incorporate all of the needed changes. (This is at no additional cost to ABC.)

Unfortunately, a possible strike at Premier Printing's main facility may delay the publication of the CSP. Because the CSPs need to be produced in time for the training, if the strike does occur and lasts longer than a week, we may have to go with Zippy Print, our second choice for printing. Zippy costs approximately 5 per cent more than Premier, but we are confident they can complete the job even on a rush basis if need be. Every effort will be made to inform ABC's management about a delay if one is imminent, and no printing with Zippy will go forward unless we have the express permission of ABC's CEO.

2.4 Schedule

As of July 30, we are on schedule in terms of the research, consultation, and preparation of drafts phases of the CSP project, despite a small delay as noted previously. Even in light of a possible strike at Premier Printing, we are confident that we can still meet the publication deadline with a week to spare before the CSP training begins.

Remaining work is expected to meet agreed-upon timelines even in the event of a strike at the printer.

Delay briefly noted after positive news, and resolution immediately following to reassure reader.

Challenges noted after "good news" so reader is comfortable problems being managed.

Delay noted but also solution—and reader will be happy—"at no additional cost."

Possible problem noted but also solution to keep reader confident in progress.

If contingency plan necessary, reader is reassured project team will inform decision-makers.

Note sentence starts with good news, then resolution of the bad news (delay).

Writer again notes potential problem but also solution to mitigate challenge for reader.

3.0 Future Plans

The following tasks are still to be completed on the Customer Service Plan project:

- Final content and copy edits by appropriate, designated managers incorporating their last-minute changes to the content
- Graphic design and prepress preparation
- Printing and binding of 100 copies
- Distribution of the CSPs to all sales and service staff, as well as managers
- Planning of customer service training, which will incorporate the new CSP
- Delivery of the training to all sales and service staff in the last week of August
- Evaluation of training by staff and managers

The entire project up to the delivery of training is expected to be completed, as agreed, just before the Labour Day weekend. The evaluation questionnaires will be distributed to training participants in the first week after the holiday, to be collected and put into a final evaluation report by September 30, 2011.

4.0 Conclusion

ABC Corporation's Customer Service Plan is nearing completion in the final phases of editing, design, and printing. Despite a possible strike at the printers, we are confident that we can contract another printer to provide service if this occurs, keeping the entire project on time. The CSPs will be delivered to all appropriate staff at ABC well in advance of their customer service training at the end of August.

> Work to be completed written in point form for easier reading and follow-up.

> Neatly restates introduction, progress, work to be done, and challenge/resolution.

5

Want to see more examples?

For more examples of formal reports, see this text's website at www.oup.com/Luchuk.

Checking Your Work

CONTENT EDITING, COPY EDITING, AND FORMATTING REVIEW

Return to Chapters 1 and 4, and review the content editing, copy editing, and formatting guidelines to ensure that you have met the requirements for your report. There are some special instructions for formal reports, however, that you need to take into account when preparing your final printed document.

FINAL PREPARATION OF THE FORMAL REPORT

Because it is a *formal* report, your final copy should be professionally presented to make the best possible impression. This is particularly important if your report is intended for an external audience (not for readers within your company or organization). These readers may not know you well (or at all), and the report is representing you and your level of professionalism. It's also particularly important if your formal report is unsolicited, because you want to make a very strong first impression with the physical presentation of the report.

First, choose a paper that is slightly heavier in weight than or in a texture different from the paper you use for printing routine materials. For your colour, choose a conservative but classy off-white or light cream colour.

In terms of the print colour, black is the standard. Dark brown (almost black) on cream paper can look classy as well. However, when in doubt, go with black.

You should print your report at home only if you have a laser printer, because inkjet printers do not always produce great results, especially on high-quality paper. One option is to take it to the nearest printer or business supply store and have it professionally printed on the paper of your choice. It's a good idea to have a dark, sober-looking cover that will cover your title page. If you choose this option, attach a label to the front cover, stating the title of the report; on the other hand, some cover stock has a small window through which the report's title and date can be seen (the title information on your title page would have to line up with the window on the cover).

The most appropriate colours to consider for your cover are blue, burgundy, green, grey, brown, or black. Colour psychology has shown that these colours give the impression of dependability, stability, trustworthiness, and high intellect—and you want to impress upon your readers that you have all of these qualities and more!

If your actual title page will be your cover, you should choose a lighter colour, such as beige, cream, light grey, or light blue so that the print is easy to read.

Finally, there is the question of binding and other types of covers. If your report is fairly short, and particularly if you have separate attachments (such as a resumé or relevant supporting materials), a two-pocket portfolio cover would suffice. Again, dark colours are best. Attach a label on the front (title, date), but do not apply any logos or designs other than a company logo. Place your report in the right pocket, because this is where the reader's eye will travel first when he or she is opening it. Then place your business card in any card slots on the pockets.

If your report is more lengthy, you might consider Cerlox binding. Cerlox is the plastic, semi-ring binding used for more weighty reports or informally published books. Most copy centres, business supply stores, and printing houses can apply this kind of binding.

Very large reports that cannot be Cerlox-bound should be put into a ringed binder. Again, the cover of the binder should display the report information, attached as a label or inserted into a clear sleeve on the front cover.

It's always a good idea to give your known readers a few extra copies, because they may want to share the report with others in their organization. But use discretion when handing out extra copies—you wouldn't want anyone to steal your work and use it for their own credit or to obtain sensitive company information.

If you are to make an oral presentation, be sure to have extra copies on hand. Take along the number of copies needed for the people you know will attend, plus a few more for others who may show up.

Oral Presentation of the Formal Report

Often, you will be asked to present your formal report orally to the person for whom it was written, and other people may attend the presentation as well. Because it is a *formal* report, you will want to ensure that you conduct your oral presentation in a formal format and tone. See Chapter 12 for assistance in creating an appropriate oral presentation.

Preparing and Sending Your Report

Usually (although not always), the preparation of a formal report takes a fairly long time, and the report is quite detailed and lengthy. In most instances, you will be expected to produce it in hard copy as well as electronically—and in order to ensure that what you see on your screen is what your reader will see, you should save it in a PDF format (unless it needs to be modified by the receiver, in which case it should be saved in a word-processing format like MS Word or Rich Text Format). Find out how many copies are needed, and print as many as required, plus a few extras just in case other people need to see it.

If you have to mail it and time is of the essence, use a courier or priority speed mailing service to ensure that it will reach the destination on time. If it's a large document, use a sturdy padded envelope or even a small box designed for the purpose.

If it's enormous (hundreds of pages, with graphics) and you're sending it electronically, you might want to consider sending it in the compressed format available on your word-processing or computing software (for example, Stuffit) or uploading it to a secure, receiver-accessible FTP (file transfer protocol) site. Another alternative is to mail the hard copy along with a CD that you burn, label, and package with the copy.

CHECKLIST FOR formal reports

- ☐ Have you applied the Starting Point questions so that you will know your readers better? Do you know what they hope to learn from your report?

- ☐ Are you clear about the message or information you need to communicate? The purpose and the desired outcome? (See Chapter 1 for help with this.)

- ☐ Do you understand the purpose of your report and whether it's an evaluation, information, progress, incident, or expense report?

- ☐ Have you included all the information the reader is looking for?

- ☐ If applicable, is your report persuasive enough to persuade the reader of the merits of your information?

- ☐ If this is a budget report, have you included all of the financial information your reader requires? Have you included a spreadsheet budget or report, if required?

- ☐ If this is a progress report, have you organized the information into summary, background, progress, future plans, conclusion, and evidence (if required) sections?

- ☐ If this is an incident report, have you organized the information into introduction, investigation, assessment, conclusion, and recommendations (if required) sections?

- ☐ If this is an incident report, and if you are *not* to evaluate or give your recommendations on the situation, have you been careful to include only the facts and not your evaluation of the situation? Have you avoided laying blame?

- ☐ If this is an expense report, have you organized the information into introduction, activities (or items purchased), benefits, cost(s), conclusion, and recommendations sections?

- ☐ If this is an information or evaluation report, have you organized the information into introduction, overview (or background), methodology, findings, assessment, and conclusion sections?

- ☐ Are you quite sure that your letter does not contain any grammar or spelling errors? Including the recipient's name and other names within the text?

- ☐ Is the report in the correct format as described in this chapter?

- ☐ Is the tone of the writing suitably formal?

- ☐ Have you produced the document in a professional format befitting the formality of the report? (Cerlox binding? Card stock cover?)

Chapter Summary

In this chapter, you have learned the differences between formal and informal reports and in which business situations to choose the formal report rather than the informal one. You learned the method and importance of researching and organizing information. Since information is the basis of all report-writing, you also learned how to select information based on the reader's needs and how to develop the amount of information expected in a formal report. You found that organization is the foundation of good writing and learned how to organize your research into an appropriate format for a formal report. Finally, you learned how to edit and review your formal report to ensure that it meets the needs of your readers and fulfills your purpose in writing.

■■▮ SUGGESTIONS *for Further Reading*

Bentley, T. (2002). *Report writing in business.* Toronto, ON: Elsevier/CIMA Publishing.

Blicq, R.S., and Moretto, L.A. (2000). *Guidelines for report writing.* (4th ed.). Toronto, ON: Pearson Education.

Bovee, C.L. (2007). *Techniques of writing: Business letters, memos, and reports.* (2nd ed.). Toronto, ON: Oxford University Press.

Lesikar, R.V., and Pettit, J.D. (1997). *Report writing for business.* (10th ed.). Toronto, ON: McGraw-Hill/Irwin.

Reid, M. (2012). *Report writing.* New York, NY: Palgrave Macmillan.

■■▮ PRACTISING *What You Have Learned*

1. Write a formal progress report on your work at college or university during the last full school year to justify your standing as the recipient of an award from the Most Deserving Student Scholarship Foundation. The board of this organization requires an annual formal progress report on your scholastic and intellectual activities in order to award you money for another year at college or university.

2. Write a formal progress report on your search for work in the months leading up to your graduation from college or university. Describe the steps you have taken in terms of resumé development for specific jobs and careers, letter-writing, submission of letters and resumés, research into the hidden job market, and networking you have done with people suggested by family, friends, and professors. Include any interviews you have had and the outcome of these interviews. In short, note all the steps you have taken to find a job you will begin after graduation and the tasks that you must complete to achieve your goal.

3. Write a formal incident report on something serious that happened at your paid or volunteer workplace, assuming that you have been asked to report on the details so that your supervisors or the board can assess the situation before deciding what to do about the consequences of the incident.

4. Write a formal incident report on an accident you witnessed, describing details and facts as you saw or experienced them as though you were writing a report to support a police or workplace health and safety investigation. Remember that in an investigation, you are generally not asked to provide your assessment of blame or cause but are to provide all of the details and unbiased facts to help others determine cause or blame.

5. Write a formal expense report to the Most Deserving Student Scholarship Foundation board of directors documenting your expenses at school over the past year. This report is required for you to obtain further funding. The board also wants you to note any paid work you have done over the past year (but remember, if it seems that your marks were lower because you worked, you will have to present this information in a relatively positive way).

6. Write a formal expense report to your parents outlining how you spent the money they gave you for college or university over the past year, considering such expenses as tuition, books, rent, utilities, Internet, cable, food, telephone, transportation, and, of course, entertainment (but you may want to downplay how much you spent on beer). Parents like to know that their money was well spent on the essentials you need to survive and be educated, but that doesn't mean you should lie. For instance, you could simply put the figures for your beer budget into an overall category called "entertainment." As an added touch (and to show them how much you are learning), provide a spreadsheet outlining expense categories and income from other sources, broken down by month.

7. Write a formal evaluative report on why you decided to attend your particular college or university, noting the other schools you considered and the criteria you used to decide on the one you are currently attending. (If you are considering several colleges or universities for further education after this school year, you might want to focus this report on that decision-making process.)

8. Write a formal evaluative report on everyone you have dated over the past three years, noting the strengths and weaknesses of each relationship and what you learned. Outline the ideal person you are seeking now that you have had a cumulative learning experience from dating a few people. Describe the steps you will take to improve yourself or make yourself better prepared for a good relationship.

   Variation: If you are a mature or part-time student who is already working full-time, think of situations for which you would write a progress, incident, expense, or evaluative report on something real or possible in your workplace. This will make the exercise even more relevant for you.

CHAPTER 10

Informal Proposals

LEARNING OBJECTIVES

In this chapter, you will learn:

- ⊙ The rationale for the writing and formatting of informal proposals

- ⊙ How to research and prepare information for informal proposals

- ⊙ How to write the proposal persuasively so that readers endorse, support, or fund a proposed project, work, or activity

- ⊙ A generic format for writing informal proposals

- ⊙ Specific tips for oral presentation of informal proposals

ESSENTIAL EMPLOYABILITY SKILLS

2ooo+ Employability Skills The Conference Board of Canada has identified certain essential employability skills (EES) as benchmarks for performance in the workplace. You will learn the following EES skills in this chapter:

COMMUNICATE
- ⊙ Can write and speak so others pay attention and understand
- ⊙ Can listen and ask questions to understand and appreciate the points of view of others
- ⊙ Can share information using a range of information and communications technologies (e.g., voice, email, computers)
- ⊙ Can use relevant scientific, technological, and mathematical knowledge and skills to explain or clarify ideas
- ⊙ Can read and understand information presented in a variety of forms (e.g., words, graphs, charts, diagrams)

MANAGE INFORMATION
- ⊙ Can locate, gather, and organize information using appropriate technology and information systems
- ⊙ Can access, analyze, and apply knowledge and skills from various disciplines (e.g., the arts, languages, science, technology, mathematics, social sciences, and the humanities)

USE NUMBERS
(depending on the nature of the report)
- ⊙ Can decide what needs to be measured or calculated
- ⊙ Can observe and record data using appropriate methods, tools, and technology
- ⊙ Can make estimates and verify calculations

THINK AND SOLVE PROBLEMS
- ⊙ Can assess situations and identify problems
- ⊙ Can seek different points of view and evaluate them based on facts
- ⊙ Can recognize the human, interpersonal, technical, scientific, and mathematical dimensions of a problem
- ⊙ Can identify the root cause of a problems
- ⊙ Can be creative and innovative in exploring possible solutions
- ⊙ Can evaluate solutions to make recommendations or decisions
- ⊙ Can check to see if a solution works and act on opportunities for improvement

Case Study

Informal Proposals: A Case Study

Recently, one of the trainer-facilitators at the Aspire Adult Education Centre in Nanaimo, BC, left her one-year, 20-hours-per-week contract position for a more lucrative permanent position with a similar organization in Burnaby. The contract still has six months to go, and the manager of Aspire is considering advertising in the community for someone to fill the position for the remaining months.

Tony Galston, a part-time trainer who worked closely with Katherine Goodheart on the work skills development program, feels qualified to move into this position, thus creating a full-time opportunity for himself. Tony has worked with Aspire for the past five years on various training contracts and has more than 10 years' experience working with career changers and displaced workers. His experience also includes three years as a program supervisor at another training centre in Penticton (he left that position because his wife got a better-paying, high-school resource teacher job with the board of education in Nanaimo).

He would like his employer to consider taking him on for the six months left in Katherine's contract as a pilot project so that he can prove to Aspire's management team that he is a major asset and should be hired full-time on a permanent basis.

1. What are the persuasive points Tony can use to convince his employer to endorse the proposed six-month pilot combining his current work with Katherine's former workload? List these points. (These points create Tony's case for himself.)

2. What are the advantages to the employer in hiring Tony versus advertising and hiring someone from outside the organization? Think of as many advantages as possible, and list these. (These points illustrate why hiring Tony would be an advantage to the employer over hiring someone from the outside and are very important in persuading the employer to agree.)

3. Based on what you have read—and any other possible reasons you can think of— what might be the disadvantages to the employer in hiring Tony, if any? (These are the possible objections the employer might have to hiring Tony. Tony has to anticipate what these objections might be and address them proactively in his proposal so that he minimizes any reason the employer might have to say no.)

4. With these points in mind, write a brief informal proposal from Tony Galston, Work Skills Development Trainer, to Fred Kogawa, Programs Manager at Aspire Adult Education Centre.

Before You Begin . . .

An **informal proposal**, like a formal proposal, is a written offer to someone internal to your organization or business to perform some work or a project. It is written either as a solicited proposal—one that another department or your boss has requested from you, based on your position or expertise—or as an unsolicited one but with content the internal reader will understand or know something about.

It is a **persuasive form of writing**, and in terms of tone and style, it's written in a moderately informal way, somewhat less formal than a formal proposal, because you are writing to someone who presumably knows you or at least knows *of* you in the organization. (In the case of a large, multi-department or multi-branch organization in which the person you are writing to may not know you—much as when you are writing to an external reader—you would write a formal proposal.)

In terms of format, the internal proposal follows a fairly simple organizational template, but you can vary the headings if you feel that others may be more relevant to the specific proposal. The basic format is as follows:

- introduction (including purpose, scope)

- background (which tells the reader what led to writing the proposal—answering *why* you are writing)

- proposal (the who, what, where, when, and how of your proposal—i.e., four of the "5 Ws and how" questions)

- conclusion (which wraps up the proposal by restating your purpose, scope, and what is involved in a very brief few points)

As with any other report, using subheadings to keep the reader moving through the proposal and keep them from becoming bogged down in a lot of text is a good idea if you have a lot of information to include. Write the proposal first using the basic template for an informal proposal. Then, if your text seems to be getting excessively wordy, you can break it up further into additional subsections to avoid overwhelming your reader.

Brief proposals of one or two pages are often set in memorandum format (see Chapter 2 for this format). You would use the same template for organizing the information, but you would use the memo banner and information before presenting the information for the proposal. Proposals more than two pages in length are usually written in non-memo format. Brief proposals usually involve very short-term projects or jobs, such as the planning of the company picnic or a proposal to determine benefits and costs of new equipment.

If your proposal is more than five pages long, a table of contents is strongly recommended; the goal is to keep the reader moving through the reading of your proposal and focused on what you are proposing. A title page is a good idea for a longer proposal, and the format for it is included in this chapter. In this respect, the informal proposal becomes more like a formal proposal in length, but again, it does not require the same level of formality or organization as when you are writing for an external reader.

Longer proposals are usually concerned with longer-term projects or work, such as the implementation of a pilot project that you or your department will start, monitor, and assess at the end of a period of several months or a year. Usually, such projects include the proposal itself, a project and assessment plan, progress reports, and, finally, an evaluation report so that the organization or the person to whom you are writing can assess the success of the project.

Idiom Alert

bogged down – Dealing with a lot of work, stress, or projects—having way too much to do, which holds you back from moving on with whatever you have to do. Bogged down refers to people being caught in a bog—a very wet, soggy, and mucky experience in which it's hard to move forward or backward.

all the bases are covered – All the details of a plan, project, or ongoing operation are attended to, leaving no detail out; you are making sure that you are not missing any detail in a project that might cause problems later.

no stone left unturned – All possible options, ideas, or opportunities have been researched or thought of; someone has been very thorough in his or her work.

get your mojo running – Operate as your best, most energetic, and creative self; be enthusiastic and ready for anything.

great bone structure – In reference to a building, means sound walls, foundation, and other aspects of the building. In reference to a person, means a lovely figure, beautiful cheekbones, and so on.

splash out – Spend extravagantly, not thinking much about cost.

has gotten out of hand – Is out of control, unmanageable, or extravagant; the expression often implies that it will take a lot of effort to correct the situation, if that is even possible.

Your Starting Point

As with any other form of business writing or oral presentation, you need to know as much as possible about the reader(s) or receiver(s) of your communication. You need to know why you are writing and/or presenting.

To get started with an informal proposal, apply the Starting Point questions to your reader(s). Answer these questions first before you begin collecting information for your informal proposal and certainly before you start writing. The answers will help you to stay on track with the purpose and scope of your proposal and keep you from wasting time on research or writing that is not relevant to the task.

Concurrently, be very clear on why you are writing this proposal—what you or your organization wants to have happen as an outcome of the proposal. This will also determine the information and message you want to convey.

Creating the Written Product: How to Do It

PREPARING TO WRITE

Research

In order to be persuasive—to prove that the proposed project, work, or expense is justified and desirable—you will often need to do some research.

Based on the answers to the questions noted previously, you will know what kind of information the reader needs in order to be convinced of the merits of your proposal. For example:

- If the reader is budget-conscious and your proposal involves buying some new technology or products, you will need to obtain at least three verifiable price quotes and determine the benefits of each item you are proposing to buy or implement.

- If the proposal is to implement a pilot project, you need to find documented, verifiable information or reports about how the project has been beneficial to other organizations like yours.

- If you are proposing a new product or service that the business can offer, you will need to find recent, relevant statistics about the benefits to customers and the company to prove that the product or service will increase profitability, create customer recognition and retention, and improve the fortunes of the company or department.

Think about the timelines for your proposal, and work backward from the deadline to determine how much time you will need to write and edit your work—and ahead of that, how much time you will realistically need for research.

Doing research usually takes a lot more time than writers think. Don't rush the process, because the success of your proposal depends on the quality of the information and statistics you use to persuade the reader. If you think it will take a certain amount of time to do research, double that time to allow for dead ends in your search, interruptions, and, of course, some mini-breaks so that you won't burn out in the process.

Use the Internet for research, but don't rule out using your local library or a larger reference library in a university, college, or major city. Perhaps you don't like reading—but with help, you can get a lot of information for most projects through a couple of focused visits to the library.

Get to know the reference librarians at the reference or business information desk. They can help you cut through the dizzying array of print information and the many online, exclusive databases of information that libraries have to get exactly what you need. All you need to do is make a list of exactly what you are looking for—and screw up the courage to ask!

Libraries have online, searchable databases of information pertinent to all sorts of businesses and organizations; depending on the size of the library, many have such resources as trade or business journals and publications, newspapers, brochures, catalogues, directories, and, of course, books on a wide range of topics that will be helpful to you.

Trade or business-sector associations, chambers of commerce, business improvement associations, and business advisory centres in your nearest town or city also offer a wealth of information for the business writer putting together a proposal or report. Do an Internet search to find out what's available locally in this regard or which organizations you can email and contact remotely for help.

You may also interview or obtain information orally from a person—primary information that can't be found anywhere else. You should record this information in notes to use later.

When you are doing Internet research, be sure to consider where the information you find comes from to ensure that you are relying on reputable sources. See the box below for tips on how to optimize your Internet research.

More efficient research using the Internet

Before the advent of the Internet, students and business people often found research quite time-consuming and daunting. They would go to the library to find whatever they could in the stacks and reference section, spend a fortune on photocopying the very best reference material, and take out a pile of books only to glean just a few kernels of relevant or useful information.

Thank goodness for the Internet and the way it has cut down on the running around involved in research! However, research on the Internet has its own challenges.

First of all, there is the issue of search terms. Many people think that if they enter the most obvious search terms, their results should include exactly what they need. Not always! You will have to review each of the entries on the results page to see whether the information is what you need for your proposal or report.

You will *have* to look at pages "deeper in" rather than just the first page of results. The first pages tend to include websites for which their owners/hosts have invested serious money to ensure high ranking. While some of these sites are indeed the best possible sources of information, look carefully at what motivated them to include the information you are interested in—to ensure credibility and lack of bias (see below).

Depending on how esoteric or specific your research is, you may find useful information buried several pages of results "in" from the first page. You have to cultivate patience, because this kind of search takes time; you need to take time to look at as many likely websites and sources of information as possible to determine whether it will be helpful.

You may find that some of your search terms aren't as helpful as others might be. One of the best ways to do Internet search is to give free rein to your imagination when you first consider likely search terms and scribble these terms down so that they're close at hand and you can enter them when one of your searches turns up less or when you are done with it.

Once you have found useful websites, bookmark them—*and* record the home page URL (or copy them into a Word document) in case you have any computer problems or otherwise miss your bookmarks. Another good idea is to print the articles or homepages and put them in a file folder—again, in case your technology fails you and you have to retrace your steps.

As discussed in Chapter 1, before you use any Internet source, you must verify its credibility. To do that, you need to:

- Determine when the source was written (web text or article on a website, for example): it has to have been written recently—within the past four to five years—to be considered credible, unless you are researching something that happened before that point.
- Determine authorship: who wrote the article? If there is no author, what is the sponsoring agency or organization? Who has sponsored or is hosting the website? If you can't determine the author, sponsor, or host, the source is probably suspect. You want to be sure that the author/sponsor/host of the information is a credible, unbiased source with appropriate educational or experiential credentials. You also want to be sure that the sponsor or host is not a company or agency with a commercial agenda (i.e., trying to sell something) that would make any information suspect.
- Determine the reason that the article or information is included on the website: is it to promote a product or service? In that case, the information is biased and therefore not as credible as material written from an unbiased point of view, such as scientific studies. Even if you find what looks like an academic-style report or study about a product or service online, be sure to double-check the author's, sponsor's, or site host's credibility. Big companies with a major stake in convincing you their product or service is the right one sometimes sponsor expensive research to "prove" efficacy!
- Avoid using blogs or discussion boards as sources, except to support more credible, unbiased source information such as reports or articles. These sources are typically individuals' opinions or thoughts about products/services or information. They are worth considering, but not as empirical sources of information in and of themselves.
- Do not use Wikipedia as a research source (Chapter 1 explains why you should avoid doing so).

PREPARING FOR CITATIONS

The professionalism and quality of your proposal depends on your information sources. You must be able to tell the reader where you got the information in order to prove that you are not making any assumptions and have taken the time required to make a definitive case in favour of the proposed work, expense, or project. Nothing will sink your proposal faster than general statements about benefits or features without any indication of where you got the information.

Further, if you are perceived as having merely copied and pasted large amounts of information into your proposal, you will appear not only lazy but dishonest as well. Your reputation is on the line.

When you have located information that is useful for your proposal, immediately write down everything you can about the source, either on the same printed page or on an easily locatable piece of paper:

* the website address, date accessed, date of the most recent update or the launch of the website, any authors of materials you are using, the name of the organization hosting the website, the titles of articles or information sections, the section or paragraph number of the webpage where the reader can find the information if desired;

* the title of the print source, chapter name/number (if relevant), names of authors, volume or issue number (if relevant), series name/number (if relevant), publisher name, publication date;

* the full name and title of the person you spoke with, the organization or business the person works for or with, the date you spoke with this person, their contact information.

In short, keep as much information as possible about each source in one location. While for most business audiences you don't need to cite this information as you would in an academic research paper, you may be asked for more information about your sources after you present the proposal, so you should have it close at hand.

If you have time, you may want to produce a citations page with all of this information ahead of time, just in case one of your readers requests it. Take it with you when you present the proposal, or have it ready to give to any readers who ask for the information after reading your proposal.

ORGANIZING INFORMATION AND WRITING: FORMAT

As mentioned previously, the format of an informal proposal is simple—introduction, background, the proposal, and conclusion. If it's one to two pages and an internal document, it's safe to say that it can be presented in **memo format**, unless otherwise specified by your reader (e.g., see Figure 10.2). If it's more than two pages, you would put it in **"non-memo" format**, which has a title page as a cover; if it's five or more pages in length, you would also add a table of contents immediately after the cover page.

Proposal in memo format

Proposal in memo format guidelines

MEMORANDUM

To: Name and position of reader(s)
From: Your name and position (if a group project, names of group members)
Date: Date of submission
Subject: Title of your proposal, which should reflect your purpose for writing or why you were asked to write; should be short and to the point

---

Introduction

In this section, describe why you are writing (purpose) and the scope (what you will or will not cover in the proposal). Refer to the answers to the questions noted previously in this chapter to help you write this section.

Background

In this section, provide a history or background of what led to the writing of the proposal. For example, you could mention that the reader or your boss asked you to write the proposal; historical facts or a situation that led to the proposed work, project, or expense you are about to write about in the proposal; or past experience you have had with the proposed work, project, or expense.

The proposal (or a more specific title related to its purpose, if appropriate)

In this section, you detail the 5 Ws of the proposed work, project, or expense and explain how it will work and how it will be implemented. Don't make any sweeping assumptions about the merits of the proposed work or expense; instead, try to prove to the reader that the work or expense is justified, has merit, and/or will make money for the organization, using solid facts, statistics, and so on to demonstrate the strength of the proposal. You will, of course, have to cite the source of this information.

If the proposal is for a longer-term project, you would also indicate that you are willing to provide documentation such as budget and progress reports at regular intervals to keep the reader(s) up to date on work completed.

You may also want to explain how you will evaluate the project, work, or expense once the process has been completed.

Remember to write this section in short, succinct paragraphs so that the reader can easily follow your proposal information. However, do include all the details that are important to the reader so that he or she can make an informed decision about your proposal.

Conclusion

The conclusion should do just that—conclude your proposal by restating the main purpose, scope, background, and proposal points. This is your last chance to win the support of the reader for your proposal, so a reminder of its potential benefits to your organization or the reader in one short, memorable sentence at the end of the conclusion is an excellent idea.

Proposal in non-memo format

A proposal in non-memo format is just that—not a memo. It is divided into the same sections as those of a memo-format proposal. It's generally longer, more than two pages. You would write in this format for an internal reader when there is more detail than can be contained in a two-or-fewer-page memo or (seldom) for an external reader you know well. Such an external reader would be almost like an internal reader, such as a regular supplier or a strategic partner of the company. Make sure you know that the relationship with the external reader is appropriate for an informal proposal.

Differences between non-memo and memo format

SUMMARY

If your proposal is longer than two pages, you probably should write a summary so that the reader will know at a glance what's included in the document.

The text sums up your entire proposal, start to finish, on one page only. It is written *after* you write your proposal, drawing on all parts of it, and in short paragraphs.

To ensure that the reader is clear on your main points, you may even want to write a short paragraph for each section of your proposal (introduction, background, etc.), in the same order. Include your contact information and an invitation to the reader to ask you for more information if he or she needs it. Finally, attach the summary to the cover page of your proposal with a paper clip.

TITLE PAGE

If your proposal is in non-memo format, create a title page that includes the title of your proposal (drawn from the purpose of the proposal), the date, and your contact information. Staple or bind it at the beginning of your proposal.

TABLE OF CONTENTS

A non-memo format proposal longer than five pages should have a table of contents (T of C), which would be the next full page following the title page. The T of C leads the reader through the parts of your proposal by indicating on which page each section begins. Compile this page after your proposal is completed and you know where each section is located.

APPENDIX

Sometimes you might have additional information that would further reinforce your proposal and win your reader's approval. This information, if not included within your proposal (because the documents are oversized or too lengthy, for example), can be placed in an appendix section. However, be sure to mention these items somewhere in your proposal; otherwise, the reader might miss them or not understand how they relate to your proposal.

All appendix items should be preceded by an appendix title page that divides the appendixes from the proposal itself.

Proposal in non-memo format guidelines

Summary	**Background**
Title page	**The proposal**
Table of contents	**Conclusion**
Introduction	**Appendix**

Sample Documents

Figure 10.1 shows a short proposal—fewer than two pages—so it's written in memo format and does not require a summary, cover page, title page, or appendix section.

A summary can introduce a proposal, as in Figure 10.3. It would be attached to the front of your proposal with a paper clip.

FIGURE 10.1 **Proposal in Memo Format**

MEMORANDUM

To: Jose Ramirez, Vice-President

From: Jane Van Loon, Social Committee Chairperson

Date: May 1, 2014

Subject: Locations for company picnic

The introduction should state briefly what the proposal is about and why it was written.

Introduction

At your request, the social committee has obtained details and costs for three different sites for our company picnic on July 15, 2014, and proposes to hold the event at one of them.

Background provides history of past events as context leading to proposal.

Background

As you know, we held our company picnic at Belle Park last summer. Much fun was had by all, but unfortunately, this year the park is not available because of an Asian long-horned beetle outbreak, which has required that trees be clear-cut and burned.

There has been a bit of a mad scramble to find a new location, since we only found out about the park closure in mid-April. We needed to find a site where there would be plenty of parking, swimming, a picnic shelter, well-marked trails to walk, and ample field space for our company's annual Summer Olympics event.

The following are the three parks we reviewed for suitability for our picnic:

Enchanted Forest Park

Enchanted Forest Park is closest to the city, offering enough parking, a heated swimming pool, and some short, well-marked trails. There is also a picnic shelter in case of rain and a large field for our Olympic events. The only potential issue with this location is that a couple of family reunions are already booked there, so it could be crowded. To book the park, we would need to make a 20 per cent down payment on the $500 booking fee.

Subheadings like this help reader see information about each option at a glance.

Locations rated according to criteria in Background to help reader process information easily.

Summer Glade Park

Summer Glade Park is located about 20 km outside of the city and has all the required amenities. The shelter has a massive built-in gas barbecue and facilities for cleaning up. However, several of our families don't have cars to get there. We could remedy the situation by renting a bus or a couple of large vans for the day or asking people to car-pool. This private park requires a $50 down payment on a total fee of $200 by June 15.

Swift River Conservation Area

This park is located 10 km from the city and has all of the needed amenities. Because the beach is unsupervised, we would need to hire a lifeguard. The other issue is that there are no outhouses or bathrooms; we would have to rent a couple of portable outhouses for the day at a cost of $200. The park costs $300 for the day, which means a total cost of booking and outhouse facilities of $500.

The Proposal

Outlines the core of the proposal.

Upon review of these three choices, we propose use of Summer Glade, since it provides excellent swimming, eating/food preparation, games, and hiking facilities and has flush toilets and sinks at the site. To address the transportation issue, we will set up a car-pooling list so that everyone has a ride to the picnic. With this provision, Summer Glade is not only the best choice in terms of space and facilities but is also the least expensive of the three. This means we can use the extra money in the picnic budget for better Olympics prizes than we handed out last year, which should raise the stakes considerably for the family teams involved!

We will need to book Summer Glade ASAP with our down payment. I have already contacted them and assured them we would be in touch by the end of this week so that they will know whether we wish to make a reservation.

Action required immediately, so mentioned here.

Conclusion

Conclusion usually requests action; provides contact information for questions or concerns.

I would appreciate it if you could indicate whether you agree with our choice ASAP, since I need to make a booking within the next week or so.

If you have any questions or concerns, please contact me at my extension (x 123) or by email (jvanloon@thecompany.ca).

FIGURE 10.2   Proposal in Non-memo Format

A separate cover page is required for a longer report.

TORONTO YOUTH CENTRE

Strategic Planning, Policy/Procedures Development, Fundraising Planning, Board Development, and Programming/Operations Facilitation and Oversight Services

DECEMBER 2013

Youth Workers International Incorporated
79 Bridge Street
Ottawa, ON K9F 1TJ

Table of Contents

(continued)

Introduction states what proposal is about.

INTRODUCTION

The following is a proposal for the research and writing of a strategic (business) plan, board policy and procedure development, and board development, as well as operational consulting for a proposed youth centre in Toronto, Ontario.

Background provides history and informs (unsolicited proposal) or reminds (solicited proposal) reader why written.

BACKGROUND

In October 2013, John Jones, chair of the board of governors of the Toronto branch of Youth Workers International Inc. (YWI), asked me to create a preliminary proposal for a youth centre in downtown Toronto for the consideration of the Greater Toronto YWI board. He indicated the proposal was to cover all aspects of planning for and implementation of the new centre.

Source noted in the sentence itself, and website from which it comes is noted in parentheses.

This youth centre is to be modelled on the Nepean Youth Centre in Nepean, Ontario. The Nepean Youth Centre serves a similar youth population to that of downtown Toronto in terms of ethnic diversity, social issues, and programming interests, according to a review of Statistics Canada's 2006 Report on Urban Youth, *Youth in Cities* (www.statscan.ca/youth2006).

In my capacity as organizational consultant to the Ottawa YWI, I provided all start-up services for the Nepean centre, including a five-year strategic plan, a comprehensive board policy and procedures manual, and board of directors training. I also provide ongoing facilitation and consulting services for the Nepean Youth Centre, including board liaison and facilitation, oversight of operations management, and funding source research and proposal writing.

It is from this experience that I present this preliminary proposal for the youth centre in Toronto for your consideration.

The Proposal outlines all work to be completed in easy-to-read sections with subheadings.

THE PROPOSAL

In order to proceed with the groundwork for the new downtown Toronto youth centre, I propose to provide the youth centre committee with a professionally researched and produced strategic plan, a comprehensive policies and procedures manual, consultation on board development and ongoing governance, board training, and a fundraising plan.

Which details should be included? Apply Starting Point questions to intended readers.

I am also pleased to offer ongoing board facilitation and proposal-writing services to assist the board with the development of sustainable funding on a separate service contract.

This and following sections offer specific, relevant details to keep reader moving through proposal.

Strategic plan

The strategic plan will cover all aspects of start-up and early-phase growth over the first three years of operation. This plan will include a mission and values statement, an organizational concept, market and youth community analyses and projections, and marketing, operational, financial, and funding plans for the centre. (Please see the Nepean plan as an example of a strategic plan at http://www.nepeanyouthcentre.ca/strategicplan. You will need to supply your YWI password to access the secure area of the site.)

Policies and procedures manual

A comprehensive policies and procedures manual will be researched and modelled on best practices in community youth programming and facilitation (which is required by law for not-for-profit corporations) as well as on the successful operation of the Nepean Youth Centre. This will provide the board with all the information needed to competently manage the operations of the new centre with confidence, knowing that "all the bases are covered" in terms of operations. (Again, see the *Policies and Procedures Manual* of the Nepean centre at the website specified previously for an example.)

Governance policies

As a framework for organizational governance policies, the manual will address the rationale for and background to the founding of the Toronto youth centre. It will also provide:

- An organizational constitution and bylaws
- Mission, vision, and values statements (which will also be echoed in the strategic plan
- Objectives (also echoed in the strategic plan)
- Operating structure (a description of how the organization will be managed, lines of authority and accountability)
- Board and officers' roles and responsibilities
- Description of committee structure and roles (such as the HR committee)

Ultimately, your organization will have to provide articles of not-for-profit incorporation to include in the final copy of the policies and procedures manual once you have conducted the necessary registrations with the province. This can take several months, so you will want to pursue this as soon as possible; we can recommend legal firms who can help with this process, if required.

Administrative policies

This section will address such aspects of administration as:

- Membership
- Access to information
- Record retention and archives
- Conflict of interest guidelines
- Communications
- Insurance (third party, bonding, directors and officers)
- Meetings—voting, cancellation
- Board–employee relations

Financial policies

In this section of the manual, we will provide policy to govern:

- Accounting methods and reporting
- Assets (valuation and disposal policies or guidelines)

Persuasive writing used in this and following sections: words like "comprehensive," "modelled on best practices," "successful," "competently."

4

(continued)

- Annual audit and year-end procedures (criteria for and process of hiring outside accounting firm to do so)
- Banking (based on the bank information you supply)
- Budget preparation and management (what, who is involved, and monthly reporting procedures to the board)
- Legal requirements, such as remittance of HST, secure retention of financial records
- Expenses—what will be considered reimbursable expenses, method for filing expense reports
- Cash management
- Fundraising management and reporting (to adhere to provincial not-for-profit corporation rules)
- Cheque control and safeguard (signing authority, approval process, etc.)
- Contract tendering process (RFPs)
- Use of credit (what it can be used for, authorized users, etc.)

Human resources policies

This section of the manual will address:

- Employment (paid) positions and descriptions (if available)
- Hiring process and procedure
- Training policies for paid employees
- Holidays/sick time
- Discipline and dismissal procedures
- Recruitment process for volunteers
- Orientation and training of volunteers
- Recognition of volunteers (events, awards, etc.)
- Board of directors recruitment process
- Orientation, training of board members
- Board management (meeting attendance, committee work, participation at events)
- Evaluation and recognition of directors (including any honoraria)
- Resignation/replacement of board members
- Public participation in board meetings

Facilities and property policies

In terms of facilities and property management policies, the manual will address:

- Use of the building—rentals, access, maintenance, keys, summer or holiday use or rental
- Rental contracts, insurance, and cleaning/maintenance obligations of renters
- Purchase, storage, and maintenance of equipment—tables, chairs, AV equipment, etc.
- Office and program use (participant) computers—access, safeguards, storage, record retention
- Insurance—required coverage and terms for centre activities and/or renters

5

Board development and training

Based on my experience with the development of the Nepean centre's board, I will assist Greater Toronto YWI in selecting a board that will not only reflect the diversity of the downtown Toronto community but also provide the skills and expertise needed to oversee all aspects of operation. With a well-developed recruitment, screening, and selection process, I will be able to help you establish the new youth centre board within a two-month period.

Any board, regardless of individual members' previous experience, will require specific training in governance relevant to the organization's particular mandate and mission. In addition to this training, I will also ensure that the new board is very familiar with the strategic plan and the policies and procedures manual.

This training will be provided within a month of board selection so that the Greater Toronto YWI and the new board can get on with the exciting business of starting up the youth centre.

Fundraising plan

Fundraising for any new not-for-profit organization, particularly at a time when so many other organizations are also out in public to raise money in lieu of government grants, can be a daunting task. The key to fundraising success is to have a well-researched plan with achievable goals and measurable outcomes, which provides for a diversified approach for developing sustainable funding. I will provide detailed, no-stone-left-unturned research into corporate, philanthropic, and government funding sources for sustainable operational funding; in addition, a local fundraising strategy will be developed, building on the specific interests and strengths of the local downtown Toronto community.

The Nepean centre's fundraising has gone extremely well, and all of the goals of the initial fundraising plan have been achieved. The Nepean Youth Centre's fundraising plan can be viewed on our website as an example of what was planned and what has been achieved to date.

ADDITIONAL SUPPORT SERVICES

Professional and comprehensive planning, and then ongoing, professional consultation and facilitation, is what has led to the success and ever-increasing growth of the Nepean Youth Centre's constituency, mandate, and programming since its inception in 2000.

In order for the proposed downtown Toronto youth centre to succeed, professional board management of operations and human resources must be sustained—and sustainable—and shorter-term funding must be obtained on an ongoing basis.

In this regard, I am pleased to offer the following services for your consideration on an annual service contract basis.

Fundraising plan situated here so reader is persuaded of proposal before confronting challenging information.

Writer assures reader of success with "well-researched plan," "achievable goals and measurable outcomes," and sustainability.

Section added by writer; not necessary unless it provides relevant additional information.

Terms of contract only briefly mentioned so that reader stays focused on what is offered.

6

(continued)

Board support and consultative services

Consultative and support services would be provided for the board as needed. This could include such services as facilitation of board meetings; liaison with other youth centres and organizations in the city and local, provincial, and federal government organizations; assistance with planning and implementing human resources strategies; and other ongoing aspects of operations.

Proposal writing

Once suitable funding sources have been identified for the needs of the Toronto youth centre, it will be essential to proceed with proposal writing as soon as possible, since many funders' processes are quite detailed and time-consuming.

Having written successful proposals for a myriad of not-for-profit agencies under the auspices of my company, Smith Communications Consulting, since 1999, I would apply this expertise to achieving funding levels specified in the fundraising plan.

Writer convinces reader she is right person for job.

CONCLUSION

Neatly restates proposal details, extras available, and final assurance of success.

As your professional partner in the proposed Toronto youth centre, it would be my pleasure to provide a professionally researched and produced strategic plan, a comprehensive policies and procedures manual, board development facilitation and training, and a fundraising plan.

I would also be pleased to provide ongoing board support and facilitation, as well as proposal writing services to not only help get the downtown Toronto youth centre started but allow it to thrive in its inception and look forward to a bright future. Should you have further questions about this proposal, please contact me at (613) 555-5555 or by email at jane@smithconsulting.ca.

7

FIGURE 10.3 Summary Page for Proposal (non-memo format)

December 5, 2014

Jane Smith
Smith Consulting Inc.
454 Royalty Road
Toronto, ON T4A 1G6

John Jones
Chairperson, Greater Toronto Youth Workers Inc.
254 Adelaide Street
Toronto, ON T4J 2H5

RE: Preliminary proposal, Downtown Toronto Youth Centre

Dear Mr. Jones,

It is my pleasure to provide you with the preliminary proposal for the downtown Toronto Youth Centre.

In keeping with your request, the proposal outlines all aspects of planning for and implementation of the new centre. Strategic planning is essential to the success of any youth centre, as is the development of a well-trained and organized board of directors and resources for those board members, as well as a fundraising plan. What follows is a proposal for consulting services for a professionally researched and produced strategic plan, a comprehensive policies and procedures manual, consultation on board development and ongoing governance, board training, and a fundraising plan.

Once these important planning pieces have been completed, I also offer ongoing board facilitation to assist with start-up operations and proposal-writing services to assist the board with the development of sustainable funding on a separate service contract.

Introduces and sums up proposal on one page; written in short paragraphs.

If you have any questions about this proposal, please do not hesitate to contact me at 613-555-5555 or jane@smithconsulting.ca.

Contact information and an invitation to the reader to ask for more information if needed.

Yours truly,

Jane Smith

Encl: Proposal, Downtown Toronto Youth Centre

Want to see more examples?

For more examples of informal reports, see this text's website at **www.oupcanada.com/Luchuk**.

Checking Your Work

CONTENT EDITING

Once you have written your proposal, the first review you conduct will focus on whether you have answered all of the preliminary "5 Ws and how" questions in your writing.

Did you deliver what your reader needs, wants, and understands and the specific instructions for the proposal (purpose and scope)—or did you get off-track at some point? Revisit the Starting Point questions to ensure that you are meeting your reader's requirements.

COPY EDITING

Once you have done a careful content edit, you must do an equally detailed and focused copy edit. Start with a spelling and grammar check, using your word-processing program. Put the document aside for a while, and then come back to a printed copy and read it carefully for grammar, spelling, punctuation, and mechanical errors or problems. Make sure that your paragraphs are short and to the point in order to keep your reader moving through the document. Get someone else in your organization—ideally, someone you can trust who is not involved in the proposal—to read it through to ensure that your writing is not only error-free but also understandable, clear, and concise.

FORMATTING REVIEW

Next, address format issues, if any. Choose an easily read, businesslike font, such as Times New Roman or Verdana.

Ensure that the proposal is organized with appropriate headings and subheadings so that the reader is guided through the entire document. If you are submitting a short proposal in memo format, ensure that you have followed memo format before launching into the proposal itself.

Make sure that you have used different sizes of font and emphasis to indicate to the reader where major sections or subsections begin and end.

Because your proposal should be single-spaced and left-justified (no indents on paragraphs), make sure that you have left a space between paragraphs. Ensure that there are no headings or subheadings at the bottom of pages, with text on the next page.

PRESS PRINT . . . OR *SEND*!

Once you have confirmed that everything is thoroughly edited and in the correct place, you can proceed with printing and sending it—or emailing it as an attachment.

Oral Presentation of the Informal Proposal

You may be asked to present your proposal to the person who requested it or to a wider audience.

WHO IS YOUR AUDIENCE?

In order to be well-prepared beforehand, be sure to find out as much as you can about who is attending, their positions in your organization (or others!), the nature of their interest in your proposal, their knowledge of the background or the proposal information itself, and what biases or objections they may have even before you present the proposal. This information is *critical* to presenting your proposal in such a way that it will meet their needs and concerns—ensure their "buy-in" to the proposed work, project, or expense.

Remember: Knowing your audience/readers = being able to prepare what they will want to hear = the success of your proposal.

Whether or not you're using AV resources to present your proposal, be sure to prepare your speaking points in advance. Practising your presentation should help you to project confidence and speak convincingly as you stress the benefits of your proposal. Remember to speak clearly and slowly and to be natural with your gestures and movements.

WHAT ARE THE LOGISTICS?

Find out from the person who asked you to present the proposal how much time you will have, where you will be presenting, the layout of the room, and whether there will be audio-visual (AV) resources available (and what they include). You also need to know how many people will be attending.

Once you have this information, you can plan the length of your presentation, decide whether you will use AV resources, work with the layout of the room so that everyone can see and hear you, and make enough copies of the proposal for everyone who shows up for your presentation.

PRESENTATION FORMAT

Whether you use AV resources or merely speak at the front of the room, introduce yourself and any colleagues you have with you, and then ask each person in the audience to introduce himself or herself, unless you already know who they are. That way, you will know who is who, and you will be able to address everyone's particular background, hopes, and concerns in the presentation and questions session.

Tell the audience what you will speak about, how long the presentation will be, that there will be a time for questions at the end, and that you will circulate copies of the proposal after the question period.

NO AV RESOURCES?

You can make an informal presentation of your proposal without AV support, particularly if the proposed work, project, or expense is of short duration or minimal cost. Follow the procedure noted below for slide presentations in order to make a persuasive pitch.

WORKING WITH (OR WITHOUT) AV RESOURCES

If you have access to a computer, projector, and screen (or blank wall)—and have at least 20 minutes to present—it is strongly recommended that you provide the main points of your proposal in a slide presentation. Because most people are visual rather than audio learners (or a combination of the two), providing a brief yet informative and persuasive slide show is an excellent way to generate excitement and buy-in.

Slide presentation software programs such as PowerPoint are widely used in the business context and can further highlight your proposal and provide visual reinforcement for what you are saying—that is, your pitch. However, slides should be an *enhancement* for what you say: do not read from your slides, and do not merely cut and paste the points from your proposal onto your slides. The goal is to get your audience to listen to you, not to read your slides while you blather on, so only put a few points—even one important point—on each slide and then elaborate on it.

To achieve this goal, review your proposal for the most important points that briefly sum up the purpose and background of the proposal, and spend more time on the benefits of the proposal to the organization or company. This may seem a bit daunting, since it means deviating from what you have already written—but your audience will receive a copy of your hard work to read when they leave. The object of making an oral presentation is to generate excitement and enthusiastic endorsement of your proposed work, project, or expense.

To come up with the best benefit points that will meet the needs, concerns, potential objections, and biases of the audience, refer to the information you have gathered about who is attending. Use the most relevant benefits you have stated in the proposal to address all of these needs and concerns, and the audience will feel that you understand them—and will be more likely to see the merits of your proposal.

QUESTIONS

Once you have made your presentation, ask whether there are any questions. Try to remember who is who and their reason for coming to your presentation as you answer their questions.

HANDOUTS

You want to keep the attention of the audience as you speak, so don't hand out copies of the proposal until the *end* of the presentation; otherwise, they will read it while they should be paying attention to you—and you are presenting them with the most important details, the *benefits* of the proposal!

FOLLOW-UP

You need to give your audience time to read and digest your proposal before you follow up with a phone call or email—whichever you feel is most appropriate. Give your audience at least a week before you contact them for feedback.

For in-depth information on planning and delivering oral presentations, see Chapter 12.

CHECKLIST FOR informal proposals

- ☐ Have you applied the Starting Point questions so that you know your reader(s) better? Do you know what will persuade them to endorse, support, or fund your project, idea, or work? Do you know what potential objections readers may have to your proposal—and how you will meet these objections before they arise?

- ☐ Are you clear about the message/information you need to communicate—and that it will be persuasive? Are you clear about the desired outcome? (See Chapter 1 for help with this.)

- ☐ Have you included all the information the reader needs to be fully convinced that your proposed work, project, expense, or idea is worth endorsing?

- ☐ Have you considered what format you should use for your proposal (memo or non-memo), based on the level of formality expected by the reader and/or its page length?

- ☐ Have you included in an appendix any statistics, illustrations, graphs, or related materials that will help to persuade your reader? (Only the most important and relevant should be attached; otherwise, you should probably be writing a lengthier formal proposal.)

- ☐ If there are costs involved in your proposal, have you included all of the financial information your reader requires? Have you included a spreadsheet budget or report, if required? (This is a good idea even if not requested or required; showing how you can save money is a good idea!)

- ☐ Have you included timelines and deadlines, if applicable?

- ☐ Have you clearly indicated the benefits of your proposed work, idea, or project to the organization or individual?

- ☐ Have you provided contact information so that readers can respond to you about your proposal? An offer to provide more information, if requested?

- ☐ Have you conducted a comprehensive edit for grammar, spelling, and mechanical errors?

- ☐ Is the proposal written in an appropriate tone and style for your workplace? (Generally, a moderately informal tone is best.)

Chapter Summary

In this chapter, you have learned that an informal proposal is *usually* an internal document and that it is usually solicited—that is, someone has specifically requested it. You also built your skills for researching and organizing information. Although relatively informal in tone, such proposals require a persuasive form of writing so that readers will endorse, support, or fund a proposed project, work, or activity. You found that informal proposals can be formatted as memos if they are quite short or as short reports with a contents page if they contain greater detail. You read about the many sources of information available to you when you conduct research for your proposal, and you were given tips on Internet searching. This chapter also reminded you to keep track of your sources so that they can be properly documented. You were shown a template to follow in organizing your materials, and you were given guidance on oral presentations of informal proposals.

■■ SUGGESTIONS *for Further Reading*

Coher, S.J., and Dickson, L.S. (2009). *Effective planning strategies and proposal writing: A workbook for helping*. Lanham, MD: Rowman and Littlefield.

Lister, L. (2009). *Proposal writing for smaller businesses*. Ipswich, UK: Biz Guru.

Miner, J.T., and Miner, L.E. (2008). *Proposal planning and writing*. (4th ed.). Santa Barbara, CA: ABC-CLIO/Greenwood Press.

Murthy, V. (2006). *Effective proposal writing*. Thousand Oaks, CA: Sage.

Sant, T. (2012). *Persuasive business proposals: Writing to win more customers, clients, and contracts*. (3rd rev. ed.). New York, NY: AMACOM Publishing.

■■ PRACTISING *What You Have Learned*

1. You are the chairperson of the Flin Flon Family Centre, an organization that provides early childhood enrichment programs for children and their caregivers on a drop-in basis. As such, you are actively working with a fundraising committee to obtain funding for operational and program costs.

   You are also an employee of Shopease Foods Inc., also based in Flin Flon, Manitoba, and you have been invited by your boss, Shelley White (the district manager), to apply to the company's marketing department for funding and food supplies for a "cooking for kids" program. Shelley's children, although now in public school, attended the centre with her when they were preschoolers, and she knows of your involvement there—and, more important, the value of the programs offered to Flin Flon families.

   While Shelley has offered to advocate for the centre in its application to the marketing department for support for the cooking program, she also has to run the proposal past the company's community outreach committee, which will also be looking at applications from other worthy organizations in the community. She needs a really persuasive proposal based on facts and statistics about how the centre is effective in providing invaluable early childhood education and supporting families emotionally, socially, and psychologically as well as intellectually. She also needs you to prove that the local community needs this program (e.g., statistics on how much people need to learn about nutrition for their kids).

   Write a non-memo format proposal (more than two pages) to Shelley White to share with Shopease Foods' marketing department, and include a budget page that outlines how much money is needed for each item for the cooking with kids program. (In terms of donated food items, you will detail in your proposal section what the program needs that the company can supply free of charge.)

Variations:

- If you are preparing the proposal for your instructor, be sure to include a cover page.

- If you are working on this assignment in small groups, prepare to present it to the rest of the class (in an oral presentation) as if they were the community outreach committee of Shopease Foods.

2. You are employed as a graphic designer in a creative department at a small advertising agency, and you and your colleagues are finding it hard to "get your mojo running" in the environment you work in. The workspace is drab—painted a depressing pea-green and devoid of artwork, with large beige curtains covering the windows at either end of the long room and hideous linoleum on the floor. The boss has noted that productivity in your department has gone down of late, so he has asked you to come up with some solutions to this problem in a proposal.

   The company is situated in a century-old building that has "great bone structure." You are sure that if the nasty linoleum were lifted, the original wood floor would be revealed and could be refinished. A historical photo you found in a dusty closet indicates that there are decorative brick walls beneath the poorly applied, lumpy drywall. A dropped ceiling partially covers the very tall windows, and if it were removed, there would be significantly more natural light.

   You and your colleagues have decided to propose a renovation to the space to make it warmer, sunnier, and more user-friendly. You know that the company is in its early phase of growth, so there isn't a lot of money around for the owners to splash out on contractors. Therefore, you all have decided that you will do whatever work can be done without specialized skills. Fortunately, one of the graphic designers worked in construction when he was at college, so he will be able to provide the expertise to ensure that the floor, walls, dropped ceiling, and window renovations will be done properly by the rest of the group.

   Write a proposal in non-memo format (more than two pages) to Jacques Bellefair, your boss (and co-owner of the company), proposing the work that is to be done, timelines, and what you and your colleagues are prepared to do to make it happen. You also need to ask for a certain amount of money for materials and equipment rentals and for three Fridays or Mondays off so that you can have three long weekends to get the job done. You know that this project will go a long way toward building solidarity in your work team, which will help the company be even more successful.

   This proposal will require a cover page, table of contents, and possibly budget pages at the end of it. Present it with a memo introducing the proposal, attached to the front of the proposal with a paper clip.

   Prepare to present the proposal to the rest of the class as though you were presenting it to Jacques Bellefair and the other co-owner of the company, who is also the financial comptroller.

3. At your company, holiday gift-giving has gotten out of hand. Because it's a family-owned company and everyone feels like part of the family, people have started to buy each other increasingly expensive gifts. This trend is difficult for some of the workers who really do not have the extra money to spend on a gift for a colleague when they have so many other expenses during the holiday season within their own households.

You have decided that it's time for the company to do something different. Recently, two of the managers of the company returned from a business trip in South Africa where they were investigating new sources of raw materials, and they were very moved by their visit to an AIDS centre for children and women. They made a presentation to anyone interested at the company in October, and now many people are talking about how they might help. On the other hand, the presentation also prompted a lot of discussion at work on Canadian social justice issues in terms of the food insecurity in many homes. Some say, "If we want to help someone, we should start at home."

In your position as the executive assistant to the president of the company, write a short proposal (up to two pages) in memo format to the chairperson of the social committee of your company, Lucy Lim, proposing that the company stop the regular gift exchange and instead collect what employees would normally spend on gifts to donate to the Stephen Lewis AIDS Foundation and the Ontario Association of Food Shares.

4. You are the assistant manager of Scores and Sports, a sporting goods store specializing in providing equipment, clothing, footwear, and accessories for almost every team and individual sport imaginable. In your city, Scores and Sports is best known for offering the widest range of brands, sizes, and features in hockey equipment and skates in the region. The local Junior A team gets all of its equipment at your store, as do minor hockey teams.

Recently, however, an American big-box chain store, Sports Unlimited, has set up shop on the outskirts of town. Their prices are hard to beat, but they have limited choice in brands and sizes. Last year, local residents who were worried about the area's independent shopkeepers did manage to dissuade a big-box store from building, so you know that the community is on the side of the small retailer. You are concerned about how the new store will affect your store's sales, so you have come up with a proposal for the owner and manager of Scores and Sports to build on this "support small business" sentiment in the community and reinforce your store as the place to buy sporting goods.

The proposal is for the store to provide financial sponsorship for minor hockey teams. Scores and Sports would provide team sweaters *at cost* for all teams that are sponsored and would donate $5,000 to the local minor hockey association to help kids who can't afford fees or equipment to participate in hockey.

As assistant manager, write a short (up to two pages) proposal in memo format for your immediate boss—Johan Richersohnn, Store Manager—and the owner of the store, Morris Pipher.

5. In your role as a junior designer working with an eco-fashion designer, you are responsible for contributing to design and tailoring as well as managing the boutique. Funk by Nature sells trendy, fashion-forward work and party clothing for women between 18 and 40 who appreciate one-of-a-kind clothing and like to make an "eco-statement" with what they wear. These women generally work at well-paying jobs, so the clothing is priced accordingly. The mark-up on production costs for garments is between 100 and 200 per cent.

Recently, with increasing sizes on the part of customers (because of growing obesity in North America), many women are unable to find clothing in the boutique that will fit them. The senior designer, Trixie Starr, has been producing clothing between sizes 00 and 10, which means that a lot of inventory is not being sold because it does not fit the larger-sized women coming into the store. Sales are down since this time last year.

You have been making a note each time a larger-sized potential customer comes into the boutique and goes away disappointed. At this point, it appears that one-third of the shopping traffic consists of women who wear sizes larger than 10. (To your trained eye—and from the conversations you've had with some shoppers—you estimate that most of these women would wear sizes 12 to 18.) Several items that Funk by Nature produces every season sell out regularly, so you think that creating just these pieces in a wider size range would be a good pilot project to determine the market for plus-size clothing in the store. It would also go a long way toward extending the company's mission of providing quality design to "everywoman."

Write a short, informal memo format proposal to the senior designer, Trixie Starr, to have her design and the company fabricate larger sizes in the most popular designs. (Tip: It would be a good idea to use numbers, such as the loss of sales in recent months, potential increases in sales with an expanded size range, and the means you will use to determine whether the pilot project has been a success.)

6. You are the owner and operator of a professional tiling installation subcontracting business that provides services to a prestigious tiling and flooring company, Underfoot Ltd., in Toronto. Wealthy customers come to Underfoot to select tiles from an array of materials (such as ceramic, granite, and, increasingly, marble) for bathroom and kitchen floors, and your company provides the skilled tradespersons to perform the installation.

Recently, a particular brand of marble tile from Italy (a very expensive brand!) has been breaking up or cracking when installed, even with every precaution and safeguard built into the installation process. This has led to costly replacement of many tiles on some major residential jobs in the past couple of months and has understandably annoyed and angered the customers, who have prepaid half the cost of the tiles.

You decided to do some investigation and research into the source of the tiles, and you found that the quarries from which this marble is taken have not produced consistent quality tile for the past year or so. (Thank goodness you took Italian in college—a great help in your review of many Italian websites!) You have translated the most important details and are prepared to share them with Underfoot's management for their attention and action.

Rather than just deliver the bad news, though, you want to provide Underfoot with some quality alternatives to their current marble supplier so that customers will be satisfied and the company can save money. You have found three other suppliers from the same region in Italy—smaller quarries, family-owned and -operated, so you think they would have better quality control. While you are not exactly fluent in Italian, you can get by while negotiating with a supplier. You want to propose that Underfoot's president and CEO, Julia Tran, take you with her on a quick visit to the quarries you have investigated to negotiate a new deal for tiling.

Write a brief (two pages or less) informal proposal in memo format to Julia Tran.

7. You manage the shipping of North American orders purchased through the online store of Green Thumb Garden Tools Inc. Orders are normally processed and mailed through

Canada Post to the customer within five business days of ordering, but over the past two months, you have received several complaints from US customers that their orders have been taking up to two weeks to arrive; in three cases, packages never arrived at their destination.

Because prompt delivery is key to keeping a loyal US customer base, you need to take action and find a new means to ship orders south. You have investigated several courier companies, and after comparing the advantages and disadvantages of each shipping method and company, you have decided that one of the companies is best for Green Thumb's US shipping needs. This company provides online tracking for customers and a guarantee of delivery within five business days to any location in the continental United States. (Their shipping guarantee is seven days to Hawaii, Puerto Rico, Guam, and US military installations around the world—but your company's guarantee did not extend to these areas previously. This would be an improvement on your offer of delivery within 14 business days.)

The cost of shipping, however, will be higher than it is currently, so you will need to meet this potential objection with some suggested strategies for implementation. Your strategies could address a price increase in shipping passed on to customers and how it would be done from marketing and customer service perspectives, or they could involve offering a price freeze on shipping for loyal customers. Think of how a price increase would affect both the company and the customer, and then consider what could be done to soften the blow.

Write a brief (two pages or less) proposal in memo format to Zachariah Stein, Vice-President, Operations, and Alexander Onassis, Vice-President, Customer Relations and Marketing, to switch the company's US shipping to the new courier company.

8. You are the manager of a local animal shelter that has a "no euthanize" policy. Because your organization is not-for-profit and government funding covers only the rent and utilities of the facility, you rely heavily on individual and corporate donations of money or supplies to keep the shelter operating.

Currently, the shelter has reached capacity; over the past winter, many cats and dogs were brought to the shelter, straining capacity to the maximum. At this point, you cannot take on any more unwanted or abandoned pets, so you have implemented a fostering program for people to take in these animals temporarily until homes or space in the shelter become available.

The municipality has agreed to finance an addition to the shelter building—but only if the shelter embarks on a community-wide public education campaign regarding spaying or neutering of pets to prevent the abuse or abandonment of unwanted animals.

It's clear that you need some major corporate funding to hire a PR consultant to research and produce a communication plan for this initiative and to produce materials for distribution in the community and at events, schools, and speaking engagements around the region.

Write a brief (less than three pages) proposal in memo format to Steve King, the vice-president of community relations and marketing of a major corporation in your area, to ask for assistance in funding this project. It will cost a total of $40,000, including $25,000 for the consultant to be hired on a six-month contract and $15,000 for promotional materials development, participation in community events, and a website. You could ask the company for all of the amount or just for part of it (perhaps either the consultant portion or the promotional materials and events portion of the total budget).

FYI—The vice-president loves animals and has adopted many strays or abandoned pets over the years, but the executive of the company will still have to be convinced of the value of endorsing this donation. You will need to document some solid benefits to the community and to the company in your proposal to help the vice-president persuade them.

CHAPTER 11

Formal Proposals

In this chapter, you will learn:

- The difference between formal and informal reports

- How to work effectively with a request for proposal (RFP)

- How to research and prepare information for formal proposals

- How to write the proposal persuasively so that readers endorse, support, or fund a proposed project, work, or activity

- Formatting guidelines for formal proposals

- Specific tips for oral presentation of formal proposals

ESSENTIAL EMPLOYABILITY SKILLS

2ooo+ Employability Skills The Conference Board of Canada has identified certain essential employability skills (EES) as benchmarks for performance in the workplace. You will learn the following EES skills in this chapter:

COMMUNICATE

- Can write and speak so others pay attention and understand
- Can listen and ask questions to understand and appreciate the points of view of others
- Can share information using a range of information and communications technologies (e.g., voice, email, computers)
- Can use relevant scientific, technological, and mathematical knowledge and skills to explain or clarify ideas
- Can read and understand information presented in a variety of forms (e.g., words, graphs, charts, diagrams)

MANAGE INFORMATION

- Can locate, gather, and organize information using appropriate technology and information systems
- Can access, analyze, and apply knowledge and skills from various disciplines (e.g., the arts, languages, science, technology, mathematics, social sciences, and the humanities)

THINK AND SOLVE PROBLEMS

- Can assess situations and identify problems
- Can seek different points of view and evaluate them based on facts
- Can recognize the human, interpersonal, technical, scientific, and mathematical dimensions of a problem
- Can identify the root cause of a problems
- Can be creative and innovative in exploring possible solutions
- Can evaluate solutions to make recommendations or decisions

Your company, Management Training Consultants, is seeking requests for proposal (RFPs) to develop, design, and facilitate training for medium-sized to large not-for-profit organizations. You have worked in the not-for-profit sector in project design, management development, and volunteer training for several years, most recently with the United Way, providing training in team-building and project management. Others in your company with less experience are able to work with you on various aspects of programming design and facilitation—providing supportive services. You find an RFP on the Charity Village website (http://www.charityvillage.com) that looks promising (see Figure 11.1).

FIGURE 11.1 Example of a Request for Proposal (RFP)

THE CENTRE FOR ONTARIO CHILD CARE

MEASUREMENT CONSULTANT

Position type:	Request for Proposal
Date ad posted:	Aug. 29, 2014
Job region:	ON (London area)
Application deadline:	Sept. 15, 2014
Location(s):	London

REQUEST FOR PROPOSALS

Description of the work

The Centre for Ontario Child Care is seeking a senior consultant with *proven experience in outcomes-based methods of project design and management and knowledge transfer/training for organizational teams.*

The consultant will design and deliver training sessions to enhance individual employees' and overall organizational capacity in outcomes-based project design, planning, management, and evaluation. He or she will use current or planned organizational projects as a hands-on means of training to help participants fully integrate and retain key concepts.

Target audience

The consultant will train 25 staff members of the centre. It is important to note that the staff's experience with project design and planning varies.

Required deliverables

An environmental scan: The consultant will design and deliver training to staff in methods for conducting an environmental scan (evaluating strengths and weaknesses and opportunities within an organization). He or she will provide guidance to staff as they complete a comprehensive environmental scan on the centre.

An outcomes-based project design and management plan for upcoming projects: The consultant will design and deliver training in the production of outcomes-based project proposals, including project implementation plans, monitoring and evaluation methods, and comprehensive budgets.

Required proposal format

The proposal must contain a list of five to 10 recent contracts or employment activities relevant to training and outcomes-based project design and management experience. A list of three references from relevant positions or contracts conducted within the past two years is required.

The proposal must also include timelines, projected required personnel, schedules, and costs/resources required to complete the project.

ASSUMPTIONS FOR THE PROPOSAL

- Project completion by January 30, 2015.
- Consultant bids may not exceed $65,000, including GST.
- The centre's manager will act as liaison and support for the consultant to ensure appropriate resources and supports are made available.
- All materials developed by the consultant are the exclusive property of the centre.
- The consultant will invoice the centre monthly, at the end of each month.
- Invoices for approved expenses (such as travel, postage) will be invoiced separately at the end of each month.

SUBMISSION DEADLINE
September 15, 2014

AWARD DATE
September 30, 2014

JOB CONTACT INFORMATION
Joan McAllister
Administrative Assistant
The Centre for Ontario Child Care
143 Queen Street
London, ON L8A 3V6

1. What would you do to prepare for writing this proposal?

2. Review the RFP carefully. What do you think are the most important points that you would need to address in the proposal? List these points so that you have a clear idea of what you would need to address.

3. How would you structure (format) the proposal?

4. How much detail do you think is required?

5. What tone or style would you employ to write the proposal?

Before You Begin . . .

A formal proposal is very much like an informal proposal except that it is a written offer to someone who is *external* to your organization or business.

However, some formal proposals *are* internal. This exception to the rule is when the proposal requires a lot of money, is a longer-term project, involves fundamental change for your organization, or is, in general, of major magnitude.

The proposal may be solicited by the other organization (a person from the other business may have asked you to write the proposal) or it may be unsolicited—a proposal that will benefit your organization *and* have equal or even more impressive benefit to the external organization. A formal proposal written within your organization also may be solicited or unsolicited.

SO HOW IS THE PROPOSAL FORMAL?

As the name suggests, a **formal proposal** is written and organized in a more formal way, including tone, word choice, style of writing, and formatting. Because more detail and explanation are required, as well as more formal style and tone in writing, formal proposals are generally longer—sometimes much longer—than informal proposals. They are never written in a memo format, even if they are brief and intended for an internal readership.

TABLE 11.1	Informal vs. Formal Proposals	
	INFORMAL	**FORMAL**
Solicited	Yes/no	Yes/no; often RFP
Covering letter	No (memo format)	Yes
Executive summary	No	Yes
Cover page	No (memo format)	Yes
Table of contents	No (memo format)	Yes
Introduction	Yes	Yes
Background	Yes	Yes
Proposal section	Yes	Yes
Benefits	Yes	Yes
Conclusion	Yes	Yes
Appendix	Possibly (few pages)	Yes (usually)
Sections	A few main sections	Several sections/subsections
Section numbering	Usually not needed	Recommended (longer proposals)
Writing tone/style	Moderately informal	Moderately formal to formal

ASSUME THAT YOUR READER KNOWS NOTHING ABOUT THE PROPOSAL TOPIC

If you are writing an unsolicited proposal, you should give even more emphasis to providing proof of the benefits of the proposed work, project, or expense. Because the person or people reading your proposal will have never seen it before—and because they were not involved in the lead-up to its creation—you cannot assume that they know anything about your topic. Instead, you need to assume they know *nothing* about the proposed work, project, or expense—even if the readers are experts.

TARGETED RESEARCH PERSUADES READERS

Whether your formal proposal is solicited or unsolicited, internal or external, you must conduct very targeted research to back up any statements you make about the benefits of the proposed work, project, or expense to the people you are trying to persuade. Your persuasiveness very much depends on the quality of your research and the way you express the relevant findings to prove the merits of your proposal.

As with an informal proposal, you must always indicate your sources in a complete citation at first mention and then in an abbreviated citation or reference every other time you use that source.

WHO ELSE MIGHT READ THE PROPOSAL?

Always keep in mind that unlike when you are writing an informal proposal, you probably do not know who all of the readers of your proposal will be. Although you are submitting it to one person or department, it may be circulated to a number of other people or departments whom you know nothing about. Assume that whoever reads your proposal has no knowledge of what you are proposing and that you will be doing a bit of educating in order to persuade your readers of its merits.

WHAT'S AN RFP?

In business and in the not-for-profit world, proposals are often written in response to a **Request for Proposal (RFP)** that may be circulated by the requesting organization to you, to your organization, or to several organizations like yours, or it may be posted in a newspaper, in a journal, or online. For example, municipal governments often post RFPs in community newspapers in order to attract local businesses to tender (offer services) through a formal proposal process. The RFP is often very specific in what the proponent (you, the writer) must provide in the proposal, sometimes down to the details of length and even how it is to be formatted. There are usually strict rules governing what questions you can pose to the organization putting out the RFP so that everyone who submits a proposal has equal access to information, thus creating a level playing field for everyone applying.

Other organizations that often post RFPs include businesses seeking certain services on contract or not-for-profit entities seeking another company, organization, or individual to provide specific contracted services (usually for a certain time period). An example of a website on which not-for-profit organizations post RFPs is Charity Village (http://www.charityvillage.com). The website includes job postings for work in a variety of charitable and not-for-profit organizations, as well as RFPs to attract proposals from related businesses and organizations that could provide certain services.

FORMATTING THE PROPOSAL

The formal proposal follows an organizational template similar to that of an informal proposal. The headings may be varied if you feel that others are more relevant to the specific proposal, but note that the headings may be specified in the RFP—that is, the solicitor of the proposal may have a very specific format in mind that takes in all of the information required. In other words, you will need to restate your potential client's needs and tie them into your proposal as you write it. If you stick to the expressed list of what is required, you will give them what they want rather than surprising them with details they don't really need or want. You will need to carefully study the RFP and any specifications that have been given for the proposal to ensure that you conform to what the readers expect. In fact, if you ignore the specified format for your proposal, it may not even be read, let alone considered!

The following sequence of elements and information make up the basic format for a formal proposal:

- covering letter (introducing the proposal, attached with a paper clip to the front of the executive summary or proposal package)
- executive summary
- cover (title) page
- table of contents
- introduction (including purpose, scope)
- background
- proposal
- benefits
- conclusion
- appendix (including references page and other supporting documents; follows its own cover page immediately after the conclusion)

As with any other report, it is advisable to use subheadings to keep the readers moving through the proposal and keep them from getting bogged down in a lot of text. If you have no specified format or outline for your proposal, use this template, and create appropriate subheadings to break up and organize your information, particularly in the background, proposal, and benefits sections. It is also highly recommended that you use a numbering system to organize headings, subheadings, and sections of information: for example, 1. HEADING, then 1.1 Subheading, 1.2 Subheading, 1.3 Subheading, and so on.

USE THE FORMAT TO ORGANIZE INFORMATION

Even if you have a specific format to follow, you might want to start your writing by organizing information points under the general headings of the basic template so that you have a good idea of where to go next with your writing. Insert the specified headings where you think they should go, or substitute them for the basic template headings, so that you can see how all the information you have gathered fits together.

INTRODUCE THE PROPOSAL WITH A LETTER

Once you have written the proposal, you will write a letter of transmittal that introduces the proposal, explains details briefly, and concludes by thanking the reader for receiving it and with an offer for more details along with your contact information. Note that even internal formal proposals should be accompanied by a transmittal (covering) letter—*not* a memo.

Idiom Alert

fromage – The French word for cheese. If something is referred to as *fromage*, it is likely something that stinks—something that is not quite right; it can be a case of someone trying too hard to influence someone else.

cheesy – When something is cheesy, it is much like what the word *fromage* describes—someone is trying too hard to impress someone else, usually in a showy or over-the-top way.

Your Starting Point

As with any other form of business writing or oral presentation, you need to know as much as possible about the reader(s) or receiver(s) of your communication. You need to know why you are writing and/or presenting. Make sure you apply the Starting Point questions to the known (and unknown, or possible) readers of the proposal.

In order to learn more about the readers of a proposal you are preparing for an external organization, you will need to do some research to answer these questions. The information you need can come from business directories and associations, from business advisory centres in your nearest town or city and your local library, and, of course, directly from the business or organization you are writing to.

Getting information from the organization or business directly can, however, be a bit challenging. First of all, if you are responding to an RFP, there may be rules about what you can and cannot ask for in terms of information so that the requester can maintain a level playing field for everyone who submits an application. Find out what these restrictions are—and *don't* press for more information beyond the stipulated areas. If you do, you may find your proposal discounted before it is even read.

However, if your proposal is unsolicited, or if it is solicited but there are no restrictions on access to information, then you can visit the business, use any contacts you have there to get information, or, best of all, get to know the person you will be writing to by becoming acquainted with his or her administrative assistant. Nicknamed "gatekeepers," assistants usually know at least as much as their bosses do, and it is often part of their job to keep people from bothering their supervisors with questions and requests for information. On the flip side, assistants are often extremely helpful if you genuinely try to get to know them and provide them with good reasons to give you information. These "good reasons" can include clear benefits for the company or the assistant's boss—but should not involve bribes!

In any case, when you are gathering information from the company or organization directly, remember to be respectful of the time, effort, and work of the people you are consulting for answers to your questions. (If you need more guidance on how to gather information about an organization or business, see Chapter 14, Job and Informational Interviews. Following the guidelines for conducting an informational interview will help you to get the information you need.)

If you are responding to an RFP, you need to determine what, specifically, the requester of the proposal wants to see in your proposal. What information is the organization looking for? What is it *not* looking for?

Whether the proposal is solicited or unsolicited, once you have as much information as possible about readers, the organization, and the project, you can create a purpose statement, focusing on why you are writing.

- What is the purpose of the proposal?

- What is the scope of the proposal—what will be addressed? What will not be addressed? What are the limitations of what you will include or address?

Creating the Written Product: How to Do It

PREPARING TO WRITE

Research

With a formal proposal, particularly if it is unsolicited, you will have to do your homework in order to truly prove the benefits of the proposed work, project, or expense to the reader. You cannot afford to make assumptions—or to make assertions about benefits you cannot prove. If you cannot prove benefits, you will not get the job or project—some other organization or business will.

In order to be persuasive—to prove that the proposed project, work, or expense is justified and desirable—you will definitely need to do some research.

Based on the answers to the questions noted previously, you know what kind of information the reader needs in order to be convinced of the merits of your proposal. (For examples of the kind of considerations your readers or the requester of your proposal might have, see the Preparing to Write section in Chapter 10, Informal Proposals.)

Think about the timelines for your proposal, and work backward from the deadline to plan for the time you will need to write and edit your work—and ahead of that, how much time you will realistically need for research.

Research for a formal proposal must be exhaustive, so it is likely to be very time-consuming. Don't underestimate how long it will take. Preparation is key, and the actual writing of the formal proposal takes the least amount of the time and work involved. It's much like painting a room in your house. Before you paint, you put in a lot of time: carefully taping around baseboards, windows, and door frames; moving the furniture or covering items that cannot be moved; spreading drop sheets on the floor; removing cover plates for switches and outlets; finding "work clothes" that you don't mind getting paint on.

Even more than for an informal proposal—which your reader is probably aware of or has solicited—your success depends on how effectively you prove the merits of your proposal. This means you have to provide quality information and statistics to prove that what you are proposing is a good risk or will deliver rewards to the reader and his or her company. Count on spending more time than you expect to find the highest-quality, verifiable, and credible sources of information to support your proposal.

Just as you do for informal proposals, you need to consult a variety of research sources, including the Internet, specific business or topic/sector databases, oral interviews with known experts, trade or business organizations, and print sources. Again, as suggested for informal proposals, it is strongly recommended that you get to know your reference librarian and ask for help. Sometimes, depending on how much the proposal is worth to you or your company, you may hire someone with specific expertise in research to find the best possible information needed to convince the reader(s) of the merits of the proposal.

For more tips on using the Internet for researching your proposal, please see Chapter 10, Informal Proposals.

Time management is a key factor in business communication, particularly when you're working on formal proposals. Create a work schedule based on your proposal deadline, leaving enough time to edit and polish your work. You might also set automatic reminders via your email account or your mobile phone to keep yourself on track with project goals.

PREPARING FOR CITATIONS

It bears repeating: the professionalism and quality of your proposal depend on your information sources. The success of your proposal—and winning the contract—depends on how well you defend the benefits with verifiable, current sources that your readers can easily look up for themselves. Again—nothing will sink your proposal faster than blanket statements about benefits or features with no indication of where you got the information.

Plagiarism is a serious offence in a college or university, and it is equally serious in a business or organizational setting, but with different consequences. If you are perceived as having merely copied and pasted information in large chunks in your proposal, you will come across as lazy and dishonest. Further, you could end up in legal trouble for having used someone else's work, quickly acquire a bad reputation for yourself or your company, and effectively eliminate yourself or your business from any future dealings with your target organization. Further, bad news spreads faster than good news, and when there is less than positive information circulating about you or your company, you may be surprised at what a small world the business sector you work in suddenly becomes in terms of how many people find out.

Once you have found good information for your proposal, immediately write down everything you can about the source, and keep the information in a safe place for future reference. This information should include, but is not limited to, the following items:

- the website address, date accessed, date of most recent update or launch of the website, any authors of materials you are using, the name of the organization hosting the website, the titles of articles or information sections, the section or paragraph number on the webpage where the reader can find the information if desired;

- the title of the print source, chapter name/number (if relevant), names of authors, volume or issue number (if relevant), series name/number (if relevant), publisher name, publication date;

- the full name and title of the person you spoke with, the organization or business the person works for or with, the date you spoke with this person, their contact information.

You don't need to cite information sources within the document as you would in an academic research paper (but mention them in full the first time you use them and thereafter in an abbreviated way every time you use them). Your paper record of all of your information sources will also be essential in preparing a references page in your appendix section.

Sometimes an RFP will specify that you must provide a works-cited, sources, or references page so that the reader can see at a glance where you got your information if he or she wants to verify facts or do further research. Even if not specified, you may want to produce a references page based on the needs and profile of the reader you are addressing or on the actual project, work, or expense. (See Chapter 1 for guidance on how to create in-text citations and a works-cited, sources, or references page, as well as Appendix B.)

ORGANIZING INFORMATION AND WRITING: FORMAT

As mentioned previously, the basic format of a formal proposal is simple: executive summary, cover/title page, table of contents, introduction (including purpose, scope), background, the proposal, benefits, conclusion, and appendix (including references page and other supporting documents). The appendix is usually headed by its own cover page, which immediately follows the conclusion, thus separating this section from the rest of the text.

However, most formal proposals can and do deviate from the basic outline. In terms of organizing your information before you write, it's a good idea to start with the basic template. If you are writing for an RFP, you should look at the headings you are directed to use, if any, and then put these into the sections in your basic template to which you feel they most closely correspond. You may need to insert subheadings within larger sections, such as the background, proposal, or benefits sections, based on what the requester of the RFP has asked for.

If you are writing a non-RFP proposal, you may want to use subheadings to break up text in a logical way to keep the reader moving through the document, as you would in a longer informal proposal. Again, use the basic template until you have all the information organized where you want it, and then think about logical subheadings in various places within the larger sections of the report.

Once you have finished writing the proposal, you will write a letter of transmittal, which introduces the proposal and briefly notes all of the main details.

Basic formal proposal outline

(In order of appearance)

LETTER OF TRANSMITTAL

The letter of transmittal, like any other letter, follows the basic format (see Chapter 3, Business Letters) of introduction (purpose/scope), background, body/content, and conclusion but is *not* a memo and does not have subheadings. Keep the tone moderately formal—more formal than that of an informal proposal or memo—and do not use first-person pronouns (*I, me, we, us*). It is best printed on letterhead.

EXECUTIVE SUMMARY

Depending on the requirements of an RFP—or the research into your reader—you may decide to position the summary page before the title page or immediately after it. Either way is acceptable, but for the purposes of this text, it is suggested that you attach it to the cover page of your formal proposal.

The summary is just that—a summary of your entire proposal, start to finish, stating introduction (purpose/scope), background, main proposal points, main benefit points, and then a conclusion.

It is written in a moderately formal tone and assumes nothing about the reader's knowledge of or experience with the proposed work, project, or expense.

If it's placed after the title page, it is still considered entirely separate from the body of the proposal, because it comes just before the table of contents and is not a numbered page.

COVER PAGE

The cover or title page is a neatly formatted page with the title of the proposal, the date, and your complete contact information. It often includes your company logo or logotype with your contact information, and it is best produced on card stock (both the front and back pages of your proposal), bound to the rest of the report with Cerlox or similar binding or stapled and included as part of a presentation portfolio or package. In any case, it needs to stand out as a clean, professional presentation of what is to come.

TABLE OF CONTENTS

The table of contents is another separate page following the title page (and possibly the summary, which would immediately precede it). It clearly sets out the various sections of your proposal—with headings and subheadings—and lists the page number where each section begins.

This page needs to be formatted so that the headings, leader dots (the dots connecting the headings to their page numbers), and page numbers are aligned neatly; otherwise, your proposal will look sloppy and unprofessional. First impressions count when you are trying to persuade someone to contract your services, spend a lot of money, or make another form of major investment in the proposed work.

INTRODUCTION

In this section, describe why you are writing (the purpose) and the scope (what you will and will not cover in the proposal or its limitations). Remember that you are writing either to an external audience—and the readers may include many people other than the person you are writing to—or to an internal audience who may or may not know much about the proposal you are presenting to them. Assume that your readers know very little about what you are about to propose.

Details are important—but these will be taken care of later on in the proposal itself. The idea at this point is to generate interest on the part of the reader, so you must write in a persuasive manner. Choose information that is attention-grabbing without being sensational: facts, statistics, a news item, or something mildly amusing to get the reader's attention (but be very careful with humour unless you know the reader will appreciate the joke).

Note that while you want to engage the reader, you should not come across as "too familiar." Keep your tone moderately formal, and never use first-person singular or second-person pronouns (*I, me, mine, my, you, your*).

BACKGROUND

In this section, you provide a history or background of what led to the writing of the proposal. This could include details of the RFP posting found online or in a newspaper; mention of you being asked to write the proposal by the reader; historical facts or a situation

(continued)

that led to the proposed work, project, or expense; or past experience you have had with the proposed work, project, or expense.

However, the background should never be very personal—your passion, your interest, or your hobby in the field of interest should not be mentioned here except briefly and only if it is important in impressing your reader with your academic or work experience in the field.

Again, refer to the answers to the "5 Ws and how" questions to help you put this section together. As in writing an informal proposal, you must not make any unsupported assumptions about the merits of the proposed work or expense. Prove to the reader that the work or expense is justified, has merit, or will make money for the organization, for example, with solid facts and statistics that will demonstrate the strength of the proposal. You will, of course, have to cite this information.

In fact, throughout the formal proposal, you should make liberal and regular use of citations from sources you have consulted. It shows that you are a thorough researcher and writer and, more important, a highly competent person capable of following up on the work of the proposal. However, if your proposal mainly consists of quotations and very little of your own writing, it may annoy the reader and make you look less competent. Remember, use of other people's writing and ideas must be carefully balanced with your own writing, your own perspective, and how you integrate all the information into a proposal that is worth considering.

THE PROPOSAL (OR A MORE SPECIFIC TITLE RELATED TO THE PURPOSE OF THE PROPOSAL IF APPROPRIATE OR DEMANDED BY AN RFP)

Based on the information provided in the previous sections of your proposal, you are now ready to explain the actual details of what you are proposing. In this section, you describe the proposed work, project, or expense with lots of detail and many citations in as neutral a way as possible.

The proposal section outlines the who, what, where, when, why, and how of the proposed work. It gives the reader all the features and elements of the project and leads directly to the *pitch* or *sale* in the benefits section.

In this section, you should also indicate how you will monitor the project, particularly if it involves a long period of time, many people or departments, and/or a lot of money. These monitoring methods often include regular documentation to the person or organization for which the work is being done, such as budget, progress, and information reports. Not only are you telling the reader the details of the project, you are assuring him or her that it will be carefully managed and monitored for best results.

As well as the interim reports on work, you may also offer a final evaluation report that would assess all the work done on the project or the merits and results of the expense incurred.

Remember to write the proposal section in short, to-the-point paragraphs so that the reader can easily follow your proposal information—but do include all details that are important to the reader so that he or she can make an informed decision about your proposal. Use appropriate or requested subheadings to keep the reader moving through the information and to highlight important points of your proposal.

BENEFITS

This is the section where you really *sell* your proposal to the reader by writing—as factually as possible—about its evident benefits to the target individual, company, or organization. Benefits can't be vague—they must be very specific and clearly based on facts, statistics, and verifiable information that the readers themselves would have access to. With this in mind, you should not make any statement that you cannot back up with facts. See Figure 11.2 for an example of a **benefit statement**.

You can determine which benefits will really get the attention of the readers by reviewing what you have learned about them from your 5-Ws-and-how research and answers. Find out what excites the readers: Is it cost savings? Increased revenues? Stronger recognition in the industry or by the consumer? A better profile in the community? Helping those who can't help themselves?

Learn what the readers' psychographic tendencies are (their motivation and what demotivates them), as well as their biases and pet projects, and you will be well on your way to writing convincingly of proven benefits that will interest them—and win their buy-in.

FIGURE 11.2 **Benefit Statement**

The proposed work will increase revenues of XYZ Corporation by 100 per cent. —— Statement.
We are confident in making this prediction, since ABC Corporation, a direct
competitor of XYZ, experienced a similar revenue increase in the fourth quarter of 2005 based on its implementation of the same proposed system (ABC
Corporation Annual Report 2005). —— Proof.

CONCLUSION

The conclusion neatly restates the purpose, background, and main points of your proposal. It also makes
a final pitch about the benefits of the proposal to the
readers and their organization or business. This final
pitch is much like the introduction—you want to leave
your readers as excited about your proposal as they
were in the beginning, feeling that they really *must*
engage you or your company to do the work or project
involved.

However, a word of caution: avoid *fromage*. That is,
avoid cheesy or sweeping closing statements, such as
"This project will take XYZ Corporation into the next mil-
lennium and beyond" or "With this community project,
XYZ Corporation will forever have a place in the hearts
of the people of Anytown." Keep it short, sweet, and to
the point—get to the heart of what the reader is really
looking for. Even if your proposal was unsolicited, make
a case for it based on what you have found out about
the reader's needs, wants, concerns, or dreams.

Sample Documents

The following proposal (Figure 11.3) was written in response to an actual request for
proposal (RFP), which can be found on the textbook's website (www.oupcanada.com/
Luchuk). The proposal was to encourage decision-makers in a county in Ontario to
hire the proponents (the company writing the proposal) for the research and development of a tourism marketing plan.

For confidentiality reasons, the proposal sample does not include a spreadsheet
budget or financial statements.

The organization issuing the RFP also provided additional, previous reports and
information leading up to the proposed work for background reference, which the
writer drew on heavily to persuade the reader(s) to hire her team.

Because the proposal is a response to an RFP, and the RFP included supporting
documents to which the readers of the proposal would also have access, the writer
considered that these readers had a good understanding of what needed to be done in
terms of developing a marketing plan for the region as a tourism destination. Therefore,
the proposal only briefly reiterates what the readers already know, and it then elabo-
rates on what her company can offer in terms of services to establish an effective marketing plan.

FIGURE 11.3 Example of a Proposal Written for an RFP

March 19, 2012

Victoria Millpond
President, Millpond Communications Inc.
RR #3
Peterborough, ON K9J 1G2

The Corporation of the Municipality of Prince Edward County
123 Water Street,
Picton, ON K0L 1V0
Attention: Greta Swenson, Clerk

RE: RFP-146, Development of a Tourism Destination Marketing Plan

Dear Ms Swenson,

Please find attached Millpond Communications Incorporated's proposal to develop a tourism destination marketing plan for Prince Edward County (PEC).

Per the specifications noted in the RFP document, we have provided a detailed background section highlighting the municipality's and local businesses' concerns and challenges in reference to tourism business development, as well as brief, complete details of our plan to research, write, edit, and present the final marketing plan. Consultation with stakeholders in PEC's tourism industry and related businesses and organizations will be a part of the entire plan development process.

A complete budget in both narrative (within the proposal) and spreadsheet format (within the Appendix) is also provided, as well as our team's qualifications (in the Appendix) per the RFP instructions.

Should you have any questions, I would be pleased to speak with you at (705) 555-6677, or entertain queries by email at president@millpond.ca. We look forward to hearing from you soon.

Yours truly,

Victoria Millpond

Attachments: Executive Summary and Three-Year Tourism Marketing Plan Proposal

EXECUTIVE SUMMARY

While Prince Edward County (PEC) offers sun, water, beaches, fine dining, wineries, and most of all, a relaxed place to get away from it all, it isn't as widely known to Ontario tourists as it could be. Those "in the know" quickly become regulars, returning year after year or season after season to relax and restore—but word of mouth advertising hasn't quite helped PEC's tourism businesses and services become a premier destination for tourists close to home or from further afield.

The municipality, along with such key stakeholders organizations as county chambers of commerce, the Picton and Bloomfield Business Improvement Associations, and individual business owners and operators have mutually agreed that a Three-Year Marketing Plan would be a great start to build capacity in the tourism sector. Specifically, such a plan should build a brand for what PEC has to offer, as well as "buzz" in all media channels to attract a diverse range of tourists from Ontario and beyond.

The plan will also address education of the target tourist group, those interested in the attractions of the county and located in Ontario. In several surveys to date, the majority of Ontario tourists did not identify PEC as a "destination of choice." In order to educate tourists, our proposal outlines how stakeholders will be engaged in consultations with our team to identify key attractions and their features of relevance/interest to the target tourist group.

Concurrently, Millpond Communications will conduct research to identify or confirm the primary and secondary customers for PEC's attractions and, specifically, their demographic and psychographic profiles to better communicate about the key features and attractions identified in consultations with stakeholders. Further, a customer survey will be developed in consultation with stakeholders; this will generate consistent, regular feedback from visitors to be used not only in future marketing but also in development of existing businesses and new entrepreneurial enterprises catering more closely to visitor needs and wants. Contact information of those participating (where permission is granted) will be included in a database to assist PEC's businesses to effectively market directly to primary and secondary customers.

Throughout, consultations with diverse stakeholders will also help to generate a sense of community solidarity and commitment to working together to create the Three-Year Marketing Plan. Once brought together by the process, our team will work with those interested to form a central, cohesive tourism marketing organization to work with the marketing plan and to develop a process and guidelines for working as a committee for maximum mutual benefit and minimal conflict.

(continued)

THREE-YEAR TOURISM MARKETING PLAN AND STRATEGY PROPOSAL

RFP-146

Millpond Communications Incorporated
RR #3
Peterborough, ON K9J 1G2

Table of Contents

The Table of Contents gives the reader a guide through the proposal pages by sections and subsections.

(continued)

The introduction states what the proposal will address and why it is being written.

INTRODUCTION

Sun, water, sand . . . and wineries, fine dining, bed and breakfasts, historical sites, and miles of trails and roads for meandering and driving at a leisurely pace.

Sounds like the perfect weekend—or longer—getaway for the frazzled in need of some R&R, but for the most part, idyllic Prince Edward County (PEC) is a well-kept secret as a destination.

While those "in the know" return repeatedly to seek respite from everyday life, tourism in the county could be greatly enhanced by a targeted marketing plan that builds on the strengths of the business community and natural assets.

The following is a proposal to research and establish a Three-Year Marketing Plan for Prince Edward County, based on specified requirements of a recently released Request for Proposal.

Background addresses all of the information and events that led to the Request for Proposal—usually represents writer's research into the reasons for the project; therefore, it is longer/more detailed than the rest.

BACKGROUND

Prince Edward County is starting its tourism marketing process with a number of major strengths, including research into tourism destination branding and market analysis in county, regional, and provincial reports produced over the past year. This information is an excellent base from which to pursue further targeted research into markets and competition, consult with stakeholders on future directions and marketing strategy, build capacity in the tourism industry with a consolidated, unified tourism marketing organization, and develop an appropriate and dynamic brand for the region. This previous research will help in the development of a three-year plan to effectively market PEC's many premier destination activities, amenities, and experiences to an enthusiastic marketplace.

The core attractors for PEC's target tourism market (primarily Ontario-based tourists seeking overnight/extended stays and day trips) include beaches and the Lake Ontario waterfront, wine and culinary experiences, and outdoor activities. Supporting attractors (which will be further developed in a Three-Year Marketing Plan) include arts, heritage, and cultural experiences, several festivals and events, and specialty shopping. The PEC tourism "product" has been determined by CTS/ITS data to be relevant to visitors from regional, provincial, national/US, and international markets. There is enough for people to do to keep them occupied for more than 24 hours. PEC is easily accessed via Hwy. 401 and other well-maintained highways, as well as from Lake Ontario.

Acronym used here without explanation because reader used it in the RFP.

In summary, there is certainly potential to expand on these activities or venues of interest to optimize economic success for the region's tourism and much more when it comes to developing supporting attractors as primary streams of income and capacity to further diversify PEC's appeal to visitors.

Further, PEC has had significant critical acclaim in third-party published articles and reviews and has certainly come to be known as a destination of interest by those interested in wine and culinary experiences. As Ontario's newest wine region, PEC has a range of fine dining establishments, a cooking school, and an expanding culinary scene in which many of Canada's best-known chefs are deliciously presenting a wide range of cuisines. PEC is also recognized in the media and anecdotally as a significant destination for outdoor activities, particularly those associated with being on or near a lake, as well as cycling, running, hiking, and other pursuits. Sandbanks Provincial Park continues to be recognized internationally as an environmentally unique venue for water-based pursuits and is very frequently booked solid by families, individuals, and groups for camping.

Commitment from stakeholders in PEC's tourism economy has been encouraging, as over the past five years a significant investment has been made in facility renewal or expansion. Individuals seem committed to reinvesting in programming and infrastructure. The county and municipalities have committed to improving road, transit, and parking infrastructure in high-traffic tourist areas with an official plan for roads in PEC and a Picton Downtown Revitalization Plan.

However, there is plenty of room for improvement.

Branding

To start with, PEC's brand, "A Beautiful Island Adventure," does not express the region's unique appeal to target and secondary markets. The branding issue will be addressed in this project through careful, in-depth research into target and secondary markets and their interests and expectations of a tourism experience. Consultation with stakeholders will ensure that the brand is one that expresses the culture and "personality" of not only the county but also individual businesses and organizations.

Other marketing challenges

In addition to the brand issue, there are several other challenges in attracting primary and secondary markets that will be addressed in the Three-Year Marketing Plan. (These challenges have been articulated in the supporting documents to the RFP, as disseminated by the county.)

First, there is a distinct lack of knowledge on the part of the target market about what PEC has to offer. When queried in a variety of provincial government–sponsored surveys, the majority of Ontario tourists did not identify Prince Edward County as a "destination of choice."

According to the *2005 Eastern Ontario Tourism Sector Study* (The Tourism Company), part of the reason for the lack of recognition by tourists is an underdevelopment of PEC's culture and rich heritage product. There is tremendous potential to bring out the hidden gems of the county by exploring communities' and attractions' appeal to the target and secondary tourist. The consultation process with stakeholders who are particularly involved with these "gems" will help to create a strategy to appropriately develop and then market these products.

Subheadings are used to highlight key areas of information the RFP indicated should be addressed.

2

(continued)

In terms of the identified core and supporting attractors (as well as the unidentified, as just mentioned), there has not been any unified or cohesive promotion. Marketing efforts have been sporadic, not concentrated enough on the demographics and psychographics of the target and secondary tourist market. Matching the appeal of the attractions to what the target or secondary customer is looking for in a vacation experience will be key to developing an advertising and promotional strategy that will effectively boost the tourism economy. One of the causes of the minimal promotional activity may be that insufficient funds have been directed to this work. Because marketing efforts of the magnitude needed for PEC are expensive, obtaining financial support from all sectors of the PEC economy will be critical.

In the *Premier Ranked Tourism Destination Report* (The Tourism Company, 2005), it is noted that overnight or extended-stay opportunities have not been promoted in the advertising and promotional activities that have been undertaken. This has led to a lack of recognition of PEC as a weekend or holiday destination. When a cross-section of Ontarians were asked about where they could go for a weekend or longer stay, very few identified PEC as a destination of choice, according to provincial tourism market research (Ministry of Tourism study, 2005). The marketing plan will certainly identify the appeal to the target and secondary customer (based on demographics and psychographics) of overnight and longer stays and match this to what is offered in terms of accommodation and meals to come up with a comprehensive strategy to get the word out about PEC's B&Bs, lodges, cabins, hotels, guest houses, and dining opportunities.

In terms of those tourists who do make their way to PEC, The Tourism Company's reports indicate a lack of regular customer satisfaction survey processes. No focus groups or questionnaires concerning the PEC tourism experience have been held or disseminated and collected across the county, with the exception of some individual destinations' or attractions' own customer satisfaction measurement tools.

In consultation with stakeholders, a comprehensive set of questions for a customer satisfaction questionnaire will be developed, and this questionnaire will be distributed to all stakeholders across the county to ensure a comprehensive, wide-reaching gathering of information. Once the information has been gathered in hard copy, the yet-to-be-organized tourism organization for PEC will input these responses on an ongoing basis into a database. The database would be created for the collation and processing of such important marketing information as tourist address and demographic information; attractions, accommodations, services, and restaurants visited; and guidance to improve the PEC tourist experience.

According to the reports supplied by Prince Edward County, there is a low internal awareness of the importance of tourism in PEC's economy. In other words, PEC's communities, particularly the business community, are not aware of how their venture fits into the tourism economy, nor of how to market themselves effectively

3

within a broader brand and marketing effort. Few business owners understand the importance of marketing to the tourism market, instead focusing efforts on a limited, local customer base.

In conducting consultations, it will be critical to get the message across that there is a quantifiable, economic benefit for businesses to participate in PEC's tourism marketing efforts. Proving "what's in it for them" will be essential not only to obtaining endorsement of the county's tourism marketing activities but to ensuring financial support from all stakeholders for the costs of the marketing program.

Once the marketing plan has been completed, there will be a need for the creation of a central, cohesive tourism marketing organization. This will be no small task, since it will be important to take into consideration as many perspectives as possible from stakeholders across the county in the consultation process.

Once a picture emerges of what the stakeholders feel will work in this organization, best marketing practices from other similar destinations and the needs of the county as a region will also have to be taken into consideration. There may be differing ideas as to how this organization should be set up; in light of this, it is recommended that the interim marketing entity be evaluated after one year so that all interested stakeholders can assess future directions for marketing in the county. A conflict resolution method should also be implemented at the start of the new organization so that issues are worked out in a timely and appropriate manner.

These areas are of specific concern when considering market analysis and subsequent marketing strategy, and they will be addressed in a Three-Year Marketing Plan.

Infrastructure concerns

While a marketing plan to attract tourists is critical, the infrastructure of the county must be sufficient to accommodate and support major growth in the tourism economy. "If you build it, they will come"—but if everything that is being marketed is not available to tourists, they will leave with a negative impression, and bad experiences are communicated far more broadly and quickly than positive ones.

A strategy to address the following concerns will be included in the plan, following consultation with all stakeholders:

- Limited accommodation offerings (no brand-name hotels).
- Underdevelopment of culture and heritage product by stakeholders/communities.
- Core and supporting attractors not easy to purchase at a distance.
- Product offerings primarily available only between June and October, leading to poor tourism performance in the rest of the year.
- No investment made in animating public spaces.

4

(continued)

- Primary tourism experience involves day trips.
- Destinations and stakeholders do not conduct surveys or use other information-gathering tools to track and assess customer satisfaction.
- Key experience, service, and prices are not monitored, which is essential for a cohesive marketing effort for PEC.
- Visitors must use automotive transportation to get to the county.
- Underfunding of county and stakeholder marketing efforts.
- General lack of awareness on the part of PEC residents of tourism's importance.
- No county-based customer service training.
- Lack of investment in developing underdeveloped/secondary attractors and assets, as well as in revitalization of underperforming assets.
- No plan in place to manage tourism carrying capacity in PEC.

While the challenges to tourism marketing and sector-specific economic development are sizable, it is important to see them also as *opportunities* to build PEC's tourism capacity. While we will acknowledge and detail the challenges in the consultative process, we will also present them as opportunities for stakeholders to rise to the occasion and work collaboratively and creatively to come up with PEC-appropriate solutions. During and following the consultation process, relevant research will be applied to resolve areas of concern in order to prepare a strategy for success for the PEC tourism economy as well as address stakeholders' interests.

It is expected that the process and the final plan and strategy will capitalize and expand on current strengths in PEC's tourism economy and further develop the potential of secondary streams of tourism income for the county and stakeholders.

Objectives

As specified by the RFP, there are several objectives to be achieved in the development of a Three-Year Marketing Plan:

1. To provide Prince Edward County with a highly marketable destination brand, recognized by primary and secondary tourism markets.

2. To create a cohesive, truly representative tourism organization to market and support tourism marketing efforts in Prince Edward County (through consultation with stakeholders).

3. To research/determine stable funding for tourism marketing efforts from within the county and through any available government/other grant schemes.

4. To create a Three-Year Marketing Plan and Strategy based on in-depth research into markets and competition, existing market research from previous reports,

5

consultation with stakeholders within Prince Edward County, and best tourism marketing practices.

5. To establish a promotional and advertising plan, including graphic, print, media, and online promotional activities and products.

6. To determine an appropriate budget for all marketing and promotional activities, balancing advertising and promotional execution costs with available funding resources.

Method

Building on the previous research into the development of Prince Edward County as a tourism destination, the proposed work of this proposal will include branding, tourism organizational development, and research into sustainable funding for tourism development and marketing initiatives. The culmination of these efforts will be a Three-Year Marketing Plan produced with the support and guidance of stakeholders in PEC's tourism sector so that it is endorsed and achievable by all involved.

Branding

Appropriate branding of the county's varied tourism opportunities, concurrent with the county's tourism profile itself, will require consultation with stakeholders such as owners/managers of accommodations and cultural/historical/sports/outdoor attractions, and facilitators of events, festivals, and other tourism activities.

It appears that a concerted effort has been made to date to engage stakeholders in the process leading up to the issuing of the RFP, and information and feedback from this process will be included in the branding process of this contract.

To continue this critical consultation process, one-on-one, small-group, and larger-group meetings will be held throughout the first three months of this contract (January to March, approximately). We have planned for 10 small- and larger-group meetings in this segment of the process to be held in various communities throughout the county. These meetings will allow us to meet with as many people as possible while minimizing costs and time to obtain necessary information for branding.

To further the effort to be inclusive, we will be contacting stakeholders through telephone, mail, and online surveys to collect further input for a comprehensive consultation that will lead to a truly representative branding for Prince Edward County as a tourism destination. Where possible, particularly in conjunction with scheduled consultation meetings, we will meet with key stakeholders as identified by PECTDA or through this process itself.

6

(continued)

Collected information, as well as previously solicited information from earlier county, regional, and provincial tourism reports, will be combined to determine an appropriate branding to represent Prince Edward County as a tourism destination, as well as its constituent tourism and related businesses and organizations.

The final draft of the branding process will be presented at meetings in April, along with a proposal for a countywide tourism marketing and planning organization (see below for details). Because the process to arrive at the branding will be based on extensive consultation, it is assumed that only minor changes to the branding statement(s) suggested by stakeholders will need to be incorporated at this point.

The new Prince Edward County tourism brand will be included in the Three-Year Marketing Plan and Strategy, to be completed and submitted by the end of May 2013.

Tourism organizational development

Prince Edward County would like to develop a representative, cohesive tourism marketing structure/organization that will implement the Three-Year Marketing Plan, identify issues of common interest to tourism stakeholders, solve problems as needed, and develop further capacity in the tourism economy of the county.

Consultation through the meetings, one-on-one consultations, and surveys mentioned previously will also be an opportunity to solicit stakeholders' suggestions and ideas for developing a countywide tourism development and marketing organization/structure to represent themselves as well as the county as a destination.

This feedback, obtained through professional facilitation of targeted questions to determine the structure that would be most appropriate for this organization, will be collated and included, along with *relevant* best practices of tourism marketing organizations elsewhere. Utilizing the specific expertise of our team members in organizational development and behaviour, an organizational structure will be created and presented back to stakeholders in meetings in April (see Timeline) for final review and changes.

Through the above-noted meetings, one-on-one consultations, and surveys, we will identify key stakeholders of interest. Once a representative tourism marketing organization has been determined and planned, these key stakeholders will be asked to participate to ensure that implementation of the marketing plan is equitable and representative of the many and varied business and cultural tourism interests in the county.

7

The structure of the proposed tourism marketing and planning organization will be unveiled in meetings with stakeholders in April 2013. It is anticipated, with extensive consultation and reference to other previous research, that only minor changes or adjustments to this plan will need to be made before it is presented as part of the Three-Year Marketing Plan and Strategy in May of 2013.

Research/development of stable funding

In order to establish stable funding for Prince Edward County's tourism marketing efforts and implementation of the Three-Year Marketing Plan and Strategy, a two-pronged approach will be used.

The first part of the research and establishment of stable funding will be to get a sense of what kind of funding can be pooled, consistently, from all stakeholders and individuals with an interest in tourism in the county. This feedback will be obtained through professionally facilitated meetings and consultations as noted above.

Individual follow-up to obtain financial commitments from stakeholders across the county will be important. Telephone, mail, and online methods as appropriate will effect this.

The second part of this process will be to research government and other grant monies available for tourism marketing. We will have a dedicated researcher on our team who will conduct this research in (approximately) March 2013, following research into target and secondary markets and competitive analysis.

Financial commitments from within the county and potential sources of funding from elsewhere will be presented as part of the Three-Year Marketing Plan and Strategy.

THE PROPOSAL: THREE-YEAR MARKETING PLAN AND STRATEGY

Overview

The Three-Year Marketing Plan and Strategy will be the culmination of the consultation process; extensive research into target and secondary markets, competition, and best practices in tourism marketing; and previous county, regional, and provincial tourism reports and studies.

From our review of PEC-related provincial, regional, and county-level tourism studies and reports, we have ascertained that there is a solid, basic understanding of target and secondary markets, competition, and overall placement of PEC within the tourism economy of Ontario. This information will be invaluable as a base from which to further research and acquire more critical demographic and consumer habits

8

(continued)

information about target and secondary markets and tourists, as well as to conduct a detailed analysis of the competition's strengths and weaknesses in reference to the PEC tourism brand.

Of course, no marketing strategy will be effective unless the stakeholders involved articulate their vision and concerns regarding marketing of their own interests as well as those of the county. An extensive consultative process, as noted previously, will harvest stakeholders' input into the process to create a strategy that all can endorse and support.

The consultative process will include receiving feedback from stakeholders on tourism development and marketing efforts. We will be assessing the stakeholders' overall business objectives as well as the market environment. Business and community profiles will be developed based on this thorough process to assist with the development of a tailor-made tourism strategy for each PEC community and the county as a whole as well as branding.

An essential part of our consultation work will be to identify resources (monetary and otherwise) available in each PEC community. The success of any venture really depends on how committed stakeholders are to the process, and through sincere consultation, we are confident that we will also be able to obtain commitment for financial and other support of PEC's tourism plan implementation. Resources will also include a thorough skills assessment of the stakeholders in order to determine who can assume various aspects of leadership as the plan is implemented in the years to come.

Because implementation of such a comprehensive tourism plan will require perhaps more capital than the community can afford, we will investigate all possible corporate, government, and charitable sources of funding available to PEC.

The plan will clearly identify the segment of the overall Ontario (and Canadian) tourism industry that PEC fits into. From this overall identification, we will then focus more closely on the segments and portions of the PEC tourism market to develop appropriate marketing objectives for them. Marketing strategies and mixes will then be developed for each segment, focusing on product, price, placement, and promotion.

A timeline and specific tasks will be outlined in an implementation plan, as well as suggestions for a tourism marketing organization structure. Again, we will be working very closely with stakeholders to create an implementation plan and organizational structure that will work with the county communities' and businesses' unique needs and situations to ensure compliance to the plan.

A marketing budget will be carefully created, based on worst-case scenario expenses and income. By planning for the worst and hoping for the best, the plan will be feasible even if several key factors of the plan do not come to fruition. While we will most certainly plan for the best outcomes, it is realistic to plan a budget around possible challenges so that the plan can go forward regardless.

Evaluation of the marketing plan and strategy on a regular basis will be essential to ensure success of the tourism industry in PEC. Evaluation methods that are easily implemented and assessed will be executed at various time intervals (at six months, the first year, and annually thereafter).

Proposed format of the marketing plan and strategy

The information and data collected from past reports, the consultation process, and our research will be distilled into a comprehensive marketing plan that will include the following:

1. **Stakeholder-determined objectives**

2. **Situation analysis** (including analysis of target and secondary markets; competitive analysis; overall tourism market analysis of regional, provincial, federal, and international levels; county tourism infrastructure analysis; and funding analysis)

3. **Marketing strategy** (based on analysis)

4. **Marketing program for a three-year implementation period** (including advertising and promotional products and activities, media/PR plan; in particular, per the RFP, we will provide a print and graphic promotional strategy and costing as part of the marketing program)

5. **Marketing program management structure** (the suggested tourism marketing and planning organization, which will be determined through consultation and best practices in tourism marketing)

6. **Marketing evaluation and controls** (how Prince Edward County's tourism marketing and planning organization will be able to determine whether their efforts and the marketing plan implementation are effectively achieving desired outcomes)

7. **Funding analysis** (committed funding from stakeholders, municipal/county governments, and other identified grant and funding sources)

8. **Marketing budget** (including narrative explanation)

Proposed time frame: January to May 2013

January–February

Between January and February, we will host 10 consultations as previously described regarding tourism organizational structure, branding, and funding support from local communities, businesses, and organizations. These meetings will be held in communities across the county to best connect with local businesses, organizations, and individuals with an interest in the tourism sector.

10

(continued)

Because meetings (particularly considering winter travel issues) will not obtain all the feedback needed from stakeholders, we will conduct online, mail, and telephone surveys and interviews to obtain further information and guidance from those stakeholders who were unable to attend consultations.

During these months, we will also begin research to identify PEC's target and secondary tourism markets and direct and indirect competition. This information will help to determine an effective marketing and competitive strategy and will contribute to the branding process.

March

In March, we will conduct research into funding sources outside of county sources. We expect to investigate provincial and federal government funding as well as broader tourism sector and organizational funding, corporate sponsorship, and foundations grants.

As our dedicated researcher undertakes this research, other members of the team will be working on the distillation of information from consultations and questionnaires held or disseminated in January and February.

Branding ideas for PEC based on the research and consultations to date will be explored and developed, with a short list of options produced for further consultation with stakeholders in April.

Based on research to date and further research into best tourism marketing practices from similar communities and regions, a working structure for PEC's tourism marketing organization will be developed to present to stakeholders in meetings in April.

April

In April, research to date, including target and secondary market information, competitive analysis, branding ideas, and tourism marketing structure, will be presented to stakeholders in a couple of major, well-advertised meetings (suggested locations: Bloomfield and Picton). Distilled information in an interim report on the process will be presented at these meetings, and feedback and, potentially, endorsement will be sought from those in attendance.

The interim report will also be distributed via email or other methods to stakeholders who have been actively involved in the process to date for their response and feedback before a stated deadline.

Once we have the final stakeholder feedback (and while this consultation is taking place), we will compile all of the researched and consultation data and produce the Three-Year Marketing Plan.

Further, we will work to finalize financial commitment to support the plan from the county's stakeholders and external funding sources. Based on the level of financial commitment and projected, highly probable financial sources, we will develop a realistic marketing budget.

May

The final product of this proposal, the Three-Year Marketing Plan, will be presented to stakeholders at a well-publicized, centrally located meeting (suggested location: Picton). All stakeholders who have been involved in the process to date will be invited via email, telephone, or mail. Copies of the plan will be made available to all who attend, and several copies will be given to the relevant county departments and officials. Additional copies will be generated for the purposes of funding applications and proposals.

BENEFITS

Short-term benefits and goals

Based on the expressed needs stated in the RFP, we are confident that we can deliver the following short-term benefits aimed at establishing PEC as a tourism destination of choice. These goals would be achieved within a year of receipt of this proposal, and we would provide complementary support during that year as the PEC tourism structure (as outlined below) is selected and begins its work.

The first short-term goal and benefit will be a strong, well-articulated Three-Year Marketing Plan and Strategy reflecting the unique needs of Prince Edward County's tourism industry. This plan, as noted earlier, will be based on our work with the Tourism Development Alliance and, most important, extensive consultation with a broad cross-section of the tourism industry in the county.

Within this plan, we will present a proposed organizational structure for PEC's tourism stakeholders to act as a single tourism destination marketer for a co-ordinated and unified industry effort to increase collective success in tourism for all stakeholders.

In order for the proposed structure to work, we will set in place clearly defined processes by which the tourism marketing organization can manage and execute the tourism marketing plan/strategy.

The strategy and plan itself will be focused on a centralized yet representative approach to marketing PEC while simultaneously marketing individual businesses, organizations, and events in PEC. This will ensure the "buy-in" and support of the business community and the energy to make the strategy and plan succeed.

12

(continued)

Branding is essential for everyone involved to "sing from the same song book"—in other words, a unified message must be adopted by all stakeholders in terms of marketing tourism in the county. This branding will provide essential focus for all marketing activities, thus creating a strong image of the unique attractions of the county in the minds of potential visitors and tourists.

Finally, the tourism marketing structure will be able to implement the plan, strategy, and branding with a carefully planned budget. This budget will take into consideration financial commitment levels from the business community as well as potential sources of grant money to assist in implementation of the marketing plan/strategy.

The achievement of these short-term goals will lay the groundwork for major growth in the tourism sector of PEC's economy in the years to come.

Long-term benefits and goals

In the long-term (up to five years after the tourism plan is adopted), several benefits will accrue.

With the implementation of the tourism plan and branding by all stakeholders, PEC's municipal government and business community can expect solid tourist/visitor/customer recognition of Prince Edward County as a destination.

The Prince Edward County brand will resonate with tourism stakeholders and primary/secondary market/tourists alike, leading to strong brand recognition within target and secondary markets in Ontario and increased brand recognition outside of Ontario. The Prince Edward County brand, when applied and endorsed universally by all stakeholders, will effectively communicate the Prince Edward County experience ("Regional Complex," as stated in the PRTD) concisely.

The implementation of the plan and consistent branding will ensure success in marketing, leading to increased tourist traffic and revenues for PEC's tourism industry. PEC's tourism industry will appear to potential visitors and competitors alike as a co-ordinated, unified effort.

The conclusion section in this proposal sums up what the proponent hopes to achieve, restates benefits as final persuasion for reader to accept proposal.

CONCLUSION

The development of a Three-Year Marketing Plan and Strategy, as well as the initiation of a central marketing organization representative of a wide range of stakeholders, will help PEC establish a brand, educate potential visitors from the primary and secondary markets about what the county has to offer, and effectively target market to customers' psychographic and demographic interests/needs. With the county brand and marketing plan as a focal point, the central tourism marketing organization should be able to effectively market the tourist "gems" to an even wider range of visitors in both the short and long term.

13

DISCLAIMER

While efforts and methods as noted previously are planned with the best possible outcomes in mind, Millpond Communications Inc., its shareholders, officers, and contractors will not be held liable for any perceived or actual lack of success in branding, marketing, or financing Prince Edward County's tourism initiatives or activities. The aforementioned will not be held liable if the planned and suggested tourism marketing organization does not achieve perceived or actual success in marketing Prince Edward County's tourism opportunities.

The disclaimer section is often added to the document to absolve the proponent from any liability.

BUDGET

(The budget for this proposal, developed in an Excel spreadsheet format, was originally included here, as well as a brief budget narrative so that the readers would clearly understand the costing and expenses of the proposed work. However, because of confidentiality concerns, it has been removed from this version.)

An appendix list (on separate page) is included here to demarcate this section. Appendix items are not numbered but could be—with Roman numerals.

APPENDIX

Budget (Excel format)
Qualifications

The budget, as mentioned previously, is not supplied here because of confidentiality.

14

Want to see more examples?

For more examples of formal reports, see this text's website at **www.oupcanada.com/Luchuk**.

Checking Your Work

CONTENT EDITING

Once you have written your proposal, check whether you have communicated effectively with your primary and secondary readers by applying the Starting Point questions to the proposal. Then you will need to check the proposal against the stated required outcomes and needed information specified in the RFP, if applicable, or against the stated purpose for the proposal. Does the proposal meet the needs of the RFP? Does it achieve the purpose as determined by you or someone you work for?

COPY EDITING

After your careful content edit, you must do an equally detailed and focused copy edit, since the formal proposal is your first—and last—opportunity to make a persuasive impression. Making spelling, grammar, or mechanical mistakes in a formal proposal is like chewing gum while giving a presentation. Make your first impression a good one!

Start with a spelling and grammar check, using your word-processing program. Print a copy of the proposal, then put it aside for a while. When you come back to it, read it carefully for grammar, spelling, and mechanical errors or problems. Make sure that your paragraphs are short and to the point in order to keep your reader moving through the document. Get someone else in your organization—ideally, someone you can trust who is not involved in the proposal—to read it through and ensure that your writing is not only error-free but also understandable, clear, and concise.

FORMATTING REVIEW

The formatting of a formal proposal is a very important element in persuading the reader of the merits of your proposal, much like choosing the appropriate clothes for a first date or a job interview. Unfortunately, human beings can be superficial in their judgments—and just as we tend to judge people on their appearance, we judge a document on how it looks. So don't skimp on careful formatting!

Choose an easily read, businesslike font. Ensure that the proposal is organized with appropriate headings and subheadings so that the reader is guided through the entire document. If the RFP specifies the headings and subheadings or areas that must be addressed, make sure that you have included them.

Make sure that you have used different sizes of font and emphasis to indicate to the reader when major sections and subsections begin and end. Because your proposal should be left-justified (no indents on paragraphs), make sure that you have left a space between paragraphs. Make sure as well that there are no headings or subheadings stranded at the bottom of a page.

PRESS PRINT . . . OR *SEND*!

Once you have confirmed that everything is thoroughly edited and in the correct place, and if you have written a short proposal, you can proceed with printing it—or emailing it as an attachment.

If you are going to email it, try emailing it first to someone else in your organization or to a friend, and have him or her open the document and print it so that you can be sure it appears exactly as you intend it to. Once you confirm that the document can be transmitted and received properly, go ahead and send it to the intended recipient or destination.

Make sure that it is appropriate to email the document before sending it. Many RFPs specify that a certain number of copies, bound or unbound, must be couriered or mailed to an address. The other issue is that emails sometimes get "lost," so when in doubt, rely on courier or mail.

PRESENTATION GUIDELINES

A formal proposal should appear formal. If you are trying to make an impression as a professional,

How do you impress readers with your proposal? Attention to detail! In addition to creating well-researched work, be sure to present a polished document that is neatly and professionally bound.

competent person, your report should be printed on better-quality paper (cream or white, not coloured), have the title page (front) and blank back cover in card stock, and be bound in some way. Ring binding is a good way to go, and it can be done at most office supply stores, copy centres, or printing businesses; however, there are other forms of binding that may be more appropriate. Sometimes the transmittal letter, proposal, and accompanying documents are placed in a portfolio (which may or may not have graphics or information on the cover).

When in doubt about the appropriate presentation of the formal proposal, consult the RFP instructions (if any) and/or check similar formal proposals that were produced in your industry or business sector to see how they are presented.

Oral Presentation of the Formal Proposal

You may be asked to present your formal proposal to the person who requested it or to a wider audience. Often, you won't know everyone who will attend your presentation—perhaps only the person(s) who received your proposal. Your oral presentation may be the first opportunity some will have to receive your proposal, and it may be the first time those who have read it will get to meet you.

Make sure that your first (or first face-to-face meeting) impression is favourable by following the instructions in this section carefully and closely to ensure a professional result. You will also want to dress appropriately for the occasion; find out how others dress at the organization where you will be presenting, and try to emulate that look as much as possible. (See the "Dress for success!" box in Chapter 14 for further help.)

WHO IS YOUR AUDIENCE?

In order to be well-prepared beforehand, be sure to find out as much as you can about who is attending, their positions in the organization, the nature of their interest in your proposal, their knowledge of the background or the proposal information itself, and what biases or objections they may have even before you present the proposal. This information is critical to presenting your proposal in such a way that it will meet their needs and concerns—and ensure their endorsement of the proposed work, project, or expense.

Knowing your audience or reader = being prepared regarding what they want to hear = the success of your proposal.

WHAT ARE THE LOGISTICS?

Find out from the person who asked you to present the proposal how much time you will have, where you will be presenting, the layout of the room, and whether audio-visual (AV) resources will be available (and what they include). You also need to know how many people will be attending.

Once you have this information, you can then plan the length of your presentation, decide whether you will use AV resources, work with the layout of the room so that everyone can see and hear you, and make copies of the proposal for everyone who shows up for your presentation.

PRESENTATION FORMAT

Whether you use AV resources or merely speak at the front of the room, introduce yourself and any colleagues you have with you, and then ask each person to introduce himself or herself, unless you already know who they are. That way, you will know who is who, and you will be able to address everyone's particular background, hopes, and concerns in the presentation and questions session.

Tell the audience what you will speak about, how long the presentation will be, that there will be a time for questions at the end, and that you will circulate copies of the proposal after the question period.

WORKING WITH (OR WITHOUT) AV RESOURCES

If you have access to a computer, projector, and screen (or blank wall)—and have at least 20 minutes to present—it is strongly recommended that you convey the main points of your proposal in a slide presentation. Because most people are visual rather than audio learners or are a combination of the two (see Chapter 12), providing a brief yet informative and persuasive slide content is an excellent way to generate excitement and buy-in. For best results in planning, organizing, and presenting your slide presentation, see Chapter 12, Oral Presentations.

To convince the audience of the merits of your proposal, review it for the most important points that briefly sum up its purpose and background, and spend more time on the benefits of the proposal to the organization you are presenting it to. This may seem a bit scary, since it deviates from what you have already written—but your audience will receive a copy of your hard work to read after they leave. The object of making the oral presentation is to generate excitement and enthusiastic endorsement of your proposed work, project, or expense.

To come up with the best benefit points that will meet the needs, concerns, potential objections, and biases of the audience, refer to the information you have gathered about who is attending. Use the most relevant benefits you have stated in the proposal to address all of these needs and concerns, and the audience will feel that you are speaking "their language"!

QUESTIONS

Once you have made your presentation, ask whether there are any questions. Try to remember who is who, their background, and their reason for coming to your presentation as you answer their questions.

HANDOUTS

You need to keep the attention of the audience as you make the presentation. Don't hand out copies of the proposal until the *end* of the presentation; otherwise, your listeners will read it while they should be paying attention to you—and you are presenting them with the most important details, the *benefits* of the proposal!

FOLLOW-UP

You need to give your audience time to read and digest your proposal before you follow up with a phone call or email—whichever you feel is most appropriate. Give your audience at least a week before you contact them for feedback.

CHECKLIST FOR formal proposals

- [ ] Have you applied the Starting Point questions so that you know your reader(s) (and the organization to which you are addressing the proposal) better? Do you know what will convince them to endorse, support, or fund your proposal?

- [ ] Do you know what potential objections the readers or the organization may have to your proposal—and how you will meet these objections before they arise?

- [ ] Are you clear about the message/information you need to communicate—and that it will be persuasive? Are you clear about the desired outcome? (See Chapter 1 for help with this.)

- [ ] Have you included all the information the reader needs to be fully convinced that your proposed work, project, expense, or idea is worth endorsing? Have you reviewed the RFP to determine exactly what is required?

- [ ] Have you included in an appendix any illustrations, photos, graphs, statistics, or related materials that will help to persuade your reader?

- [ ] If there are costs involved in your proposal, have you included all of the financial information your reader requires? Have you included a spreadsheet budget or report, if required? (This is a good idea even if it is not requested or required; showing how you can save money is always a good idea!)

- ☐ Have you included timelines and deadlines, if applicable?
- ☐ Have you clearly indicated the benefits of your proposed work, idea, or project to the organization or individual?
- ☐ Have you provided contact information so that readers can reach you with responses to your proposal? An offer to provide more information if they request it?
- ☐ Have you conducted a comprehensive edit for grammar, spelling, and mechanical errors?
- ☐ Is the proposal written in an appropriate tone and style for the situation?
- ☐ Have you double-checked that you have met the information demands of the RFP—all the points that the organization or readers require?

Chapter Summary

In this chapter, you learned the difference between formal and informal reports in terms of their style and the amount of information required. The longer the report, the more formal it becomes. You learned that formal proposals are usually written for an external audience in response to a request for proposal (RFP) and how to read a request for proposal effectively to identify the key issues that must be addressed in your proposal to persuade your intended audience to accept it. You were shown a template that you can use to organize the information in your proposal in a conventional but effective manner. Then you discovered how to research and prepare information for formal proposals and how to write the proposal persuasively so that readers endorse, support, or fund a proposed project, work, or expense. Finally, you were given specific tips for an oral presentation of your proposal.

■■▌ SUGGESTIONS *for Further Reading*

Chambers, K.D. (2007). *The entrepreneur's guide to writing business plans and proposals*. Santa Barbara, CA: ABC-CLIO/Praeger Publishing.

Freed, R., Freed, S., and Romano, J. (2010). *Writing winning business proposals*. (3rd ed.). Toronto, ON: McGraw-Hill.

Geever, J.C. (2007). *The Foundation Center's guide to proposal writing*. (5th ed.). New York, NY: The Foundation Center.

Hamper, R., and Baugh, L. (2010). *Handbook for writing proposals*. (2nd ed.). Toronto, ON: McGraw-Hill.

Holloway, B.R. (2002). *Proposal writing across the disciplines*. Don Mills, ON: Prentice-Hall.

Reeds, K. (2002). *The Zen of proposal writing: An expert's stress-free path to winning proposals*. New York, NY: Random House/Crown Publishing/Three Rivers Press.

■■▮ PRACTISING *What You Have Learned*

1. Go to http://www.charityvillage.com, select Browse Jobs from the Jobs menu, and click on Requests for Proposals to find an RFP related to your sector, discipline, or future career direction that you can follow up on to create a formal proposal.

2. Go to http://www.merx.com to investigate tenders and RFPs for work within your sector, discipline, or future career direction. (Note: Some of the RFPs on MERX require a membership—which your instructor, college, or university should be able to arrange—and/or a fee to obtain the RFP. If this situation arises, discuss it with your instructor.)

3. Visit the website (or look at a hard copy) of a national newspaper, and look for tenders or RFPs in your sector, discipline, or future career direction. Create a formal proposal to address the tender or RFP.

4. Consider what it would take to start up a new venture, program, or service at your college or university (for profit or not). Write a formal, unsolicited proposal to the appropriate administrators and decision-makers at your school.

5. Consider a new venture, program, or service that your local government (municipal, county, or regional) could start, such as a recreational program or facility, a drop-in centre for youth, a seniors' centre, or a similar initiative. Write a formal, unsolicited proposal to the appropriate administrators or decision-makers in your local government.

6. If you belong to a community group, club, or organization and you think there is a program or service it could offer to the public or to specific groups of people, write a formal, unsolicited proposal to the appropriate decision-makers or executive.

7. Within your workplace, if you think there is a program, service, or product your employer could offer to customers or clients, write a formal, unsolicited proposal to the appropriate manager(s).

8. If your current employer, workplace, or volunteer organization has a service or product it could offer to another business or not-for-profit organization, write a formal, unsolicited proposal to the other organization proposing details of the service or product and how it would benefit that organization.

CHAPTER 12

Oral Presentations

LEARNING OBJECTIVES

In this chapter, you will learn:

- How to assess the needs and expectations of receivers of your presentation

- How to research, plan, and outline a three-point/part presentation to communicate effectively with an audience

- How to grab and keep the attention of your audience and how to avoid common errors in slide preparation and presentation

- How to work with the venue and resources available to make a presentation that is well received, understood, and appreciated

- Presentation tips to help you speak in a calm, cool, and collected way while keeping your audience engaged

ESSENTIAL EMPLOYABILITY SKILLS

2000+ Employability Skills The Conference Board of Canada has identified certain essential employability skills (EES) as benchmarks for performance in the workplace. You will learn the following EES skills in this chapter:

COMMUNICATE

- Can write and speak so others pay attention and understand
- Can listen and ask questions to understand and appreciate the points of view of others
- Can share information using a range of information and communications technologies (e.g., voice, email, computers)
- Can use relevant scientific, technological, and mathematical knowledge and skills to explain or clarify ideas
- Can read and understand information presented in a variety of forms (e.g., words, graphs, charts, diagrams)

MANAGE INFORMATION

- Can locate, gather, and organize information using appropriate technology and information systems
- Can access, analyze, and apply knowledge and skills from various disciplines (e.g., the arts, languages, science, technology, mathematics, social sciences, and the humanities)

THINK AND SOLVE PROBLEMS

- Can assess situations and identify problems
- Can seek different points of view and evaluate them based on facts
- Can recognize the human, interpersonal, technical, scientific, and mathematical dimensions of a problem
- Can identify the root cause of a problem
- Can be creative and innovative in exploring possible solutions
- Can evaluate solutions to make recommendations or decisions

Oral Presentations: A Case Study

Angie Lau, Human Resources Manager, recently completed a management training course in effective teamwork, paid for by her company, Coastal Organics, a natural foods company. Now her boss, CEO Ken Kobayashi, would like her to make a presentation to department managers at their annual retreat on how and why to build team contracts for a more efficient, harmonious workplace.

Coastal is considered a progressive company, one of the top 100 employers in Canada. It has created a supportive, **affirming workplace** and offers excellent benefits, such as three weeks' annual vacation, a comprehensive health benefits package, full compensation for continuing education, and **flextime** or home-working arrangements. It's a relatively small company (105 people), so the workplace environment is quite casual and easygoing.

The company has recently added a new line of organic, EcoCert-verified cosmetics and skincare products. The production of these new products has placed employees of the company under additional stress, since many are putting in overtime currently because new employees have yet to be hired. If all goes well, the company is about to make its biggest profit ever (and employees stand to benefit, because they are all shareholders), but the strain is really starting to show—work teams are in conflict, and production is often interrupted.

There has never been a formal team-building process in the company. Coastal started small eight years ago, with Ken Kobayashi and his business partner, Jane Palace, working from their homes to produce home-style baby food and, later, organic soups. Coastal's success came so fast that Ken and Jane just did what needed to be done on the fly to take the business to the next level of success.

Angie's presentation is scheduled for 11 a.m. to noon on the Saturday morning of the weekend retreat, which means that people might be getting a bit hungry and distracted by the prospect of lunch. There will be 15 managers attending, all at the same level of responsibility as Angie on the company organizational chart, so she will be presenting to peers. The venue for the presentation is a small meeting room (seats 50) with movable chairs, small tables, and one large table at the front of the room. The room has plenty of natural light, and there is a projection screen, a computer for slide presentations, a flip chart, and a blackboard.

1. **You are Angie. Describe the receivers of the presentation and what their needs or expectations would be. (Hint: Take the information from the case and apply the Starting Point questions from Chapter 1 for the answer.)**

2. **Once you have a clear idea of the receivers' expectations and needs—and what Ken Kobayashi expects from the presentation—review the information in Chapter 6 on the importance of team contracts, their content and format, and how such contracts can be applied for best results. Create an outline of points of the information you should present, organized in a logical and receiver-friendly order.**

3. **You have an hour to make the presentation, and it's just before lunch, so participants will be distracted. How could you engage participants in the presentation**

and effectively educate them about team contracts and their application in the workplace? Brainstorm some ideas you could use to make the presentation engaging and interactive.

4. Considering all of this information, create a final outline of your presentation, including main points and activities to fill the presentation time, with consideration of the best use of the resources and space available in the room.

Before You Begin . . .

Oral presentations are a part of the normal activity in most workplaces. At one time or another, you will probably be asked to speak to at least a small group of people, if not many more.

Oral presentation skills are needed when you make a presentation on written business communications (such as reports or proposals) or when you are simply asked to give a stand-alone oral presentation, such as in a training seminar or a public-speaking event. If you are presenting a report or proposal, your presentation will consist of the highlights of the written product.

Regardless of whether your audience is from your own organization (internal) or not (external), prior to organizing your talk and making your presentation you will need to do the same kind of research that you would when writing business communications. In other words, using the Starting Point questions is essential to planning and organizing relevant information to present to your receivers so that your presentation is effective and makes an impression.

Our attention span is limited because of all the information and mental stimuli we are exposed to—and in the case of listening to a presentation, this is even more so. Even a person with an amazing memory often finds it difficult to remember points someone else has made in a conversation just moments before. With this in mind, imprint on your oral presentation process the concept of three:

- three main parts of your presentation (introduction, discussion, conclusion);

- three main points in the discussion;

- three repetitions of each point (in different words, of course).

Most people can retain at least three points in their heads when presented with information orally. Any more than that and they lose track of what was said.

However, even with the emphasis on three in a presentation, it's essential that throughout your presentation, you remind your audience of the points you have and will cover. You gently direct them through the material you have prepared to help them remember.

Great speakers research their audiences to find out what they want, need, or will understand. They find out what the venue will be, and the time constraints, so that their presentations are appropriate and not hindered by these factors. They inject humour, storytelling, and up-to-date, relevant research to keep their audiences' attention and respect.

By doing the appropriate planning, research, organization, and practice, these speakers make giving presentations look effortless and entirely natural. With attention to the points that follow, you too can plan and deliver an excellent presentation—internally or externally, to a small group or a large one.

Idiom Alert

on the fly – Acting quickly, in the moment, without much attention to details or process in order to get a task or job done.

lose track – Forget what you were talking about or doing, much like a train that derails or goes off its course.

decision-makers or opinion-makers – Actual or perceived leaders in any group who have the power to make decisions or to influence them.

dig up (further information) – Conduct further investigation and research.

stand-alone – Not related to or connected to anything else.

main event – The most important event, more important than whatever else is happening at the time.

get uptight – Become annoyed or upset.

junky-looking – Substandard, poor quality

cutesy – Not serious or mature enough for a business context; would be more appropriate for children.

Your Starting Point

ASSESS THE REASON AND RECEIVERS

As in preparing to write a business communication document, you need to know who will be receiving your presentation—hearing, watching, and participating in it. Answer the Starting Point questions in Chapter 1 to help you determine everything you can about them.

Some specific questions to address before you begin to research, organize, prepare, and deliver your presentation include the following:

- Are you informing or persuading?

- What kind of receivers/audience will you have? How large will the group be?

- Who are the key decision-makers or opinion-makers? What are their needs and concerns?

- What do the receivers already know? What should you explain?

- What kind of resistance might you encounter? How will you deal with it?

- How diverse are your listeners in terms of educational level and understanding of the topic?

- How interested are they in your topic?

- Do the receivers know you, either in person or by reputation? (If not, be prepared to provide your credentials or evidence of your credibility.)

ASSESS THE CONDITIONS

In order to prepare an oral presentation, it's important to know under what conditions you are to present. How you deliver the oral presentation will depend on the venue. For example, if you are presenting in a large lecture theatre where many people are seated in the back, far away from you, you would not hold up a small illustration for them to see. You would instead use a projector and overheads, PowerPoint™ slides, or photo slides so that everyone would be able to see your illustrations. However, in a smaller presentation situation, such as when you are making a proposal to a few people around a boardroom table, your visuals can be handheld or, better still, distributed as copies.

How much time will you have?

Knowing how much time you have is critical. You don't want to speak for too long, nor do you want to say too little. When preparing your presentation material to fit a certain timeline, you generally have more information than you can use. You then reduce the information to the most important points, the ones you can reasonably cover in the time allowed. You may have to do a few trial runs of the material to see how long it takes to present, and you may have to make modifications as you do so. (This means that you need to work in extra preparation time to rehearse your presentation before you spring it on your audience.)

What time of day will you be presenting?

The time of day can have a big effect on how well your audience receives your information. If you have any control over when you present, avoid presenting right after lunch, when people have what is known as "fuzzy sandwich head," or around 3:30, when many people's blood sugar takes a dip and concentration is not at its peak. Near the end of the working day, people's attention often switches to the upcoming commute and the evening ahead. The best time of day to make a presentation is when people are fresh—in the morning, but *after* the first coffee of the day.

If you can't set the time yourself, then knowing that your audience may be less than attentive at certain times means that you should be proactive in planning the presentation so that it keeps the attention of a sleepy audience. For example, if you were to present right after lunch, you might want to include some active component in your presentation to get people moving around. Try humour or do something silly to make them laugh. Use shocking or provocative statements to get their attention (within reason). While it's true that you want to capture and keep the audience's attention in any presentation, if you are battling audience fatigue you should be sure to include dynamic elements in all parts of your presentation: the introduction, the middle, and the conclusion.

In a smaller, less formal setting and you feel it's appropriate, you could bring coffee and light food items if you think your receivers are going to need a break or a snack to stay focused. (If you do this right—if you ask people in advance how they like their coffee or at least bring along all the options—you further impress your receivers with your thoughtfulness and good planning!)

Creating the Oral Presentation Product: How to Do It

PREPARING TO PRESENT

Research

Because oral presentations are often based on a report, proposal, letter, or memo you have written, the information you use will come mostly from the written document. You will obtain your main points for the presentation from the report, and the presentation will highlight the contents of the written document that your audience may have already received or will receive as you make the presentation.

However, you may want to enhance the content of your written document by adding information that will further emphasize or support what you have written. This can be particularly important when you are presenting a proposal or other persuasive written product. To do this, you dig up further information and data, and, as usual, you must document your sources carefully so that you can let the audience know where the new information came from.

Sometimes your presentation is a "stand-alone" communication product—that is, one without a written report—such as when you are asked to be a guest speaker at an event or conference. In this case, you would conduct research using the same kinds of sources that you would for a written report, proposal, letter, or memo. Then, of course, you would give the audience information on your sources. (In a slide or overhead presentation, this can be done by creating a works-cited or similar page as the last slide or overhead, which can be printed and handed out to the audience so that they can do further research if they desire.)

PREPARING FOR CITATIONS

Why do you have to care about citations if it is an oral presentation—especially if your audience already has or will have your written report or document with citations?

There are a few good reasons for citations in an oral presentation. First, citations show that you have done wide-ranging, relevant research; receivers will feel satisfied that you are a professional and possibly even an expert on the topic you are speaking about.

Second, even if the receivers are given a copy of the document with citations before, during, or after the presentation, some will simply not read it. It's sad, but true: after they have heard the presentation, some people merely skim the written document and may miss your citations.

Finally, you want to differentiate very clearly between the information that is original to you and what you obtained from someone else, because the consequences of plagiarism and misrepresentation of others' materials as your own also apply in the business world. The repercussions can be destructive and costly.

Review the information on citations in Chapter 1 of this book.

ORGANIZING INFORMATION AND WRITING: FORMAT

Organizing the material

Begin with an introduction that is a preview of your presentation—a brief layout of what you are going to say and the order in which you plan to say it.

Using a few main points, develop what you are going to say in the body of your presentation—generally, no more than three main points, all related to your topic. Any more than three and you risk losing your audience's attention; any fewer points and you risk sounding uninformed or ill-prepared to address your topic fully. (See the box below on the *three-part presentation*.)

Close your presentation by reviewing (that is, repeating, but in a different way) in summary what you have just said.

Try to grab your audience's attention when you deliver a presentation. Opening with an anecdote or even by polling your listeners on a relevant topic can engage the audience and help set the right tone for the rest of your presentation.

Planning the body

1. Establish your theme or main topic, and try to break it down into three sections (see #4 below).

2. Choose the best method of organization for the purpose of your presentation, the setting, the time constraints, and your audience:

   a. Order of importance: Three main points presented from most important to least important

   b. Chronological order: Three main points presented according to when these points will occur (e.g., Step 1, Step 2, Step 3 in a process)

   c. Geographic or spatial order: Items organized according to their physical arrangement (e.g., an oral report on three different locations for a new office could present information on the Toronto office first, Montreal second, and Whitehorse third.)

   d. Division or classification order: Information organized into three divisions or categories, with material that has a common "thread" or relationship grouped together

   e. Comparison order: Three main points compared and/or contrasted

3. Choose either a direct or an indirect approach. Remember how information is organized in good and bad news letters? How to deliver good or bad news in a report? The persuasive style you need to employ in a proposal?

   a. For any presentation that is good news, use the direct approach (good news delivered fairly early in the presentation).

   b. For any presentation dealing with bad news, use the indirect approach (give neutral news or a statement first, then the bad news, then any remedy to the bad news).

4. Create three main sections, which cover three main points (for example, three ways to improve your marketing or three ways to reach your clients). If you include

any more than three, your audience will likely miss them. Studies have shown that most people cannot take in more than three main points—unfortunately, people's attention spans are limited!

5. Help your audience to remember your points by using frequent numerical reminders ("*First*, I'd like to discuss X, *second*, Y, and finally, for my *third* point, I'll share . . .")

6. Support all your points with *specific* examples and information from a variety of sources—present facts, not opinions, and back them up with citations.

7. Draw "word pictures" for the audience; that is, put your examples in visual terms. This helps to keep the audience engaged in your presentation and helps the visually oriented receivers to fully understand it (see box on Learning Types).

Beginning and ending

1. Spark the audience's interest with an exciting, shocking, or otherwise thought-provoking beginning (use humour, a fact or statistic, or a quote, for example). Boring introductions are guaranteed to not grab your receivers' attention and to ensure that they will sleep—perhaps with their eyes open—through your presentation.

2. Reveal your plan for the presentation in your introduction. Introduce your three main points so that the audience knows what is coming up. Remind your audience where you are in the order of presentation by mentioning which point you are on (e.g., "To conclude my first point" or "Moving on to the second feature of this project . . ."). Repetition helps to keep people's minds focused.

3. At the end of your presentation (the conclusion), close quickly. Simply summarize your main points, and then finish in as forceful a way as you started with another compelling fact, statistic, humorous thought, or quote. A boring conclusion, like a boring introduction, will lose your audience's attention and make it less likely that they will remember any of the points you so carefully and thoughtfully presented.

Using audio-visual aids

If you are going to use **audio-visual aids** such as slides or overheads, remember the following points:

- Don't put too much information on each slide. You don't want to encourage your audience to merely read and not listen. The points on your slide are there as visual reminders to guide listeners through your presentation and as a memory device so that they can remember what you just said.

- Don't read from your visuals. Use them as points to elaborate on.

- Limit any slide or overhead to no more than six lines of print.

- Use a large font for visibility.

- Use a horizontal layout, not a vertical one.

- Use colours carefully and appropriately.

- Don't overuse visuals—if you hide behind them, your presentation will be less effective, and you will come across as nervous or unprepared.

- Stand to the side of any projection equipment you are using, and whenever possible use a remote control for changing the slides.

The three-part presentation

This is a general format for a presentation. But first you should think about the purpose of your presentation and determine whether your approach should be direct or indirect, as discussed earlier in this chapter.

In a ***direct format presentation*** in which you are delivering good or neutral news, you can introduce your topic and three main points right away, in the introduction. You don't need to hold back on describing, in detail, what the three main points are, because your message is positive.

In an ***indirect format presentation*** involving a negative message, you should briefly mention, in a neutral way, the bad news you will be presenting—at the end of the introduction section of your presentation—and then expand on these points using emotionally neutral language in the discussion section.

For example, if you have to present to shareholders three challenges that your company is facing, then in the introduction you would not specify what each of these challenges is but merely say something like "My presentation today on plans for our company in 2014 will focus on three challenges we are facing."

Then in the discussion section, you would introduce the three challenges but mention these as neutrally as possible: "The first issue we are facing is a supply issue; the second is human resources; and the third is competition from Asia."

Then you would elaborate on each of the problems, one by one—but if possible, as you present each one you should also offer solutions or describe efforts that are being made to solve the problems.

Without further ado, here are the three main parts of an oral presentation:

INTRODUCTION

In your introduction, you

- begin with a startling fact, statistic, anecdote, quotation, or similar attention-grabbing statement related to your topic;
- introduce your topic and the background to it;
- introduce your three main points in the same order you will present them in the body of your presentation.

DISCUSSION

In your discussion section, you present your three main points in the order you used in your introduction. You provide examples (illustrations) to help your audience understand your information. You mention each point of information in at least three different ways to reinforce the information in the mind of your audience.

- point one (stated in at least three different ways, plus examples)
- point two (stated in at least three different ways, plus examples)
- point three (stated in at least three different ways, plus examples)

Repetition is important, because people generally need to hear something at least three times before it even begins to make an impression on their grey matter!

CONCLUSION

In your conclusion you in essence repeat what you started with in your introduction, although in different words. Restate what your presentation was about, the background, and the points you covered, in the same order. Then close as you began, with a compelling, startling, humorous, or interesting fact, story, or quotation so that the audience leaves feeling they have just learned something interesting or were at least entertained!

You may also make some recommendations in your conclusion, particularly if you are trying to help a client or company solve a problem or make a decision.

Learning types and your oral presentation

We all take in information and learn differently. This is an important factor for you to consider as you plan an oral presentation to a large group of people.

Harvard University psychologist Howard Gardner has defined eight different **learning types**, which he calls Multiple Intelligences (MI) theory (Smith, 2008). If you can address the learning and information needs of as many types as possible in your oral presentation, you will get your message across more effectively.

Linguistic: thinks in words; learns best through storytelling, materials they can read (slides, overheads, handouts)

Logical-mathematical: learns by reasoning; learns best through demonstrations of products and services, logical flow charts, and scientific presentations

Spatial: learns in images and pictures; learns best through illustrations, art, visualizations, doodling

Bodily-kinesthetic: learns through movement; learns best through action, moving around (dancing, jumping), role-playing, tactile activities

Musical: learns through music; learns best through music, singing, clapping, rhythm, music in background

Interpersonal: learns by discussing with others; learns best by talking to other people, small-group or pair discussions and activities

Intrapersonal: learns by relating information to own needs/feelings; learns best through self-reflective activities, writing down thoughts, goal-setting, planning, making lists

Naturalist: learns by contact with nature/environment; learns best by anything to do with nature, the environment, the outdoors, animals

Using PowerPoint effectively

PowerPoint is the accepted standard for business presentations today, and presentations have become a standard form of communication in fast-moving businesses. That said, many people complain about the overuse or poor use of PowerPoint; some corporations have limited or even banned the use of PowerPoint. Just as Word cannot make you a better writer, PowerPoint cannot make you a better presenter. Start with sound basics of presenting as outlined in this chapter, and then consider the following.

First, let's consider what *not* to do with a slide, as illustrated in Figure 12.1.

In the figure, it seems that the presenter included everything he or she wanted to say in one slide! Wordy text like that should never appear on slides—no one can possibly read that much at a glance. People attend your presentation to listen to you, not to read your slides. Keep the number of points limited, and keep each point . . . *to the point!*

Note, however, that there are no animations or sound effects on the slide. Animations and sound

A slide presentation can considerably enhance your oral presentation. However, it's important to ensure that slides don't overwhelm the audience or muddle the ideas you are trying to convey. See the next section for tips on how to create effective slides.

FIGURE 12.1 ❌ **Ineffective PowerPoint Slide**

THE THREE-PART PRESENTATION

The Three-Part Presentation is the best way to speak to large groups of people, so they focus on the main points of what you have to say. People's attention span is really limited, so you have to keep reminding them of what you want them to think about. Today will we will look at why we use the three-part presentation format, how the three-part presentation is structured, what to include in each slide, and tips for more engaging presentation to a diverse audience.

- Why people don't remember anything in a presentation
- Why we use the three-part presentation format
- How we use the three-part presentation format
- How to keep people laughing
- How to keep people from falling asleep
- What to do if people start snoring

Wordy paragraphs should never be included.

Too many points listed here, and too wordy.

Text is too small.

effects may amuse children, but they have no place in a business presentation. You could add a picture if it's very relevant to your topic, but don't do so just because you think the slide looks boring. You don't have a lot of space for text on your slides, so anything else you add must enhance the value of the points, not distract the audience from you, the main part of the show.

Figure 12.2 depicts a more effective slide. Note that it contains just three items—to model the three-part presentation as you go through it so that the audience can follow

FIGURE 12.2 ✓ **Effective PowerPoint Slide**

THREE-PART PRESENTATION AGENDA

- Why use three-part presentations?

- How to set up

- How to keep people engaged

Only three points here—to model the three-part presentation as you talk about it.

Points are brief.

Notice the larger type font? With fewer words, text is easier to see!

the flow of your talk. Each line is very brief, which frees the audience to focus on you and use the slide only as a reminder of what you will talk about.

You've got the audience's attention. You can now follow up on the impact of the slide, clarify the point it makes, and get them pumped with your enthusiasm for the idea.

Follow these simple rules for connecting with an audience through PowerPoint:

- Keep text simple—no more than six lines, no more than six words per line, key words and phrases only, commonly understood words. Just a picture, with no text at all, can also be good.

- Slides are limited. If you have a complex idea or a series of important points, break it into its smallest parts, and devote one slide to each part. Your audience will more readily grasp your meaning as you go along, and you can then sum up the entire process on one slide at the end of the sequence.

- The minimum typeface size for your text is about 20 points for most presentation situations. Make it easy for your audience to read the text.

- Sound can be added to PowerPoint if your computer is connected to audio technology, but don't overuse it. Audiences have a limited tolerance for sound. At most, use short audio clips to help your audience to identify objects or to set a mood for your comments.

- PowerPoint can accommodate short video clips. Use file formats compatible with PowerPoint, and check that the technology is available. When running the clip, stand aside so that the audience can focus on the video.

- You can add **hyperlinks** to your slides to bring up applications external to PowerPoint. Ensure that the application software is available on the computer you are using and that it is compatible with the files you want to show. Documents or spreadsheets can be shown in this manner, as well as websites that may include audio or video content.

- Speak directly to your audience. Use cue cards if necessary to keep you on topic. Never read text from a PowerPoint slide.

- Practise your presentation to make sure that the slides accurately and completely connect with what you have to say.

Strategies for presentations to an international audience

As markets continue to globalize, you may have to deliver a presentation to an international audience. In general, the instructions in this chapter about planning, organizing, and delivering a quality presentation that receivers will appreciate and understand apply to presentations you might make anywhere around the world. However, you must keep several factors in mind when addressing an international audience to ensure that your presentation is culturally appropriate.

First, be extremely careful to avoid any jokes or comments that might be offensive to the religion or culture of your audience. To find out what might be considered offensive, consult print or online resources specific to the country or cultural group you will

Posting presentations on the Web

Posting a PowerPoint presentation on the Web is a way of making it accessible to a wider audience 24/7. The method you choose will depend on the PowerPoint features you want to include in the presentation and the software your visitors have on their computers.

You have a number of options:

- The simplest method is to upload your PowerPoint file directly to a website with a link to it on a **directory page**. Note that your visitor will need PowerPoint on his or her computer and that the download can take a long time if your file is large. Note also that you're giving the file away, so anyone who wants to modify and use it for their own purposes can do so. Adding a separate voiceover file in .mp3 format will help to guide your visitor through the slides and provide important detail.

- Save the presentation as a slideshow. This allows you to add transitions between slides and an audio track. Note that these additions will greatly increase your file size and download times for visitors. If your visitor does not have PowerPoint software, he or she can download a free PowerPoint Viewer from Microsoft.

- Save the presentation as an Adobe PDF file. Most people have free Acrobat Reader software to read your file, and it can be printed easily. However, the PDF file will be limited to the slides: no audio, animations, or speaker notes.

- Save your presentation as a webpage. PowerPoint creates an HTML index page linked to a folder with a series of files, so be sure to upload the whole folder! Speaker notes below slides are included. Download speeds are quick.

- Save the presentation slides as a series of pictures that can be uploaded to a folder.

- Save your presentation as a movie. PowerPoint for Mac will do this. Windows users will require additional software such as Camtasia. Your visitor will need movie-viewing software appropriate for the file type you used.

- Save as Adobe Flash. This will require special Adobe software on your computer. However, the resulting file will be smaller and faster for your visitors to download using the free Adobe Flash player.

Uploading files on a company **intranet** is often a simple matter of clicking and dragging the files into an Htdocs folder or directory. Uploading to a remote server can be more complicated. Websites like Slidestory and Microsoft SkyDrive require logging in to an established account and installing new software on your computer. Note any required limits on file size and type.

---

be presenting to. Do not use humour unless you research what is appropriate for your audience—which means first researching who will attend your presentation. If you do decide to include a light note, self-deprecating humour (making fun of yourself) would likely be the least problematic.

Second, learn about the cultural group's or business community's expectations for non-verbal communication, such as eye contact, physical gestures, and dress code. For example, in some cultures looking directly into someone's eyes for any length of time is considered confrontational or inappropriate.

Third, learn about gender relations and interaction in the other culture(s) you may be interacting with. In some cultures, for example, women are seated in a separate area for religious or cultural reasons, and it may not be appropriate for a man to speak directly to an unmarried woman.

Knowing as much as you can about your receivers by applying the Starting Point questions will help, but be sure to question the person who asked you to speak about the specific circumstances. Pose the Starting Point questions to him or her, but also ask whether there is anything that might be considered taboo or inappropriate by your audience. (There's no such thing as a stupid question, but there are definitely many stupid—and sometimes costly—mistakes!) Read up on the business and social culture of the group you will be addressing, and be willing to adapt your presentation to suit your audience.

Using handouts

In general, giving people anything other than an outline of your presentation will merely encourage them to read rather than listen or pay attention to your presentation in which you will probably elaborate on the written material. Considering all the work you have put into the presentation, you want them to listen and grasp the very important information and elaborations you have added so that they can better understand the report or printed material when they take it away for further consideration.

When speakers offer a slide presentation, particularly in a large lecture theatre, they often provide a printed version of the slides so that the reading-oriented members of the audience can follow along. Three slides per page is reasonable, printed with vertical lines on the right of the slide image where your receivers can make their own notes. Check out the printing features of your slide-generation software (e.g., PowerPoint) for more information on how to create this type of handout.

Save distribution of your report, proposal, or research materials for the end of your presentation. Your oral presentation is an introduction—and an interest-generator—for the materials that receivers will take away to read.

Checking Your Work

CONTENT EDITING, COPY EDITING, AND FORMATTING REVIEW

Unfortunately, many speakers feel they don't need to edit the printed or visual materials used in a presentation. They may have created a meticulously edited report, proposal, or research piece to hand out to their audience but feel that any errors in slides or overheads—or handouts!—will be overlooked because the "main event" is the written document.

First, remember that some listeners will *not* have read your report, perhaps because of time constraints or simply a disinclination to read anything. For these people, your oral presentation visuals represent the only opportunity you will have to make a professional impression.

Further, if your visuals or handouts are riddled with spelling and grammar errors, many receivers will not be inclined to follow up with you or your materials, because they will write you off as less than informed, unprofessional—or unintelligent. (It's not just communications instructors who get uptight about grammar and spelling; many people in business will also be put off if your message is poorly presented.)

Finally, make sure that anything you hand out or create as a visual is clean, neat, and visually organized so that it's not cluttered and distracting. Less is definitely more when it comes to slides, overheads, and handouts. Give just enough information to keep the receivers' interest and attention and to guide them through your presentation, but no more. Cluttered screens, cutesy graphics (avoid fluffy kitten pictures unless you are a pet food manufacturer!), or standard, boring PowerPoint template formats will immediately detract from the professional message you are presenting.

Delivering the Presentation

Here are some proven tips for a polished presentation:

- Do not memorize! Use notes listing the main points you want to cover, and practise delivering your presentation a few times before you actually do it for an audience.

- A key to success is knowing your material ahead of time. Study it thoroughly so that you can elaborate confidently and clearly on each point with relevant information.

- Radiate confidence. Arrive early to avoid getting jitters from running late; maintain good posture; don't fidget or bite your nails; do establish eye contact with at least a few people in your audience at different points in the room.

- Speak clearly and slowly. Pause when needed!

- Be natural with gestures and movement. If you are an "expressive" speaker, use your hands—but if not, keep your hands behind a lectern or together in front of you (don't wring your hands or clasp too hard, though). Don't put your hands in your pockets!

- Wear clothing that will suit your audience and makes you feel professional. If you are presenting to executives, dress the way an executive in that organization does. If you are presenting to teenagers at a career day, then dress as you would in your workplace (but not too formally—you want them to relate to you). If you are speaking at a company retreat, wear the casual style of clothing everyone else is wearing.

CHECKLIST FOR oral presentations

- ☐ Have you applied the Starting Point questions to get to know the receivers of your presentation? Do you know what they need to fully appreciate and learn from your presentation?

- ☐ Are you clear about the message/information you need to communicate? Are you clear about the outcome you want from the presentation? (See Chapter 1 for help with this.)

- ☐ Have you included all the information the receivers will need in order to understand your message—but not so much that they are overwhelmed and lose interest?

☐   Have you organized the presentation with the three-point/part model in mind? (Three main sections; three main points of information; information repeated three times, in different ways within each section; three main points restated in the conclusion.)

☐   Have you investigated the venue and resources available for the presentation?

☐   Have you planned for the use of audio-visual resources and practised with these? Do you have a back-up for these resources in case a computer or overhead projector doesn't work on the day of your presentation?

☐   Have you conducted a careful spelling and grammar check on any handouts, slides, or overheads?

☐   Have you created enough handouts for your audience (to be handed out after your presentation)?

☐   Have you practised and timed the presentation to ensure that it flows smoothly and fits into the time allowed?

☐   Have you planned what you will wear? Have you developed your personal strategy for dealing with nerves?

Chapter Summary

In this chapter, you learned how to assess the needs and expectations of receivers. Knowing your audience is the key; it will determine what you will say and how you will say it. You also learned the steps in researching, planning, and outlining a three-point/part presentation to communicate effectively with a business audience. In addition, you discovered that not all presentation situations are the same, so you learned how to work with the venue and resources available to make a presentation that is well received, understood, and appreciated. You found that knowing how to make PowerPoint slides is not enough in itself, so you learned how to connect with your audience using PowerPoint and similar software to create effective presentations. Finally, you were given some tips for presenting to help you speak in a calm and collected way while keeping your audience engaged.

■■■ SUGGESTIONS *for Further Reading*

Bradbury, A. (2010). *Successful presentation skills: Build confidence; understand body language; use visual aids effectively*. (4th ed.). London, UK: Kogan Page.

Coughter, P. (2012). *The art of the pitch: Persuasion and presentation skills that win business*. New York, NY: Palgrave Macmillan.

Lucas, S., Simeon, L., and Wattam, J. (2007). *The art of public speaking, Canadian edition*. Toronto, ON: McGraw-Hill Ryerson.

Novis, M. (2003). *Canadian public speaking*. Toronto, ON: Pearson Education Canada.

Reynolds, G. (2010). *The naked presenter: Delivering powerful presentations with or without slides*. Berkeley, CA: Pearson/New Riders Press.

Steele, W.R. (2009). *Presentation skills 201: How to take it to the next level as a confident, engaging presenter*. Parker, CO: Outskirts Press.

◼◼▮ DEBATE *and Discussion Starters*

1. As a recent graduate, you have been asked to make a presentation on college or university success strategies to 200 incoming students. These students have just graduated from high school or are mature students coming back for more education, so the age range and experience level is mixed. You have only 20 minutes to present, and you have access to a lecture theatre with fixed seating, projection equipment (projector and computer and traditional overhead projector), and your presentation is for 3:00 p.m. on a Friday. How would you plan for this presentation, considering the needs of your audience, the venue, the time of day, and the amount of time you have to speak? What would be the three main points you would cover?

2. You are facilitating a meeting with the marketing department and are making a presentation about a new product your company is about to launch. The department needs to know what the product is, its benefits and possible negatives, what the competitor products are, which companies offer a similar or the same product (and their strengths, weaknesses, opportunities, and threats), and who the target customers are so that they can effectively plan a marketing campaign that will sell the product. You are facilitating in a boardroom with chairs around a large table that is hard to move, and you have projection equipment. There is not a lot of light in the room, and you are presenting from 11:30 a.m. until 12:00 noon, when people will break for lunch. What will you do to plan a presentation that effectively communicates the information about the product? What other factors might you have to take into consideration, given the time of day and the venue? Will your style be informal or formal?

◼◼▮ PRACTISING *What You Have Learned*

1. Visualize yourself in your dream job 10 years from now. You have been asked to come back to speak at a graduation ceremony at your old college. The organizers would like you to talk to the graduates about what you do now: how you got there (and how your time at the college helped you with that) and what you think are the most critical pieces of information graduates need to get ahead, based on your experience. Your Starting Point questions are going to focus on the graduating students. You already know why you are speaking to these students—to share your story and to motivate them as they take the next step into careers. The presentation will be given in a large lecture hall that holds 800 people; it is equipped with a computer projector, so you can use slide-generation software, if you like.

2. As human resources manager, you have been asked to evaluate three different new uniform styles for employees of your company (but you didn't have to write an evaluation report). You are to present these three choices to a small group of company executives in a small boardroom where there is no projector or screen (so think about alternative visual aids to keep your receivers moving through your presentation). Starting Point questions will focus on the executives who will attend your presentation. You have 10 minutes to make the presentation, and then you will receive questions for five minutes.

3. Imagine a business you would like to start—the products and services, operations, customers, competitors, competitive and risk management strategy, marketing, and financial plan. (For an outline of what is in a business plan and to help you consider all the parts of a business for this question, see the supplementary business plans chapter available on this textbook's companion website: www.oupcanada.com/Luchuk). Think about how much money the business would cost to start, and consider how much you might need to borrow. Based on your business concept/outline/plan, create a presentation to potential investors (venture capitalists, a bank manager, or investors from your community or family) to persuade them of the merits of your business and show how they not only will recoup but will make money on their investment.

4. Based on a marketing plan you have created for course at school, make a presentation to potential investors about how you plan to effectively market to your target and secondary customers and successfully compete with competitors.

5. Using any report or proposal you have written in this course or another (as your instructor directs), create an oral presentation based on this report to deliver to your seminar group or class. Your instructor will provide direction on AV resources available, the venue, and the amount of time you will have to present.

6. Research, create, and deliver a presentation on health in the workplace to your classmates. Focus on diet, fitness, and stress management techniques.

7. Imagine you are a college or university liaison officer. Research, create, and deliver a presentation to a group of students about to graduate from high school, outlining the programs, services, and special features of your school to persuade them to enrol in any program or in your program in particular.

8. Research, create, and deliver a presentation on how to conduct an effective job search. Consider that your classmates are close to graduating from your particular program of study. Besides the general information they need to know about job search techniques, provide some specific details on how graduates from your program can find job opportunities. (See Chapter 13 for information on resumés and cover letters, but consult as well with instructors and co-ordinators of your program, and search the Internet for further specific tips and strategies for job searching in your discipline.)

Communications for Career Development: Resumés and Covering Letters

LEARNING OBJECTIVES

In this chapter, you will learn:

- ⊙ How to envision your ideal job or career and how to conduct research into the career of your choice

- ⊙ How and where to research job opportunities

- ⊙ How to assess personal skills, abilities, qualities, and education in reference to job postings and ads or for a resumé

- ⊙ How to relate personal skills and qualifications to the needs of the employer in a letter or resumé

- ⊙ How to organize and write a clear, concise, effective covering letter and an industry- or sector-focused, functional resumé

- ⊙ A functional resumé format and tips for professional presentation of your letter and resumé

ESSENTIAL EMPLOYABILITY SKILLS

2000+ Employability Skills The Conference Board of Canada has identified certain essential employability skills (EES) as benchmarks for performance in the workplace. You will learn the following EES skills in this chapter:

COMMUNICATE

- ⊙ Can write and speak so others pay attention and understand
- ⊙ Can listen and ask questions to understand and appreciate the points of view of others
- ⊙ Can share information using a range of information and communications technologies (e.g., voice, email, computers)
- ⊙ Can use relevant scientific, technological, and mathematical knowledge and skills to explain or clarify ideas
- ⊙ Can read and understand information presented in a variety of forms (e.g., words, graphs, charts, diagrams)

MANAGE INFORMATION

- ⊙ Can locate, gather, and organize information using appropriate technology and information systems
- ⊙ Can access, analyze, and apply knowledge and skills from various disciplines (e.g., the arts, languages, science, technology, mathematics, social sciences, and the humanities)

THINK AND SOLVE PROBLEMS

- ⊙ Can assess situations and identify problems
- ⊙ Can seek different points of view and evaluate them based on facts
- ⊙ Can recognize the human, interpersonal, technical, scientific, and mathematical dimensions of a problem
- ⊙ Can identify the root cause of a problem
- ⊙ Can be creative and innovative in exploring possible solutions
- ⊙ Can evaluate solutions to make recommendations or decisions

Communications for Career Development: A Case Study

Gerti Lindeman is about to graduate from a Bachelor of Business Administration program with a specialization in human resources (HR) management. To gain experience in HR, she has worked as a volunteer managing human resources at a local food bank for the past year and has also worked as an HR administrative assistant for the past two summers.

With graduation only a couple of months away, she is starting to panic, because she hasn't seen any suitable HR consultant job ads in her hometown weekly newspaper.

Now she has finally seen an ad for a human resources consultant at TLC Medical Supply Inc., a well-established, medium-sized company. The position requires a diploma or degree in human resources management as well as two to three years' relevant employment experience.

Because she is in a hurry, she buys a book about writing covering letters and uses a sample letter from the accompanying CD to apply for the human resources manager position. Gerti changes the date and employer information and, of course, adds her own name and address. She addresses the letter "To whom it may concern" because the job ad does not specify to whom the application package should be directed. Gerti then gives a quick outline of her educational qualifications. She does not include any details about what she has learned at university that is relevant to the specific position and organization she is applying to, nor does she include any information that would indicate to the employer that she knows something about the role of the human resources department at that company.

In thinking about what to say in relation to the work experience requirement, Gerti panics, because she has only been employed as an HR administrative assistant over two summers and she wasn't a consultant. Although she does have two years' significant volunteer experience doing exactly what she would be responsible for at TLC, she doesn't think volunteer work would be acceptable as work experience. She writes that she doesn't have any work experience in HR other than the summer work but that she would love to learn on the job.

Because the application package is due tomorrow, she does not check her letter for spelling or grammar errors, nor does she conduct a copy and content edit—and she hasn't even looked at her resumé since she graduated from high school, because she obtained her volunteer and paid work through family and friends' contacts (no application required). Arrghhh! Gerti pulls up her chronological resumé on the computer screen, adds her most recent work experience and her educational details, and prints the letter and resumé on white paper. She can't find a stapler, so the two pages of her resumé are not stapled. Gerti races off to deliver the package to TLC's reception desk.

1. Given what Gerti has included (or not included) in her application package, what do you think the result will be? What should Gerti have done differently?

2. Can volunteer work be regarded as equivalent to paid employment? How should it be included in a resumé or covering letter?

3. Is it ever acceptable to use a form letter for your covering letter? Why or why not?

4. Should you use the same resumé to apply for every job? Why or why not?

5. Is "To whom it may concern" an appropriate way to address the reader of the covering letter? What if the reader's name is not included in the job advertisement? How would you handle this situation?

6. Where could Gerti have looked for jobs besides in the local newspaper?

Before You Begin . . .

You have graduated—and you've got the "piece of paper" you needed to take the next step in your career. Perhaps along with your diploma you have a hefty student debt.

Stop! Rewind! Go back a few months. Before you graduate, it's important to take the time to think about and plot your job search. Waiting until the last minute is going to mean major stress when your bills come in or when the student loan people start to want repayment.

It's strongly recommended that when you are in your last year or semester of college or university, you begin a job search plan. You need time to gather the resources needed to land your first "real" job, one that, you hope, will be rewarding—and even fun.

Start by envisioning your ideal job. Where would it be located? What kind of organization (or which specific organizations) would you like to work for? Who would you like to work with? How will your work fit your personal core values and your vision of who you are or would like to be? What kind of working conditions would you work best in—for example, indoor or outdoor work, flexible schedule versus set hours? How much money would you like to make? How much will you *need* to make to cover your budget needs? How much responsibility would you like to have in your work?

Once you have gone through this visioning process—and committed the details to paper or computer—you can then start to search for work that might fit what you are looking for. Remember, unless you are truly desperate to pay bills immediately, you should look for work that more or less fits most of your vision of your ideal job. You don't want fit yourself to a job that won't suit you over the long term, because you will soon find yourself unhappy and you will not perform at your best.

Obviously, however, if you can't get the job you want right away, you should do your very best with the job you do get in order to build a good reputation. Meanwhile, continue to look for what you want, and find out if there's anything else you can do to gain experience—such as volunteering (see the box "Build your resumé by volunteering").

The next step is twofold: you need to do research into the organizations or businesses where you would like to work while concurrently looking at job postings and advertisements in the media and at job search agencies and channels. Landing a job somewhere you really would like to work would be ideal, but you don't want to miss out on another possibility you might not have thought of that could pop up in a job ad. The key to doing both parts of this step is to remind yourself of your goals for your career and life, as well as your budgetary needs.

The research into organizations where you want to work must be driven by the Starting Point questions found in Chapter 1. Answering these questions will help you to determine whether the organization is one you would be comfortable working for, and it will also help you to figure out what the people who will be screening and interviewing you are looking for in an employee or contractor. Researching the organizations that you are applying to or that you hope to work for is critical not only to landing the job but also to ensuring a good fit between you and the organization.

Part of the research you should do—and this is why you want to start the process early—is to conduct informational interviews with decision-makers at the organizations where you would like to work. This process is covered in Chapter 14, Job and Informational Interviews, and is basically an opportunity to ask Starting Point questions and have them answered directly by those you might want to work for.

Once you have narrowed down where you will apply and have done the research (possibly including informational interviews), you are ready to take the next step, which is to create your resumé. The resumé is a paper or electronic version of you—your qualities, skills, experience, and education. As such, it has to make a good—yet truthful—first impression. The resumé is usually accompanied by a well-written, to-the-point covering letter that highlights your particular skills and education for the

Idiom Alert

rewind – Go back to the beginning where you started.

pop up – Arise unexpectedly (usually, not something terribly negative).

one-size-fits-all – Generic; meets the needs and concerns of everyone. A one-size-fits-all toque might work for most heads because the material stretches, but it would be hard to imagine a one-size-fits-all bra or set of underwear. Your resumé and covering letter should be tailored to the specific career, or even the specific job, that you are applying for, *not* one-size-fits-all.

cross-referenced – Relevant in more than one area or subject. Some courses at university or college can be considered to be cross-referenced; for example, a course might be listed in the calendar under both history and Canadian studies because it contains material that is relevant to both programs of study.

brainstorm – Think of as many ideas and options to solve a problem as you can or make a plan without censoring any of the thoughts. The goal is to generate as many ideas as possible that could be helpful and then narrow them down to the best ones.

being stuck – Being unable to proceed with work or a task until another action occurs or until more information or resources are obtained.

pull off (a quality job) – Accomplish or complete, usually despite challenges or obstacles.

detail-oriented – Paying a lot of attention to all aspects and facets of a project.

workaholic – Someone who works to excess.

generalist – Someone who is good at many things or areas of expertise that are broadly related; a *specialist* is someone who works in a more narrowly focused range of expertise.

tossing out – Disposing of; throwing into the garbage.

urban legend – A commonly accepted and widely disseminated story that may or may not be based in fact; although not documented with proof or evidence, urban legends always contain some compelling, believable aspect.

hook – Attention-grabber or persuasive element.

bricks-and-mortar – Having a tangible building or structure. A store located downtown or in a mall is bricks-and-mortar, while a store selling online is a virtual store (i.e., there is no actual physical store location).

specific position you are applying for (and is *never* written as a one-size-fits-all, generic covering letter that you use to apply for every job!).

Creating a good resumé requires that you ask yourself a lot of hard questions about your skills, abilities, personal qualities, job experience, volunteer experience, and education in order to showcase what you have that the employer will want. It's not a bad idea to begin with the Starting Point questions. Put yourself into the position of the employer, and ask yourself questions that would elicit a lot about you. From the answers to the Starting Point questions, you can create an inventory of your strengths and weaknesses, your personal qualities, any and all relevant work and/or volunteer experience, and your relevant educational achievements.

Using the job description as a guide to what the employer is looking for, you then write a covering letter that relates your relevant skills, abilities, experience, and education to what the job requires. The letter is a "teaser" to get the employer interested in you as a potential employee and encourage him or her to read more about you in your professionally crafted resumé.

Chapter 14 will help you with an interview—and the aftermath of the interview—to seal the deal.

Your Starting Point

ENVISIONING YOUR JOB OR CAREER

Before you can start an effective job search and do research into where you might like to work, you need to be really clear on what you want out of your work life.

It's strongly recommended that you visit a college or university career counselling centre, an employment centre, or a similar organization for help with this process, because they can provide basic information to help you envision your career—and to help you with research for and the writing of covering letters and resumés.

Questions that you should ask yourself about your ideal job include the following:

- Where do I want to work (geographical location)?

- What kinds of organizations or business sectors would I like to work for or in?

- Who would I like to work with? Who do I work best with, personality-wise?

- How much supervision would I like—a lot of guidance or to be left to my own devices?

- How will my ideal career fit my personal core values and ethics and my vision of who I am or would like to be?

- What kind of working conditions would I work best in—for example, indoors or outdoors, a flexible schedule or set hours?

- How much money would I like to make? How much do I need to make to cover my budget and contingency needs?

- How much responsibility would I like to have in my work?

Before you start job searching, you should work out your minimum salary requirements based on your current expenses and plans for saving. See the box below for guidance on what to consider when budgeting.

If you can wrap your head around asking yourself these questions, you may find the process triggers more information that will help you to define what your ideal career would be.

RESEARCH INTO ORGANIZATIONS AND BUSINESSES

When you have determined what kind of job or career you are aiming for, you need to do some research into which organizations or businesses will meet your criteria for the right job and employer.

Internet search engines can be helpful: type in any combination of search terms using words or phrases from your visioning process, and see what comes up in terms of employers.

Another good idea is to check out *Canada's Top 100 Employers*. This survey is published annually, and you should be able to find it in hard copy at the library or online at http://www.canadastop100.com. It includes thoughtful descriptions of the leading employers in Canada, detailing not only the "who, what, where, when, and how" of the companies but also why people want to work for them.

Ask your career counsellors or professors to recommend employers who would meet your career criteria. Chances are that your professors, in particular, have current contacts at many of the organizations or businesses you would like to apply to or would consider for employment. These contacts are people with whom you could try to arrange an informational interview for more detail on what the company is looking for and whether they might be hiring in the near future (see Chapter 14 for details). Informational interviews are a primary source of information that can be invaluable to you as you craft covering letters and resumés to submit to these organizations.

Get into the habit of reading the newspaper. The front section usually focuses on news of the day, and this can be a major tip-off in terms of finding out what organizations in your field of expertise are doing, activities that can lead to job openings that are never advertised.

If you are a business student, focus particularly on the business section; read the business profiles, and find out what companies are expanding operations, are planning to hire new people, or might require someone with your expertise to resolve a problem or challenge. Because most of the job market is hidden, it pays to keep up on what is happening in the business world and with any employers you are interested in to see whether the news indicates that they are hiring or would be looking for the kind of help you can provide. If you are not a business student, you should still keep up on business news, but also read sections that pertain to your field of expertise. For example, such sections as health and well-being, family, or local news can yield a lot of information of interest to a graduate of a health sciences or community services program.

Watching television can be good for your career search—in particular, watch educational shows, news broadcasts, and investigational journalism shows such as *W-Five* and *Marketplace* for information that may alert you to new developments in your field of expertise.

How much money do you really need?

When you are searching for a job, part of the process should include a realistic appraisal of the income you need to make in order to cover your expenses. While we would all love to make hundreds of thousands of dollars annually, chances are that as a recent graduate or career changer you will have to build your way up to the big bucks.

Sometimes people think they will "make do" with a job that pays less than they realistically need, counting on Mom, Dad, or a significant other to cover the shortfall—or a credit card at a high interest rate!

On the other hand, job-seekers sometimes have an unrealistic notion of what is an essential expense (a need) and what is a luxury (a want). As a consequence, they turn away perfectly reasonable work and a decent paycheque because they want to live in luxury.

One way to think seriously and realistically about what you will need in terms of pay is to work out a personal budget. Being realistic about costs means considering the worst-case scenario—such as when an item or service is at its most expensive—rather than what you could "get by with." That way, if your costs are lower than expected, you can save some for the future—or enjoy a small splurge!

In this scenario, you would need to earn the total amount ($2,739) from your pay each month *after* taxes and deductions. If you received an offer of employment, you would want to find out what the gross amount per pay would be and then how much your "take-home" (net) pay would be after deductions and taxes to see whether you would have enough to meet the expenses noted here.

Note that there are other expenses that you would be wise to consider **amortizing**—that is, spreading out as a monthly expense—and the ones that come up unexpectedly or infrequently, like dental care,

TABLE 13.1	Sample Monthly Budget
EXPENSE	**AMOUNT ($)**
Groceries	300
Housing (rent)	500
Utilities	125
Car (lease)	200
Car insurance	110
Gasoline	320
Car maintenance	80
Telephone	100
Internet	49
Student loan	250
Debts (credit card)*	200
Clothes	75
Personal care	80
Entertainment	100
Savings (RRSP)	150
Savings (other)	100
TOTAL	**2,739**

*(for 12 months, to pay off plus interest)

prescriptions, major car repairs, and so on. Think about how much you could spend in a year on such expenses—or how much you have spent on them annually in the past—then divide the worst-case scenario amount into 12 equal amounts. Add these amounts to your monthly budget, and plan on putting the money aside for the time when you *will* need to spend it.

Local chambers of commerce and business associations publish directories and post this information online, so visit your local library for the hard copy, as well as for access to the many databases on businesses there to do research into potential employers. In fact, joining a chamber of commerce as a recent-graduate or student member will give you an opportunity to get to know potential employers in your community and find out more about possible job openings.

Let your family and friends know what you see as your ideal job, and ask them to be on the lookout for potential employers or job openings that might fit what you are looking for.

Finally, be sure to look at job postings daily—in newspapers and online and at employment centres, career counselling agencies, and associations in your business or trade sector. Bookmark websites or job search engines so that you can do this quickly and easily.

RESEARCH FOR ADVERTISED JOBS

If you see a job posting that you would like to apply for right away, you still need to do as much research as possible on the potential employer, even with a tight application deadline. Ask the Starting Point questions to determine what the employer will be looking for in your application, using them to guide you through research to get the right information.

As soon as possible, "get thee to a library!" Tell a helpful reference librarian that you want all available information on the company. It could come from directories such as *Scott's Directory*, which lists information about companies across North America, or even from newspaper articles or online databases available in the library. In many cases, the print sources cannot be taken out of the library, while anything you find online must be printed. So take lots of change for copying and printing.

Contact the chamber of commerce in the community where the business is located. Ask them whether they have any information on the business that you can borrow, take, or copy. You may have to buy one of their annual business directories, but it's probably worth the money if you plan to apply to a number of organizations or businesses in that community.

If you have time, visit the business, and speak with someone there. Receptionists and administrative assistants can often give you a lot of information—if you are very pleasant, use their first names, and show respect for their position. They often know more than the typical CEO does! They may also be able to give you brochures, newsletters, or other promotional or informational literature on the business. If you do obtain help from someone in the organization, be sure to get their contact information and send them a thank-you card—or perhaps even flowers, depending on what he or she did for you.

If the company has a website, use that as a research source. Look around the site to see whether there is any information pertaining to the position you are applying for.

If you know anyone who works at the organization, contact him or her and ask some of the Starting Point questions. If anyone has been able to help you in this way, send the person a thank-you note or even a quick thank-you email.

If the business or organization is open to the public—such as a store or health centre—visit and take a look at how people are dressed, note the atmosphere and vibe, and, particularly, observe what employees are doing and how they interact with the public. This is also primary research.

RESEARCH AND THE RESUMÉ

In order to write your resumé well, you need to:

- do research on what employers in your industry, sector, or discipline are looking for in general;

- brainstorm your own personal qualities, skills, education, and work experience relevant to jobs in your field;

- research what your target organizations are looking for in employees in general—and specifically, what qualities, experience, and education are required in the positions you would like to have.

You should do as much research as possible into your business or organizational sector, the leading organizations or companies, and what these employers are looking for. For example, in numerous studies conducted by government and college and university business departments, the vast majority of managers and business leaders state that strong oral and written communication skills are essential, followed closely by excellent interpersonal dynamics and customer service skills. When you write your resumé, be sure to highlight your strong skills in these areas.

Of course, you can't describe yourself as a brilliant public speaker if you are not—that would be lying. But you will need to brainstorm lists of your strengths and weaknesses, skills, personal qualities, educational achievements, and work experiences relevant to working in your sector. These lists will be the foundation of information about yourself and what you have to offer a potential employer. If you do have qualities, experience, or education that the employer is looking for, you will definitely highlight these qualities in your resumé so that he or she can quickly identify you as a strong candidate for a job.

If you find yourself stuck when it comes to brainstorming your personal qualities, strengths, and weaknesses, ask trusted friends or family who can give you honest feedback. Often, others see things in us that we cannot see. In terms of your weaknesses, of course you would not say to a potential employer, "I procrastinate far too often." Your weaknesses, however, can be turned into strengths if you view them differently. For example, rather than saying you procrastinate, you could say that you "produce quality work to deadline" (perhaps at the last minute, but somehow you always manage to pull off a great job).

Finally, every resumé you produce should be tailored for a specific type of job, if not for each specific employer. If you feel that the resumé you crafted for a particular job needs to be altered to suit another potential employer and position, then apply information about that employer—and what that specific organization is seeking—to what you write in your resumé.

RESEARCH AND THE COVERING LETTER

Before you write a covering letter when applying for a job, you again need to apply the Starting Point questions. Once you have answered the Starting Point questions about the potential employer, you will have the information and background to write a strong, to-the-point covering letter that will open the door at the business you are applying to. Knowing the company's position in the community, its alliances, its major business moves, and what it is looking for from its employees will help you to frame the letter so that it will be well received.

For example, if you learn that the business has recently begun an environmental initiative, you could open your letter with that information, suggest a way that you can help with the initiative based on

You can gain work experience and grow your professional network by volunteering. Making a good impression on the organization(s) you volunteer for could help you secure a good reference to use when you apply for paying jobs. See the box on volunteering for additional details.

Build your resumé by volunteering

You can't get a job without experience, but how do you get experience without a job? Volunteer!

Volunteering in a position that gives you work experience relevant to the type of career or job you want will get you through the door of an employer faster than just your degree or diploma alone.

There are many not-for-profit organizations that can offer you resumé-building work experience. Look up volunteer centres in larger communities; these central organizations act as agents for not-for-profits, interviewing, screening, and matching appropriate volunteers to jobs or positions, thus filling both the organizations' needs and those of the volunteer. You can also volunteer at a workplace where you would like to work. The employer may not have an opening yet but would love to have a young, talented person like you to pitch in and work with someone with more experience. It's a great deal—free labour for the employer, a chance for you to show him or her what you can do, and an opportunity for you to be mentored by others in your business sector or industry.

See Chapter 14 for suggestions on how to conduct an informational interview with an employer you'd like to work for. At the end of the interview, ask whether he or she would ever consider having you as a volunteer working in the business. Let the person know that you would like to do some job shadowing, be part of a mentoring program, or have an opportunity to learn more about the company or the industry in general. (However, don't push the idea that you hope to get a job out of this. The goal of an informational interview is to get information, not to press for a job.)

something you have done in the past, or talk about your own personal commitment to environmentalism. It's like getting to know a few things about a person before you have a first date so that you can launch a conversation that will break the ice.

In fact, such research will enable you to present information that the reader will find both interesting and intriguing; the information indicates that you cared enough to do research into the company. You can use this information to write an excellent opening paragraph. Like the lead of a well-written news story, the first sentence in your letter must hook your reader from the outset with a provocative, helpful, interesting, or informative point that relates to something he or she cares about.

The job posting or advertisement should provide a list of skills, abilities, experience, and educational credentials that candidates seeking the position should possess. Using this list, refer to your own skills, abilities, experience, and educational credentials that you have identified (and have put into your resumé), and cross-reference the two lists. In other words, relate what you can offer to what they are looking for as preparation for writing the covering letter.

Creating the Written Product—How to Do It

PREPARING TO WRITE

As mentioned in the Starting Point section, you first conduct research to determine your own strengths, weaknesses, personal qualities, experience, and education and to find out more about potential employers.

Resumés do not require citations, but of course you need to be truthful about what you claim to be or what you have written in your resumé. If you decide to use a quote to open your covering letter or anywhere else in the letter, be sure to give credit to the source (e.g., "A little neglect may breed mischief"—Benjamin Franklin). This shows your integrity—and how brilliant and well read you are!

ORGANIZING INFORMATION AND WRITING: FORMAT

Resumé format

A good resumé starts with the preparations noted in the Starting Point section, beginning with lists of your strengths and weaknesses.

When you have compiled your list of weaknesses, take a close look at each one, and think about how that particular weakness could also be considered a strength. For example, if you wrote "ultra-picky" as a weakness, you could also see this quality as "detail-oriented." If you feel you are a "workaholic," position this quality instead as "hard-working."

Once you have come up with a more positive spin on your weaknesses, add these new positives to your list of strengths. Check to see whether there is a theme, or repetition of qualities. If you have "hard-working," "diligent," and "committed to getting the job done" on your list, these qualities all speak to your ability to work hard. Consolidate these qualities into one strong, enthusiastic statement.

Put this list aside for a moment, and consider your skills, experience, and education as it relates to the type of job you are applying for. Create another list including these points, and, again, check to see whether there's repetition of certain points, then narrow the list down to carefully worded, strong, positive statements about your qualifications.

Create a list of qualifications the specific employer—or type of employer—wants from someone working in the type of position you are applying for. Put this list aside.

Draw up an outline for your resumé. There are many resumé formats to work with, and most people create resumés based on whatever combination of types works best for the jobs they are applying for. You may have learned how to write a **chronological resumé** in high school or through career counselling. This type of resumé lists your work and academic experience, showing the most recent first. It does not focus on transferable skills, experience, or volunteer work, for example, that would make up for a lack of actual work experience.

Generally speaking, people who haven't worked for many years or who are at the beginning of a new career should consider a **functional resumé**—because a chronological resumé only points to your lack of work experience. A functional resumé profiles your particular mix of skills, experience, personal qualities, and education that relates to the type of job you are applying for rather than focusing on when you worked, the length of time you worked, and where. The functional resumé tells your story better to a potential employer.

The box below shows a functional resumé format that works well for a variety of applicants, ranging from recent graduates to folks with a variety of experience and qualities. You should create your resumé in an assortment of font sizes and styles to provide definition for each section (but use no more than two different fonts—perhaps one for your headers and another for text). Your instructor may also share with you some variations on this format.

Functional resumé format

PERSONAL CONTACT DETAILS

Your contact details should be centred as a header in following format:

YOUR NAME
Street address
Town, Province, Postal Code
Phone number(s) with area code(s)
Email address

SUMMARY

In the summary, you list direct experience with the type of work you want to do, transferable skills from other work or volunteer positions that would apply to jobs you are applying for, relevant personal qualities, and any related hobbies or interests.

Consult your lists of strengths, skills, experience, and education to come up with the points for your summary. It is extremely important to choose energetic, dynamic words to express all that you have to offer. Use a thesaurus if you are stuck on word choices to describe your skills (don't use "good," "excellent," "great," and similar words too much; look for more dynamic word choices that show your brilliance and creativity).

The summary must be brief, only *one* paragraph in length. Therefore, it's important to choose only the best, most descriptive words and phrases that will briefly but effectively grab the reader's attention.

ACCOMPLISHMENT

In this section, you use as subheadings what the employer is looking for in terms of qualifications or experience. Under each subheading, you list what you have achieved or done in relation to that specific qualification or experience type and where you acquired the experience.

Qualification/experience heading #1

Place where you got the experience
- Blurb regarding what you did there, specific to the qualification/experience heading

Another place where you got the experience
- Blurb regarding what you did there, specific to the qualification/experience heading

Another place where you got the experience (and so on . . .)
- Blurb regarding what you did there, specific to the qualification/experience heading

Qualification/experience heading #2 (and more if needed . . .)

Place where you got the experience
- Blurb regarding what you did there, specific to the qualification/experience heading

Another place where you got the experience (and so on . . .)
- Blurb regarding what you did there, specific to the qualification/experience heading

RELEVANT EMPLOYMENT/BUSINESS HISTORY

In this section, you only need to note when you worked and where, since you have already listed all of your relevant qualifications and/or experience in the previous section. List your employment career in chronological order, starting with your most recent (or present) job.

If you have a lot of work experience, you need only list jobs that are relevant to the job experience/skills you have already described. In other words, list only the jobs where you acquired the relevant experience for the positions you are applying for. If you do not have a lot of work experience yet, then it's not a bad idea to list all the jobs you have had so far.

Years or dates	Name of employer, address	Your job title
Years or dates	Name of employer, address	Your job title
Years or dates	Name of employer/ address	Your job title

EDUCATION AND TRAINING

In this section, list where you obtained educational qualifications such as diplomas, degrees, or certificates. Show these qualifications in chronological order, starting with the most recent. Include only educational qualifications from high school onward.

Years or dates	Name of institution, address or location	Title of educational achievement (e.g., Bachelor of Arts, History)
Years or dates	Name of institution, address or location	Title of educational achievement

VOLUNTEER WORK

In this section, list your positions at and the locations of the organizations where you did or are doing volunteer work. Because you will draw from your volunteer experience as well as work experience and personal qualities when you create your summary and accomplishments sections, you don't need to go into detail about what you did at each of these volunteer positions.
- Title/position, name of organization, location/ address, when you volunteered (e.g., "current" or, if in the past, dates)
- Title/position, name of organization, location/ address, when you volunteered

(continued)

REFERENCES

In this section, list the full contact information, including position/organization, for each of your references. Whether you provide references depends on whether the organization or business has asked for them; if you are not asked, it is usually fine to simply state, "References available upon request."

References can be personal or professional. A personal reference is someone who has known you, your reputation, and your work in the community. Personal references can include such people as your religious leader, former professors or instructors, or others who know you well. A professional reference is someone who has experienced your work and can vouch for it, including former employers or volunteer agency leaders with whom you have worked.

If the kind of references required is not noted in the job posting, contact the employer to find out whether he or she wants personal or professional references, or both. If you can't get this information, provide both types.

Warning: Always, always contact the people you would like to have as references *before* you give their names and contact information to a potential employer. It's extremely rude and unprofessional to give someone else's name as a reference without getting their permission first. Further, you risk getting a very negative reference from anyone who is unhappy that you "sprang" the responsibility of providing a reference on him or her. It's also a good idea to fill your references in on what the potential employer might be looking for and what is involved in the position for which you are applying. If you are required to supply references in your resumé, here is a format to use:

Name of person, title
Name of organization he/she works for
Street address
Town, province, postal code
Telephone (the number[s] where the reference can best be reached, with his or her permission)
Email (the email address[es] where the reference can best be reached, with his or her permission)

Covering Letter Format

Once you've put your resumé together, you will have a good idea of which of your skills, qualifications, and personal qualities match what an employer is looking for.

Using the job advertisement or, better still, a job description for the position you are applying for, make a list of qualifications the employer is seeking, as well as any specific educational or job experience that is mentioned. Looking at your resumé, make note of what you have to offer that relates to what the employer is looking for.

Once you have created this list, you are ready to write the letter. In terms of tone, the letter should be moderately formal, because it's most likely that you do not know the person you are applying to and you want to make a professional first impression.

The words you choose should be descriptive but to the point. Avoid repetitious use of words; use a thesaurus if you are stuck on word choice. Use a variety of sentence lengths, but avoid very long sentences. In terms of paragraphs, make sure these are short and to the point as well—no longer than two or three sentences.

TABLE 13.2	Employer Needs and Applicant's Qualifications
EMPLOYER NEEDS	**MY RELATED POINTS**
• Proven customer service skills	• More than five years' experience as customer service rep; three-time winner of XYZ Inc.'s customer service excellence award
• Solid problem-solving ability	• Addressed customer concerns and complaints in a proactive way, working collaboratively with customers and fellow employees to resolve problems

Applying for jobs internationally?

While every employer around the world wants to learn about you and what you can do for him or her, international employers (outside of North America) require some additional or different pieces of information to consider your application.

In many other countries, such as those in the European Union, a resumé is a CV—**curriculum vitae**. It's typically longer than in North America, because employers want more information about you. Therefore, include your most important details on the first page (the functional resumé format highlights your strongest points immediately). This is to engage the potential employer's interest in you sufficiently that he or she will want to read the rest of your resumé and review other supporting documents.

WHAT INFORMATION DO I NEED TO PROVIDE?

Highlight any international experience or education you may have. Assume that international employers are more formal, and write in an appropriate tone.

In addition to focusing on the obvious skills and credentials sought, carefully scrutinize the job posting to see whether the employer wants any additional information. To be even more on the safe side, do some research into resumés for your industry or sector in the country you hope to work in.

CONTACT INFORMATION

As in a North American resumé, you provide your name, full address, telephone (and possibly fax) number, and email address at the top of the CV.

PERSONAL INFORMATION

You shouldn't include any personal information, such as marital status, age, sex, and nationality or cultural background, right? In some countries or cultures, it is legal to ask for this information, and in other cases, it's expected. For example, indicating your cultural background can help you to land the job. If you leave out personal information, you may not be considered for an interview.

If you determine that personal information is helpful and/or required when you apply for work, include a brief section, Personal information, just below your contact information and just before the Summary of qualifications.

Working in many countries around the world requires a visa, so note your visa status in this Personal information section.

SUMMARY OF QUALIFICATIONS

Provide a brief summary of qualifications, particularly if you lack employment experience in your field.

EMPLOYMENT OR WORK HISTORY

We've indicated that a functional resumé is best if you have limited work experience or have switched jobs several times. However, in your employment history or work history section, list all the jobs you have had since high school. This indicates to a European employer breadth of experience and that you have adjusted to change accordingly. Note *any* international work experience, demonstrating your ability to adapt to other cultures.

What if you have had many jobs? Document details of the most recent, including a description of duties,

(continued)

supervisor(s), and full address. The least recent you may document more briefly, with fewer details.

Have more work placement or volunteer than employment experience? Insert a Volunteer/work placement experience section ahead of Employment or Work history. Organize information about each volunteer or work placement position the same way you would for employment positions as described above, with more detail for most recent work and fewer details for less recent.

EDUCATIONAL HISTORY

What if you don't have a lot of work experience yet? Most of you reading this are currently in college or university and will be graduating in a year or two. Because this is your current situation, put your educational history on the first page.

An exception to this order would be if you acquired professional designations, certifications, or memberships before, during, or after schooling. International employers may be more impressed by these qualifications than employers in North America are, so insert a section on Professional designations and memberships just ahead of Educational history. In the professional designations or educational history section (depending on which category the information better fits), add any cross-cultural or language training.

Attaching copies of diplomas, certificates, and even educational transcripts is helpful, particularly considering that the employer may not be familiar with the schools you attended or the professional designations you acquired. While North American employers are not generally interested in marks achieved in school, European and other international employers may well be.

NOTES ON TONE, EDITING, AND FORMAT

Your CV and covering letter should be written in a more formal tone. Avoid any cultural references, slang, or colloquialisms, and definitely do not include industry-specific jargon unless you know the potential employer expects it and/or understands it. Print on off-white or white paper if you are mailing your application (colours are not considered appropriate).

COVERING LETTERS

An international covering letter summarizes what you have to offer and what you are looking for in terms of experience in the first paragraph or two. This quickly and succinctly answers employer questions, "What can this person do for me and my company better than any other candidate? Why should I bother to read more?"

If the potential employer wants to know your salary requirements, put this information in the letter. Research typical salaries in the organization before specifying, or, if you can't get this information easily, try to find out the range of pay for the position in that country's industry or sector. But don't provide your salary expectations *unless* you are asked to do so.

Keep your letter to one page if at all possible. When you stray beyond two pages, you can lose the attention of the reader. If you find that your letter is getting too long, check to see whether you are merely reproducing what the reader can find in your resumé. The letter should be an invitation to learn more about you from the resumé (and an interview); it should not overwhelm the reader with information. Reading a long, wordy letter is a little like meeting someone who runs on at the mouth, with hardly a breath between words—it can be very annoying, not to mention boring.

Remember, your reader (the potential employer) will probably have to wade through a lot of letters and resumés to create a shortlist of candidates to be interviewed. Impress your reader with strong, enthusiastic, yet concise language, sentences, and paragraphs. Sometimes less *is* more!

The sample letter format in Figure 13.1 is formatted in the full-block business letter style and is set up without letterhead.

FIGURE 13.1 Covering Letter Format

Date	
	Leave five line spaces.
Your name Your address City, province, and postal code	
	Leave three line spaces.
Name of person you are writing to (and position) The company/organization name (in full) Company address City, province, and postal code	
	Leave three line spaces.
RE: Title of job (and any relevant job code or number)	
	Leave two line spaces.
Dear (name of reader—Mr./Ms plus last name):	
	Leave two line spaces.
Introductory brief paragraph 1: In this paragraph, include an attention-grabber to hook the reader's interest. For example, if you have done research on the company, you could include some information that the company might use for a new operation or initiative, a quotation appropriate to that employer's work or mandate, a statement about some social or business issue you know about that is of interest to the employer and/or related to the job, or some other thought-provoking statement to intrigue the reader enough to read more.	Paragraphs are not indented.
	Leave two line spaces.
Brief paragraph 2: In this paragraph, state your purpose (to apply for the position), and briefly describe your background as it relates to the position.	
	Leave two line spaces.
Brief paragraph 3: In this paragraph, briefly outline qualifications or skills the employer is looking for and what you can offer in that regard.	
	Leave two line spaces.
Brief paragraph 4: In this paragraph, briefly outline more qualifications or skills the employer is looking for and what you can offer in that regard.	
	Leave two line spaces.
Brief paragraph 5: Ditto	As above, as needed.
	Leave two line spaces.

(continued)

As above.

Leave two line spaces.

As above.

Leave two line spaces.

Leave three line spaces before complimentary close.

Leave three line spaces in which you hand sign the letter.

Leave two line spaces.

Brief paragraph 6: Ditto

Brief paragraph 7: Ditto

Closing paragraph: This brief paragraph includes a thoughtful statement, perhaps referring back to the one you made in the first paragraph or carrying that thought through to a satisfying conclusion. The paragraph restates your purpose (your enthusiasm for a position with the company), reiterates your main strengths in reference to the job, and invites the reader to contact you for more information (and an interview).

Yours truly,

Your name

Attachments: Resumé (and any other application forms or materials required to apply for the job)

Sample Documents

FIGURE 13.2 Resumé

KATHERINE WILKEY
69 Queen Street West
Ganges, BC V8K 2T1
(250) 555-4223
kwilkey@wotmail.com

An enthusiastic generalist with significant experience in project management; writing, editing, and production; managing print projects; problem solving/conflict management; business counselling and planning; office operations and administration; human resources and volunteer management; and adult education/training.

ACCOMPLISHMENTS

Marketing

The Marketing Centre

- managed all marketing projects for various clients in retail/service industries
- developed media plans; liaised with media representatives
- oversaw all development of advertising, including creative, production, and proofing processes

Salt Spring Island College

- taught marketing and sales courses to college diploma and continuing education students
- created curricula for marketing, sales, and promotional planning courses

The Ganges Media Group Inc.

- managed sales of advertising in local newspaper
- developed annual advertising calendars for newspaper
- assisted with proofing process of advertising prior to printing
- maintained customer database

Management Skills

The Marketing Centre

- managed office staff of 10 people
- oversaw all aspects of administration and operations
- worked with management team on three- and five-year business plans
- provided customer service and problem-solving services

The Government of Canada

- developed, delivered, and managed four 16-week federal government marketing and sales training programs through the local employment centre
- managed budget and administrative paperwork for this program

Always include full name and contact information at top.

Subheadings represent the specific skills/abilities required in job posting/ad.

Under each employer, list relevant tasks performed relating to job posting/ad.

(continued)

The Ganges Media Group Inc.

- supervised a sales team of five people
- co-ordinated production of advertising with graphic design and web design team
- worked with other members of management team on three- and five-year plans for newspaper sales and editorial
- managed annual marketing department budget of $100,000

Business and Consulting Skills

Kate Wilkey Consulting Inc.

- organizational assessment, counselling, and troubleshooting
- marketing and early-stage business growth consulting/training
- customer service and retention assessment, planning, and implementation
- event management
- sales planning, training, and troubleshooting
- marketing project management (including all creative services)
- marketing plan review and analysis
- financial systems management
- media and public relations planning

EMPLOYMENT EXPERIENCE

List in descending chronological order job positions, where worked, location.

2004–present	**Owner**, Kate Wilkey Consulting Inc., Ganges, BC
2004–present	**Marketing Co-ordinator**, Marketing Centre, Ganges, BC
2003–present	**College Instructor**, Salt Spring Island College, Ganges, BC
2002–2004	**Advertising Sales Manager**, The Ganges Media Group Inc., Ganges, BC
2002–2005	**Co-ordinator/Manager**, Essential Marketing Skills Program, Government of Canada (Service Canada), Ganges, BC

List relevant education in descending chronological order; include qualification earned, then where/location.

EDUCATION

2001–2004	**Bachelor of Business Administration (Marketing)** Bishop's University, Lennoxville, QC

List in descending chronological order position/title, where worked.

VOLUNTEER EXPERIENCE

2004–present	**Vice-Chair, Salt Spring Island Economic Development Board** Ganges, BC
2001–2002	**Marketing Co-ordinator, Local Economic Trading System** Lennoxville, QC

Best to state "on request" so that you can provide best references for specific job.

REFERENCES

References available upon request.

FIGURE 13.3 Covering Letter

August 4, 2014

Note cover letter follows business letter format.

Katherine Wilkey
69 Queen Street West
Ganges, BC V8K 2T1

Jane Beckett
Vice-President, Marketing
Salt Spring Island College
500 Lower Ganges Road
Ganges, BC V8K 2T1

RE: MARKETING CO-ORDINATOR, CONTINUING EDUCATION

RE line should include title of position (and any file number if requested).

Dear Ms Beckett:

Always address a woman as Ms, since you don't know her marital status.

According to a recent *Globe and Mail* article, job seekers are advised to engage in post-graduate and continuing education for an edge in today's challenging job market. Salt Spring Island College's Continuing Education school, with over 25 market-ready and relevant programs, offers the relevant education these job seekers need to land the job of their dreams. With a background in both post-secondary education and marketing, I am ideally suited to help Salt Spring College tap into this market as Marketing Co-ordinator, Continuing Education.

Information here is a hook, proving writer knows about market and what college offers.

As a contract instructor in the marketing diploma program at Salt Spring College, I was delighted to learn about this job opening in the marketing department, where I could put my extensive experience in communication and adminis-tration and my business management skills to work in a dynamic, fast-paced environment.

Writer gives reason for reader to read on with summary of relevant qualifications.

Through my work at this college, I have kept up with the latest developments in marketing to an ever-changing student demographic and have integrated this ongoing learning into my work in the classroom. I am confident I would be an asset to the marketing team in the role of continuing education marketing

Writer's qualifications noted in this and next paragraphs let reader know she is qualified.

(continued)

co-ordinator, since I also maintain solid involvement with the Gulf Islands communities' economic and social agencies through my own business, Kate Wilkey Consulting Inc., and through work with the Salt Spring Economic Development Corporation's board.

I am also currently employed (part-time) as marketing co-ordinator for The Marketing Centre in Ganges. In this role, I have developed extensive administrative and management skills and have further enhanced my relationship with local businesses and individuals. This experience would provide a wonderful base for networking and marketing the college's continuing education programming.

In short, I offer a portfolio of exceptional marketing, management, and administrative skills and experience, and I invite you to review my resumé for further details. Should you have any questions, please contact me at (250) 222-5437 or at kwilkey@wotmail.com. I look forward to sharing with you how my particular mix of skills, education, experience, and community networking will be an asset to the college's marketing department.

Yours truly,

Katherine Wilkey

Attachment: Resumé

Relates applicant's specific skills/experience of relevance to the job.

Summarizes what applicant has to offer that is relevant to job; persuades reader to follow up.

Always provide contact information, even if in resumé.

Affirmation of interest and what applicant offers as assets functions as final persuasion.

Yours truly is most appropriate way to sign off.

Note that resumé is attached.

Want to see more examples?

For more examples of covering letters and resumés, see this text's website at **www.oupcanada.com/Luchuk**.

Checking Your Work

CONTENT EDITING, COPY EDITING, AND FORMATTING REVIEW

As has been said many times before in this book, careful content editing and copy editing will make your brilliance and intelligence shine through in all business communication applications. However, flawless writing is even more important when you are applying for a job.

It's not an urban legend—employers still toss out (into the recycling bin, not the garbage!) resumés and covering letters that contain even one error. One error can sink your chances of getting an interview or of being considered seriously for a position you really want, because you are perceived as lacking attention to detail or just plain lazy.

Before you send anything out, make sure not only that you put the paperwork aside and return to it later for close editing but also that you give it to a friend or two to review. Several pairs of eyes are better than one set, particularly since you have such a stake in how your resumé and covering letter will be received.

Resumé

In content editing your resumé, be sure to ask yourself the following questions:

- Did I include the most relevant of my personal qualities, skills, experience, and education? (Cross-reference with the lists you created.)

- Are the points about myself totally relevant to the job or type of job I am applying for? (Eliminate all information that is not relevant to the job you want to land.)

In copy editing your resumé, check the following:

- parallel construction for lists of qualifications, skills, and similar information;

- proper use of semicolons, colons, commas, and em dashes;

- correct grammar and spelling, especially the spelling of people's names, positions, and company names;

- no jargon—if you have used jargon, and even if you are pretty sure the reader will understand it, eliminate it, and replace it with a better word (use a thesaurus);

- abbreviations and acronyms spelled out the first time you use them—never assume that the reader understands the short form;

- no slang—as in the case of jargon, eliminate it; and replace it with more formal language;

- appropriate writing style—is it moderately formal, suitable for a professional, intelligent presentation?

The formatting of the resumé is also critical. Make sure that you have closely followed the template in this book or another model, being sure to use different sizes of one or two easy-to-read fonts to demarcate major headings and subheadings. Be sure that all text lines up properly—that left-justification, indents, or tabs are uniform and presenting your verbiage neatly.

Do not print your resumé on plain white paper—but don't go to the other extreme and use neon-coloured paper. To make a good impression, print it on an off-white, beige, light grey, or light blue paper, preferably of a heavier weight than the usual and perhaps textured. Office and business supply stores carry a variety of classy-looking resumé papers; some even come with matching envelopes. (Print your covering letter on the same type of paper.) If you know that the resumé is going to be photocopied many times, fasten the pages together with a paper clip; if not, neatly staple them. It's also a good idea to attach your covering letter to the resumé with a paper clip so that both pieces stay together.

Covering letter

As in the case of your resumé, you should check your letter thoroughly for content, copy, and format.

- Did you focus your letter on the main qualifications, skills, and/or academic criteria the employer is seeking, and did you back up what you have to offer with examples? (To be sure, check both your list of qualifications and skills and the list of what the employer is looking for.)

- Is the content written tightly, briefly, and in a dynamic way, highlighting what a great match you would be for the job?

- Are your phrases and sentences varied—shorter and longer but none too long?

- Are your paragraphs brief—no more than two or three sentences in length?

- Does your introduction provide a hook to get the reader's attention—something thought-provoking or helpful?

- Does your conclusion restate your interest in the job, your main strengths in reference to what the employer is looking for, and a final closing, thought-provoking statement to seal his or her interest in you?

- Have you avoided repetition of certain words?

- Are there any spelling, grammar, or punctuation errors?

- Have you used the correct spelling for names and positions?

- Is your letter left-justified, with paragraphs double-spaced? Does the format follow what is in this book or an alternative format suggested by your instructor?

As noted above, you would print the letter on the same type of paper as your resumé for best results. If it is more than one page, be sure to staple the pages together (unless you are certain it will be photocopied, in which case it's a favour to the receiver not to have to remove a staple).

Sending Your Application Pieces by Email, Snail Mail, or Fax

In many cases, you can send your resumé, covering letter, and other required information by email or fax in addition to or instead of "snail mail." However, *do* check to see whether email or fax is acceptable, and never assume that it is, because if you are wrong, that could mean that no one will see your carefully written and presented application.

If the employer is willing to receive your documents by email, it's strongly recommended that you save your resumé and letter in PDF format. Sending in this format "freezes" your information in place so that it is less likely to become unformatted at the other end. Depending on the technology the potential employer has, a word-processed document saved in a program like Word could appear with different formatting when it arrives. You will never know this, but if the documents look messy, they may be rejected.

Particularly if you are sending your application package internationally, though, you might want to make sure that the receiver at the other end has Adobe Acrobat Reader so that your PDF can be opened easily. If you have to send your documents in Word or a similar word-processing program, make sure that the receiver has the same program and version of it. A quick email or polite phone call requesting this information would not be frowned upon.

If some of your documents must be supplied in hard copy, indicate in your email that hard copies of them will follow. If you don't have an electronic copy of a document, you might consider scanning it and emailing it as a PDF so that it can be read at the other end (provided that they have Adobe Acrobat Reader).

When you send any documents by email, always introduce the package with a brief, polite message following the rules you have learned in this text for writing a neutral/positive email. You might ask for confirmation that the documents have been received if the employer has not indicated that you will receive an auto-response confirming receipt.

In terms of sending your covering letter, you should check with the potential employer whether he or she would like it sent in the body of an email or in an attached document. Don't assume it's okay to send it within the body of an email. If you do include it in the body of the email, it's even more important to keep it short and to the point. Often, the employer will expect the covering letter as an attachment to your email, usually produced in Word or PDF format.

In some cases, you will be expected to fax documents. Make sure that any documents you send are very crisply printed so that there is no blurring, because fax machines, particularly thermal, may distort the image at the other end. Be sure to create a cover sheet with the date, to whom the documents are directed and all their contact information, your full name and contact information, and a note about how many pages, including the cover sheet, are to follow. You might want to follow up with a phone call to make sure that the documents were received if you don't have a confirmation report from your fax machine.

If you have time, regular mail can be a better bet to ensure that your package arrives by any stated deadline and in the condition and presentation form you want the employer to see. You can print your documents on nicer-quality, resumé paper that will make your application stand out from the rest. You may opt for regular mail particularly if you have to supply such items as transcripts, certificates, or diplomas so that all of your pieces arrive at the same time, thus minimizing the risk of some important information going astray. If the deadline is tight, consider using a priority mail service or a courier.

CHECKLIST FOR covering letters

☐ Have you made notes about how your skills, experience, and education relate to requirements for the position or job?

☐ Have you done research on the organization to learn more about it and to relate your qualifications to the company's operations, needs, or concerns?

☐ Have you done research or contacted the company to obtain the decision-maker's name so that you can address your letter appropriately?

☐ Have you double-checked your letter to ensure that you have not missed any key qualification? Have you indicated how your qualifications match those being sought?

☐ Have you conducted a thorough edit of the letter?

☐ Have you printed it on high-quality, neutral-coloured paper?

CHECKLIST FOR resumés

☐ Have you done research on what employers in your industry, sector, or discipline are looking for in general to determine what to put in your resumé?

☐ Have you brainstormed your own personal qualities, skills, education, and work experience relevant to jobs in your field?

☐ Have you researched what employers in your sector or industry are looking for in employees in general—and, specifically, the qualities, experience, and education they seek for the positions you would like to have?

☐ Have you drafted the resumé using the headings indicated in the suggested format?

☐ Have you created the resumé with appropriate font styles, font sizes, and spacing to reflect the format suggested in this chapter?

☐ Have you conducted a thorough content edit and copy edit of the resumé?

☐ Did you produce the resumé on high-quality, neutral-coloured paper and staple the pages together if there are more than one?

Chapter Summary

In this chapter, you have learned how to develop a set of career objectives and the jobs that will get you there and create a personal budget to determine how much you need to earn. You've seen the importance of conducting research into organizations and businesses you might like to work for, how to find advertised jobs and learn more about organizations or businesses you are applying to for advertised postings, and how to identify the most important information you need to provide in a covering letter and resumé to persuade an employer to hire you.

In this chapter, you've also learned how to organize information for, write, and format a functional resumé specific to the stated requirements for an advertised position and the needs of a prospective employer and how to organize information for, write, and format a covering letter specific to the stated requirements for an advertised position and the needs of a prospective employer.

■■■ SUGGESTIONS *for Further Reading*

Graham, S. (2010). *Best Canadian cover letters*. Toronto, ON: Sentor Media.

Kessler, R. (2012). *Competency-based interviews*. (rev. ed.). Toronto, ON: Career Books.

Kessler, R., and Strassburg, L.A. (2005). *Competency-based resumes: How to bring your resume to the top of the pile*. Toronto, ON: Career Books.

Noble, D.F. (2011). *Gallery of best resumes: A collection of quality resumes by professional resume writers*. St. Paul, MN: Jist Publishing.

Parker, Y., and Brown, B. (2012). *The damn good resume guide: A crash course in resume writing*. (5th ed.). New York, NY: Random House/Crown Publishing/Ten Speed Press.

Schuman, N., and Nadler, B.J. (2012). *The resume and cover letter phrase book: What to write to get the job that's right*. Avon, MA: Adams Media.

■■■ DEBATE *and Discussion Starters*

1. Why would it be important to research careers you are interested in and then the industry or sector these careers are found in?

2. Why would it be important to research specific employers you might like to work for? What information would you be looking for in this research, and how would you apply it in your application for an advertised or unadvertised job?

3. When applying for an advertised or unadvertised job, is there any time when a chronological resumé might be a better format than a functional resumé? Why would either format work better for *you*?

4. Is it ever a good idea to simply write a form covering letter and submit it to employers? Why or why not?

5. What else could you do or supply in addition to a covering letter and resumé to persuade a potential employer to hire you for work in your desired career or industry sector?

■■ PRACTISING *What You Have Learned*

1. Find a commonly used online job search engine that posts jobs in your discipline or career area (some good ones to try are Workopolis and Monster). Locate a job posting for the kind of job you would like to apply for. Print it, and follow the instructions in this chapter to write a covering letter and resumé that you would send to apply for this job.

2. Alternatively, look in the careers section of a national or major regional newspaper, either online or in hard copy, and locate a job posting for the kind of job for which you'd like to apply. Follow the instructions in this chapter to write a covering letter and resumé that you would send to apply for this job.

3. Find some industry-specific or trade publications relevant to your discipline, future career, or business sector (for example, *Marketing* magazine if you are in marketing; *Communication Arts* if you are in graphic design, advertising, or marketing; *Quill and Quire* if you plan to work in communication or writing/editorial services). Locate a job posting for the kind of job you would like to apply for, and write a covering letter and resumé that you would send to apply for this job.

4. For a week or two, a month, or most of a semester, read the first (news) section, the business or financial section, and any section pertaining to your discipline or business sector of a few major newspapers (online or in hard copy). Look for articles about companies or organizations that you would like to work for, and read carefully to learn their current status and future plans. Keep the articles in a file folder, and take notes in a journal, recording the dates of articles, the publication information, and the main points.

   By reading these stories—and reading between the lines—you can often uncover a hidden job opportunity. You may see that the organization could use someone like you to fill a position the decision-makers haven't even thought of yet, literally creating your own position and job description.

   Using the notes generated from reading the articles, identify a potential job or position at a company in your industry or business sector. Make notes about what you think this position would entail, and write a job description as if you were the employer creating the position, noting qualifications needed, duties, hours, and any other relevant details.

   Then note how the company would benefit from the addition of the new position—such as making more money, improving efficiency, or providing better customer service. In order to prove these benefits, review your notes and the articles, and identify any information that indicates a need for your services.

   Incorporating this information, write a covering letter and resumé following the instructions in this chapter.

5. Do some research into the types of jobs you are interested in applying for, first by identifying commonly used job titles and then by checking the websites of companies that hire for such jobs. You can also search for information on these occupations on Industry Canada's Strategis website or through Service Canada (commonly known in bricks-and-mortar offices in your community as "the employment centre"), which should be able to provide information about job titles, related job titles and opportunities, the education needed, and other relevant details. Practise writing letters and resumés as though you were applying for a job with one of the job titles featured.

6. Interview someone who has the type of job in your industry or business sector that you would like once you graduate. If you don't know anyone with a position you would like, ask your program co-ordinator or professors to suggest past graduates you could interview. Before passing on their contact information to you, however, the co-ordinator or professor should first contact these individuals to make sure that they are willing and able to talk to you.

   Once you've made contact, set up an interview time, and ask this person how he or she got the position. You would also want to know required education and experience (qualifications), the job description, and the hours or type of employment (full- or part-time, permanent or contract). More important, ask this person what he or she has learned about what it takes to succeed in the job. Official job descriptions and postings rarely include all that is required of you once you are in the job. What additional skills or experience can the person suggest you include in your resumé or covering letter that an employer would appreciate? This information could give you an advantage over others applying for your dream job.

   Based on your interview, write a covering letter and resumé for your job application.

7. Working with another student in your class, exchange the covering letters and resumés you created for one of the previous exercises. Review your colleague's letter and resumé as though you were the potential employer, reading first for content. Does the content cover all of the information you need to know about this person, including relevant personal qualities, education, work experience, and volunteer experience? Once you've read the letter and resumé, are you convinced that he or she is a strong candidate for the position you are hiring for?

   As an employer might do, make notes of the positives and negatives of the person (your fellow student) applying for the job. On a scale of 10, how would you rate the covering letter? The resumé? Review the materials for grammar, spelling, and mechanical errors. Identify any errors with a coloured pen or highlighter.

   Return the materials to your classmate, and then debrief each other about the strengths and weaknesses of your application packages. At the end of the discussion, offer specific, constructive guidance about what each of you could do to improve your letter and resumé.

8. Using your own contacts or those of your professor or program co-ordinator, arrange to spend a day or longer with someone working in a position you would like to be hired for after graduation. This is known as *job shadowing*. While spending time on the job with this person, make notes about what he or she actually does in a typical day. What are the challenges and rewards of the work? What are his or her primary and secondary responsibilities? What does the person do that is not, strictly speaking, part of the job description but is assumed to be a responsibility or obligation of the position? What is the work environment like?

   Use this information to help you write a covering letter and resumé for a similar employment situation.

Job and Informational Interviews

LEARNING OBJECTIVES

In this chapter, you will learn:

- ◉ The differences between job and informational interviews

- ◉ How to conduct relevant research into potential employers to prepare for a job or informational interview

- ◉ How to use your contacts to land an informational or job interview

- ◉ Typical questions asked in a job interview and what to ask in an informational interview

- ◉ Step-by-step how-tos for job and informational interviews

- ◉ Etiquette and follow-up for informational and job interviews

ESSENTIAL EMPLOYABILITY SKILLS

2ooo+ *Employability Skills* The Conference Board of Canada has identified certain essential employability skills (EES) as benchmarks for performance in the workplace. You will learn the following EES skills in this chapter:

COMMUNICATE

- ◉ Can write and speak so others pay attention and understand
- ◉ Can listen and ask questions to understand and appreciate the points of view of others
- ◉ Can share information using a range of information and communications technologies (e.g., voice, email, computers)
- ◉ Can use relevant scientific, technological, and mathematical knowledge and skills to explain or clarify ideas
- ◉ Can read and understand information presented in a variety of forms (e.g., words, graphs, charts, diagrams)

MANAGE INFORMATION

- ◉ Can locate, gather, and organize information using appropriate technology and information systems
- ◉ Can access, analyze, and apply knowledge and skills from various disciplines (e.g., the arts, languages, science, technology, mathematics, and the humanities)

THINK AND SOLVE PROBLEMS

- ◉ Can assess situations and identify problems
- ◉ Can seek different points of view and evaluate them based on facts
- ◉ Can recognize the human, interpersonal, technical, scientific, and mathematical dimensions of a problem
- ◉ Can identify the root cause of a problem
- ◉ Can be creative and innovative in exploring possible solutions
- ◉ Can evaluate solutions to make recommendations or decisions

Job and Informational Interviews: A Case Study

Jason Green is about to graduate from a computer programming program and has been applying for a variety of advertised programmer positions at companies in the area. He has had six interviews to date, but thus far he has not had any second interviews or offers.

Swallowing his discouragement, he applied hopefully for a position at the Pleasant Valley Board of Education. He was offered an interview within a week of submitting his resumé and covering letter. The resumé and covering letter were very carefully prepared to reflect not only the qualifications and profile wanted in the industry but also the stated requirements in the job advertisement.

Jason feels he knows quite a lot about what the board of education—or any employer—needs from him as a programmer, so despite the urging of his girlfriend, he does not conduct any research to learn more about the school board's mission, mandate, operations, programs, and people. Besides, he's busy working on some coding for a program that will revolutionize the industry!

On the day of the interview, Jason can't find his khaki pants, so he pulls a pair out of the laundry basket, sniffs them to see if they smell okay, and puts them on. He puts on a wrinkled white shirt and leaves it untucked (he can't stand the constrained feeling of a belt). It's business casual at most workplaces—right?—so Jason pulls on a pair of white tube socks and his high-top, somewhat smelly sneakers. He also keeps in his multiple earrings, since hey, he's a creative guy, and they should appreciate that.

Having forgotten what time the interview is, he arrives 10 minutes late. He also realizes he has left his portfolio of work and copies of his resumé at home. A woman from the interview team has to make photocopies of the resumé for the other three team members.

The interviewers ask most of the standard interview questions Jason learned about in his college communications courses, but they also throw in a few queries that are hard to answer. Jason had not thought about potentially tricky questions.

"Why are you applying for this job?" asks one woman. "To pay off my student loan," Jason replies. "What would be your weaknesses?" asks another interviewer. "Well, I tend to procrastinate, because I am often distracted by my other programming hobbies . . . but did I mention I'm working on code that will revolutionize programming?" "How would you describe yourself?" a third interviewer asks. "Well, I'm a creative guy. I would say I'm a nonconformist, so I have to do things my own way." "What are your goals for yourself?" "Basically, I see this job as a stepping stone to bigger and better things."

At the end of the interview, the co-ordinator of the interview team asks Jason if he has any questions. "Yes. How much does this position pay?" Jason asks. "What are the benefits like?" Another team member responds, "The salary is commensurate with experience and education, so we can't really say at this time."

A week passes and then another. Jason calls the school board's HR department. He is told that no, he did not get the job.

1. **What went wrong with Jason's preparation for the interview? List possible factors he could have improved on.**

2. What about how Jason dressed? Was it appropriate for an interview?

3. At the interview, what mistakes do you think Jason made? What could he do to improve his performance at his next interview?

Before You Begin . . .

You have decided on the types of jobs you want to apply for and have narrowed down a list of employers you would like to work for. You've begun to search posted job ads in newspapers and online, and you're watching for opportunities through your college or university career counselling centre and professors. It's now time to consider getting in the door to get more information—and acing the interview.

RESEARCH IS CRITICAL TO SUCCESS

As mentioned in Chapter 13, it's extremely important that you do research on the organizations and businesses you want to apply to, whether for a specific job or just to conduct an **informational interview**. You need to know as much as possible about the organization to give a potential employer the strong impression that you are competent, knowledgeable, and—most important—an unbeatable potential asset to the organization.

When you have determined which companies you want to work for, you can then look at their websites or do a search online through career and job search organizations such as Monster.com or Workopolis.com to see whether they are hiring. Chances are, though, that the type of position you would like to land at a particular company is not posted. In fact, the vast majority of jobs are never advertised. People are hired through their own initiative, which involves getting in touch with the company directly to find out more about it and get to know decision-makers who do the hiring.

This often means going to the company in person—after you have done the research needed to find out as much as you can about the organization and who the decision-makers are—in a cold-call situation. You may speak with what is known as a "gatekeeper"—usually a receptionist or administrative assistant in smaller companies—but you should avoid contacting the human resources department, because their main job in recruiting is to screen out people before they get to the "big kahuna" in the corner office.

In this cold call, you would try to get in to see a decision-maker who has the authority to hire people. You may have to negotiate with the gatekeeper to find a good time to meet with the boss, or you might actually get to walk in and chat briefly if the organization is small and informal enough.

USE YOUR CONTACTS TO GET IN THE DOOR

An even better way of getting an informational interview would be to use your contacts. "But I'm a student," you protest. "I don't *have* any contacts yet!" Believe it or not, you *do* have many contacts who "know people." It may take time to dig up the appropriate connections to get you in the door, but start with your professors, who are probably well connected to the very industry or field you want to work in and know many people from their years of experience. Then speak to other professors or leaders in your college or university department about where you want to work and what you're interested in doing.

Talk to everyone and anyone about what you want to do, being specific about the type of job and places where you want to work (not "I'll take anything"). You'll be amazed; even your grandma might know someone who knows someone who works at the company you want to work for. (Read on and find out how to create your "elevator speech" about what you want. In this context, an elevator speech is a very short and quick presentation of the most important details of the type of work you want. It's brief, because you want the person you are speaking with to remember the most important information—don't overwhelm them with too many details!)

CONDUCT INTERVIEWS TO OBTAIN MORE EMPLOYER/SECTOR INFORMATION

Once you are in the door, you will conduct what is known as an informational interview. An informational interview is not unlike a job interview, except that in this case, you are asking the questions and the decision-maker is responding. Your goal is to get as much information as possible about the company, the industry or **business sector**, and future job opportunities. Even more important, you want to give the decision-maker the opportunity to see that you are very interested and could be a highly competent addition to the company. *You are not going to ask for a job!* The goal is to let the decision-maker know that you are interested in his or her company and to find out, in a relaxed, non-demanding way, about possible job openings that may be coming up. By asking intelligent questions that highlight your stellar qualities, education, and experience, you pique the interest of the person talking with you.

Once you've made an impression in an informational interview, ask the person you are interviewing whether you can stay in touch about any upcoming openings that might be appropriate for you. Be sure to stay on top of any contacts you have made this way, networking with them on a regular basis. It's your job search, so it's up to you to check in with them; don't wait for them to take the initiative, because they may simply forget to call you when a job comes up. (You may have made a great impression, but people are busy.)

THE BIG EVENT: THE JOB INTERVIEW

Let's say that you have landed a job interview, either through an informational interview process or by applying with resumé and covering letter to a **job posting** advertisement. The next step is a formal interview with decision-makers in the company—in which *they* will ask *you* the questions. However, being in the hot seat doesn't have to be a nerve-wracking experience. With the solid research you have done on the company, notes from an informational interview (if you had one), and a clear understanding of what you have to offer that will benefit the company, you can be confident and enthusiastic. It's all about what you have to offer that will help them—not whether they will take pity on you and hire you! (However, arrogance is *not* the way to go—present with confidence *and* humility.)

With research, preparation, and enthusiasm, your chances of being hired are good. Even if you don't land the job this time around, with further practice in interviewing and by addressing any mistakes you made, you will eventually end up in the right job.

TABLE 14.1   Job vs. Informational Interview

	JOB	INFORMATIONAL
To get hired	Yes	No
To get information about employer/ sector/industry	Somewhat	Definitely
Employer calls you (Solicited)	Yes	No
You call employer (Unsolicited)	Possibly	Definitely
Requires advance research	Yes	Yes
Employer asks most questions	Yes	No
You ask most questions	No	Yes
Panel or group interview	Very likely	Possible
Interview with one person	In a smaller company	Very likely
Close with pitch to be hired	Yes—sum up what you have to offer/benefits	No
Business dress required	Yes	Yes
Resumé required at interview	Good idea	Possibly send in afterwards (as part of follow-up)
Thank you note afterwards	Yes	Yes
Follow-up	Phone call a week later if you haven't heard yet	E-mail/mail, maybe phone call, depending on your conversation

Idiom Alert

narrow down – Choose a few best choices from among many. For example, of the 10 men Janie was considering in the online dating service, she narrowed down her choice to two with whom she wanted to have an actual first date.

getting in the door – Being allowed to come into a business or organization or to speak to someone in authority in your quest for more information.

acing – Doing something extremely well or making a great impression. An ace can be an expert, an unbeatable tennis serve, a very effective military pilot, the highest playing card in the deck, or a hole-in-one in golf—in other words, all high achievers.

chances are – Something is very likely to happen (short for "the chances are good").

big kahuna – The boss, owner, or major decision-maker in a business or organization.

dig up – Do research and find the correct information needed—like digging up buried treasure.

in the hot seat – At the centre of attention.

FYI – Short form of *for your information*.

cold call – An *unsolicited* call that is made in order to sell something, obtain information, or persuade someone to do something. This is opposite to a *warm call*, when some sort of relationship already exists between the parties; they are either known to each other or have been referred by a third person. Cold calling is common in sales—calling a potential client or customer (in person or by phone) to generate a sale or at least create some interest in buying the product or service.

Going in with the attitude that you want the job that is meant for you—not whatever you can get—will put you in the right frame of mind to interview for—and select—the job that is right for you, right now.

Your Starting Point

ENVISIONING YOUR JOB OR CAREER

As mentioned in Chapter 13 on resumés and covering letters, it's very important that you take the time to really get to the bottom of what you envision for your work and personal life. You need to know—*really* know—what it is you want before you begin looking at potential employers or job postings. That way, you can better ensure that the job you get is as good a fit as possible. (Of course, if you need a job right away because you can't buy food or pay bills, you may not be able to be so picky. However, you should still do the work of figuring out what you do want—and keep applying for that kind of work while doing your very best in the job you have.)

Envisioning your ideal job or career also involves getting to know which businesses or organizations will most likely offer you the best opportunities.

RESEARCH INTO ORGANIZATIONS AND BUSINESSES

If no jobs that reflect your ideal career path are currently being advertised online, in newspapers, or in other job posting media, then you will need to look into the "hidden job market." Most jobs are never advertised—the people who land these jobs have made themselves known to the decision-makers in the organizations they want to work for. Before successful hidden job market applicants land their jobs, they do a lot of research into the companies or organizations they want to work for, and they even research, as much as possible, the **key decision-makers** in the company.

Armed with this information, these smart people approach their company or organization of choice and ask to talk with a key decision-maker about the organization or company. This is an informational interview—one in which *you* ask the questions to find out more about the company, the types of jobs they have, and what people need in order to be employed in these jobs. (This is not a time to pitch your skills and abilities, although you should demonstrate how brilliant you are by asking good questions, which the decision-maker will remember when filling positions later on.)

To come up with the smart questions—which will highlight your brilliance—you must do research into the companies or organizations that you want to work for.

As mentioned in Chapter 13, there are several ways to get the information you need without having to go to the place of business:

- Use Internet search engines to search the company name, keywords about the company's products or services, names of decision-makers (if you have them), and anything else related to the company and type of job you are looking for. Use this information to help you prepare for the informational interview (or for questions you might be asked in a job interview). Look for information on the key decision-maker you want to meet with, the business activities of the company, any recent

Get your motor running—put search engines and job boards to work for you!

Back in 1855 ... err ... 1985, the only way you could find a number of job postings related to the career you wanted was to (a) read countless newspapers' want ads and careers sections; (b) visit an employment centre that might have a really horrible, DOS-based computer database of jobs that will burn your eyes out to look at; (c) repeatedly visit an employment centre to see whether any new postings were added to the jobs available board; or (d) pay big bucks to a **career search agency** that claimed it could help you to find the kind of job you wanted. (The latter was often a huge cash grab, because the agency would actually do very little except look up the postings offered by employment centres and similar government agencies!)

Fortunately, while the newspaper is still a source of job ads and, of course, word of mouth and **networking** are still primary ways to find out about jobs (particularly unadvertised ones), you can now use your own Internet access to connect with a "virtual" career search agency—a vertical job search engine (VJSE).

A vertical job search engine is like Google in that it uses search terms, but it only looks for job listings. A few of the best ones in North America these days are Indeed.com, SimplyHired.com, and Jobster.com.

A VJSE "crawls" through the Web to find job listings that meet your criteria based on keywords you supply. These search engines generally don't engage in job transactions themselves (i.e., they don't set you up with a potential employer), but they do provide you with the source of information, and they can even connect you with specific job opportunities or postings within

your industry—jobs you might never otherwise learn about.

As mentioned elsewhere in this chapter, another way to find job postings is through a job board website. These are websites that employers use, paying to post employment opportunities, while you (the job seeker) usually see these postings for free.

Two of the biggest online job boards accessed by job seekers in Canada are Monster.com and Workopolis.com. Monster is a fabulous resource in that it connects you with job search engines in a number of countries around the world—handy if you are looking for work overseas—and Workopolis shines in that it helps you to find work in Canada, even notifying you of potential jobs that might meet your criteria through an email notification system. Job search engines like these have questionnaires you can fill in to generate a profile of who you are, your qualifications, and the types of jobs you are seeking and where, for example. You can post your resumé so that any employers seeking someone like you can look at your resumé online, which means that the site can not only help you to find job postings but enable potential employers you might not have even thought of or considered to find you and possibly offer you an interview.

If you are looking for a more specialized, industry-specific job board, you can Google "job boards" in association with key search terms describing your business, such as "job boards electricians." If you typed that in, you'd get a first page of results listing many job boards featuring opportunities for electricians. Such job boards could be a great source of current job postings in your field of expertise.

---

changes in operations or production, the size of the workforce, any job postings ... really, everything and anything about the company.

- Google the key decision-maker(s) you will meet with for your informational or job interview. Knowing about their interests, hobbies, and activities outside of work may help you to find common ground for a friendly icebreaker. For example, you might find out that the person you are meeting with is an avid gardener, and because you are also passionate about gardening, you could start your conversation by talking about gardening. This builds rapport. You could also find out what this person doesn't like—an equally important bit of information that will help you to avoid touchy or inflammatory subjects!

- *Canada's Top 100 Employers*, published by Mediacorp Canada (for more information, see http://www.canadastop100.com), is a good place to start looking for the employers who are considered the best to work for in your field or discipline.

- Search newspapers and magazines online or at the library. Many newspapers, from national dailies (e.g., *The Globe and Mail*) to community newspapers, carry articles of interest about the companies or organizations you want to work for. If you are a business student, focus on the business section—and read it regularly. If you are in another sector or field, look at sections that pertain to your area of expertise, such as health and wellness or lifestyle sections if you are in health services. Knowing what's in the news about the company or organization gives you an edge when you are talking to a decision-maker, because you will appear well informed on issues and the concerns of that decision-maker and his or her company. This information can make the difference between being considered for jobs that open up and being passed over in favour of someone else who is better informed on current issues and the concerns of the company. (FYI—this is the kind of information you can also use as a lead-in for a covering letter when you are applying for a job.)

- Career counsellors and professors can recommend employers who might offer career opportunities that would fit what you are seeking. In particular, professors who have worked in the industry or sector often know who is a good employer or a less-than-great one by reputation. They can also give you inside information on the companies and decision-makers you may approach for an informational interview. Buy a teacher a coffee, and ask for a few minutes of his or her time to share some industry or sector insights with you.

- How often does a textbook suggest that you watch television? Watching television—with the purpose of finding out more about companies, organizations, and issues that affect the sector or industry you plan to work in—can give you a lot of good information that you can use as the basis for the questions you ask in an informational interview. Watch educational, business, news, or investigative journalism shows (such as *W-Five* and *Marketplace*) to learn more about current issues and events affecting the people with whom you will do an informational interview.

- Check out chambers of commerce directories (either local or those of the city you want to work in) for basic information. Join a chamber of commerce as a student or associate member to network—and to learn about jobs before they are advertised. Look up business and organization directories at the public library, or ask the reference librarian to help you look up information on the companies or organizations you want to work for.

- Don't forget to tell family and friends about your job search; see whether they know anything about companies or organizations you would like more information on. Chances are, if they don't know anyone at the company or much about it, they know someone else who might know. Eventually, even these leads can turn into solid information about companies or organizations.

Finally, when possible, go to the company or organization, and gather as much information as you can from "gatekeepers" such as receptionists or administrative assistants or from any employees you know. Look up the company website, and gather information there. If the company has a physical, publicly accessible location, go there and ask for brochures, pamphlets, flyers, information packages, and even—if you can get them—annual reports produced for shareholders (this is usually public information). Thank the person who helps you obtain this information profusely, and send him or her a thank-you note—or at least an email—as soon as possible.

QUESTIONS TO ASK ABOUT COMPANIES OR ORGANIZATIONS

Here are some questions you can ask your information sources or as you look through your gathered information. You would also come up with your own questions that are specific to what you want to know about the company, the careers available there, and other details.

Remember to search the Web when you start job hunting. You can search online job boards, research prospective employers, and even "follow" companies that may post job opportunities on LinkedIn and Twitter.

- What is the full name of the company or organization?

- What does the company or organization do, provide, or sell?

- How long has the company or organization been in business?

- What is the reputation of the company or organization?

- Who are the key decision-makers (e.g., CEO, chief administrative officer, managers, etc.)?

- What are these decision-makers' interests, concerns, pet peeves, volunteer work outside of the company, and so on?

- How many people does the organization employ?

- Do people work there full-time, part-time, on contract, seasonally?

- What kinds of positions are available at the company?

- What qualifications (education, experience, skills) does the company look for in any employees? In people applying for specific jobs?

- Has the company recently hired more people? Has it recently laid off employees or eliminated positions?

- How well is the company doing in terms of profits and profile in the industry or sector it is in?

- How has the company been affected by the macro-economic situation (positively or negatively)?

Let your fingers do the walking: Social media networking for jobs

There are many online tools, both stand-alone and integrated with Facebook, Twitter, or LinkedIn, that offer opportunities for networking both within your local community and internationally. The best way to start is to go back to your list of businesses or people you are currently following on your social networks and see what organizations or groups they are a part of. Traditional business groups such as your local chamber of commerce (a great place to meet many business owners in one place, if you can go there with someone who belongs), union halls, or other industry or sector-specific organizations may use social marketing, which may be a good way to start networking with other members outside of regular meetings.

The best way to network on your own is by adding/following people you want to network with. By doing this, you are not only showing your interest in their business, but you will receive their updates in your news feed/Twitter feed, which will provide information you can use to properly pitch yourself when the time is right. Once you have added them to your network, be sure to say hello and strike up a conversation on some kind of common ground. This conversation could be industry-related or perhaps just based on the fact that you live in the same community. Even a quick message to say that you are a fan of their business will go a long way toward turning a new online acquaintance into a networking opportunity.

Once you have built up your network on Facebook, take the initiative and host an event for networking. There are options within Facebook for setting this up and sending invitations as well as updating information for attendees. Outside of the Facebook/Twitter/LinkedIn platforms, there are many other Internet applications for networking. One popular platform is www.meetup.com, where you can find meetings hosted by like-minded individuals to attend or host your own.

The best way to network through Twitter is to join conversations with people you are following and comment on topics of interest to you. This can be an invaluable resource when it comes to people within the industry or business sector you want to work in. Sharing tips and ideas could impress those in a position to hire you. In your profile, be sure to note any special training or abilities you have within your field in case a current employee doesn't have what you can offer.

- Has the company recently added any new products or services?

- Has the company recently revised its production, operations, or management?

- What is it like working for the company? (Ask this question of someone who works there, or consult *Canada's Top 100 Employers* or a similar source.)

- How are people paid? Salary or hourly wage? By the contract?

- In terms of salary or hourly pay, how does it compare to that of other companies in the field?

- Is the company a subsidiary or branch or in some other way connected to another company or organization? What about that company or organization (apply the same questions as above)? If there is a relationship with another company, how does it affect the company you want to work for?

- What are the long-term prospects for the company? Short-term? (You can usually get an idea from an annual report that is issued to shareholders, but you might also find this information in a news article or on the company website.)

These are just a few of the questions you should ask to obtain general and more specific information as background to your informational or job interview, and it's clear that there are many more questions you could pose. Generate your own questions by reviewing these ones, and apply the entire list as you conduct your research.

SUMMARY OF INFORMATION

So what do you do now with all this information? It's a good idea to make a summary of what you have found out—kind of a "cheat sheet"—that you can review and re-review before you meet with a decision-maker for an informational interview *or* a job interview. Making a list of the key points about the company will also help you to create more targeted and intelligent questions to ask the decision-maker and will give you an excellent knowledge base when you are answering questions in a job interview. If you can drop into your answers information that shows you have "done your homework" and learned as much as possible about the place where you want to work, you will make a strong and positive impression on your interviewer(s).

Using whatever format works best for you, formulate a list of the necessary information and study it—*integrate* it—so that by the time you go to the interview, the information is second nature to you.

REVIEWING THE JOB POSTING BEFORE A JOB INTERVIEW

If you are preparing for a job interview where people will be asking you the questions, in addition to the information you have gathered about the company you must be very clear on what the employer is looking for from you—and how you can deliver it.

In other words, you need to memorize the qualifications the employer is seeking and be able to quickly and without hesitation relate your skill set to those qualifications.

For example, if the employer is looking for "proven customer service skills," use the research you have done to figure out what this qualification might mean to the employer. For a retailer, it means direct service to customers in a store. For a service provider like a graphic design business, it could mean a lot of behind-the-scenes work that the customer never sees until the job is done.

Generally speaking, though, if an employer lists this skill as a required qualification, it means they are looking for proof that you have had customer service experience—*and* that you have done a good job serving customers in jobs (or volunteer work) you have had to date. You know they are going to ask some questions about this, so think about what you have done, specifically, that would answer such questions. If you have a specific episode in mind when you went "above and beyond" for a customer, make sure that you will be able to relate it in an interview, very clearly and in detail, highlighting how your approach to the customer helped the company *and* made the customer happy and satisfied.

The goal in this preparation is to ensure that you don't blank out in the interview and that you can quickly and accurately answer interview questions *according to how that company views the skill or qualification!*

RESUMÉ (AND COVERING LETTER)

To complete your preparation for either an informational or a job interview, you must completely familiarize yourself with your resumé (and covering letter, if applicable).

Read and reread your resumé and covering letter, particularly if someone else helped you to create it, so that you remember what you wrote—what you said you had to offer. Believe it or not, sometimes people get an interview as a result of a well-crafted resumé and/or covering letter they haven't reviewed at all, and when the interviewer asks questions related to the resumé or letter, the applicant freezes up. Don't be like a deer caught in the headlights—stunned. Make sure that you—and your resumé and covering letter—are "singing from the same song book"!

Why bother with this review if you are conducting an informational interview? Knowing what's in your resumé will allow you, if asked by the decision-maker, to elaborate on your skills and qualifications. While you wouldn't mention that you are looking for work (at least not at the beginning of the interview), the person you are interviewing might ask you the obvious question: why are you there? If you can respond that you are doing research on potential employers and places where you would like to work, and if you can drop in some information about your qualifications and career ambitions, so much the better. That way, the decision-maker has some idea of who you are and what you could potentially offer the company if the right position were to come up.

ARE YOU READY TO GO FOR IT?

You are ready for a job interview or informational interview if you have

- envisioned your ideal job or career and can clearly articulate what you want;
- done research on target companies or organizations that you want to work for—or that you are about to have an interview with;
- summarized your research into a list of main points that you have studied and can easily refer to in an interview;
- reviewed the qualifications required by the employer, know how your skills relate to them, and can give concrete examples if required.

Job and Informational Interviews: How to Do Them

SETTING UP AN INFORMATIONAL INTERVIEW

To set up an informational interview, contact the decision-maker's administrative assistant or receptionist—or contact the person directly if he or she does not have an assistant.

Tell the person you are booking the interview time with that you want to speak with the decision-maker to gather information about the company and what it's like to work there. It's very important that you tell the person why you are interested:

- You are a recent graduate or about-to-be-graduate of X college or university and are starting to research companies and organizations in your field as part of your career search. State that you are not going to ask for a job and that you merely wish to collect information to help you with your career search process. This way, the person will not see you as a potential annoyance to his or her boss.

- You are making a career change and are researching companies and jobs in your field of interest. State that you are conducting an informational interview, not seeking a job.

To add more sweetness to your bid to get some interview time, tell the person you are talking to a little about what you have found out about the company and why you are so interested in finding out more about it—these are flattering points, which also show your enthusiasm for the company. If you can share in the company's enthusiasm for what it does, you will be genuinely flattering the person you are speaking with. For example, "I was doing some research on marketing companies recently as part of my career search, and I was really impressed by your company's commitment to ethical advertising. I understand that when your company was approached by a beer company for a major ad campaign targeting college students, it turned the work down—and instead decided to support a campaign of the Canadian Students Federation aimed at reducing binge drinking on campuses."

Make it clear that you only want a few minutes of the person's time. A general rule of thumb is 10 to 20 minutes (and make sure you stick to this—keep track of the time with a watch!). Ask whether the person can spare this amount of time in his or her schedule. Find out whether the decision-maker likes coffee or tea (or a snack, or other beverage) at that time of day and how he or she likes it prepared. Bring that beverage or snack with you as a goodwill gesture so that he or she can relax a bit.

Finally, before you leave or hang up the phone, get the full name of the person you are speaking with for the interview booking if this person is a receptionist, assistant, or other gatekeeper. Make sure you have the full mailing address of the company. As soon as you get home, write a thank-you note, and send it to that person. Better still, tuck in a small gift certificate (such as from Tim Hortons or another coffee or food vendor). If you will be seeing the person on your way into the interview, bring him or her a treat (find out ahead of time what he or she likes).

PREPARING FOR THE JOB INTERVIEW

The circumstances of the job interview are set for you—the time, the date, and any preparations the potential employer wants you to make beforehand.

In order to prepare, make sure you have done the following:

- confirmed the date, time, and location of the interview;

- found out how to get to the interview (directions) *and* gone there at least once so that you are familiar with how long it takes to get there, park, and so on;

- planned extra time in your schedule so that you get to the interview at least half an hour early;

- found out how many people will be interviewing you and who they are;

- printed good copies of your resumé, covering letter, and any supporting documentation for yourself and all interviewers;

It's critical that you dress sharply for an interview. You'll want to choose an outfit that looks professional and makes you feel professional too. See the "Dress for success!" box below for more details.

Dress for success!

First impressions count when you are interviewing for a job or for information.

- Find out how people dress where you are going for the interview. Do they have a casual **business dress code**, or are they more formal? You can find this out by going there personally or by asking your contacts who know the organization. Dress the way the bosses or managers do.
- Choose understated colours. If you plan to wear a suit, choose grey, black, brown, or navy blue—but of these colours, pick one that suits you best so that you don't look tired or ill!
- Wear a bright colour near your face (e.g., in a shirt, tie, blouse, scarf) so that the person you're with focuses on you and what you are saying. Pick a colour that makes you feel powerful, one that makes you look energetic and healthy.
- Pare down your accessories and jewellery. Wear one statement piece, be it a watch, a pair of classic earrings, a striking pendant, or cufflinks. Don't wear a great deal of jewellery—one ring will suffice, for example.
- Wear shoes and stockings that co-ordinate with your clothing. For example, don't wear white tube socks, sneakers, or platform shoes with a suit! In fact, don't wear anything too trendy unless you are interviewing for a creative job in the arts or design. Make sure that any bags or shoes you are carrying or wearing are in good repair.

- If you are a woman, don't pile on makeup; too much may make it appear that you are insecure or are dressing for a night on the town rather than for a professional office environment. Go with natural-looking colours; you want to look good but understated, as though you were not wearing makeup at all.
- Smell good, but not *too* good! Bathe or shower and use an appropriate deodorant. If you tend to sweat heavily, think about layering a t-shirt or undershirt under your shirt or blouse or consider a prescription-strength antiperspirant. When you are already nervous, you don't want to have to worry about soaking through your carefully selected interview garb. Don't wear heavy perfume, cologne, or aftershave—think of other people's sensitivities, even allergies.
- Wash and style your hair so that it is neat, tidy, and looking good.
- This is not the time to look "individual," which means no multiple or unusual piercings, no visible tattoos, and no unnatural hair colour or style. Save the individual expression for holidays or for after you have been hired (unless there's a dress code).

- prepared any work samples or portfolios for the interviewer or interview team to review;
- determined some of the potential questions the interviewer(s) may ask from the job description or job posting/ad, as well as some of the more generic questions;
- practised answering these questions with family and friends;
- planned—and prepared—your interview outfit and accessories the night before (see the "Dress for success!" box for tips and tricks on what to wear for interview success).

POTENTIAL QUESTIONS: INFORMATIONAL INTERVIEW

In the informational interview, *you* will be asking the questions of a potential employer, a decision-maker in the company you want to work for. At the end of the interview, or even during, the person you are interviewing may ask you some questions about yourself and why you are there.

Here are some basic questions you might ask the potential employer:

- Can you tell me what the company does? What it sells, provides, or does for its customers and clients?

- How long has the organization been in business?

- Who is the competition? How do you deal with them?

- What are the company's goals and objectives?

- What is the mission statement?

- Tell me about the employees who work here. How many are there? What do they bring to or offer the company? How are their contracts structured—are they on salary, on commission, or paid an hourly wage?

- What types of jobs does your company offer?

- What are the qualifications (education, experience, skills) that the company expects in its employees? In people applying for specific jobs?

- Are you planning to expand your workforce?

- Can you describe your company's customer service policy?

- What are some of the key economic factors that affect the company?

- Has the company recently added any new products or services? Can you tell me about them? Have there been other positive changes here?

- What's it like working for the company?

- Does the company work closely with other companies?

- What do you, in your position, see in the future for the company? If you had a crystal ball, what would things look like around here in 10 years?

It's also really important that you do your homework to learn more about the organization and person you are going to speak with to come up with additional questions pertaining directly to the company. Going beyond the generic questions listed above shows that you are truly interested in the company or organization. Asking generic questions only is like giving the employer a generic resumé for every type of job. It won't impress the potential employer!

Your interviewee may ask you a few questions, particularly if you have shown interest by asking intelligent and specific-to-the-company questions. The first one that may come up is "Why are you here?" Answer this question honestly, but be sure to get across that the decision-maker's company has interested you so much that you had to find out more. *Don't* say, "I need a job"! Do say that you are doing some career planning and that in your research you came across this company or organization and were impressed by what they do, sell, or provide. Do say that you are researching all of your career options and that you think this company would be a great place to work in and a great fit for your plans, but leave it at that. Don't press for a job or for consideration for a job.

If the person asks you whether you would like to work there, answer honestly, "Yes." Then the ball is back in his or her court, either to ask you for a resumé or other materials or to ask another question related to the first. Again, be cool, and don't show any desperation to get a job with the company or organization. Showing desperation is a major turnoff—and you weren't there in the first place for a job interview, so stick to your original mission. If you start to talk about getting a job there, the person you are interviewing may be annoyed and think that you asked for the meeting under false pretences.

If the opportunity comes up and the person asks whether you have a resumé with you, be cool and say something like, "Yes, I think I have one in my briefcase. Let me take a look." Then give it to the decision-maker. If you want to be even cooler about it, you can ask whether you can drop one off later or email it.

POTENTIAL QUESTIONS: JOB INTERVIEW

As mentioned previously, if you have done your homework and learned all you can about the employer, you will be well positioned to answer questions in a way that will appeal to the interviewers. Knowing what the company does and how it operates, the decision-makers' biases and concerns, and so on will help you to understand the kinds of answers the employer is looking for when asking certain questions.

You can count on many interview questions pertaining directly to the skills, qualifications, and other information in the job posting or ad. Obviously, certain skill sets will be very important to the employer, so you will be asked about them. Make sure that you can answer any question about how your experience and education relates to the desired skill set—and can give specific examples.

Here are some of the generic questions asked in most interviews. Be aware, however, that there are many variations on how these questions are asked:

- Tell me about yourself.

- Why are you applying for this job?

- What do you know about this job or the company?

- How would you describe yourself?

- Can you tell me what your strengths are?

- What would be a weakness you have?

- What types of work do you like best?

- What are your hobbies and interests?

- Can you tell me about an accomplishment or achievement that made you feel great?

- What was your worst mistake on the job?

- Why did you leave your last job?

- Please tell me how your education and experience relate to this job and to this company.

- Where do you see yourself in the future, say five to 10 years from now?

- What are your goals?

- What do you feel you can contribute to this organization?

Some of these questions are tricky and can be a bit of a trap. Here's how to handle them:

- *Why are you applying for this job?* Be honest, but never say "because I need money." That implies desperation; if you are willing to do almost any job, you're probably not the best fit for the job.

- *How would you describe yourself?* Don't lie, of course, but focus on what you are and do that is very positive. Even if you think of something that can be considered negative (such as "I'm nit-picky"), try to turn this quality around into something positive ("I have strong attention to detail").

- *What would be a weakness you have?* Ah, there's honesty and then there's honesty. Share only a weakness that can also be seen as a positive. For example, you might say that you are a workaholic—which may mean to the employer that you work hard and are willing to put in the time it takes to do something well—but you could also say that you are working on finding balance between your quality work output and your home life so that you can do it *all* well. In other words, give them an answer, but choose the answer that will be best perceived as a positive. Telling them that you are a procrastinator is not good. You could, however, say that you are good at getting work done at the last minute.

- *What types of work do you do best?* Well, be honest, but at the same time, be aware of the demands of the job you are applying for and the company itself. If you say, "I hate working outdoors" and the job involves mainly outdoor work, then you are pretty much closing the door to getting the job.

- *Where do you see yourself in the future?* The employer may be asking this because he or she wants to know whether you might stay in the job for only a little while. Answer honestly, but consider what the employer is looking for: "In five years, I hope to have demonstrated that I am an asset to your company and to have been promoted to general manager. On the personal side, I hope to have completed additional management training and bought a house." This kind of answer shows determination, commitment, and that you are willing to make big, long-term investments, such as buying a house, based on your commitment to the company.

- *Why did you leave your last job?* Ouch. This one can be a hard one to answer if you were fired. If this is the case, state quite simply that you made a mistake (if it was your fault), and briefly describe what the mistake was. Then spend *way* more time talking about how you learned from that mistake (using examples) and have moved on to doing things differently. What the employer wants to hear is that you took steps to accept blame, did some soul-searching, and have learned from the mistake so that you can now work better for a new employer.

- *What are your goals?* While it's good to mention some personal goals, what the employer really wants to hear is what your *career* goals are. Again, you should not imply or state that the job you are applying for is a mere steppingstone to something else.

WHAT TO EXPECT: INFORMATIONAL INTERVIEW

As mentioned previously, do *not* let the interview last longer than you said it would. Keep a watch handy, and stick to the time you promised. If the person seems very enthusiastic and has started to ask you questions, ask whether it's okay for the interview to last longer than the number of minutes you promised originally. Don't assume that it's okay—ask. If he or she doesn't have any more time but would like to talk to you more later on, try to arrange a time that would be convenient when you can continue the conversation.

As in a job interview, be sure to dress the part, as though you *were* on a job interview. Wear the kind of attire that you know people in the position you would like to have do. Dress the part and be the part—and win the part! See the "Dress for success!" box in this chapter for guidance.

Always, *always* thank the person for his or her time, and ask whether you can get in touch at a later date if you have more questions. Usually, the person will say yes, so it's an opening to check about jobs or information in the future.

As soon as you get home, write a thank-you note to the person you interviewed. While you can send an email, and particularly if you decide to email your resumé, a hand-written note is a very classy touch. Hand-written notes stand out for people because so few people actually take the time to write them anymore. It's another way to be memorable—the person you talked to will be more likely to remember you when he or she finds that a job is coming up in the very field you showed interest in.

WHAT TO EXPECT: JOB INTERVIEW

In order to ace a job interview, make sure that you

- Eat! Don't go with a growling stomach. If you can't eat a lot, at least have a piece of fruit or something light.

- Arrive with at least 15 minutes to spare so that you won't be stressed out about arriving just in the nick of time.

- Dress appropriately (see the "Dress for success!" box).

- Know—down cold—your own information and the information you've gained about the company.

- Turn off your cellphone before the interview.

- Keep your answers focused; be descriptive but brief.

- Take a notepad in case you want to write down information or questions that come up.

- Prepare questions that you would like to ask (at the end of the interview and only if asked).

- Get everyone's full name and title before you leave (a good way to do this is to ask for business cards)—and then send *everyone* a thank-you note, hand-written.

Most job interviews range in time from half an hour to one hour. If there are any tests or written work to do as part of the selection process, you may be there for another half to full hour. Usually, the employer will let you know about this ahead of time.

Cultural considerations: Making the right impression

IF YOU ARE A NEW CANADIAN . . .

Job interviews with a Canadian employer may be quite different from any you have had previously in your homeland. For example, you might have provided just the basic details in answering an interview question, since the potential employer did not want to hear a story in response to the query. You might not have made much eye contact with the interviewer(s), because direct eye contact would have been seen as confrontational or rude (as is the case in some Asian countries). Certain hand movements and gestures might not have been acceptable—might even have been considered offensive—in the interview environment in your previous community. You might have been encouraged to be deferential and to talk about how you could do something to fit into the existing hierarchy.

In the Canadian context, interviewers want you to make direct eye contact (but not constantly!), to assume an enthusiastic and optimistic tone of voice (to convey confidence and competency), to speak clearly and at a moderate pace (not to be soft-spoken), to be as natural as possible with facial expressions (but not overly expressive!), to greet the interviewer(s) with a firm (not sweaty or limp) handshake, and to allow for brief pauses and silence (not to talk constantly). Most of all, the impression you need to leave with a Canadian employer is that you are competent, assertive, and professional and that you, more than anyone else they interview—are the candidate that will contribute the most to the success of the business.

If you are in this position and are nervous about your presentation in a job interview, it's strongly recommended that you practise interviews with other students. Doing informational interviews before any job interviews is also great practice—in fact, you could even ask the person you are doing the informational interview with how you performed during the interview and whether he or she has any tips for you when you are involved in a job interview. Most of the time, these people are more than happy to give you feedback and offer advice for future job interviews.

Another consideration in your presentation to a Canadian employer is your command of English (and/or French, if you are seeking work in Quebec). If your spoken English is still quite accented and native English speakers have a hard time understanding you (such as other students in your classes), then you should probably see whether there is an ESL (English as a Spoken Language) program at your college or university that can help you improve your oral English skills or find ESL programs in your community designed for newcomers to Canada. (Most of the community programs are free, funded by various levels of government.)

. . . OR IF YOU ARE A CANADIAN SEEKING WORK OVERSEAS . . .

You need to do research on the culture of the country you plan to work in and, additionally, consult books and online resources with guidance on business protocol and customs—before you do an interview or even prepare your resumé, covering letter, and supporting documents. The variations on what is expected of you in interviews and applications among countries or regions of the world are far too many to note here. As in the above advice for new Canadians, you too need to find out what is expected of you in terms of tone/volume of voice, eye contact, gestures, greeting, and the directness or details of answers you would give in response to interview questions.

You will find some ideas about what to include in a European or UK CV in the chapter on resumés, but these are guidelines only. To succeed in your job search, be sure to customize your application documents to the demands of the culture or business environment you want to work in—and this means being extra diligent in your research not only on the company where you will be interviewed but also on the business environment in which it operates. Never assume that what works in Canada or North America will work elsewhere!

You can ask when the employer will get back to you with a decision. If the employer does not get back to you within the specified time period, give it another week, and then call to find out, politely, if a decision has been made. If so, usually someone will tell you the details—that an announcement will be made soon and you will be notified or that another person was hired.

If you are not hired, you can ask whether there were any specific reasons for your rejection so that you will be better prepared for your next interview. If you ask nicely, the interviewers will usually comment on what they felt you had to offer and what they feel you need to work on to apply again in future or for other jobs elsewhere. Generally, they feel badly that they were not able to hire you—because saying no to people is a difficult thing—so if they can help you this way, it makes them feel better about the process.

So . . . when do you ask about money?

You may not know how much your potential employer is willing to pay, or perhaps he or she has suggested a range of pay based on experience. How do you find out what that actually means, and when should you ask? Here are some points to consider:

- If you ask too soon about what you would be paid, the employer may think you are either desperate or so focused on the money that you would not do a good job for him or her. If you ask *after* you have accepted the job, then it may be too late to negotiate.

- Never ask during an interview or even at the end of it. Wait until the potential employer offers you a job. Before the offer is made, think about what you want or need for income. Ask politely what is being offered, including any benefits in addition to the pay. Do *not* let the employer know what you want yet!

- Then ask how you would be promoted or advanced in terms of pay and responsibilities. When the employer responds with a salary figure, refer back to your worst-case scenario budget (see Chapter 13) for your minimum income. Would the proposed pay suffice? Would benefits cover some expenses to make up for lower pay? Would you receive a guaranteed pay raise at regular intervals? How hard would it be to advance into other positions that would pay more? If you are guaranteed annual pay increases or promotion for work or activities, you may be able to make up any shortfall by budgeting carefully in the meantime.

- Get as much information as you can before you make a decision, but do ask all of your questions in one phone call or email. If you keep going back to the employer with yet another question, he or she may think you are stalling, are not really interested, or would be a problematic employee. Peppering him or her with questions over a few days might even make the employer retract the offer!

- Ask for a reasonable amount of time to consider all of the information, and stick to the deadline you agree to for a decision. Any employer concerned with hiring the right employee for his or her organization will give you some time to think about it. Be wary of anyone who demands a decision right away—this could mean that the workplace is dysfunctional or experiencing major challenges.

CHECKLIST TO prepare for informational and job interviews

☐　Have you confirmed the date and time of the interview?

☐　Do you know how to get to the interview (directions)?

☐　Have you planned extra time to get to the interview in case you run into difficulties?

☐　Have you planned what you will wear? Have you made sure that your clothes and shoes are clean and neat?

☐　Have you found out how many people will interview you and made copies of your resumé and other hand-outs for everyone?

☐　If applicable, have you prepared your portfolio for your interview?

☐　Have you carefully reviewed the job ad (if applicable) to anticipate possible interview questions?

☐　For an informational interview, have you created a list of questions according to this chapter's suggestions and your own research into the organization?

☐　Have you considered any difficult questions that might be asked and practised how you would respond?

Chapter Summary

In this chapter, you discovered the differences between job and informational interviews. You learned how to conduct relevant research into potential employers to prepare for a job or informational interview and how to use your contacts to land an informational or job interview. You also found out how to network with family and friends to help you seek out opportunities and how to use social media to assist with that networking. To help you prepare for interviews, this chapter showed you typical questions you will be asked in a job interview and information-gathering questions for you to ask in an informational interview. Then you learned the practical steps for taking job and informational interviews, including how to handle difficult questions in a job interview. Finally, you learned how to dress and conduct yourself for best results, tips for interview etiquette, and how to follow up a job or informational interview.

■■▌ SUGGESTIONS *for Further Reading*

Bolles, M.E., and Bolles, R.N. (2011). *What color is your parachute? Guide to job-hunting online.* (6th ed.). New York, NY: Random House/Crown Publishing/Ten Speed Press.

Burns, D. (2009). *First 60 seconds: Win the job interview before it begins.* Naperville, IL: Sourcebooks.

Darlington, J., and Schuman, N. (2008). *Everything job interview book: All you need to make a great first impression and land the perfect job.* Avon, MA: Adams Media Publishing.

Krannich, C., and Krannich, R. (2007). *I can't believe they asked me that! Tips and techniques to quickly prepare for a tough job interview.* Cottesloe, WA: Impact Publishing.

McDermott, J., and Reed, A. (2006). *Top answers to 121 job interview questions.* La Vergne, TN: Ingram Book Company.

Schuman, N., and Nadler, B.J. (2012). *1,001 phrases you need to get a job: The hire me words that set your cover letter, resume, and job interview apart.* Avon, MA: Adams Media Publishing.

■■▌ PRACTISING *What You Have Learned*

1. a. Working with a partner, find a company you would *both* like to work for, and do as much research as possible on that organization to learn all you can.

    b. On your own, formulate a list of the main points. Create a list of questions you would like to ask a decision-maker in that company.

    c. Get together with your partner. Take turns asking each other your informational interview questions. Since each of you has researched the company, it should be easy to be both the interviewer and the decision-maker. Try to make the experience as true to life as possible. Critique each other's approach as interviewer after you have completed this process.

    d. Role-play the scenario in front of your entire class or seminar group—you should get plenty of constructive criticism!

2. a. Working with a partner, find a job posting online or in a newspaper that you would both like to apply for. Do as much research as you can on the potential employer to prepare for a job interview.

    b. On your own, formulate a list of the main points you have discovered about the employer. Create a list of questions you think the employer would ask based on this information and the job posting or description.

    c. Take turns being the interviewer and the job applicant, and interview each other. Since you have both researched the same job and company, you should be able to play both roles well. Critique each other's answers and presentation as the applicant.

    d. Role-play the scenario in front of your entire class or seminar group, and ask for constructive feedback.

3. In pairs, and using the "do's and don'ts" information in this chapter, make a list of points to remember in order to do well in any interview. Based on this list of points for success,

make a list of points that would be almost guaranteed to *not* get you the job or the information you are seeking.

Role-play the interview with all the *wrong* choices for success. Be prepared for a lot of laughter! Once each pair is finished role-playing, have the class or seminar group list all of the factors they witnessed that would contribute to the failure to get the job or the information.

4. a. Write a job description and advertising text for a job you would like to have at an employer of your choice. Consider the educational qualifications, work experience, volunteer experience, and personal qualities that would be sought for this position. (Review a job posting online or in a newspaper if you need a template or outline for how to set this text up.)

   b. Trade job descriptions and ads with another person in your class or seminar group. Write a covering letter and resumé in response to the ad the other person has written. Critique each other's letters and resumés based on what you were "seeking" in your job description and posting. Taking turns as employer and applicant, conduct job interviews for your respective job openings. Critique each other's interview process.

   c. Circulate copies of the job descriptions, ads, covering letters, and resumés to other class members, and give them a few minutes to quickly read the materials. Then conduct the interview in front of the class. Have the class critique the interview based on the materials and the interview itself.

5. If you know someone who is working in the career or job of your choice, ask whether you can conduct an informational interview with him or her to learn more about the position, the company, and what is required to be hired for such a job. Record your notes, and keep them for reference to use when you apply for such a job or position.

Grammar Handbook

Parts of Speech 101

For the purposes of your writing in business, here are the basic parts of speech you need to be most concerned with when writing sentences.

Noun: a person, place, or thing; can be a subject of the sentence—doing the main action of the sentence—or can be an object of the sentence—having something done to it, receiving the action.

Verb: asserts or asks something about the subject; can be a verb that represents the main action of the sentence done by the subject.

Pronoun: a word that stands in for a proper or defined noun. For example, the pronoun "he" can stand in for the noun "John," and the pronoun "it" can stand in for the noun "cat."

Preposition: a word that indicates a relationship between a noun/pronoun and other words in a sentence (such as "by," "like," "as," "to," "toward," "of," "for," "out of")

Interjection: an emotional or emphatic exclamation "injected" into a sentence and followed by an exclamation point, such as "Ouch!" and "Good!"

Article: a word that defines a subject or object, such as "a" or "an" (an indefinite, not specific, noun, such as "*a* cat") or "the" (definite, very specific noun, such as "*the* cat").

Adjective: a word that describes and gives more detail about a noun (e.g., the subject or the object of the sentence), such as colour, size, shape, and so on. Examples would be the adjective "yellow" with the noun "house" or the adjective "bohemian" with the noun "rhapsody."

Adverb: a word that further defines the nature of an action (the verb). For example, dancing "erratically" (verb + adverb), or jigging "frantically" (verb + adverb). A tip: adverbs often end with "-ly," but of course, since this is the English language, not always.

Conjunction: the helpful "connector" in a sentence, connecting words, phrases, or clauses. These words can be remembered as FANBOYS: *for, and, nor, but, or, yet, so*. A co-ordinating conjunction, along with a comma, "co-ordinates" two phrases or ideas in a sentence (see sentence structure and parallel structure further on in this appendix).

Subjects and Verbs: A Review

And now . . . (the audience is hushed) . . . the award for the most important word in an English sentence goes to two actors . . . the subject and the verb! (Loud applause. . . .)

The subject is the noun (person, place, or thing) that is doing the action (the verb). To write a complete sentence, you can't have one without the other. The subject and the verb are, in a sense, married to each other. They can be separated by other modifying information in a clause, but they still must agree with each other.

For example:

The yellow cat excitedly chased the squeaking mouse across the floor.
          (S)   (V)

For example:

Jane waited three hours for her date to show up, but in the meantime, was entertained by
(S)   (V)   (V)
three other attractive young men.

For example:

The weary student, exhausted after writing three essays in one week, slept for 24 hours
         (S)   (V)
straight.

Confusing a Subject with an Object

One of the most common errors people make in identifying subjects and verbs is confusing them with objects, or adjectives or adverbs. It's easy to be confused about which word is the subject (the noun doing the action) and which is the object or objects (the noun or nouns having the action done *to* them). Both are nouns!

Consider the following example:

The professor told the class that a pop quiz would be held at the end of the lecture.

"Professor" is the subject. He or she is doing (did) the action "told" to "the class," which is the direct object (or main receiver of the action). The "quiz" is also a noun, as is "lecture," but these are indirect objects involving further details about what is going on.

Remember: the **subject** is the noun (person, place, thing) doing the action (verb) to the **direct object** (noun: person, place, or thing receiving or being affected by the action of the subject) and the **indirect object** (further nouns that define more of the details of the sentence—the object[s] of the direct object!)

Therefore the previous sentence could be described as below:

The professor told the class that a pop quiz would be held at the end of the lecture.
      (S)   (V)   (DO)   (IO)   (IO)   (IO)

EXERCISES

Identify the subjects and the verbs in each sentence below by writing out the sentence in your notebook or on paper and then putting an "S" above the subject and a "V" above the verb.

1. Jorge's car died on the side of the busy highway last night.

2. The car was jammed with too many passengers—students who needed a ride home from the pub.

3. So overloaded was the car's rear end, it was scraping the asphalt, and sparks were flying from the exhaust pipe.

4. The billowing smoke coming from under the hood was a sign that the students should vacate the car immediately.

5. They all leapt out of the car and dove into the snowy ditch; this was just in time, as the car burst into flames.

6. All Jorge could think about was his parents' reaction when they found out the car was totaled and he hadn't been maintaining it properly.

7. Someone had called 911, but the fire trucks arrived about 20 minutes later, only to find a smouldering hulk of twisted metal.

8. The police arrived around the same time and recorded the details of the incident, then arranged for a van to transport the students back to their residence.

9. It was difficult to determine the cause of the blaze, but the fact that Jorge had not changed the oil in a year probably had something to do with it; he had also neglected to take the car to a mechanic when he was seeing puddles of oil under the car in the residence parking lot.

10. Needless to say, Jorge's parents were not pleased, but he and his friends decided instead to buy shares in AutoShare for future transportation so that he wouldn't have to worry about maintenance again.

Pronoun-Antecedent Agreement

Another sticky situation for writers is ensuring that a pronoun agrees with its antecedent. The antecedent is the word (a noun, pronoun, or other substantive) to which a pronoun refers in a sentence. Here is a sentence in which the writer got horribly muddled in connecting the pronoun with the antecedent:

> After the long, hot convocation event, when they had finally gotten rid of their steamy robes and donned cooler clothing, cars of students and families headed to the town's many restaurants.

Read this long sentence carefully. Because the pronoun *they* is used in the second clause we aren't sure who *they* are. It appears that the **cars** were attending the convocation and were wearing steamy robes. Chances are the writer intended to say that the **students** had disrobed and changed into cooler duds.

Now the sentence makes sense, though it's still a bit longer than you'd want to use in a business communication:

> After the long, hot convocation event, when STUDENTS had finally gotten rid of their steamy robes and donned cooler clothing, cars of students and families headed to the town's many restaurants.

If pronoun-antecedent agreement is one of your particular problems in writing, try changing the order of the sentence or just use the noun instead of a pronoun. Here are two modified examples:

After the long, hot convocation had ended and students had gotten rid of their steamy robes, they headed out in cars with their families to the town's many restaurants.

After the long, hot convocation event ended, students got rid of their steamy robes and donned cooler clothing. Then they headed out with their families in cars to the town's many restaurants.

Bet you were dying to break up that long-winded sentence into two shorter ones, because reading it aloud would probably have left you breathless!

EXERCISE

Mark the pronouns in the following sentences with a "P" above or below and the antecedents with an "A." Tip: read slowly and carefully, because you might miss which pronoun goes with what antecedent.

1. Tonia diligently applied for jobs in her field of accounting after graduation from college.

2. Seeing few opportunities advertised in the newspaper, Tonia applied her knowledge of informational interviews to meeting with key decision-makers at employers she wanted to work for.

3. At one business, the manager said she would be happy to talk to Tonia in another six months, since she would be expanding the workforce when the company added a new product line.

4. Tonia didn't stop her job search at that point, though, because this hopeful conversation wasn't a guarantee of a job in six months.

5. After she had completed a dozen informational interviews and applied for a number of hard-to-resist positions found on the student job bank, Tonia got an interview with the company that was interested in expanding and adding positions.

6. Tonia was surprised, because she had not expected to hear from Ms Telka for several months, if at all; apparently, Kierkegaard Enterprises' executives decided to take advantage of some tax incentives from the government to upgrade their equipment ahead of schedule.

7. The position Tonia interviewed for was senior accountant, and she couldn't believe her luck, having just graduated (although at the top of her class) from college.

8. Clearly, being relaxed and showing interest (with questions based on her research) in Kierkegaard Enterprises' operations during the informational interview had demonstrated Tonia's brilliance to Ms Telka.

9. A week after her formal interview and after she had chewed off many of her fingernails in anticipation, Tonia received the good news that the job was hers if she wanted it—at $65,000 per year to start!

10. Tonia immediately called her communications professor at the college to let him know that everything he had taught her about informational interviews had paid off handsomely.

Subject-Object Pronoun Confusion

Ever wondered whether to use "I" or "me" as the pronoun in a sentence that involves you? Not sure about when to use "he" or "him" as a pronoun when a guy is involved?

You may be caught in the twilight zone of trying to figure out whether the pronoun you want to use is for a subject or an object. Remember, the subject is the main "doer" or "actor" engaged in the action (verb), and the object is the person, place, or thing that is receiving or is being affected by what the subject is doing.

Personal pronouns in English have three forms or "cases" that indicate whether they are being used as a subject, object, or possessive. Writers mainly become confused (yes, even great writers!) when deciding whether to use the subject or object case, particularly since in our spoken English, we often use these cases incorrectly and don't even think about it.

The subject form of pronouns are: *I, you, he, she, it, we, you, they*. The subject case is used when you are using a pronoun to replace the proper name of the subject that is doing the action (verb) in a sentence.

For example:

Duarte pulled muscles in his back when shovelling the driveway.
(*Duarte* is the subject—proper noun)

He pulled muscles in his back when shovelling the driveway.
(*He* is the subject—subject case pronoun)

The object form of pronouns are: *me, him, her, it, us, you, them*. The object case is used when you are using a pronoun instead of the proper noun for the direct or indirect object of the sentence or when the pronouns are the object of a preposition.

For example:

The ferocity of the snowstorm surprised *me*.
(*Me* is the direct object)

Professor Starkowicz sent *her* the results of the final paper by email.
(*Her* is the indirect object)

The university sent a notice to *us* about the impending strike.
(*Us* is the object of the preposition)

EXERCISES

In the following sentences, choose the correct pronoun within the brackets, and then indicate whether the pronoun you chose is the subject or object case.

1. (We, Us) rallied for lower tuition fees at the provincial legislature.

2. Eating too much chocolate wires (me, I) up.

3. Should (he, him) use the ticket to the game even after breaking up with Jane?

4. Show (them, they) that you care.

5. Are these delicious pastries for (we, us), or are they for the faculty meeting?

6. My doctor gave (me, I) a prescription for antibiotics for my chest infection.

7. (She, her) loves to scour eBay for excellent quality vintage coats.

8. The student with the top marks in online marketing is (he, him).

9. Not getting into the program I applied for is a disappointment to (me, I).

10. The supervisor asked (me, I) to cover for Ahmed, who was ill with the flu.

Problems with Possessive Case Pronouns

While we will deal with the use of the apostrophe in the section on punctuation, let's tackle possessive pronoun problems (try saying that fast!) now—with a review of what a possessive pronoun is and then the incorrect use of the apostrophe.

The third pronoun case in the English language is those pronouns that denote ownership, and there are two types of these particular pronouns.

The first type refers to pronouns that are used as adjectives to modify nouns: *my, his, her, its, our, your, their*.

For example:

> *My* room needs a serious cleaning, because it's covered in old pizza boxes and heaps of smelly laundry.

The second type refers to pronouns used as predicate words, subjects of verbs, or objects of verbs or prepositions: *mine, his, hers, its, ours, yours, theirs*.

Examples:

> The responsibility for this problem is *yours*. (Predicate word)
>
> *His* is the highest mark in the class. (Subject of verb)
>
> Juanita needs *hers*. (Object of verb)
>
> There's something missing in *mine*. (Object of preposition)

EXERCISE

Select the correct word within the brackets to complete the sentences below.

1. (Our, ours) hair was long and silky.

2. The fault for the accident was (their's, theirs).

3. Those purple shoes are (her, hers).

4. The train rattled along (its, it's) track to the final destination.

5. The stack of textbooks abandoned at the back of the classroom was (my, mine).

6. The letter was on (its, it's) way to England but was intercepted by CSIS.

7. The larger piece of pie is (our, ours), because you are on a diet.

8. The missing coat is (their, theirs).

9. The fabulous curry recipe was (her's, hers), developed over years of study with excellent Indian chefs in Mumbai.

Verb Tense

As covered earlier in this chapter, verbs are the action words of the sentence, so they also indicate to the reader **when** the action takes or took place.

There are six different tenses (or times) that can be contained in sentences: present, past, and future (simple tenses) and present perfect, past perfect, and future perfect (perfect tenses).

The present tense of a verb is exactly the same as the name of the verb.

Walk, jump, soak

The past tense of a verb describes action that has taken place in the past and is generally written by adding a *d* or *ed* to the present tense root.

Walked, jumped, soaked

As usual, there are some exceptions to this rule—it's the English language, remember? When you write a past tense of an irregular verb, you change the spelling of the word. (You'll just have to look it up if you're stuck on a more exotic, irregular verb—sorry!)

Stink in the past tense is *stank*.
Go in the past tense is *went*.

The future tense of a verb, describing action yet to be performed, inserts **shall** or **will** before the present tense version of the verb.

Walk in the future tense is *shall walk* or will walk.
Jump in the future tense is *shall jump* or *will jump*.
Soak in the future tense is *shall soak* or *will soak*.

If you have to communicate that action took place at two different times, one earlier than the other (as in an incident report), you need to use a perfect tense. You create a perfect tense verb by adding "has," "have," or "had" to the past tense verb.

For example, the verb **soak** is **soaked** in the past tense, so add **has, have,** or **had** to **soaked** for a present or past perfect verb; if you are writing a future perfect tense verb, you would use the future tense of **soak (will** or **shall soak**) and inject **have** between **will/shall** and **soak**:

Present perfect: *has soaked, have soaked*

Past perfect: *had soaked*

Future perfect: *will have soaked, shall have soaked*

Are you soaking this up yet? Here's an exercise to see if it has sunk in yet.

EXERCISE

In each sentence, underline each verb, then indicate whether the verb is in the present, past, or future tense or in the present perfect, past perfect, or future perfect tense.

1. When he heard the crash in the other room, Raoul leapt from his chair to see what had caused the noise.

2. Students will go to the financial aid office if they need an emergency bursary to make ends meet.

3. We enjoy dark chocolate on a daily basis because it's good for us.

4. Shall I go and call the others?

5. Professors at the college will go on training next week to learn how to help their students deal with test anxiety.

6. A group of forestry workers in Prince George, BC, has won the jackpot of $10 million.

7. They have gone the distance in their efforts to improve student life at the college.

8. Freezing rain had coated the highways, creating hazardous conditions for the homeward commute.

9. The protesters shall have reinforcements arriving in the next couple of days.

10. Bjorn yelled downstairs to his girlfriend, "Where have you hidden my favourite t-shirt?"

Passive and Active Verbs

In business writing, it's important to write more in the active than in the passive version of a verb, because using an active verb keeps the reader engaged and interested in your writing. Using active verbs also decreases wordiness in your sentences and paragraphs—and keeps you writing clearly, concisely, and efficiently for the busy business reader.

So what the heck is the difference between passive and active verbs?

Active verbs are those whereby the *subject* of the sentence performs the action. *Passive verbs* are those created *by using a form of "be" with the past tense verb* (participle). Verbs with *objects* can be changed from active to passive.

For example:

Active verb: *Professor Singh facilitated the debate.*
                 (S)   (V)   (O)

Passive verb: *The debate was facilitated by Professor Singh.*
                 (S)   (V)   (IO)

In short, you want your sentences to have the subject doing the action to/for the object, which receives the action, where possible.

How can you tell whether you are using too many passive verbs? One clue is the length of each sentence. When you read through your work (and you *do* perform a copy edit before printing or sending your writing, right?), look for sentences that appear overly wordy. Chances are that you have used the passive tense, and if you change the sentence to incorporate an active verb, then you will shorten and simplify the sentence and energize it so that the reader will be interested in what you have to express.

EXERCISE

Rewrite each sentence, changing the verb from active to passive or passive to active.

1. An absolutely delicious protein shake has been made by Chef Tomas.

2. Doug has diligently completed the bookkeeping.

3. The president of the student union has been found by fellow students to be embezzling funds.

4. The municipal government will notify ratepayers of the water tax increase.

5. The bicycle has been stolen by an unknown thief.

6. Eating protein every two hours has been recommended by Dr. Tung as a way of building strong muscle mass.

7. The elderly ladies brought their traditional macaroni casserole to the potluck supper.

8. The employer will let everyone who didn't get the job know their status following the second round of interviews.

9. A tropical vacation has been arranged by FabTours.

10. The mail will be picked up by Geordie on his way home from school.

Punctuation Perfection

Afraid of commas or semi-colons? Just what is a semi-colon anyway? When in doubt, should you just throw in an apostrophe here and there to spice up a sentence? What the heck are ellipsis points?

If you have ever wrestled with any of these issues, you are not alone. Even the most practised writers sometimes slip up on one form of punctuation or another. Most of us know where to put a period (not counting when we put one at the end of a sentence fragment), but some lesser-used punctuation can make us scratch our head in confusion.

THE PERIOD

The period (.) denotes the end of a sentence. The idea or ideas are complete, there is at least a subject and a verb (for a complete sentence), and the period signals a transition to the next thought or idea in a paragraph—the next sentence.

Using a period at the end of the complete sentence is correct; using one at the end of an incomplete or fragment sentence is not.

Incorrect: *The brochure on the floor.*
(Sentence fragment, because it is missing a verb)

Correct: *The brochure was lying on the floor.*
(Complete sentence with subject and verb)

THE ELLIPSIS

What is an ellipsis, or conversely, what is that punctuation you see in some academic or trade publications—a bunch of periods in a row?

The ellipsis is used to:

- indicate to the reader that you took a long quotation from a source and used only the first bit and something else closer to the end of the source—and that there was more "in between" the quoted passages you have used.

For example:

"The male of the species is responsible for the building of Shelter . . . He is a provider and defender" (Jones, 36).

The ellipsis lets the reader know that the quote from Jones on page 36 of the source material has more information and/or sentences in between the two lines included here. If you didn't use the ellipsis, you would be quoting your source incorrectly by not acknowledging that you are using the quote out of context of the original source material.

The ellipsis is either three periods in a row (. . .) or four (. . . .). You use the three-period form of ellipsis within a passage or sentence, as noted above; you use the four-period form of ellipsis at the end of a sentence, because the extra period is needed to denote the end of the sentence.

THE COMMA

Comma fear is one of the most common afflictions of students and writers in general. Where do you put them?

- After every item in a series and just before the co-ordinating conjunction word (*for, and, nor, but, or, yet, so*)

Example:

The flag was green, pink, and yellow.

- After the adverbs *first, second, third,* and so on, when the adverbs introduce a series of parallel (similar in subject and length) items

Example:

First, carefully open the container so as not to dislodge the content.

- When two or more adjectives precede a noun, using a comma after each adjective except the last one

  Example:

  The fuzzy, green, angora sweater was a delight to wear.

- To separate an introductory word, phrase, or clause from the rest of the sentence

  Example:

  While writing her shopping list, Gisele munched on a freshly baked cookie.

- To set off a modifying phrase that you have "injected" or placed into the sentence (interrupting the flow of the sentence)

  Example:

  Back in his youth, when he felt more spry and frisky, Mr. Musharraf would walk for miles and miles each day.

- To set off nouns used as direct address

  Example:

  Ren, come here quickly!

- To set off most appositives (a modifying word or group of words used beside another word to explain it)

  Example:

  Dr. Ben Chiang, the world-renowned coronary specialist, presented his findings on heart disease in obese teens at the recent conference.

- To set off the explanatory words of a direct quotation

  Example:

  The little girl exclaimed, "It's a magical bear!"

- Before the conjunction that joins the two main clauses in a compound sentence

  Example:

  The heat of the July day was oppressive, and we went to the beach to cool off.

- Between the day of the month and the year when writing out a date

  Example:

  The final paper is due on October 15, 2011.

- Between the name of a city or town and the name of a province or country

  Example:

  The custom-built Kevlar canoe was made in Millbrook, Ontario.

- After the salutation or complimentary close of a letter

  Example:

  Dear Ms Mishi, or Yours truly,

- To set off non-restrictive clauses (clauses that add an idea to a sentence)

  Example:

  The cat, which is missing a tail, darted across the yard when the dog chased it.

EXERCISE

Rewrite sentences, inserting commas where necessary.

1. Little Adam had a tantrum and lay on the floor and kicked and screamed in hopes that Mommy would buy him the toy.

2. First we'll go to the mall; next we'll meet in the food court; and then we will go to The Gap to check out the big sale on jeans.

3. To prepare the cake Mrs. Jones creamed the butter with the sugar beat in the eggs added the milk and then the dry ingredients.

4. For the college semi-formal you can choose between vegetarian and non-vegetarian meal options.

5. No I don't want to go that chick flick with you.

6. Next to my older sister you are the best counsellor when I have a problem.

7. Jackson a well-known lawyer will be representing him in this matter.

8. You look stunning in that new dress Nikita.

9. Dude this is my girlfriend Sarita.

10. The sweater she was knitting a turtleneck was more complicated than she anticipated.

THE SCARY SEMI-COLON

Many writers admit to being scared of the semi-colon. That's right—they have no idea what it's for, and the idea of using it and making some horrible mistake has them avoiding this perfectly good, useful form of punctuation.

First of all, the semi-colon is *not* interchangeable with a comma. Second, it's not the same as a colon (:). However, it *does* have something in common with periods.

Semi-colon versus comma: A comma is for all of the uses just noted previously—for example, between clauses that could not stand alone as complete sentences or between individual words or combinations of words (that are not complete sentences). A comma is also used in co-ordination (ahead of a co-ordinating conjunction such as "and") of clauses in a sentence or subordination of clauses (when one clause is independent and the other(s) dependent).

While the snow came down heavily, the plows were working non-stop to fill in driveways with what had fallen on the roads.

A semi-colon, by contrast, is used between phrases that could stand alone as independent clauses or complete sentences. The semi-colon is the unifier of two distinct clauses that the writer wants to connect together because they have a theme or subject in common.

In the summer session, the college offered elective courses; in the fall, more of the required courses were offered.

What the semi-colon has in common with the period is that one or the other can be used between independent clauses that could stand alone as complete sentences. For example, here's the sentence above, but with a period instead of a semi-colon between the clauses:

In the summer session, the college offered elective courses. In the fall, more of the required courses were offered.

So why bother with the dratted semi-colon if a period will do a similar job? Quite simply because you want to demonstrate variety in sentence structure and style as you write; this will impress your reader.

In short, use a semi-colon in the following situations:

- To join the independent clauses of a compound sentence when no co-ordinating conjunction is used

Example:

Joachim is the president of the student union; Michaela is the vice-president.

- When a co-ordinating conjunction is used between independent clauses of a compound sentence but the clauses are long and filled with many commas

Example:

Dr. Stokker started his teaching career at University of Victoria, with the most acclaimed English program in Canada; but when he was offered a prestigious position as chair of the English program at Oxford University, he enthusiastically moved on.

- Before a conjunction adverb (*therefore, however, hence, so, then, moreover, besides, nevertheless, yet, consequently*) that joins the independent clauses of a compound sentence

Example:

Kiki knew her trip would cost more than $4,000; therefore, she implemented a strict budget and put aside $500 a month into a tax-free savings account.

- When there are commas within items in a list or series to separate the items

Example:

Volunteers who took part in the rebuilding of Haiti were mostly from Winnipeg, Manitoba; Montreal, Quebec; and Fredericton, New Brunswick.

EXERCISE

Rewrite the following sentences; insert semi-colons where necessary.

1. Jean was appropriately dressed for a long hike in the woods however, he had too much clothing on for the warm weather.

2. One of the twins, Joyce, is a gastroenterologist the other twin, Hannah, is a gynecologist.

3. In order to be considered for the overseas internship at Siemens in Germany, she needed to be fluent in German therefore, she took part in an intensive German immersion program in the eight months leading up to the application deadline.

4. You say tomato I say tomato.

5. The qualities sought for the manager position were proven organizational skills pertaining to managing multiple work teams excellent communication skills with a variety of stakeholders and creative problem-solving and conflict resolution skills with flexibility in a quickly changing environment.

THE COLON: A HELPFUL ORGANIZER OF LISTS, GREETINGS, AND NUMBERS

The colon (:) can be considered the organizing specialist of the punctuation team. It is used:

- In sentences ahead of a list of items, letting the reader know to be prepared for that list

  Example:

  Please pack the following items for our day trip: sunscreen, a hat, and water.

- To organize a business letter by setting the content apart from the salutation, with the colon placed after the salutation

  Example:

  Dear Ms Salutin:

- To organize how we present a time in our writing by dividing hours, minutes, and seconds

  Example:

  8:52 (hour:minutes)
  8:52:30 (hour:minutes:seconds)

EXERCISE

In the following sentences, insert colons where needed.

1. Departure time is 600 a.m., with arrival at Trudeau Airport at 1200 noon.

2. In your application to the program, please provide the following academic transcripts, personal statement of application, resumé, and two reference letters.

3. When you arrive at the hotel at 300 p.m., please have the following documents ready for review passport, visa, travel itinerary, and evidence of a return airline ticket.

4. When using the washroom facilities in a Japanese household, the following steps are essential change house shoes into slippers designed to wear only into the toilet; wash thoroughly after using the toilet; and change back into your house shoes or slippers and out of the toilet slippers when returning to your hosts.

5. In order to be prepared for emergencies while travelling, bring the following items with you evidence of travel and medical insurance, information about personal medical conditions, travel immunization record, passport, visa (where required), and US money.

THE APOSTROPHE, POSSESSIVES, AND PRONOUNS: UNTANGLING A COMPLICATED RELATIONSHIP

If you want to make your communications professor grin maniacally from ear to ear, master when and where to use the apostrophe. Once you learn appropriate apostrophe use, you will see errors everywhere you look—because this is one of the most common punctuation and grammar errors made by writers of the English language!

Apostrophes are used:

- To form the possessive of a singular noun—even one with an "s" ending (apostrophe and an *s*)

Examples:

A *woman's* coat (coat belonging to one woman)
Fido's slobbery ball (slobbery ball belonging to Fido, one dog)

- To form the possessive of a plural noun that does *not* end in "s" (apostrophe and an *s*)

Examples:

Women's coats (coats belonging to several women)
Men's club (a club "belonging to" several men)

- To form the possessive of a plural noun *with* an "s" ending (apostrophe after the final *s*)

Examples:

The *Smiths'* house (the house belonging to more than one member of the Smith family)
Artists' centre (the centre "belonging to" several artists)

- To form the possessive of an indefinite pronoun (add apostrophe and then an *s*)

Examples:

Everyone's business (the business belonging to everyone)
Somebody's fault (the fault belonging to somebody)

- To form contractions—when two words are joined together to create one word. (The general rule to keep in mind is that the apostrophe replaces a vowel (a, e, i, o, u, and sometimes y)

Examples:

Don't (contraction of *do not*)
Wouldn't (contraction of *would not*)
It's (contraction of *it is*)

When the writer is thinking about using a word ending in "s," he or she often misinterprets the word as a possessive or contraction. That darn "s" leads him or her astray! Some common errors found in student (and yes, even business!) writing include:

Want's (should be *wants*) and *need's* (should be *needs*)

If this sounds like something you struggle with, keep the following rules in mind:

There should be no apostrophe before "s" unless you are writing a contraction or a singular/plural possessive. In a plural possessive ending in "s," you should add an apostrophe after the "s" ending. In such cases, adding another "s" after the apostrophe is technically correct but is not necessary.

Where many writers also get confused about apostrophes is when they don't know whether the noun is singular or plural. This requires focus!
For example:

kid's versus *kids'* items
lady's versus *ladies'*

At McDonald's you might see **kid's meals** advertised. These would be sold to **one kid**! To sell to more than one, write **kids' meals**.
When we have a noun plural with an "s" ending, like **ladies**, some writers go completely off the deep end and think there should be an apostrophe after the "e" and before the "s." When **ladie's** is written, not only is it an incorrect use of the apostrophe—sounding as though we are describing something belonging to only one lady—but **ladie** is a misspelling of **lady**. Alternatively, how many times have you seen an ad for lady's shoes or woman's coats? This would be an ad selling to **one lady** or **one woman** (one extreme shopper or a shoeaholic who will buy up the store's entire stock—imagine the credit card bill!). The correct form, in this instance, is **ladies'** and **women's**. By the way, you may note that there is no "s" after **ladies'**. You could put an "s" after ladies—ladies's, but again, while this is technically correct, it's never done. (Another instance of why the English language is so hard for people to learn—loads of exceptions to rules!)

EXERCISE

Correct the following sentences where needed, removing or moving punctuation, revising spelling, or rewriting.

1. Using transit save's commuters a lot of money on parking, not to mention the stress and hassle of being stuck in traffic.

2. This bookkeeping system need's to be overhauled as soon as possible.

3. Lady's coats were on sale on eBay.

4. The Smith's cabin was located on the edge of a lake in northern Saskatchewan; they needed to take a small plane to a nearby landing strip to reach it.

5. The wordsmiths books, while fiction and only loosely based on historical fact, were in high demand by business students seeking a keen insight into the motivations of those who survived the Great Depression.

6. Many dad's deepest desires for Fathers Day include the traditional burning of meat (barbeque), stretching out on a hammock in the shade, and frosted steins of beer; at the bottom of the list would be tacky ties and soap on a rope.

7. When you travel to another city, you can look up your banks information online.

8. There are many economic development initiative's across Canada to help with local development relevant to the community's resources.

9. Its too bad that the university has cancelled classes because of the snowstorm; we were ready to hunker down with a pile of books at the library.

10. The car blew it's engine on the freeway, probably because John had not taken it to a garage for maintenance in two years.

WHEN DO YOU USE QUESTION MARKS?

When we are asking a **direct question**, we use a question mark to end the sentence. If the sentence begins with do, who, what, where, when, why, or how, it's a direct question.
For example:

Do you want to go and see things blow up in that blockbuster movie?

Why did you go to Esmeralda's house when you said you were sick and couldn't go out to the game with me?

However, we don't always ask a direct question. An **indirect question** *does not* end with a question mark.

Incorrect: *Tell me what you think of this colour?*
Correct: *Tell me what you think of this colour.*

Incorrect: *I'd like your thoughts on the matter?*
Correct: *I'd like your thoughts on the matter.*

EXERCISE

Correct the following sentences as needed with the correct punctuation.

1. George asked whether I wanted to be in the stern or the bow of the boat?

2. Where do we go from here.

3. How long are you going to put up with this nonsense before you call a halt to what they are doing in the department?

4. "When will you have the quarterly report for me to see" his supervisor asked in an annoyed tone of voice.

5. After the train had left the station, conductors in all of the cars asked whether we had our tickets?

TO QUOTE OR NOT TO QUOTE . . . THAT IS THE QUESTION

Quotation marks are a great way to demarcate something someone has said word for word, dialogue, or, to a lesser extent, titles of written documents, but this form of punctuation is often overdone.

Writers who want readers to clearly note something important or interesting (at least to the writer!) often put words in quotations to get your attention. However, unless the word or words merit such attention, they should not be put in quotation marks. While technically correct to use in several instances, overuse of quotation marks will drive your readers bonkers—or at least leave them with a low-level, annoyed feeling.

For example, in these sentences, should the word(s) in quotation marks be singled out for your attention?

She looked a little "green" when she saw open heart surgery on television.

"Grandma Borychenko" was an "adoptive" grandmother to the neighbourhood's children.

The world's greatest cinnamon buns were made at "Delicktable Delights."

While in the first sentence the writer is using **green** in a colloquial way to describe the woman's nausea when seeing surgery, the word doesn't really merit being put into quotations. If the word **green** is not going to be understood by all readers, then the writer should rewrite the sentence to make the concept clear to readers (**nauseated**, while not as colourful a word as **green**, would suffice). Putting **green** in quotations is only pointing out that the writer is trying too hard to impress the usage of the word on the reader.

In the second sentence, the writer has decided that Grandma Borychenko's name is important. However, capitalizing both Grandma and Borychenko is enough to identify her. She is not a "special" Grandma Borychenko (although she may be a special person to the neighbourhood's kids). What about "adoptive"? The writer is trying too hard to emphasize Grandma's role. How about rewriting the sentence slightly to include **like an** before **adoptive**? This makes it far more clear to the reader the kind of role Grandma had.

In the third sentence, the bakery where the cinnamon buns were made has its name in quotation marks. While using quotation marks in this way is technically correct, it's not stylistically optimal for business writing. Putting the name of a business in quotation marks is akin to putting an individual's given names and surname into italics, which should not be done.

Do you get it now? Quotation marks are good—as long as they aren't overdone and are used in the right circumstances. In business writing, quotation marks are generally only used when the writer is including a direct quotation of someone else's writing. (Business writing generally doesn't include much in the way of dialogue—with the possible exception being an incident report when exact dialogue as it happened may be important as part of the details.)

Using quotation marks at the beginning and end of a direct quote

As was just mentioned, if you are writing a report, proposal, or study in the workplace, the most common use of quotations is around any information that is directly lifted word for word from someone else's writing—to avoid plagiarism and to give credit where credit is due. Here's an example:

"When writing financial projections for your business plan, it is helpful to have obtained at least three price quotations for each of the major appliances, equipment, and other start-up costs. Use the middle price quotation in your financial plan expenses spreadsheets, and note it in your financial plan narrative so that you have chosen pricing that is not the worst or best case scenario" (*Business Planning Journal* 2002).

Note that the end quotation mark goes after the quotation itself and does not include the citation in parentheses (brackets). Note also that the quotation marks go around all of the sentences quoted, not around each sentence in the quotation.

Quotation marks are used around a direct quote. A *direct quote* of someone's speech would be:

"I will help with the disaster relief effort," said Dr. Vasily.

The writer, perhaps a journalist, recorded Dr. Vasily's exact words and presented them in quotation marks in the story.

This is *not* a direct quote from someone:

Dr. Vasily said he would help in the disaster relief effort.

This is an *indirect quote* in which the writer is relating what he or she heard Dr. Vasily say (you could say this is second-hand information).

Using exclamation points and question marks with quotations

Exclamation points and question marks go inside the quotation marks *if* the punctuation belongs to the quotation itself. For example:

"Fritzie, get over here!" the frustrated dog owner hollered.

The dog owner was evidently unhappy and yelling at the dog, so an exclamation point indicates the tone and emotion in his or her voice. Because the tone and emotion are contained in what the dog owner hollered, the exclamation point must go inside the quotation marks.

Exclamation points and question marks go *outside* the quotation marks if they are not part of the quoted words:

Have you ever heard the expression "A bird in the hand is worth two in the bush"?

The expression in quotations is not a question in itself, but what the writer is asking you, the reader, is whether you have ever heard the saying. The saying "A bird in the hand . . ." is a statement, not a question. Therefore, the quotation marks go around the saying that is being quoted, not the question the writer is asking the reader.

Head-scratcher: What if you want to put a quotation inside a quotation?

If you want to use a quotation inside a quotation, you use single quotation marks around the inside quotation and double quotation marks around the whole sentence. Here's an example:

> "But the sign says 'No trespassing,' so why are we going inside? What if the cops come?" said the nervous friend of the gang leader.

No trespassing is what the speaker has seen on a sign; it's not the direct quote but his quote within what he is saying to the gang leader. Therefore, it's put into single quotation marks so that it stands out from the main quotation. The dialogue of the nervous friend is the direct quotation around 'No trespassing,' so it is put into double quotation marks.

When to use quotations around titles

Technically speaking, you may use quotation marks around titles of written work, songs, or TV and radio shows. This was done in the past when most business (and other) word processing was done on a manual or electric typewriter and italicizing was not possible.

However, using quotations for titles in business writing is not as polished or professional as using italics. In any commonly used word-processing program, it's easy for a writer to incorporate italicization of titles. This is particularly useful when you are including a title in the text of a sentence so that it stands out from the rest of the text.

EXERCISE

Rewrite the following sentences, inserting quotation marks, question marks, and exclamation points where appropriate.

1. I think we have a problem said one of the college's security staff, Maria Christophanes.

2. Maria was afraid her supervisor would be upset with her not keeping an eye on the Thursday night pub as she said There are some guys streaking through the halls in A Wing naked!

3. What do you mean, naked the supervisor said, not looking at all pleased.

4. Naked, as in no clothes, and they're heading our way Maria exclaimed, pointing at the security screen with views from the nearby hall.

5. The sound of fast running came to a screeching halt as the supervisor and two other male security staff tackled the guys to the floor, yelling in unison Gotcha.

6. What made you think this was a clothing-optional event said the supervisor, after security staff had obtained towels to wrap around the young men.

7. I think I'm going to need counselling for the rest of my life, because I can't get the picture out of my head now chuckled Maria as the guys were led away to get their clothes from somewhere in the pub.

8. It's fortunate we stopped them before they ran out into the −40 C blizzard, the supervisor said soberly. In only a few minutes in the cold they would have had frostbite, and being drunk, they probably wouldn't notice.

9. Yeah, we would certainly have had a frosty response from the college administration if we hadn't intervened, said one of the security guys who joined Maria and the supervisor.

10. Well, next time keep a better eye on what's going on at the pub, or you may find yourself frozen out of a job, the supervisor concluded as Maria completed the incident report form.

Sentence Structure

THE NEVER-ENDING STORY: THE RUN-ON SENTENCE

Have you ever received an assignment back from a professor who wrote exasperated red ink "ROs" or "run-on sentence" comments in the margins?

Fear not—you can escape from the hell of the never-ending sentence! A run-on sentence is one in which two or more independent clauses are fused together—without being separated by correct conjunctions or punctuation.

Technically, a run-on sentence can be short (e.g., **She runs, he walks.**), but they are often long. To catch a run-on sentence, read your work out loud. Are you breathless after reading any of the sentences? For example:

The journal article "Getting the most out of college" was required reading for all first-semester students regardless of personal interest or motivation, it was a succinct summary of the main learning outcomes to be achieved in the course and because the professor had authored the piece herself it was good preparation for that course.

Whew! Not much room for a breath when reading that sentence! If we add some punctuation to create pauses, the sentence is less demanding to read:

The journal article, "Getting the most out of college," was required reading for all first semester students, regardless of personal interest or motivation; it was a succinct summary of the main learning outcomes to be achieved in the course, authored by the professor herself.

This is better, but it's still a very long sentence. Where could we break it up into smaller sentences?

The journal article, "Getting the most out of college," was required reading for all first semester students, regardless of personal interest or motivation. It was a succinct summary of the main learning outcomes to be achieved in the course, authored by the professor herself.

But the sentences are too wordy. Where can we slash and burn words to make the text even more succinct?

Reading "Getting the most out of college" was mandatory for all first-semester students as a succinct summary of main course learning outcomes written by the professor herself.

THE CASE OF THE SENTENCE FRAGMENT: WHO DONE WHAT?

Sentence fragments are like a "who-done-it" in the midst of your other, beautifully and thoughtfully written sentences. Generally, we either don't know who is engaged in the action, or what the subject is doing, and are left wondering what exactly is going on!

For example:

The train on the tracks.
Running down the road to the free ice cream.

What is the train doing? Hurtling down? Chugging along? Is it stopped? Who is running toward the double-chocolate mocha, French vanilla, and rocky road delights?

In the first sentence, a verb is missing—in action! In his or her hurry to complete the story or report, the writer forgot to note what was happening with the train. In the second sentence, perhaps the writer was drooling so much while thinking about ice cream that he or she forgot to insert who was making his or her or their way to the frozen delectables.

Here are the corrected sentences with their missing parts (and some modifiers to make these interesting):

The train on the tracks stopped abruptly.
    (verb)

The mob of children was running down the road to the free ice cream.
    (noun)

When you are reviewing your work before submitting, transmitting, or mailing it to anyone else, look closely at each sentence to ensure that it contains a verb and a noun. A caution—just because a sentence is long and appears to be a correct compound or complex sentence doesn't mean it *isn't* a fragment. (Even wonderfully descriptive sentences can become cliff-hangers!)

EXERCISE

Correct the following sentence fragments by adding nouns, verbs, and modifiers as needed.

1. Eating delicious dragon fruit as part of the colourful bounty of fruit provided in the hotel room.

2. Dropping all of the petty cash on the ceramic floor and smashing some of the more worn tiles into tiny bits.

3. She in the doorway with the gargoyles all around.

4. The Internet service provided by InterTel in the city.

5. Send above with your payment to keep delivery coming to your door.

MAKING YOUR SENTENCES SING WITH MODIFIERS

Everything in the sentence that isn't a subject, verb, or object is a modifier. Modifiers give us the important details about the subject, verb, and object, such as when, where, how, or why somebody did something.

That doesn't mean that modifiers are not important. Often they are essential to the meaning of a sentence. However, we must have a basic idea expressed in the subject, verb, and object first upon which to hang these fascinating details, and therefore they are grammatically less important, or "subordinate."

Modifiers can be any of the following:

Single words: *The quick brown* fox jumped over *the lazy* dog.

Appositives: John, *the Master of Ceremonies*, rose to his feet.

Prepositional phrases: *In Monaco and France*, the driver *of a foreign car* is regarded *with suspicion by local police*.

Participial phrases: *Rowing hard against the wind*, the biologist approached the colony *of ducks nesting among the reeds*.

Subordinate clauses: She knew *he was wrong*, but she did not tell him *that she knew*.

EXERCISE

Locate and identify the modifiers in the following sentences by underlining them.

1. The frazzled president of the company had heart palpitations after a fire burned the main production facility.

2. Hope Sorel, president of CUPE Local 111, angrily expressed her outrage when the back-to-work legislation was announced.

3. Tyler Snelgrove, disregarding the advice of his mother, didn't put any high SPF sunscreen on before going to the beach and, as a result, was badly burned and blistered.

4. During that summer of significant and lasting heat waves, many felt the only comfortable place to be was neck-deep in the frigid water of the nearby spring-fed lake.

5. Painting a room properly takes time—precisely taping all woodwork and details is the most time-consuming aspect of the work but is essential to avoid colourful yet upsetting accidents.

MODIFIERS "GONE BAD": THE CASE OF THE MISPLACED MODIFIER

Let's look at a sentence you've already seen: "*In Monaco and France*, the driver *of a foreign car* is regarded *with suspicion by local police*."

Subject: *driver*

Verb: *is regarded*

Prepositional phrases: *In Monaco and France, of a foreign car, with suspicion, by local police*

Placement of modifiers in a sentence is important in English. The writer has placed "In Monaco and France" before the subject, "the driver," which would normally come first. This gives emphasis to the phrase modifier; it makes it more important than it would seem to the reader if placed later in the sentence. It's grammatically okay to do this.

"Of a foreign car" occurs immediately following the word it modifies, "driver," which is the usual position for prepositional phrases and other, longer modifiers. That's because your reader wants to hear the basic idea first ("driver") before we modify the general idea with more particular and specific ideas ("of a foreign car"). That's an important feature of English, because when the modifier becomes too far separated from the basic idea it modifies, the reader loses the connection.

Therefore, the phrases "with suspicion" and "by local police" both follow the idea they modify, the verb "is regarded." Note that single-word modifiers tend to come before the nouns they modify, as in "The yellow dog."

Misplacement of modifiers, then, is a major error and can be unintentionally hilarious.

"I know a man with a wooden leg named Smith."
"Oh? What's the name of his other leg?"

Better to say, "I know a man named Smith who has a wooden leg."

EXERCISE

Correct the following sentences.

1. The computer store was situated by a music hall that was selling laptops.

2. The wrangler was thrown by the wild horse in canvas pants.

3. Janelle needed several tutors to help with math seriously.

4. Mrs. Hertz returned to the neonatal unit where she gave birth to twins in 2010 in her electric car.

5. There are many pictures of past students who have studied at Brilliant University on the walls.

DANGLING MODIFIERS FLAPPING IN THE BREEZE

A dangling modifier (usually a participial phrase) is associated with a word or phrase that does not appear in the sentence; this often leads the reader to illogically connect the modifier in question with another word, often the subject of the sentence.

Example:

While eating our salads in the garden, a bee stung me.

Participle: *eating*

Subject: *bee*

The reader will connect "eating" with "bee" rather than "me" as the writer intended. Better to say "While we were eating our salads in the garden, *I* was stung by a bee."

EXERCISE

Correct the following sentences.

1. Excitedly dashing out the door, the nearest person was enthusiastically hugged by Misha.

2. To settle the matter, some paperwork was completed a week early.

3. Though only 13, the university accepted Doug's application for medical school.

4. To please Granddad, some cookies were put on the table ahead of dinner.

5. After seeing the bridge damage, our SUV stopped.

PARALLEL SENTENCE STRUCTURE PROBLEMS: "ONE OF THESE THINGS IS NOT LIKE THE OTHERS . . ."

In English, we can use the co-ordinate conjunctions ("and," "but," "or") to make lists. A list can be any grammatical unit in the sentence extended to two or more ideas: subjects, verbs, objects, single-word modifiers, phrases, or clauses . . . *this* is a list!

The trick is to keep all the items in the list the same grammatical construction. (The list above consists of nouns.) Sometimes as we write the list, we wander off into different constructions as we translate ideas from our heads into language, and this results in nonparallel constructions, greatly confusing to our readers.

For example:

Good forms of exercise include running, swimming, cycling, and long walks.

The exercises in this list are expressed as present participles: running, swimming, and cycling. The last item—long walks—is a noun. The sentence should read as follows:

Good forms of exercise include running, swimming, cycling, and walking long distances.

"One of these things is not like the others . . . one of these things isn't the same!"

Writers run into trouble with parallel sentence construction when writing long sentences listing multiple word clauses. This is known in communications circles as *faulty parallelism*.

However, you might want to remember the good old *Sesame Street* song quoted above. Reading your sentences aloud and having someone else read through them to catch anything listed in a sentence that is "not like the others" can help, but really, the key is to remember the rule that each item in the list must be in the same form. If you are listing nouns, then make sure all of the items are nouns. If you are listing verbs, make sure all of the words are verbs . . . and so on.

EXERCISE

Correct the following sentences.

1. In his quest to lose weight, Lucas not only went on a diet but also pursued weight training, yoga, and meditated.

2. In order to make bigger profits for the new retail outlet, the manager, Nick Garbanzo, read online marketing books, he met with a marketing consultant, and implementing a strategy specific to targeting customers.

3. The tropical-themed birthday cake featured hula girls, monkeys, and it also had banana filling.

4. Larry's delicious Tex-Mex pizza had jalapenos, black olives, and it was covered in three kinds of authentic, imported cheeses.

5. In the endurance race, she ran up steep mountains, swimming in cold, fast-running streams, and dodged a falling tree.

A RELATIONSHIP OF DEPENDENCE: PRINCIPAL AND SUBORDINATE CLAUSES

Principal or independent clauses are those that can stand alone as sentences. Think of these clauses as the rugged individuals in the sentence relationship. They don't *need* a subordinate or dependent clause but perhaps choose to be in relationship with them, because with a subordinate clause, their lives are more colourful and descriptive.

A principal clause is a subject–predicate combination, plus modifiers: **The leaves fall in the autumn.** Not the most exciting sentence on its own but complete and independent anyway.

If we (or that ruggedly independent clause) decide to spice up this sentence, we can add a subordinate (or dependent) clause. This clause can't stand alone as a sentence, but with the help and support of that independent clause, it can at least aspire to be a sentence. Think of it as a relationship in which one partner does most of the work or supporting and love inspires the more independent partner to look after the dependent one.

To expand on the previous example, we can add a subordinate clause:

The leaves in all of their vibrant colours *fall in the autumn.*

In all of their vibrant colours is a subordinate clause, modifying the principal clause and making the independent sentence a bit more colourful and interesting. (It's a creative relationship, this one between the independent and dependent clauses!) However, the dependent clause cannot stand alone as a complete sentence, because it lacks a subject and a verb.

Changing the relationship power dynamic: Subordinating the principal clause

Maybe the principal or independent clause is tired of being the dominant actor in the relationship and needs to take a break. Maybe it's time for a subordinate or dependent partner to step up and take charge.

If we add just one word in front of the principal clause, a word called a **subordinate conjunction**, we can change the independent clause to a dependent clause in favour of a clause that follows.

For example:

When *the leaves fall in the autumn, we go hunting.*

When is the subordinate conjunction that changes the independent clause, ***The leaves fall in autumn***, into a subordinate clause—subordinate to the principal or independent clause, ***we go hunting***.

Here's another example:

The man who had appeared briefly in the doorway ran off as soon as the cashier who was on duty rang the alarm.

The principal clause in this sentence is:

The man ran off

Subordinate clauses in this sentence are:

who appeared briefly in the doorway

as soon as the cashier who was on duty rang the alarm

who was on duty

The clause ***who was on duty*** appears twice above because it is part of the longer clause starting with ***as soon as***. It modifies ***cashier***; that is, it tells us which cashier rang the alarm. In this way, modifiers can become part of other modifiers.

Like prepositions, subordinate conjunctions are small words that tell us where, when, why, and how things happen. ***Because, if, when, although***, and ***whether*** are subordinate conjunctions.

Indeed, some prepositions can also be used as subordinate conjunctions, like ***after***. Tell them apart by looking at the words following. Is it just a noun or pronoun? That's a preposition. Or is there a noun and a verb following? That's a subordinate conjunction.

A special kind of subordinate conjunction is the relative pronoun. Words like ***who, which***, and ***that*** can introduce a subordinate clause, but they are also the subjects of their clauses: ***I know who will make a good host for the party.*** The relative pronoun, ***who***, introduces the subordinate clause and is the subject to go with the verb ***will make***.

Subordinate clauses not only modify but also act as subjects or objects. Did you notice in the preceding paragraph that the ***who*** clause is the direct object of ***know***?

EXERCISE

Identify the subordinate and principal clauses in the following sentences by underlining and putting "S" below the subordinate clause and "P" under the principal clause.

1. Although the weather was mild, Eliza still felt chilled and clammy.

2. Jonas was completing his business degree while working at a bookstore.

3. The security guard who was on duty was responsible for locking the doors.

4. The ghost, which had appeared briefly on the stairs, seemed to drift off through the window.

5. Because I am so full, I won't eat a bite of that delicious coconut cake, despite the temptation!

Spelling and Diction: Language Trip Hazards Commonly Confused, Abused, and Never-to-Be-Used Words

There are many words commonly confused in English composition that trip up even the most experienced writer, and some that are terribly common in business and student writing. And here's a newsflash: most of them will not be caught by the spell check or even grammar check that you may use as your first level of editing. You just need to know which of these words (and there may be others) cause you grief and learn the rules that apply!

Here are a few that often confuse people:

a or an: Use *a* before a consonant sound, such as a cat, a shoe, a camera; use *an* before a vowel sound or before a silent "h" sound: an apple, an idiot, an otter or an honour, an honest man.

all ready or already: All ready means completely prepared, while **already** indicates something that happened in the past, as in "She *already* packed the picnic lunch, so we are *all ready* to go."

all together or altogether: All together means something being done with everyone involved, as in "We *all together* contributed to the group gift." **Altogether** means entirely, as in "We were *altogether* shocked at his actions."

a lot: These two words are often written incorrectly as *alot*. Never write *alot*; it's never correct.

anyone or any one: Anyone refers to any person, as in "*Anyone* could have seen that was a dumb thing to do." **Any one** refers to any one thing, as in "*Any one* part of the machinery could have caused the breakdown."

bad or badly: Bad is an adjective, as in "*bad cat*," while **badly** is an adverb, as in "The little boy behaved *badly*." (Hint: The *ly* at the end of *badly* is a clue that it's used as an adverb.)

beside or besides: Beside is a preposition that means *at the side of* or *next to*; besides is also a preposition but means *except* or *in addition to*.

capital or capitol: A capital is the city where the government of a country, province, or territory is centred. **Capitol** is a term used in the United States to designate the legislative and other government buildings in Washington, DC, and in many state capital cities. **Capital** can also mean good, as in "*Capital* idea, old chap!" or can refer to wealth or resources, as in "The company required quite an investment of *capital* to launch its new product line."

choose or chose: Choose is a verb, meaning to select something. **Chose** is the past tense of that word, as in "I *chose* the white chocolate over the dark."

cite or site: To **cite** something is to quote it or to refer to it as a source of information; a **site** is a place or location.

coarse or course: Coarse is an adjective describing the rough texture of something (or rough language), as in "The *coarse* wool fabric chafed his legs." **Course** refers to a path, a unit of study, or a playing field. For example, "He stayed on *course* with studies in his psychology course."

complement or compliment: Complement means to go with or complete: for example, "The green blazer he wore *complemented* his red hair." **Compliment** refers to favourable or flattering comments, as in "He received many *compliments* on his dashing green blazer."

conscience or conscious: Conscience is a noun describing an "inner voice" or "inner guidance" that leads one to act ethically and morally; **conscious** is an adjective meaning to be alert or aware. "He was *conscious* of his role in the tragedy, and his *conscience* was urging him to go to the police with his story."

could of (also should of): These are expressions you should obliterate from your writing! **Could of** must be written **could have**, and **should of** must be written **should have**. We tend to write them incorrectly because of the way we speak (more informally than in writing, with many contractions—**could of** sounds suspiciously like **could've**, the contraction for **could have**).

emigrate or immigrate: To **emigrate** is the verb for moving *from* a country or place; to **immigrate** is the verb to move *to* a country or place; for example: "He planned to *emigrate* from Ireland to Red Deer, Alberta, in the new year to live closer to his aging parents; however, before leaving he had to contact *immigration* authorities about entry requirements for *immigrants*."

everyone or every one: Everyone is a pronoun describing an indefinite number of people but presumably many. **Every one** is two words, with the adjective "every" followed by the pronoun "one"; combined, the two words mean every individual person or thing in a group.

except or accept: Except is a preposition meaning excluding; **accept** is a verb meaning to receive; for example, "Except for the licorice candies he disliked, he *accepted* all of the goodies offered by his hosts."

farther or further: Farther describes distances, as in "Ralph's house is *farther* than Elsie's, so let's walk to Elsie's and take a cab to Ralph's." **Further** describes additional quantity or degree; for example, "*Further* renovations were needed after the home inspector found significant levels of mould in the walls."

fewer or less: Fewer refers to a specific reduced quantity of easily identifiable items, as in "There were *fewer* field hockey sticks than players." **Less** refers to an unspecified reduced quantity, usually when discussing an abstract noun or concept, as in "Geoff had *less* interest in dating when hockey playoff season began."

hanged or hung: Hanged is the past tense and past participle form of the verb "to hang" when it means to execute; for example, "He was *hanged* at dawn." **Hung** is the past tense and past participle form of the verb "to hang" when it means to fasten or suspend, as in "She *hung* the new painting on the north wall of her office."

in or into: In is associated with a condition of something, as in "She was *in* big trouble." **Into** suggests movement or a change in condition of something, as in "She got *into* trouble because her initial lie spawned additional lies, and she couldn't remember where the truth began and ended."

in regards to or in regard to: This is a confusion of two expressions: **in regard to** or **as regards**. These expressions can be used interchangeably but are never written as **in regards to**; for example, "This letter is *in regard* to your request for vacation time" or "*As regards* your vacation request, we regret to inform you we are not allowing anyone to take a break until after our busy Christmas season."

irregardless: Never, ever use this word. It's not a word! The word to use is **regardless**.

its or it's: Its is a pronoun representing a singular non-human without gender; **it's** is a contraction for **it is.**

kind of, sort of, or (aghast!) kinda or sorta: Never use these expressions in your writing, even though we all use these in our more informal conversations. Instead, use **somewhat**—a more apt and concise way to express what you really mean.

licence or license: Licence is a noun meaning a legal permit or freedom, as in "On Saturday, he wrote the exam for his motorcycle *licence*" or "Having won $5 million in the lottery, she had *licence* to spend whatever she wanted on shoes." **License** is a verb meaning to permit or authorize, as in "Without completing the written exam, he was not *licensed* to drive a motorcycle."

lose or loose: Lose is to lose something, as in "He has a lot to *lose*"; **loose** is to untighten or free up something or could describe something that is about to fall off or become disconnected. Here's a great example: "Jamie is about to *lose* his very *loose* hat."

lots or lots of: While we have often used the word **lots** in this text, that's just because we wanted to be friendly. You shouldn't use **lots** or **lots of** in your business writing unless it's to someone you know *really* well *and* someone who is not your boss! Use **many**, **much**, or even **a lot** instead.

may/might of: May of or **might of** are incorrect expressions of **may have** or **might have**. Our speech is so much less formal than our writing that we often write as we speak or hear in conversation. Always write **may have** or **might have**!

may or can: You may remember this one from public school when you asked permission to go to the washroom. If you asked, "*Can* I go to the washroom, Mrs. Grouchypants?" Mrs. Grouchypants probably replied, "*Can* you? Are you able to? Yes, you *MAY* go to the washroom, but be quick." Your teacher wanted you to know the difference between **may** and **can. May** is the word we use when seeking permission to do something, as in "*May* I eat your last cookie?" or to express that we might do something, as in "I *may* go on holiday next weekend, but it depends on who is available to cover my shift." **Can** is the word we use to describe ability: "Yes, Mrs. Grouchypants, I *CAN* go to the washroom, but *may* I?"

number or amount: Use the word **number** when you are describing quantities that can be counted, such as "There were a *number* of books on sale at the bookstore." Use the word **amount** when the quantity you are describing cannot be counted, as in "The *amount* of determination needed to succeed cannot be quantified."

OK or okay: Again, while we have used **okay** a few times in this book, it's meant to project a friendly, conversational tone—something to avoid in the business context unless it's in a quick email or text message to someone you know well. Avoid using **okay** or **OK** with the boss or anyone else you don't know well or who has the power to decide you are too "familiar" for your own good.

passed or past: Passed is the past tense of the verb "to pass," as in "He *passed* the salt after he got his elbow out of the casserole dish." **Past** is a word to describe something that happened previously or an earlier time period, as in "The *past* is but a memory, today is reality, and tomorrow is but a dream."

off of: While you might hear people say "something dropped *off of* something," this isn't good written English and is certainly not appropriate in the business setting. Don't put **of** after **off**. Just use **off**. Really!

practice or practise: Practice is a noun with three possible meanings: an action performed repeatedly to gain experience; a business; or a custom. Some examples would be: "She had choir *practice* at 7:00 p.m." or "The doctor's *practice* had too many patients, so she decided to 'fire' those who missed appointments" or "Kwame was in the *practice* of eating only the crusts on the bread and leaving the rest on his plate." **Practise** is a verb, as in "Christie wanted to *practise* singing hip hop songs, but her voice teacher had her working on classical arias instead."

principal or principle: The **principal** is the person who heads up an organization, as in "The *principal* of our college hosted a banquet for members of the student union." **Principal** can also be an amount of money, as in "Having paid off the interest in earlier loan payments, George was now paying more of the *principal*." Another use for **principal** is as an adjective, meaning most important: "The *principal* concern of the community's residents was safety on the streets at night." **Principle** is a noun meaning truth, a law, or a strongly held value, as in "Our college was founded on the *principle* that every student deserves an individually tailored approach to education."

raise or rise: To **rise** is to go up; the verb **rise** cannot be used with a direct object, and needs a subject, as in "The sun *rises* in the east." **Raise** is a verb meaning to move or cause to move upward, and this verb *can* take a direct object, as in "The oil companies *raised* the price of gas when the price of a barrel of oil skyrocketed to more than $100." **Raise** is also a noun used in conjunction with pay or salary, as in "As a reward for all his hard work, Bernard got a *raise*."

real or really: Confusion with these words arises out of adverb use errors, particularly in the spoken word. How often do you hear, "That's *real* nice!" or "You've done a *real* good job"? However, in our more formal, written language, and particularly in business communications, you don't want to write **real** unless you are referring to something being authentic or genuine, as in "He had a *real* chance for success if he applied himself." **Really** is an adverb (remember that many adverbs end in -ly?), as in

"Shaq *really* wanted a chocolate éclair, but he didn't eat one because he had to lose 10 pounds."

reason is because: While this expression is technically correct, it's awkward—and you don't want to be awkward in the business setting. Instead, you would write **reason is that** instead, as in "The *reason* for the delay *is that* there was a switching malfunction at the Bloor subway station during rush hour."

set or sit: Set is a verb that means to put or place, as in "Please *set* the table so we can eat this fabulous meal." **Sit** is another verb, but it means to be seated, as in "Everyone come and *sit* down—are you waiting for an engraved invitation?"

sometime, some time, or sometimes: The adverb **sometime** refers to an event happening in the indeterminate future, as in "*Sometime* soon we should get together for dinner." **Some**, an adjective, refers to the noun, **time**, as in "When I get *some time*, I will look at my daytimer to see when we could possibly get together." The adverb **sometimes** (yes, there are some adverbs without -ly!) modifies a verb, as in "*Sometimes*, I feel there aren't enough hours in the day to fit in time with family and friends."

Suppose to or use to: *Never* use **suppose to** or **use to** in your writing. This error comes up because we write as we speak (and our speech is far too informal to write in a business setting!). Write **supposed to** or **used to**, as in "Richard was *supposed to* get together with Tyson for a beer, like he *used to* on Fridays in the past, but life got in the way."

than or then: Because these two words look so similar, people get confused about which word to use for what. Use **than** when you are comparing items or choices, as in "This sexy sports car is faster *than* that broken-down truck you drive." Use **then** when you are describing a chronology of events: "*Then* the two guys got into a fist fight, after Osheah insulted Josh's ride."

that or which: Now this is confusion that even seasoned writers struggle with! **That** is used in a restrictive clause that limits or defines the word it's modifying, as in "In order to join the university's fitness training program, students had to pay a $50 fee *that* was non-refundable." **Which** is used in a non-restrictive clause, one describing a noun whose meaning has already been defined. **Which** is always preceded by a comma, as in "Students were forced to pay a $50 fee for fitness training, *which* was considered unfair because they had already paid an activity fee." If all of this makes your head spin, just remember that ahead of any **which**, use a comma; you don't put a comma ahead of **that**.

theirselves or themselves: Theirselves is *never* correct anywhere in the English-speaking world. It's always **themselves**! Enough said.

their, they're, or there: If we received a dollar for every time we see these three words confused in writing—on signs, in advertising, in student writing, and even in hardened professional writers' or academics' work—we'd be rich! Prove your brilliance by knowing the difference between **their, they're**, and **there**. **Their** is a possessive pronoun meaning something belonging to "them," a third-person plural pronoun. **They're** is a contraction, meaning "they are." **There** is an adverb specifying a place. Here's an example using all three in one sentence: "*They're* going to ride *their* bikes over *there*, to the warm beach packed with sunbathers."

to, two, or too: It's amazing how such small words can cause such writing grief! **To** is a word indicating the direction of movement, like toward: "Joachim was going *to* ask the new girl out for a date, but alas! His best friend made a move first." **Two** is a number, a duo or pair, as in "However, after *two* dates with his friend, the new girl asked Joachim out on a date." **Too** is an adverb describing an excess of some action: "When Joachim asked why Julia didn't want to go out with his friend again, she said, 'He was *too* needy—and you're just *too* cute!'"

utilize: You know who you are—someone trying too hard to prove your giant brain to the professor or boss by writing **utilize** instead of **use**. **Utilize** is a word that may work for those computer manuals that no one can ever read or understand or for a text that puts you to sleep, but it's not appropriate in business writing. Less is more—and way smarter—when it comes to business writing!

weather or whether: Weather is a noun, as in "The *weather* in January caused a number of class cancellations." **Weather** can also be a verb, **to weather**, describing the action of surviving or thriving in inclement weather: "Unable to drive home, professors *weathered* the storm in the university pub." **Whether** is a conjunction that refers to a choice between alternatives, as in "*Whether* you like it or not, aging is a part of life."

who or that: Who is used to refer to humans or living beings; you should never use **which** or **that**: "The president of our company, *who* put in countless volunteer hours at the homeless shelter, is being recognized with a humanitarian award." **That** is used to refer to inanimate objects but can also be used for groups of people, such as a team or class: "The award *that* she will receive is $10,000, but she has already stated that it will be donated back to the shelter to buy much needed supplies."

who and whom: So just when do you use **who** or **whom**? **Who** is used to refer to subjects and subject complements, as in "*Who* ate all of my Easter chocolate?" **Whom** is used to refer to objects: "The giant chocolate Easter bunny is awarded to **whomever** wins the egg toss."

who's or whose: Who's is a contraction of "who is", as in "*Who's* going to the concert?" **Whose** is a possessive pronoun, as in "We reminded our roommate Connie, *whose* rancid, unwashed dishes cluttered the counter, that we were going to start putting them in her room until she started to clean up after herself."

would of or would have: Would of sounds an awful lot like **would have** if you say it quickly in conversation; however, it's never correct to write **would of**. Write **would have** instead, as in "The brown colour *would have* been great, but because of the lack of light in the room, we painted it a sunny yellow."

your or you're: Your is a possessive pronoun, as in "your hat," while **you're** is a contraction for "you are," as in "*You're* silly." Here's an example using both: "*You're* looking silly in *your* purple polka-dot hat."

EXERCISE

Correct the following sentences where words are misused, are abused, or should never be used.

1. Our coarse was very difficult, but if we had fewer reading to do each week, we would of gotten a better mark.

2. Whom is responsible for the plagiarized material in your team report?

3. Unfortunately, we will have to utilize the old computer system, weather we like or not, because they're is no alternative.

4. Its plain to see getting a rise is better then being rewarded with cookies for a job well done.

5. The reason for his great performance is because he has practiced for hours each day.

6. Who's smelly socks are stinking up the laundry bin?

7. Geordie's conscious was bothering him, because he really should of given a compliment to his sister about how she looked at the party; it would of helped her feel better.

8. The vacation was real nice, since all costs were inclusive and we had lots of great meals.

9. Irregardless of how you feel about it, we are proceeding with the plan as scheduled.

10. You're textbooks have been delivered to the bookstore; your welcome to come and pick them up anytime this week.

Need to work on your writing style? To choose better, more interesting words? Don't know when to capitalize? Not sure how to write numbers, dates, or decimal amounts? Visit the Style Appendix on this textbook's companion website at www. oupcanada.com/Luchuk for how-tos and exercises!

Guidelines for Documenting Sources

Why Do We Document Our Sources of Information?

Most important is honesty. When you present information with your name on it, the audience assumes it's information that originated with you—unless otherwise stated. So when you borrow, you have to state your source, using some kind of indicator.

Second, your audience loves information, lots of specific detail. You can't tell them everything in the time or space allotted for your communication, so you provide a list of sources for them to follow up when they need more information.

Third, you want to persuade your audience to agree with your point of view, so your statements have to be verifiable and credible. Support for your claims comes from thorough documentation of published sources so that your audience can see that you're not just blowing smoke!

Principles of Documentation

Give your audience all the information necessary to find your source. In most cases, that will include the person or organization responsible for creating the information, the date it was produced, the title of your source, and where the information can be found. Record *all* the information you can about your sources.

Documentation is a two-part system. In the body of your presentation, you will have to indicate the sources of your information *at the time* and *every time* you use them. These indicators are called citations. They have to be short so as not to distract the audience from your content, so they can't contain all the information about your source. They simply provide a reference to the complete information about your source, information that can be found in a list usually placed at the end of your document. Both the citations and a reference list must be inserted into your communication to complete the documentation of your sources.

We would all like to have one, simple system for presenting this information about our sources. Sadly, such a system does not exist. Instead, there are several systems, each designed for a particular discipline or set of disciplines. They vary in details, but whichever one you choose, you must use it consistently.

Many people in your audience will have learned different documentation systems, but they will respect that you have chosen a recognizable, standard system and that you have applied it consistently.

Standard Systems of Documentation

Standard documentation systems have been created by professional associations of various kinds to bring some order to the regular process of editing and publishing information in their professional fields. As a businessperson, you may find yourself working with people in one of those fields, so it's a good idea to know how they like to document their sources. Here are the three most widely used:

MLA

The Modern Languages Association style is the oldest of the three. Most people are familiar with this system, because it is taught in high school English classes. It was designed for students of language, literature, and the humanities. Originally, it consisted of footnotes (the citations) and a bibliography (the reference list). MLA now uses an author-page style of citation instead of footnotes. The *MLA Handbook for Writers of Research Papers*, 7th edition (2009), presents a simplified version for student writers (http://owl.english.purdue.edu/owl/resource/747/02).

Works cited/references and in-text citations examples: MLA

Below are sample MLA references for common types of sources, followed by sample in-text citations for these sources.

Book (print)

Mottinger, Benjamin. *Marketing in the 21st Century*. 1st ed. Toronto: ABC Publishing Inc., 2012. Print.
(Mottinger)

Journal article (print)

Sobieski, Joseph. "Effective Customer Communications." *Business News* 5.6 (2012): 101–5. Print.
(Sobieski)

Journal article (online)

Schmorr, Philip. "Conflict Resolution 101: Basics for Work Teams." *Saskatoon Business Review*. 2012: n. pag. Web. www.saskbizreview.ca.
(Schmorr)

Magazine article (print)

Andrews, Nicole. "Financial Plans for Effective Business Planning." *Business and Finance Journal* Apr. 2012: 215–18. Print.
(Andrews)

Magazine article (online)

Gulston, Anthony. "Guerrilla Marketing on Student Radio." *Communications Today*. Mar. 2012. Web. www.communicationstoday.ca.
(Gulston)

Newspaper article (print)

Lilley, Krista. "Office Design That Works: Creating Harmonious Work Spaces." *Burlington Post* 30 Mar. 2012 weekend ed.: n. pag. Print.
(Lilley)

Newspaper article (online)

Hardie, Katherine. "Envisioning Success: Self-Coaching for Business Advancement." *Toronto Daily* 15 Apr. 2012 Spring Business Supplement www.torontodaily.com/springbusiness/envisioningsuccess.
(Hardie)

Government publication (print)

Canada. Ministry of Finance. *Taxation for Small Business*. Ottawa: Public Works, 2012. Print.
(Canada. Ministry of Finance)

Government publication (online)

Ontario. Ministry of Small Business and Economic Development. *Guide to Market Analysis*. Toronto: Ministry of Small Business and Economic Development, 2012. Web. www.sbed.on.ca/marketanalysis.
(Ontario. Ministry of Small Business and Economic Development)

Web document

"Colour for Productivity: Choosing Office Colour Schemes." *Insightful Office Design*. Insightful Office Design, 15 Mar. 2012. Web. www.insightfuldesign.ca.
("Colour for Productivity")

Blog

Taillon, Juanita. "Making Social Media Work for Your Bottom Line." *Social Media Marketing Tips*. Media Moguls Inc., 25 Mar. 2012. Web. www.mediamoguls.com/socmed.
(Taillon)

Podcast

Bonehead, Humphrey, dir. "Keeping Your Cool with Angry Customers." *Excellent Customer Service*. Boneheaded Productions, 1 Apr. 2012. Web. www.bonehead.com.
(Bonehead)

Email message

Isaac, Melanie. "Basic Instructions for Bad News Letter." Message to Ima Student. 1 Apr. 2012. Email.
(Isaac)

Film or video

Dunderlunce, Ralph, dir. *Teamwork 101*. YouTube, 2012. Web. www.youtube.com/teamwork101.
(Dunderlunce)

APA

The American Psychological Association published its most recent edition of the *Publication Manual of the American Psychological Association* in 2009. Students and professionals in the social sciences use this style guide: psychology, sociology, anthropology, politics, and economics. It uses author-date citations and an alphabetical reference list by author surname (http://owl.english.purdue.edu/owl/resource/560/02).

Works cited/references and in-text citations examples: APA

Below are sample references for common types of sources, followed by sample in-text citations for these sources.

Book (print)

Mottinger, B. (2012). *Marketing in the 21st century*. (1st ed.). Toronto: ABC Publishing.
(Mottinger, 2012)

Journal article (print)

Sobieski, J. (2012). Effective customer communications. *Business News, 5* (5), 101–105.
(Sobieski, 2012)

Journal article (online)

Schmorr, P. (2012). Conflict resolution 101: Basics for work teams. *Saskatoon Business Review*. Retrieved from www.saskbizreview.ca.
(Schmorr, 2012)

Magazine article (print)

Andrews, N. (2012, April). Financial plans for effective business planning. *Business and Finance Journal*, 24–27.
(Andrews, 2012)

Magazine article (online)

Gulston, A. (2012, March 23). Guerrilla marketing on student radio. *Communications Today*. Retrieved from www.communicationstoday.ca.
(Gulston, 2012)

Newspaper article (print)

Lilley, K. (2012, March 30). Office design that works: Creating harmonious work spaces. *Burlington Post*, pp. B10–B11.
(Lilley, 2012)

Newspaper article (online)

Hardie, K. (2012, April 15). Envisioning success: Self-coaching for business advancement. *Toronto Daily*. Retrieved from www.torontodaily.com.
(Hardie, 2012)

Government publication (print)

Canada. Ministry of Finance. (2012). *Taxation for small business*. Ottawa: Public Works Canada.
(Canada. Ministry of Finance, 2012)

Government publication (online)

Ontario. Ministry of Small Business and Economic Development. (2012). *Guide to market analysis.* Retrieved from Ministry of Small Business and Economic Development website: www.sbed.on.ca.
(Ontario. Ministry of Small Business and Economic Development, 2012)

Web document

Cooper, J. (2012, March 15). *Colour for productivity: Choosing office colour schemes.* Retrieved from www.insightfuldesign.ca.
(Cooper, 2012)

Blog

Taillon, J. (2012, April 3). Making social media work for your bottom line. [Web log comment]. Retrieved from www.mediamoguls.com/socmed.
(Taillon, 2012)

Podcast

Bonehead, H. (Director) (2012, April 15). Keeping your cool with angry customers. *Excellent Customer Service.* Podcast retrieved from www.bonehead.com.
(Bonehead, 2012)

Film or video

Dunderlunce, R. (Director) (2012). *Teamwork 101.* [Web]. Retrieved from www.youtube.com/teamwork101.
(Dunderlunce, 2012)

A WORD ABOUT AUTHOR-DATE

Author-date citations that link the name of the author with the date of publication are now the most commonly used forms of citation in standardized documentation systems. The reasons are simple. They are easier for the writer to include in a series of drafts of a presentation, and they are easier for the audience because they are not distracting when readers are scanning the presentation for content yet give accurate reference to full information on the source.

CSE

The Council of Science Editors—formerly the Council of Biology Editors—published *Scientific Style and Format: The CSE Manual for Authors, Editors, and Publishers* in 2006. It is used by professionals in the pure and applied sciences, including computer science.

It sets out two styles of documentation. The name-year style is an author-date style with author-date citations and an alphabetical list of sources by author surname. The citation-sequence style identifies each of the sources by number according to its first use in the presentation; the reference list then lists the numbers with a complete description of each source (http://www.libraries.psu.edu/psul/lls/students/cse_citation.html).

Example: Name-year style

Gulston L. 2008. Thomson Nelson guide to report writing. 2nd ed. Toronto: Nelson Publishers.

Miller M. 2012. A good social media marketing IDEA: Identify, Deliver, Empower, Amplify. Search Engine Watch [Internet]. Available from: http://searchenginewatch. com/article/2145295/A-Good-Social-Media-Marketing-IDEA-Identify-Deliver-Empower-Amplify.

Example: Citation-sequence style

1. Gulston L. Thomson Nelson Guide to Report Writing. 2nd ed. Toronto: Nelson Publishers; 2008.

2. Miller M. A good social media marketing IDEA: Identify, Deliver, Empower, Amplify. Search Engine Watch [Internet]. 2012. Available from http://searchenginewatch. com/article/2145295/A-Good-Social-Media-Marketing-IDEA-Identify-Deliver-Empower-Amplify.

OTHER SYSTEMS

The *Chicago Manual of Style*, now in its 16th edition (2010), offers a variety of documentation styles for American editors and publishers. It encourages readers to adopt one style and use it consistently.

The University of Chicago Press publishes its *Manual for Writers of Research Papers, Theses, and Dissertations*, written originally by one of its staff, Kate Turabian. It is still updated regularly.

The Institute of Electrical and Electronics Engineers (IEEE) sets standards for electrical and electronic engineering and for publishing in that field. Their documentation style uses numbers in square brackets as citations, although the reference list entries are in a modified author-date format.

How to Choose a Documentation Style

If you know the preferences of your audience regarding documentation, then use the style appropriate to your audience.

Otherwise, choose one of the widely used styles, and be consistent in its use.

Glossary

360-degree evaluation · This form of evaluation describes a process by which an individual, project, or team is evaluated by everyone involved within a project or workplace, including the individual himself/herself and other team members.

acronym/initialism · These are a "short form" of a longer title or term. Examples include TV: television; ATV: all-terrain vehicle. Use these "short forms" only after writing the entire title/term; provide the acronym in brackets the first time it's used. Capitalize the acronym. Avoid acronyms entirely if they will confuse your reader(s).

added value · This business term refers to anything that adds value or benefit for the receiver of the information or product/service. For example, an evaluation report on three options for uniforms that includes pricing lists not initially requested adds value for the reader because he or she won't have to look for this information elsewhere.

affirming workplace · An affirming workplace is a work environment free from intimidation, harassment, and discrimination. (While this is the ideal, many workplaces are not entirely affirming, so a human rights co-ordinator or committee helps to resolve situations when the work environment is intimidating, harassing, or discriminatory.)

agenda · An agenda is a list of business items to be discussed at a formal meeting. It is an ordered series of issues that require the attention of participants. The agenda's purpose is to familiarize them with the topics to be discussed and indicate what decisions need to be made.

amortizing · Amortizing refers to spreading out or apportioning work, payments, or tasks over a set time period, such as in monthly payments or an equal number of tasks/hours in each day or week of a project.

annotated bibliography or works cited · An annotated bibliography is an alphabetical list by author of the sources used to generate a report. It includes a brief summary or annotation of the content of each source. "Works Cited" in MLA documentation is the list of works cited at the end of an article, paper, or chapter.

appendix · The appendix is an optional section at the very end of a report in which the writer presents supplementary materials supporting the main discussions and arguments in the report. These materials can be statistical data, maps, computer code, legal documents, memos, or other supporting documents.

audio-visual aids · Audio-visual aids include PowerPoint, overheads, slide shows, video tapes or DVDs, or similar aids to enhance presentations. They are used to highlight what you have to present, not to replace your own sparkling presentation skills!

backgrounder · A backgrounder is a document that conveys background information, usually historical or technical, to "bring the reader up to speed" on a project and provide a context before specific detail and analysis of current issues are given.

benefit statement · A benefit statement is just that—a statement of the benefits of a project to the reader(s) based on what they want, need, or expect or what has been asked for in a Request for Proposal.

block format · Block is the most common format for business letters and memos. In this format, lines of text are single-spaced, with blank lines between paragraphs for better readability. Each line of text begins on the left margin of the page.

brief proposal · Brief proposals usually involve short-term projects or jobs, such as the planning of the company picnic or determining the benefits and costs of new equipment. Most are in memorandum format, with headings and organization the same as those of a non-memo proposal but under the memo banner.

business advisory centres · These are often found in cities as business support organizations. They provide locally relevant research sources for business, access to an excellent print library, and exclusive research databases, as well as helpful staff for guidance in using resources.

business communication product · To meet its targets effectively, a business must have people who can convey messages clearly and appropriately. The exchange of ideas within and outside the organization to achieve business goals is known as business communication. "Product" refers to any form that messages take: letters, reports, memos, emails, and so on.

business dress code · This is a set of rules governing what garments may be worn in the workplace and in specific business settings (for example, what to wear to formal meetings versus on Casual Fridays). Because you are the face of the company, you are expected to present yourself in a manner that reflects the company's image.

business etiquette · This is a code of ethical and appropriate behaviours in business and related social environments, which very much depends on your particular sector or industry. Business etiquette can vary dramatically in an international context, so you must learn what is acceptable in these contexts.

business sector · The business sector is the part of the business world your organization or company operates in—for example, Scotiabank, Royal Bank, and TD Canada Trust as financial institutions are part of the banking sector.

Canada's 100 Top Employers · This is an annual publication by Mediacorp Canada Inc. and summarized in *The Globe and Mail* listing Canada's top 100 employers in terms of such evaluative factors as pay, benefits, workplace environment, and promotion of employees. It's a great place to start when considering where you'd like to work.

career search agency · A career search agency is a professional agency that finds jobs for people seeking them and/or finds people to fill particular jobs (also called an employment agency or career recruiter).

chambers of commerce · Chambers of commerce (and business improvement associations) are local associations to promote and protect the interests of a local business community. They are a good source of primary and secondary information regarding the market and offer an opportunity to network with others.

chronological resumé · A chronological resumé organizes work and educational history in chronological order, from most recent to least. This type of resumé usually does not provide much information about transferable skills or abilities so is less helpful for anyone with minimal work experience.

collaboration model · In this model of team writing, the team defines tasks, creates outlines, and makes major revisions together, then individuals complete research, writing, and editing for specific sections of the report. The sections are combined into one document, then edited by one person.

complimentary close · A complimentary close is the way you sign off a letter, essentially a friendly "thanks for reading." The most commonly accepted complimentary close is *Yours truly*, followed by three blank lines and then your name and title, typed. You sign between the complimentary close and your typed name and title.

consensus model · In this model of team writing, the team works together throughout the document preparation process, researching and writing each section of the written document together. The consensus model requires the agreement of most participants and the resolution of minority objections on matters of form and content.

content · The content is what you are communicating—the information you want to convey to the reader. Content in a business communication can be complex, so the first rule of content is to organize the detail by grouping similar types of information under descriptive headings.

contingency plan · A contingency plan is your "Plan B" in case project or work plans run into problems. It's determined by thinking about what could possibly go wrong, then planning for damage control and a means to work around problems.

covering letter (proposal) · A covering letter introduces the proposal and is attached as a separate sheet (with a paper clip) to the front of the executive summary or proposal package. It "covers" the main points of the proposal (in the same order), especially the benefits to the reader(s).

covering letter (resumé) · A covering letter is written to a prospective employer when you apply for a job. It highlights your strongest skills and abilities in reference to what the job description requires.

curriculum vitae · A curriculum vitae, or CV, is a resumé. Resumés are often referred to as CVs in an international context. However, it's important to note that international CVs often include information different from that required for a North American resumé.

delegation model · In this model of team writing, an individual meets with team members throughout the document preparation process to ensure that everyone has input and all relevant information has been provided. Those involved offer changes to or feedback on the document; it is then returned to the writer for revisions.

direct format · A direct delivery of information means you put the good or neutral news near the beginning of your memo or email. There's no need to be indirect about the news, because it won't generate a negative response from the receiver.

direct format presentation · This is a way of presenting good or neutral news or information, with the main points presented first, because the audience is either already aware of the content of the presentation or will have a positive or neutral response to it.

directory page · A directory page is a webpage of links to other webpages with relevant or "of interest" content. They are particularly helpful when you are doing research, because they may direct you to other pages with even better content for your information-gathering purposes.

disciplinary action · Disciplinary action is a process for dealing with job-related behaviour that does not meet expected and communicated performance standards. Its purpose is to improve employee performance. Penalties for failure to meet standards can include warnings, suspension, or dismissal.

document cycling · A document may be cycled through a review chain to obtain feedback and comment. The cycle usually begins with scanning the document into an electronic form suitable for its content; technical documents, for example, will likely appear to reviewers in PDF format to retain the integration of visuals with text.

documentation · You want to document all of the sources you have drawn on for your communication product. Document all sources using the MLA, APA, author-date, or another system, depending on the needs and experience of your reader(s).

evaluation report · This document is a variation of an information report. Its primary purpose is still to present information, but the information is collected with a view to evaluating a plan, product, or person. The analysis of the data is designed to help the reader reach a conclusion or make a decision.

executive summary · The summary (otherwise known as an executive summary) sums up the main points of your report, in the same order, and is usually no longer than one page of text. It is attached as a separate sheet to the front of your report.

expense report · An expense report is a document listing costs you incurred during an authorized company assignment, project, or travel so that you can be compensated. You would also want to demonstrate that you have spent the company's money on something worthwhile.

external emails · External emails are destined for readers outside your business, such as customers, potential clients, or the media. They must be more carefully crafted and edited than internal messages. With electronic mail, people can be hasty in composing messages and may make mistakes that could lead to loss of business.

external readership · These are the people reading your document who are not members of your organization (external to your company). They are typically clients or potential customers. Since your business depends on their goodwill, messages for the external readership must be carefully written and edited.

facilitator · A facilitator in a meeting helps participants in a meeting to work together and achieve the best possible outcomes by handling the practical arrangements and by keeping the discussion on track during the meeting, summarizing when appropriate.

flextime · Flextime is a term to describe working hours set by employees, who choose their own start and finish times within agreed limits. Not all employers offer this option, but many studies indicate that it can promote better employee productivity, creativity, and morale.

formal proposal · A formal proposal is written for an external readership or for an internal readership if its scope or content will have a major impact on the company and/or involves significant expense, time, or resources. It is written in a more formal tone with more attachments and sections, since external readers need greater explanation.

formal report · A formal report is written for an external audience or for an internal audience if the topic is detailed or serious in nature, covers a long time period, or requires a lot of research. It is more formal in tone and style, includes more detail, and is more formally presented.

formal report's format · In addition to the basic informal report template (see Chapter 8), a formal report needs a covering letter, a title page, a table of contents, and a summary (or executive summary) that sums up the entire report.

formal roles · Formal roles are task-focused positions on a team for which a job or task description could be created. For example, the team leader's job comes with certain tasks and responsibilities, and a job description could be written defining them.

formal tone · A formal tone of writing is required for readers you don't know, when communicating with middle/senior management or an international audience, when delivering bad news, or when creating external communications. It may be in more passive than active style, using third-person pronouns.

full-block form · Full block is a letter form in which all lines of text begin on the left margin, including the heading, date, inside address, complimentary close, and typed signature, as well as each line of every paragraph. Paragraphs are single-spaced with a blank line between paragraphs.

functional resumé · A functional resumé presents transferable skills, abilities, and experience for a specific type of job. While you may not have specific job experience, you may have skills and abilities developed from previous jobs, volunteer work, or education that would be relevant (or "transferable") to the job you are applying for.

ground rules · Ground rules are agreed-upon procedures and limits to govern the process, conduct, and scope of a meeting. The term is derived from sport, where ground rules define the limits of play on a particular field.

hashtags · Twitter tweets use hashtags to mark keywords or topics in a tweet, like a subject line in an email. Twitter users created hashtags as a way of categorizing messages. They consist of a # followed immediately by the topic, such as #herbaltea or #summervacation.

human resources file · Also called a personnel file, this refers to any confidential record of an employee's history with the company, usually kept in a personnel or human resources office. Such files are kept for business use, employee confidentiality, medical privacy, and legal compliance.

hyperlink · Typically, titles, phrases, or words that link or connect with other text or pages on a website.

incident report · An incident report is a document describing an incident with consequences for the organization. The report can assess causes and make recommendations; you would only include an assessment and recommendations if specifically requested, because the reader may prefer to review all pertinent information and then make their own assessment and recommendations.

indirect format · In the case of delivering bad news (provided it's not seriously bad news that requires a formal and/or in-person delivery), an indirect delivery is used, meaning that a paragraph or sentence containing positive or neutral news precedes the bad news to cushion the blow of what follows.

indirect format presentation · An indirect format presentation has the main points in the middle, because you can reasonably expect the audience to view the main message as negative or unwelcome. For example, you'd want to make an indirect presentation if you had to announce to employees that lay-offs were imminent because of a supplier slowdown.

informal proposal · An informal proposal is generally a shorter proposal (could be in memo or non-memo format, depending on length) and is written in a less formal tone than a formal proposal. Informal proposals are most often for internal readers, seldom for external readers.

informal report · An informal report is written for an internal audience in a less formal tone; it is often solicited by someone in your organization and is written in memo format if less than three pages. It is shorter and less detailed than a formal report.

informal, team-support roles · In these "unwritten" roles, individuals assume responsibility for positive, effective teamwork and individual emotional and psychological support throughout a project or series of tasks. An example would be peacekeeper or cheerleader. You might fill several roles at one time.

informal tone · An informal tone of writing builds or maintains a relationship with the reader by using personal pronouns, colloquial expressions, and briefer or more concise expression—because your reader likely already knows you. Most business audiences in North America expect a moderately informal to moderately formal tone of writing.

information report · An information report is a document providing factual and timely information to reader(s) and may be solicited or unsolicited. Its purpose is solely to communicate data, and it does not imply any liability on the part of the writer for accurate analysis of the data or contain any recommendations based on the data.

informational interview · In this kind of interview, you ask for career and industry advice rather than employment. It can be an opportunity to learn more about a specific company or organization you'd like to work for—and a chance to have a key decision-maker get to know you for future job openings.

instant messaging (IM) · Instant messaging is just that—a program by which you can have a "live" conversation in real time with someone else on his or her computer via the Internet. It is the exchange of typed messages between computer users in real time.

internal communications · Internal communications are those taking place within an organization or within an approved/trusted group of external people who are affiliated with it (such as major suppliers or companies in strategic alliance). These are communications suitable for "insiders" of your company only, not transmitted to the public or customers.

internal emails · Internal emails are destined for readers within your organization or business or sometimes within your business or organization's extended relationships with suppliers or strategically allied businesses. Please remember that your tone must be formal and your message composed in brief, clear English.

internal readership · An internal readership is readers inside your organization. Internal readers may receive messages in memo format or as an informal report, while external readers would never receive them in memo format.

intranet · An intranet is a local or restricted communication network within your business or organization and often includes databases and an internal email system. It is usually accessed with a secure login and password to keep any "outsiders" out of the system and to protect potentially sensitive or proprietary business information.

jargon · Language or vocabulary specific to an industry, trade, group, or profession that others outside the group won't understand.

job posting · This is a notice posted internally in which a firm lists open positions with their descriptions and requirements. Only those within the organization with the required skills and training can apply.

key decision-maker · A key decision-maker is a person in a large organization responsible for making important decisions—for example, those with significant budget implications such as hiring or deciding which supplier to buy products or services from.

learning types · Harvard University psychologist Howard Gardner has defined eight different learning types, which he calls Multiple Intelligences (MI) theory. These types include linguistic, logical-mathematical, spatial, bodily-kinesthetic, musical, interpersonal, intrapersonal, and naturalist.

left-justified · Left-justified describes lines of text that begin at the left margin of a document. Document margins are set in word-processing software by default, but they can be altered to suit specific format requirements.

mechanics · The mechanics of writing include spelling, punctuation, word choice, and sentence or paragraph structure in your document. Mechanics constitute the framework through which you communicate the content of your writing. Errors in mechanics lead to loss of meaning in the message.

memo format (proposal) · A memo format proposal is one written for an internal audience. Because of its short length (less than three pages), it can be put into a memo format.

minutes (of a meeting) · Minutes are the formal, written record of a meeting. Minutes list those present, state the various

issues discussed by the participants, and summarize each of their responses and decisions taken at the meeting.

moderator · A moderator is someone who presides over and mediates at a meeting. This position is often considered interchangeable with the role of facilitator (see above), although "moderator" usually applies to one who presides over meetings of large groups of people.

Myers-Briggs Type Indicator (MBTI) · MBTI is a psychometric (psychological) questionnaire designed to help identify individuals' preferences in interacting with and understanding the world—including the workplace. It measures personality in four dimensions: extraversion/introversion, sensing/intuition, thinking/feeling, and judging/perceiving.

networking · Networking is making links from people *we* know to people *they* know—for a specific purpose. For example, you network at a chamber of commerce meeting to share with others what your company does/has to offer and to learn what others have to offer to your company.

"non-memo" format (proposal) · An informal proposal that is more than two pages should be written as an informal report, not as a memo. But regardless of the number of pages, if the proposal is being sent to an outside readership, it should always be written in non-memo format.

organization · Business documents are organized into logical sections and subsections. Information under each heading and subheading is ordered using chronological, levels of importance, cause and effect, classification and partition, compare/contrast, and problem/solution organization methods.

persuasive form of writing · This form of writing is used to persuade the reader of something. The most common persuasive business communications are proposals, marketing/promotional materials, expense reports—and sometimes information/evaluation reports. Persuasion is established through diction, organization of information to clearly state the benefits to reader(s), and repetition of main points of interest or benefit.

primary readers · Primary readers are those who you know will read the document and/or those who are the most important. You need to use Starting Point questions to

determine the needs and understanding of primary readers in order to effectively communicate.

primary research · This is information you gather firsthand, through your own efforts or those of your company. Also called field research, it is information that did not previously exist. Two commonly used methods are on-the-street interviews or in-the-mall marketing surveys.

progress report · A progress report details progress on a project or activity, particularly if work is to take place over time. In particular, it highlights work completed to date, any challenges or problems encountered along with potential or applied solutions, and work to be completed with a timeline for completion.

purpose statement · A purpose statement is a brief statement about the purpose of your writing, used particularly in proposals. In it you address the reason for the writing and the scope (what will and will not be addressed).

recommendations · A recommendations section of a report provides recommendations based on the information and analysis presented in the report. This section is only necessary if you have been asked to provide recommendations; check with your reader(s) to see if it is required.

Request for Proposal (RFP) · An RFP is issued by an agency, organization, government body, or business through various media. The organization asks not only for a tender (pricing) but also for project details and specifications. RFPs usually include guidelines and parameters any proponent must follow so that there is a "level playing field" for any applicants.

review chain · A review chain is a number of readers who read and comment on all or part of a business document and provide expert feedback on or response to the content of the document to the writer or writing team.

salutation · The salutation is the greeting in an email or letter: for example, "Dear Ms Raoul." Note that you do *not* use a salutation (or a complimentary close, such as "Yours truly") in a memo.

secondary readers · Secondary readers are those who may read the document, or parts of it, concurrently or subsequently to the primary readers. You often don't know who these people are, so you can't plan writing for them. You should therefore avoid jargon and use more formal language so that they understand the content.

secondary research · This is information already published, usually found in libraries, on the Internet, in corporate information centres, or in your own office filing cabinets. Since someone else researched and wrote it, you need to cite it when you use it in written or oral presentations.

semi-block form · This is a letter form in which the first line of each paragraph is indented and some letter elements are tabbed to the right of the centre line. It is not commonly used in business communications, but occasionally you may see a letter written in this way.

SMART goals · The acronym "SMART" is a mnemonic device to help a team set goals. A project or work assignment will be completed more efficiently and with less conflict when the team has goals that are SMART: specific, measurable, achievable, realistic, and time-limited.

stages of team development · Tuckman's stages of team development are forming, storming, norming, performing, and adjourning. Teams may go through these stages in sequence but more often cycle back into previous stages if conflict or challenges arise while working together.

style · The style of the document is the appropriate use of words, sentences, and paragraph structure to meet the needs of your reader(s). In general, business style is informal, brief, concise, and direct.

SWOT analysis · To help individuals think about their role in a project, they can use a SWOT analysis (SWOT: strengths, weaknesses, opportunities, and threats). SWOT analysis can also be used to evaluate the entire team and project outcomes.

team contracts · The team contract is a set of rules and operating guidelines for how a group will function. It can be organized for long-term work teams or for short-term project teams.

teleconferencing · This is a meeting by telephone of two or more people in different locations using more sophisticated technology than a simple, two-way phone connection. This technology is usually a speakerphone accessible to three or four meeting participants.

three-part presentation · A three-part presentation focuses on presenting information in three main sections (introduction, discussion, and conclusion). The introduction states the three main points you will present in the discussion; the discussion presents the three main points; and the conclusion restates the three main points but in different words.

videoconferencing · This is a meeting of people in different locations using video technology such as Skype. A videoconference requires more sophisticated technology than teleconferencing and a higher bandwidth on the Internet.

virtual teams · A virtual team is one that may never meet physically but works through technological tools for communication such as the Internet, email, wikis, telephone, and teleconferencing or videoconferencing to achieve team goals.

wikis · Wikis are websites that are developed collaboratively by a community of users who add to and edit content. The creation and browsing of interlinked webpages by multiple users on a corporate intranet is very helpful in supporting virtual team output.

References

Algeo, J. (2006). *British or American English? A handbook of word and grammar patterns*. Cambridge: Cambridge University Press.

Brown, B.L. (1998). *Learning styles and vocational education practice. ERIC Practice Application Brief*. Retrieved from www.calpro-online.org/ERIC/docs/pab00007.pdf.

Chapman, A. (2012). *Tuckman's stages of team development. Businessballs*. Retrieved from http://www.businessballs.com/tuckmanformingstormingnormingperforming.htm.

Goetsch, D.L. (2003). *Effective teamwork: Ten steps for technical professionals*. Upper Saddle River, NJ: Prentice Hall.

Pease, B., and Pease, A. (2006). *The definitive book of body language*. New York, NY: Ballentine Bantam Dell Books.

Smith, M.K. (2008). "Howard Gardner, multiple intelligences and education." *The Encyclopedia of Informal Education*. Retrieved from: www.infed.org.

Spence, R. (2007). Ed Mirvish: A true giant. *The Canadian Entrepreneur*. Retrieved from http://canentrepreneur.blogspot.com/2007/07/ed-mirvish-true-giant.html.

Tuckman, B. (1965). "Developmental sequence in small groups." *Psychological Bulletin*. 63.6: 384–99. Print.

Photo Credits

Index